The Scottish Legal System

The Scottish Legal System

Fifth Edition

Robin M White LLB, LLM, Cert Soc Anth, AIL
Ian D Willock MA, LLB, PhD
Hector L MacQueen LLB, PhD, FRSE

Bloomsbury Professional

Bloomsbury Professional Limited, Maxwelton House, 41–43 Boltro Road, Haywards Heath, West Sussex, RH16 1BJ

© Bloomsbury Professional Limited 2013

Reprinted twice 2017

Bloomsbury Professional, an imprint of Bloomsbury Publishing Plc

A CIP Catalogue record for this book is available from the British Library.

ISBN: 978 1 84766 704 5

Typeset by Phoenix Photosetting, Chatham, Kent
Printed and bound by CPI Group (UK) Ltd, Croydon, CR0 4YY

Preface to the fifth edition

The preparation of a new edition of this well-established book by someone other than its original authors is a task that calls for careful handling. The aim has been throughout primarily to update the text; but that has been a surprisingly extensive task which has on more than one occasion called for some editorial recasting of what is said about the source material. Whenever such rewriting has been required, I have sought to maintain the three goals of accuracy, simplicity and clarity, bearing in mind that the book's primary audience is undergraduate students embarking upon the study of law for the first time. Where my views may be different from those of the original authors, theirs have generally remained the position taken in this book. It can therefore be seen as still very much 'White & Willock' with no more than a dash of MacQueen; I hope still a refreshing cocktail for the reader.

I must record my very considerable indebtedness to my two editorial and research assistants, Jamie MacQueen and Tim Haddow, without whom the work would probably never have been brought to a conclusion. Their energy, insights as recent consumers of the product now being re-offered to their successors in the law school student body, and ability to meet deadlines, have been of incalculable value to me. But I, of course, am ultimately responsible for what is now presented here.

In general, the law and legal system are described in this book as they stood on New Year's Day 2013. The original authors wondered whether the previous edition might be the last published in the United Kingdom. Not so; but the possibility that this edition will have that fate is somewhat greater than in July 2007. And there is even a risk that, whatever happens to the United Kingdom, this will be the last edition needing to deal with the European Union.

Hector MacQueen
Causewayside
Edinburgh
29 January 2013

Preface to fourth edition

When the first edition of this book was published, devolution was not even a glint in politicians' eyes, while this fourth edition might just conceivably be the last published in the United Kingdom. Thus fast can things happen.

In the intervening years, there have been numerous large changes in the workings of the Scottish legal system to incorporate in this book. Most obvious, of course, have been the introduction of devolution through the Scotland Act 1998 and the embedding of human rights through the Human Rights Act 1998. They were taken account of in the third edition, but since then, quite apart from updating in relation to those changes, other sorts of change have continued apace. These range from considerable alterations to the system of complaints about lawyers (partly incorporated in the revised third edition, though the changes are still uncompleted at the time of publication) to the introduction of a Supreme Court for the United Kingdom (also, as yet, uncompleted), by way of myriad other matters such as the continuing saga of the European Union, changes in the method of appointing judges, the unification of District Courts into a 'unified' court system with a name change (again, as yet, uncompleted) and so on. (As in other parts of the law, it is clear that there never is a right time to produce a new edition).

However, what is most noticeable in this fourth edition is the splitting of a number of very lengthy chapters into a larger number of shorter ones (with a much fuller Contents page). So the change from eight chapters to 15 does not denote a near-doubling of the size of this edition (though, by the iron Law of Expanding Editions, it is slightly longer than the last). In addition to this, and less obvious, is the consequential re-location of some material. Thus, for instance, discussion of the European Court of Justice has moved from the section on 'Europe' to the chapter on courts. It is hoped that this re-organisation is helpful.

In the labour of amending, correcting and updating, we have received considerable assistance from Jamie Marshall (entering his final LLB year at the time of publication), who read the whole of the third edition to make suggestions on inclusion, style and comprehensibility from a user point of view; from our colleagues Anne Duncan and David Hart (of Dundee University Law Library) in the sections on the citation and publication of legislation and precedent; from Philip Forte (University of Abertay Dundee) and Colin Munro (University of Edinburgh) who commented on the book as users from another users' point of view; and from other colleagues (though chiefly Colin Reid) in the Dundee School of Law, who pointed out useful examples and surprising occurrences for inclusion. None bears any responsibility for what appears.

We hope the book will continue to be of use in courses on the Scottish Legal System in Scottish universities and colleges, and of interest to general readers anywhere in the world who wish to learn about its subject matter.

We have endeavoured to state the law as at 1 July 2007.

Robin M White
Ian D Willock
July 2007

Contents

CONTENTS

Table of Statutes

[All references are to paragraph numbers]

Table of Statutory Instruments

[All references are to paragraph numbers]

Table of European and International Materials

[All references are to paragraph numbers]

Table of Cases

[All references are to paragraph numbers]

1 Introduction

WHY HAVE LAW?

1.1   Law is everywhere. It is, like the air we breathe, part of our environment. But unlike the air it is man-made. Why is it made? There is no one universally agreed answer, but a plausible one that would fit most societies is this. People live together in communities. They have competing wants and limited resources to satisfy them. Therefore they make arrangements to share things out and minimise or repress conflict. These arrangements can take various forms, such as morality, etiquette, conventions and law. Law consists of rules. These are not necessarily fair or accepted by all. They may be written by a small elite who wield some form of power and impose them on a reluctant majority. But some such arrangements are indispensable. The bigger and more complex the community, the more the scope for conflict; and so the more likely there are to be rules of law. As one writer puts it, society is not a suicide club.

SOME KINDS OF LAW WE ALL KNOW

1.2   If law is everywhere about us, we must be enveloped in it from our earliest days. In a family the parents have power over young children by virtue of their greater size and strength and knowledge. Ideally the relationship is imbued with love. But it still involves the children doing what they are told on such matters as bed-time, dress, going to school, and play-mates. If the parents are consistent in what they require the children to do, then unwritten rules emerge. They can still be rules, even though exceptions may be made for special occasions or they are relaxed as the children grow older. In school too the pupils find themselves in a regime of rules, concerning time-tables, holidays, absentee notes and so on. In many schools there will be no list of school rules as such. But the children are taught by the teachers what a rule is when the consequences of unacceptable behaviour are explained to them and they are told what conduct to avoid for the future. If they still do not conform, then some

1

punishment, such as loss of privileges, will be imposed and as a last resort exclusion from the school.

As children grow older and become more self-reliant they become aware of a system of control that affects nearly everything that people do outside their homes. Probably it first impinges on them when as pedestrians they become aware of the rules that make drivers of vehicles behave more or less consistently in certain situations; stopping at a red light or giving way to someone on a pedestrian crossing or obeying the lollipop man's signal. Sooner or later they will also watch the result of not complying, when police stop and question the errant driver.

SO WHAT EXACTLY IS LAW?

1.3   Already from these simple situations we can see some of the elements of law. It seems to be the words of someone in authority who has the power to intervene in other people's affairs. It imposes patterns of conduct on other people; and if they do not comply something unpleasant is liable to befall them. A single example of these effective words is called a rule or a law. Some people would want to add that the law must be fair to be a true law. Others would say that if the law comes from a person or institution whose authority is generally recognised, then that is good enough. Some laws actually compel conduct, whether you like it or not. For example, a speeding motorist may be stopped by traffic police and warned to obey the speed limit. A persistent offender will be fined by a judge and may be disqualified from driving. But a lot of law simply provides opportunities to do things effectively. If you want to buy a house, there are rules you must observe to obtain the desired result. You don't need to go near a court. You can ignore such laws if you choose, but you are likely to find that somebody takes your house from you or you cannot get anyone to buy it from you. So some laws are primarily compelling ones and some are primarily enabling ones. But if you ignore either kind, some harm or loss or detriment is likely to befall you. Some laws are very precise; they tell you exactly what you can and cannot do. Others shade off into discretion. Thus, on divorce the matrimonial property is to 'be shared fairly' between the parties (Family Law (Scotland) Act 1985, s 9(1)(a)). The couple will be the best people to decide what will be a fair sharing of their belongings. But if they cannot, then judges are available to do it for them.

We have only just touched on some of the most profound questions in the subject called jurisprudence or legal philosophy, which university students of law will have to study later. There are many aspects of this topic which will then be examined, such as: must the law-maker obey his own laws?; is there any duty to obey the laws of a tyrant?; what law is to be obeyed during and after a revolution? But for our purposes in this book that picture of the standard form that law takes will suffice.

However, there is a variant of law that we must mention at this stage. It is law without a law-giver. It simply rests on the general observance of some pattern of behaviour. The person who steps out of line will be criticised and may suffer some harm, such as being ostracised. In a narrow street where all the cars are parked on one side to let the traffic flow, a driver who parks on the other side will soon be made to feel unpopular. This is custom or convention. It is unwritten law and is associated with an early stage of legal development, when means of making law and imposing punishments had not yet been developed. So we can call it embryonic or inchoate law. Yet, paradoxically, some of the most basic parts of the United Kingdom's constitution exist only in the form of conventions, such as the duty of a Prime Minister whose government is defeated on a matter of confidence in the House of Commons to offer his resignation to the Sovereign.

THE LAW OF A STATE

1.4   So far we have been describing a very simple model of law. But of course in a modern state it is much more complex. Indeed, to issue and uphold its own laws is one of the marks of a state. The laws of a state are arranged in a hierarchy of authority and importance. In the United Kingdom the highest tier of law has for centuries been the statutes or Acts issued by Parliament. But since the United Kingdom accepted the Treaty of Rome and entered the European Community, and the consequences of this decision were spelled out by Parliament in the European Communities Act 1972, there is a higher tier of law, that of European Union Law, which takes precedence over United Kingdom law. In theory, Parliament could repeal the European Communities Act and free itself of that level of law. But the problems of disengaging itself from the European Union make that possibility highly unlikely. Likewise, the United Kingdom Parliament has tied its hands by incorporating substantial parts of the European Convention on Human Rights in the Human Rights Act of 1998. That Parliament could repeal that Act but is most unlikely to do so except in order to replace it. Parliament has devolved some of its power to make law to the Parliament of Scotland since 1999.

3

Much modern statute law is of an outline kind. The details are provided in regulations drawn up by government departments under the authority of a parent Act. They can thus be varied easily, for example to take account of inflation. Most social security law is of this kind. As we shall see, there are many other subordinate forms of enacted law, such as laws made by courts for their own procedure, by local authorities and by transport undertakings.

Alongside the law created on purpose, there is a kind of law which is extracted as a by-product from something else. To justify their decisions in disputed cases judges issue judgments applying the existing law to the new situation which has come before them. In so doing they make law in a limited sense in that they clarify or extend the existing law, including the law emerging from the decisions of previous judges. Lawyers reading such published judgments try to formulate a brief rule of law which epitomises the reason underlying the decision. Judges in their judgments have to respect what Parliament appears to have enacted, if anything, on the subject; and their statements of the law and even (though rarely) their decisions could be overridden by Parliament. They also have to adhere to expositions of the law in courts higher than their own. So this judge-made law is also arranged in tiers of authority.

As well as this structure of enacted and judge-made law – what we might call official law – which is of general application, there are sets of law applying to people in particular circumstances; for example, members of the armed forces, of the universities, of the established Churches of Scotland and of England and of certain professions such as medicine, law and teaching. The laws of these bodies require some degree of state approval and the decisions of their courts and tribunals are usually subject to final appeal to the courts of the land.

There are also many other bodies which have a legal structure which in a limited way imitates that of the state; for example, trade unions and professional associations, the non-established churches, and sports associations. But only if they act in an oppressive way or fail to observe the basic rules of natural justice, as laid down by the law courts, do they become subject to the law of the land.

The laws of such private organisations do not have to be obeyed. If, as a member, you do disobey them the worst that can happen is that you will be made to leave the organisation. But all the other kinds of law mentioned above have a pedigree which could be traced back to the ultimate source of legal authority which in the United Kingdom we refer to by the symbol of the Crown and personify in the person of the monarch. If you come within the scope of such an official law, you have to comply or take the prescribed consequences.

IS LAW A GOOD OR A BAD THING?

1.5   A modern law system extends to every corner of a nation, and in limited ways beyond its boundaries. It touches the lives of every inhabitant and to some degree even those of temporary residents such as tourists. Most laws probably strike the law-abiding citizen as restrictive. They stop them from doing what they want to do. Yet provided laws as a whole are generally respected they create a climate of security in which people can go about their everyday affairs, confident that they are not going to be harmed in their persons or property. If they are, something will be done about it. For example, we can be reasonably sure in this country, though not perhaps in Madrid or Rome, that if we drive through a road crossing on the green light we are not going to collide with someone driving across on a red light.

The other kind of laws, those which enable us to do things and get results, are more obviously beneficial. They could be compared to the telephone network which enables us to make contact with people all over the country and even beyond. This sort of law enables us to perform transactions with people everywhere, whom we may never have seen and know little about, with some assurance that they will be honoured; and if not, we shall be able to get some redress. From Scotland we might send to a nursery firm in Cornwall for some plants, in the confidence that they would send the plants ordered to us, properly packed. If they did turn up dead on arrival, we would have a good chance of getting our money back. If we were paying by credit card or cheque we would be counting on the bank to make payment on our behalf. Again, we might get married in Scotland and, armed with a marriage certificate, we could be assured of being treated as married here and elsewhere in the world. It is this comprehensive system of law that enables people to enter transactions like these with assurance.

LAW IS ALWAYS SUBJECT TO CHANGE

1.6   One of the problems about law is discovering what exactly it is at any given point of time. If one is trying to do exactly what the law requires or to discover the law that should settle a dispute, then it is vitally important to ascertain all the rules applicable at the relevant date. Why so? Surely it might be thought the law is as clear and certain as the law-maker can make it? The trouble is that law is always subject to change so that it can be kept up to date. This is true of individual rules of law. That means that although a

5

new statute may get plenty of publicity in the media, what may not be so clear is how it amends previous statutes, or when it comes into force (for different parts of it may be operative from different dates), or whether it has any retrospective effect. So lawyers have to rely on publications such as the monthly periodical *Current Law*, or commercial databases such as LexisNexis and Westlaw, to keep them abreast of legal changes. The Internet is proving an ever more valuable aid in this regard, not least in the regular bulletins on legal developments produced by law firms and university law schools.

But although law is always evolving, it is mainly at the margins. There are broad core areas of the law, such as the law of contract and of property, and the main crimes such as murder and theft, where change is minimal or at most incremental. These heartlands of the law enable it to have a conserving and a stabilising role in societies. The very existence of the modern nation-state depends on reliable rules of law and the means to find them and enforce them. Thus, the law of companies enables property to be set apart for certain economic purposes and for the ownership of that property to be fragmented among many people and other companies, without putting at risk the rest of their assets. Without that device the capitalist or free enterprise system could not flourish.

In this book we are more concerned with structures and with broad movements and trends in the law, although some rules will be mentioned; and we shall have to strive to state them as accurately as possible at a named date. There are different kinds of legal change. There is the step-by-step kind of change, which we may call incremental. Most judge-made law is of that kind. There is innovative change, when a new area of legal regulation is opened up, for instance, by the Sex Discrimination Act of 1976 (now replaced by the Equality Act 2010); or an existing one is drastically changed, such as making divorce rest on the breakdown of the marriage, instead of the commission of a matrimonial fault. And there is evolutionary change, which takes the form of broad trends such as the increasing role of civil servants in detailed law-making. Of course, if all the laws were in a constant state of flux it would defeat the purposes of law to create certainty and security. But a certain amount of change can be lived with in the interests of keeping the law in line with people's expectations.

Another way in which a small element of uncertainty creeps into the law arises out of laws which remain on paper but are not actually enforced. Thus, in 1972 the Lord Advocate let it be known that he would not initiate prosecutions of male adults for engaging in private homosexual activities by agreement in Scotland, in circumstances such that they would not be criminal in England. The police, like prosecutors, in the nature of their duties have much discretion, but in 1982 they publicly declined to operate the powers conferred on them in the Transport Act 1982, s 27, to issue fixed penalty notices for a variety of minor traffic offences, including speeding. In 1993 (now under the Road Traffic Offenders Act 1988, s 54) they announced that they would now do so. Bodies affected by a new law may protest that they need time to prepare for it. Thus the Freedom of Information (Scotland) Act 2002 affecting all governmental and many quasi-governmental bodies did not come into force until 1st January 2005. This shows that legal institutions have the power to vary the operation of legal rules.

LAW AND POWER

1.7   Law is indissolubly linked with power; that is, the ability of a person or group to determine the behaviour of others. From what we have already said about laws, they are obviously ideal instruments by means of which to control others. Power may take many and varied forms. Sometimes it is visible and very forceful, as when massed policemen, their arms linked, try to confine demonstrators to one street and stop them marching, then handcuff those they arrest. Sometimes it is more subtle. Those who are in charge of the mass media have the power to influence what people think, and thus do, by their ability to select which facts to publicise and which opinions to advance. Power may be exercised by an individual or by a group or class. The trade union movement used to attribute its power against employers to the ability of its members to take strike action. But now strikes must be preceded by a strike ballot, otherwise the union funds are put at risk, and employees are free to join or not join a trade union. An individual employer still has the power to dismiss an employee but may have to pay the employee compensation if the power is exercised unfairly. These forms of power are legitimate in that they are either authorised by law or at least not forbidden by it. But the power a bank robber exercises when he uses a revolver to hold up the staff of a bank would be regarded as a crime and therefore illegitimate.

LAWS AS WAYS OF GETTING THINGS DONE

1.8   In a modern democratic society there is a constant ferment of debate on things that are wrong and how to correct them. For example, road accidents have long been blamed on driving with excessive alcohol in the system. Now there is concern about the effect of drugs, whether medicinal or forbidden, on driving. People who sleep on the streets regardless of the weather are seen as an embarrassment and a scandal. Pressure groups, television documentaries and articles in the newspapers draw attention to such social evils. Political parties may put them into their election manifestos. The method of correction usually uses law. It may be simply some new use of existing legal powers which have been conferred on officials such as the police or head teachers or environmental protection officers. Or it may require new parliamentary legislation. Relying on law assumes that, for the most part, people respect law and approve of the objectives that are embodied in particular laws. If they ignore a law then some sanction can come into operation to compel or persuade them to comply. It need not be as overt as imprisonment. It might be the payment of compensation to someone hurt by the failure to obey the law. In the case of professionals it might be loss of promotion or humiliating publicity. So the legitimate power of law is drawn upon to achieve reforms in all walks of life. But the job is never done. There are always calls for new laws and the amendment of existing ones. Whole new areas may be made subject to law, such as racial relations and sexual and age discrimination. The law is always on the move.

2 Scotland – nation and state

2.1   In this chapter we shall be looking in a broad-brush manner at the history of Scotland and seeing the ways in which law has been entwined with it. In so doing we may hope to find the answer to the question: how did the peculiar, indeed unique, association enjoyed by the legal system of Scotland within the United Kingdom arise?

NATION AND STATE

2.2   A nation is a cultural concept, rooted among people and their belief that they have a shared identity that distinguishes them from other peoples. It is manifested in what they produce as a people – their art, music and literature, their language, their pastimes and games, in their beliefs about themselves and their place in the world. A nation may or may not have the organs of government which signify a state; a central administration holding sway over a defined area; armed forces to defend its boundaries; police and courts to maintain order within them. That apparatus is the sign of a state and if it is functioning effectively gives it a claim to recognition by other states. It marks a society which claims independence from all others, although in the modern world of instant communications, mutual economic dependence and treaties and alliances that independence is often more apparent than real.

When we examine the law in Scotland certain unique problems confront us. Most Scots would claim that Scotland is a nation. Certainly in most sports (though not yet at the Olympic Games) it counts as a nation. But it is not in itself a state. In the Scottish Government it has only some of the apparatus of a state; part of that of the United Kingdom of Great Britain and Northern Ireland. Its representatives as MPs participate in the Parliament of the United Kingdom. Since May 1999 it has also had its own Parliament sitting in Edinburgh, composed of MSPs (Members of the Scottish Parliament) and dealing with matters devolved to it by the United Kingdom Parliament. It does have its own courts, but it shares with the rest of the United Kingdom a common highest court in civil and devolution cases. Most of its tribunals are part of a United Kingdom organisation. It has its own legal profession. Some of its laws are peculiar to Scotland, some are common to the whole of Britain (ie England, Scotland and Wales), some are shared with the rest of the United Kingdom (ie with Northern Ireland as well). Some are separate in form, but almost identical in substance. It will be one of our main tasks to tease out these similarities and differences.

THE EMERGENCE OF SCOTLAND

2.3   The emergence of a Scottish nation and later a Scottish state was a slow and painful process lasting several centuries. It began in the 11th century when four rival peoples had by warfare coalesced into one kingdom under King Malcolm II (1005–34). They were the Picts of the east of Scotland, the Angles of the south-east, the Scots of Dalriada in the west and the Britons of the south-west.

Custom

2.4   The law before David I (1124–53) was probably entirely custom and in the Celtic, Gaelic-speaking areas of the west was spoken to by hereditary oracles called Brehons. In the nature of things customary law, being unwritten, is hard to identify later. But numerous references to *leges et consuetudines* (laws and customs) in the statutes of the 12th and 13th centuries testify to the existence and recognition of some law other than the enacted written law[1]. Custom is also often referred to in charters. Some of it, especially in charters, is local[2]. Some of it is general; what in England was called the common law, a term which in Scotland is used both for the law common to the whole of Scotland and less frequently the Roman or civil law common to Europe[3]. Stair, the 17th century authoritative

---

1   Thus, the *Laws of the Four Burghs* (of Edinburgh, Roxburgh, Berwick and Stirling) are more properly the *Leges et Consuetudines Quatuor Burgorum* and were adopted by many other Scots burghs. See APS I, 333. The *Laws of the Marches* were the outcome of a process of recognition in 1249 by magnates from England and Scotland of the laws and customs of the marches (or frontiers). See APS I, 413–416, conveniently and fully translated in DM Walker *A Legal History of Scotland* (1988) vol I pp 63–66.
2   For example, Malcolm IV in a charter to the Abbey of Scone of 1164 allowed it to have three tradesmen with the same liberties and customs as those of his Burgh of Perth (Barrow, *Regesta of Malcolm IV*), No 243).
3   For numerous medieval examples, see DM Walker *A Legal History of Scotland* vol II (1990) pp 252–254. Later Stair was also to use 'common law' as the law 'common to many nations' (*Institutions of the Law of Scotland* (ed 1981) I, 1, 11).

institutional writer on Scots law, uses the term 'common law' to mean primarily, as in England, 'our ancient and immemorial customs'[4]. As examples he includes the law governing most rights of succession as being 'anterior to any statute'[5]. To these might be added the early ways of trying criminal accusations – the ordeal, trial by combat and even the early jury. Custom flourished for centuries in the law observed by mariners and traders among nations, where there was no sovereign authority to enact it, and to a minor extent this is still so. But most maritime law is now embodied in judicial precedent (the authoritative statement of the law by a court), statute and international convention. Customs of trade may sometimes be used to interpret a contract[6]. In employment law the custom and practice of a workplace may be paid regard to by employment tribunals and courts. Thus, custom had a formative role in the law of Scotland and despite the spread of written law still has a minor part to play.

EARLY MEDIEVAL SCOTLAND

2.5   Custom with its local roots could be a divisive force. But through a documentary form of law uniformly introduced and enforced from the centre the country was to become much more united. This came about through the arrival of the Normans who pacified England within a few years of their victory over King Harold at Hastings in 1066 and then began a peaceful penetration of Scotland. The marriage of Margaret, an English Saxon princess[7], to Malcolm III of Scotland and the marriages of their sons, Alexander I and David I, to English noblewomen led to the coming to Scotland of many families hailing from Normandy, such as the Bruces, the Stewarts (formerly Fitzallans) and the Grahams. Margaret's piety drew many religious orders to Scotland during her reign and thereafter. The Scottish kings then followed Norman practice in conferring lands upon these incomers, in return for their homage and the promise of armed knights in time of war. These tenants-in-chief could create their own sub-tenants. At the lowest level were the peasants, the husbandmen and cottars who tilled the land and whose return was in produce and days of labour on their overlord's land. These land rights carried with them the right to hold a court. In

---

4   Stair *Institutions* I, 1, 16. See para **5.23**.
5   Stair *Institutions* I, 1, 16.
6   See, eg, *Wilkie v Scottish Aviation* 1956 SC 198 (custom as to remuneration of chartered surveyor followed if reasonable, certain and notorious).
7   Though born in Hungary.

this way disputes as to tenure and succession could be settled. The kings also conferred on religious houses extensive lands. For them the return was usually in prayers and masses.

Feudal tenure

2.6   This system was known as feudal tenure. Worked out initially in relation to land, it was soon to be extended to towns. Burghs were royal creations, part of a deliberate policy to maintain peace and raise standards of life. This plan had three elements: royal castles manifesting the king's authority and power; sheriffs there resident to represent the king in administration, tax-gathering and law enforcement; and townships whose inhabitants were encouraged to engage in trade and manufacture. They too were given plots of land, for which they paid a return in rent and in other obligations such as attendance at the burgh court.

In this way a legal device, rooted in the staple resource of land, carried the monarch's authority throughout the country. It was a centralised form of government in that all rights derived from the Crown and the forms of land tenure were uniform everywhere. The Royal Chancery issued the charters conferring the lands or confirming them; and when any kind of dispute arose it ordered in the form of legal writs called brieves an inquiry in the local court. After hearing evidence from local people it reported back as to the true state of affairs. With some brieves (known as 'pleadable' brieves) the court was empowered to put its findings directly into effect[8]. But the system was further decentralised in so far as the monarch gave his tenants-in-chief powers similar to his own within their territories, known as 'regalities'.

Thus, feudalism reinforced class stratification, at least in the rural areas. Burghs were more loosely bound into the system. The burghers had a strong sense of community, focused on their town church and burgh court, and often maintained a doughty independence from adjacent large land-owners, even those who had the powers of sheriffs.

Feudalism in time tended to disperse power, for the successors of those who were entrusted with lands by the sovereign did not always remain faithful to him or his successors. But it did give Scotland many of the signs of statehood, even although they and that concept were not fully developed until the 16th century. It emphasised the

---

8   See HL MacQueen, *Common Law and Feudal Society in Medieval Scotland* (1993).

loyalty owed by everyone in the country to the person of the king, who was both leader and the symbolic embodiment of the nation. It facilitated the raising of an army when needed. It sustained courts in every community. Yet paradoxically, at the centre, the *curia regis* or royal court was just an informal gathering of a varying number of those clerics and titled laymen who gave counsel to the king. Out of it grew eventually the Scots Parliament, central law courts and the Privy Council[9].

The pervasiveness of the linked institutions we call feudalism has been equalled by its durability. Its concept of concurrent interests in land is still the basis of Scottish land law, for example, between landlord and tenant or owner-occupier and security holder. In 1991 the Scottish Law Commission (which is charged with the reform of Scots law) published a discussion paper entitled *Property Law: Abolition of the Feudal System*. This led to the Abolition of Feudal Tenure etc (Scotland) Act 2000 which was brought into force in stages. From this era too we derive the cleavage in Scots property and succession law between, on the one hand, the law of land, all buildings attached to land, trees and growing crops, mines and quarries and, on the other, all other items of value; that is between heritable and moveable property, respectively.

Documents of title

2.7   The distinctive form of law derived from this period is the charter, the all-important document of title which evidenced the rights over land of the wealthy, both individuals and institutions such as religious houses. The stout charter-chest can still be seen in many castles. In the 19th century, groups of (usually) titled people formed clubs, such as the Maitland and the Bannatyne, to publish the surviving charters and other documents of title, often of their own families, and these form invaluable historical records, as well as supplying a chain of ownership. Today many owner-occupiers still have their title deeds, though often deposited as security with a building society which holds a standard security (a form of mortgage) over the home. From a legal proposition of the most general kind, that the Crown is the ultimate owner of all the land of Scotland, fragments of that ownership descend to the level of the home-owner and give him legal rights. Tenants of lands, homes, factories etc likewise have the enjoyment of that property, though limited in duration and other ways.

9   See paras **2.12**, **2.14** and **2.20**.

Feudalism and independence

2.8 Feudalism also led to a growing sense of Scots independence from England, though it was from England that the feudal institutions had been imported. At one level it was a disagreement over feudal law that precipitated the Wars of Independence. On the death in Orkney en route to Scotland of the Maid of Norway, who was to succeed to the Scottish throne following the accidental death of Alexander III in 1286, Robert Bruce, the Lord of Annandale, and John Balliol, the Lord of Galloway, were in dispute as to who had the right to succeed to the throne of Scotland. Edward I of England claimed to be overlord of Scotland and in support of his claim could argue that the contenders and other Scots nobles, like the Comyns, owned lands in England for which they paid him homage. Eventually Bruce and Balliol and certain lesser claimants conceded that Edward was lord superior of Scotland and promised to abide by his decision. After many sessions of legal argument Edward gave judgment in favour of John Balliol who then paid him homage at Newcastle.

The humiliation implied in the outcome of this so-called Great Cause was emphasised by Edward who went on to hear appeals on questions of Scottish feudal rights, insisting that King John Balliol be present. When war broke out between England and France Scots envoys signed an alliance with the French. Edward invaded Scotland in 1296, stripped John of the symbols of his kingship and removed the Scots records and Stone of Destiny to Westminster. There then followed the Wars of Independence, with Scotland's defeat under William Wallace at Falkirk in 1298 and victory under Robert Bruce against Edward II at Bannockburn in 1314. This formative period in Scotland's development ended in 1328 with a peace treaty signed at Edinburgh and Northampton, prior to which Edward III accepted that Scotland was to be 'separate in all things from the kingdom of England, assured forever of its territorial integrity, to remain forever free and quit of any subjection, servitude, claim or demand'.

Beliefs sustaining legal independence

2.9 The victory at Bannockburn gave a great boost to Scotland's sense of nationhood. This is manifested in the sonorous prose of the Declaration of Arbroath of 1320. In it the nobility, the barons, freeholders and whole community of the kingdom of Scotland beseeched Pope John XXII to persuade Edward III of England to

14

allow the Scots to live in peace and liberty. They are portrayed as a nation (*nacio*) of ancient lineage, governed by a succession of 113 kings of native stock, and under the patronage of St Andrew, brother of St Peter. Mythology much of it may be, but it gave the Scots a certain pride of ancestry and confidence as a people for the future. Its rhetoric is echoed in a populist form as Scottish supporters sing 'Flower of Scotland' at international rugby and football matches. Confidence that Scotland is still a nation underlies the Scotland Act 1998 which affirms that Scotland should retain a separate judicial system from that of England[10].

The Declaration was composed by Bernard de Linton, Abbot of Arbroath and Chancellor of Scotland[11]. Leading churchmen had given their support and recognition to King Robert Bruce, speaking on behalf of the people and commons of the Kingdom of Scotland, in a declaration of 1310. A century earlier the Church had successfully fought off the claims of the Archbishop of York to jurisdiction over the dioceses of Scotland by securing from Pope Honorius III in 1218 a bull declaring the bishops of the Scottish Church to be directly subject to Rome. So the Church had an interest parallel to that of the state in proclaiming the independence of the Scottish nation.

Bernard de Linton wrote a poem in celebration of the victory of Bannockburn and later in the century another churchman, John Barbour, Archdeacon of Aberdeen, further boosted the national sentiment in his epic poem *The Bruce*. In it he gives an account of the Wars of Independence, portraying Bruce as the hero and the English kings as holding the Scottish people, rich and poor, in a state of 'thryllage' or serfdom, until led to freedom by Bruce[12].

Rather than stressing the stratification of society, imposed by feudalism, Barbour portrays one 'kynrik' or country and one folk, certain of whose members are chosen to act for the common weal (or good). This theme is to be found too in the Declaration of Arbroath. According to it, it was 'the consent and assent of all the people', as well as divine providence and (very questionably) right of succession, that made Robert Bruce King of the Scots. The class divisions of feudalism were no doubt real enough, but an attempt was being made to subsume them into a united national consciousness.

---

10 S 37. Article XIX Union with England Act 1707.
11 The Declaration of Arbroath, in Latin with an English translation, is printed in Lord Cooper *Selected Papers 1922–1954* (1957) p 334.
12 See Archibald AM Duncan *The Bruce, An Epic Poem*.

THE LATER MIDDLE AGES

2.10 The years following the Treaty of Edinburgh and Northampton were turbulent ones politically, though not without cultural achievements, in poetry, architecture and learning. Edward III went back on his word and the 1330s were a decade in which English troops captured Scottish castles and were ousted from them one by one. The Scots made an alliance with the French and thus became embroiled in the Hundred Years War. There were many dynastic feuds. Several kings such as David II and James I came to the throne in childhood. Both of these kings spent periods in captivity in England. Yet throughout these vicissitudes there was no doubt that Scotland remained a nation and had much of the apparatus of a state, though it functioned imperfectly. The chroniclers of the 14th and 15th centuries, John of Fordoun, Walter Bower, and Andrew Wyntoun, all churchmen, recount Scotland's history in strongly nationalist terms.

Emerging statehood

2.11 One way in which statehood was evidenced was in boundaries. The River Tweed and the Solway Firth became accepted natural divisions between Scotland and England, though Berwick on the north bank of the Tweed remained English. In between there were disputed marches, east, middle and west. These were policed by wardens, the Scottish ones being appointed by Parliament or the Council from the families of the Humes, the Kerrs and the Maxwells. They kept rough and ready order, at times engaging in warfare, at times upholding truces. Although raids were frequent and there was strife as to the exact boundaries, there was no doubt that here was an international frontier.

Treaties too evidence Scotland's international standing. Thus, before James IV married Margaret Tudor, daughter of Henry VII, in 1503, a Treaty of Peace was signed between the two monarchs, promising 'a true, sincere, whole and unbroken peace, friendship, league and alliance'. But no union was contemplated. If the King of England waged war against another country, the King of Scotland promised to refrain from invading England, but might still give succour to England's enemy.

Courts, central and local

2.12 By the 16th century Scotland had developed many of the judicial institutions of a legal system. Some were akin to those of

England; others adapted from continental models. The development is one from local and diverse institutions to centralised and uniform ones. Many of them emanated from the feudal system. Participation in the doing of justice was one of the returns made for the right to hold lands, large and small. At the top it meant attendance by the king's tenants-in-chief, lay and ecclesiastical, at the king's court, the *curia regis*. It advised the monarch on all matters of government. Out of it, by the 15th century, there emerged various combinations of Lords – of Council and of Session[13]. In 1532 they were placed on a permanent footing, financed out of church revenues, as the Court of Session, which remains the premier civil court in Scotland.

From the reign of the first effective feudal king, David I (1124–53), an attempt was made to maintain order throughout Scotland by travelling civil and criminal courts presided over by judges called Justiciars. These courts operated very irregularly, perhaps because the Justiciars were also magnates with more pressing interests and ambitions of their own. Repeated attempts were made over the centuries to make them travel on circuit or ayre, 'on the grass and on the corn' (in spring and autumn). The civil side of the Justiciars' work had decayed by the 15th century. The revival of their criminal jurisdiction was one of the achievements of James VI. Eventually central criminal justice was put on a permanent footing with the founding of the High Court of Justiciary in 1672, composed for the most part of Court of Session judges in the role of Lords Commissioners of Justiciary.

The inadequacies of the central courts were remedied to some extent locally. Trusted nobles and churchmen were granted from the 14th century powers of regality enabling them in their own territory to exercise justice on the gravest crimes, the pleas of the crown which normally had to await the coming of the Justiciar's court. Regality courts could repledge or recall their own subjects from other courts[14]. Some, such as those of St Andrews and the Abbeys of Dunfermline and Arbroath, even had their own chancery. The surviving regalities were finally abolished in the Heritable Jurisdictions (Scotland) Act 1746. Although they could be divisive in the hands of unruly noblemen, the records of the best regalities run

---

13 On the antecedents and creation of the Court of Session, see AM Godfrey *Civil Justice in Renaissance Scotland* (2009). For a vivid account of the part played by a leading churchman in judicial decisions, see LJ Macfarlane *William Elphinstone and The Kingdom of Scotland, 1431–1514* (1985).

14 ID Willock *The Origins and Development of the Jury in Scotland* (Stair Society, vol 23, 1966) p 84.

by religious foundations suggest that they provided a high quality of justice[15].

At the level of the shire or county, sheriffs existed as local judges, civil and criminal, from the reign of David I and remain as the mainstay of Scottish justice to this day. But like the lords of regality, the office of sheriff became a hereditary one, which could be turned against the king and his policies[16].

Sheriffs were in competition with the burghs which were created by the early medieval kings as centres of royal influence and economic development through trade and manufacturing. They enjoyed their own courts over which provosts and baillies presided. At the principal or head courts of both burgh and sheriff courts, usually held four times a year, all the adult males with a title to land had to attend. This was known as suit of court. From them jurors would be selected[17].

Until the 15th century the burgh courts were supervised by the Chamberlain, a high officer of the king's household, who also heard appeals from the burgh courts. In the later Middle Ages wealthy magnates set up their own burghs, free of the king's influence and strengthening their own power. Burgh courts are the predecessors of today's district courts. Lesser landowners, called barons or lairds, also had the right and the duty to do justice in barony courts, and usually appointed a baron-baillie to act as judge in their name. In both civil and minor criminal matters he would be assisted in establishing the facts by the suitors of court, those tenants who were bound to attend[18].

As well as these courts of the land, there operated in Scotland a parallel set of courts set up by the Church. Under the law of the Church (the Canon Law), exclusive jurisdiction was claimed in 'spiritual matters', and this claim was largely accepted in Scotland. Every bishop had his own court, with a judge called the official and in larger dioceses local archdeacons also. As well as dealing with internal church disputes, the Church courts had jurisdiction over

---

15 See JM Webster and AAM Duncan *Regality of Dunfermline Court Book, 1531–1538.*

16 For a comprehensive account of the functions of the sheriff and the records of a well-run sheriff court, see WC Dickinson *The Sheriff Court Book of Fife, 1515–1522* (Scottish History Society).

17 For a similar account of burgh courts, prefacing the earliest surviving records of a burgh court, see WC Dickinson *Early Records of the Burgh of Aberdeen, 1317, 1398–1407* (Scottish History Society). On burgh juries, see ID Willock *The Origins and Development of the Jury in Scotland* p 52.

18 See, eg, WC Dickinson *The Barony Court Book of Carnwath, 1523–1542* (Scottish History Society).

the business and affairs of the laity, such as marriage, legitimacy, wills and moveable property, and contracts made under oath. Appeal lay to the supreme courts of the Catholic Church in Rome. People also often voluntarily submitted their disputes to the arbitrament of the ecclesiastical courts[19] and registered agreements in their records.

The substantive law

2.13   Unless courts are just going to decide cases on a whim or according to what seems just and reasonable, they need law to apply, general formulae which will enable cases to be determined with consistency. Feudal law, except in the individualised form of deeds, is rather scanty; but it has a voluminous procedural law, stating the manner in which decisions are to be reached. Thus, it had an order of succession to land on the death of the holder. The procedure of determining who was the entitled successor to particular lands was commenced by a claimant obtaining a brieve, a short document issued by the chancery of the king or of a regality. It ordered the sheriff or other judge to make inquiry of faithful men, the inquest or jury, whether the deceased died 'vest and seized' of certain lands, and by what tenure, and what was the relationship of the claimant to the deceased. Most of the law was of this procedural character. When much later at the end of the 16th century the first book giving a narrative account of Scots law was written, it was the *Jus Feudale* or *Feudal Law* of Thomas Craig. Criminal law was simpler. Killing, stealing, robbing and raping were crimes. The rules of law were concerned more with detailed procedures than deciding whether certain acts constituted a crime.

Law from the courts

2.14   If law was to emerge from the decisions of courts, there had to be judges sitting regularly and giving reasoned decisions on what the law meant which were in some way recorded and stored. There had also to be people knowledgeable about the law and able to argue from it; in other words, a legal profession. Its history is described in Chapter 14. It was not until the early 19th century that such a fully fledged system of judicial precedent emerged. But in the 16th and early 17th centuries, judges began to keep notebooks, initially for

---

19 See further Simon Ollivant *The Court of the Official in Pre-Reformation Scotland* (Stair Society).

their own convenience, of decisions which demonstrated the practice of the courts, like a form of custom. These were called *Practicks*. The fullest are those of Sir James Balfour and Sir Thomas Hope, who wrote *Major* and *Minor Practicks*, and Robert Spotiswoode. All of these were eventually printed. But printing was slow to be applied to the law and for a long time they circulated in handwritten copies. Some *Practicks* are mere collections of decisions of the highest courts. Others, called by historians *Digest-Practicks*, contain extracts from statutes, Roman law and Canon law as well[20].

Written Law and Statutes from Parliament

2.15 Long before these personal collections of rules of law appeared, a book of Scots law of venerable antiquity existed. This was *Regiam Majestatem*, a rather disorderly collection of laws from various sources. Some of it is native Scots law taken from Scots statutes of the 12th and 13th centuries. But the major source is the *Tractatus* or *Treatise on the Laws and Customs of England*, attributed to Glanvill, the Justiciar of King Henry II of England (1153–1189), some of the borrowings being unchanged and others amended to fit Scottish circumstances. Other sources include writers on medieval Roman and Canon law. It is uncertain how this collection began; it may well have been merely collections made by a clerk of court for his own use. But by the 15th century it was regarded as one of 'the bukis of law of this realme'[21].

The return of James I from captivity in England produced a spurt of legislation from Parliament in 1424 and subsequent years, much of it designed to improve the quality of justice and some of it apparently inspired by English examples[22]. The substantive law was still very incomplete and a statute of 1473 deplored the 'divers obscure matters that are now in our law'[23]. The first printing press was introduced into Scotland in 1507, but it was not until 1541 with the printing of the Black Acts that it was applied to legislation. Thus, the problem of identifying the authentic text of an Act was eventually solved.

20 The largest and most authoritative *Practicks* are those of Balfour of probably 1579, but not printed until 1754. See PGB McNeill *The Practicks of Sir James Balfour* (Stair Society, vols 21, 22).
21 Records of the Parliaments of Scotland, http://www.rps.ac.uk (RPS) 1426/13; one of several such Acts.
22 On the content of that statute law, see JJ Robertson 'The Development of the Law' in Jenny Brown *Scottish Society in the Fifteenth Century*.
23 RPS 1473/7/17.

The study of law

2.16   Despite the political and dynastic upheavals, the vitality of the cultural life of Scotland in the 15th century was attested to by the founding of three universities, all under papal bulls; in St Andrews in 1413, Glasgow in 1451, and Aberdeen in 1494. All were founded on the initiative of local bishops; James Kennedy, the second founder of St Andrews, William Turnbull of Glasgow and William Elphinstone of Aberdeen were all graduates in Canon law, that is, the law of the Catholic Church. All the universities taught some law from the beginning, mainly to clerical students, who thus no longer had to travel to continental universities such as Paris and Orleans. But their existence justified a statute of 1496 requiring barons and freeholders to spend three years in the 'sculis of art and jure' (ie law) 'that thai may have knawlege and understanding of the lawis'[24]. With some interruptions the teaching of law in Scottish universities has continued to the present day.

Scots law is often said to have been influenced by Roman law – sometimes referred to as Civil law. In so far as this is true, the influences have come through academic study in the universities. The first channel was through the Canon law of the Catholic Church which provided a complete and self-sufficient legal apparatus from the 12th to the mid-16th centuries. It employed the terminology and procedures of the later Roman law which reached its peak of development under the Emperor Justinian in 6th-century Byzantium. A second channel was through the *Regiam Majestatem*, the compiler of which supplemented his mainly English materials with extracts from continental writers on Roman law (see above). The third channel was through legal study by Scots in continental universities, where as a matter of course the law worthy of study was taken to be updated Roman law and not the local customary law. In the early Middle Ages, Bologna and Pisa were favoured, in the 14th and 15th centuries, Paris and Orleans, and after the Reformation, Utrecht and Leiden in the Protestant Netherlands. Many Scots, such as William Elphinstone, also taught in these overseas universities. Their influence is to be found in the often cumbersome Romanistic pleadings used in the Scots courts and in the style and phraseology of writers such as Thomas Craig and Viscount Stair (though the latter denied that Roman law as such formed part of the law of Scotland,

---

24 RPS, A 1496/6/4. On the place of law in the first Scottish universities, see DM Walker *A Legal History of Scotland* vol II, pp 277–285.

being rather a source for its equity)[25]. The influence of Roman law on Scots law has been profound, and although limited in modern times in comparison with that of English law[26], it has shaped the deep structure and concepts of private law in particular.

THE REFORMATION

2.17   The Reformation brought about several changes in political and thus legal doctrine. The latent concept of the state emerged in England, France and Spain and a long struggle began to align nations and states. In those countries which accepted the doctrines of Martin Luther, religion became in effect a department of state and all subjects were required to follow the religion of their prince. In this respect, England followed Lutheranism. The Sovereign became the head of the Church of England, to which all subjects had to belong. Allegiance to the Pope was made a matter of treason. Scotland, on the other hand, followed the doctrines of John Calvin, as applied in Geneva. He distinguished two kingdoms, a civil one and a spiritual one, the latter with Christ as its only head. These two jurisdictions were complementary.

The magistrates of the civil power should submit to the ministers of the ecclesiastical power in matters of conscience and religion, just as the ministers submitted to the magistrates in matters of civil and criminal law. As expounded in the Second Book of Discipline, drawn up by Andrew Melville in 1578, this doctrine threw a challenge to the king, which was taken up by James VI who was something of a theologian. It lay behind many of the divisive religious conflicts of the 17th century and tended to dilute the concepts of nation and patriotism. In place of bishops, Presbyterianism chose government by committees – in ascending order the Kirk Session, the Presbytery, the Synod and the General Assembly. They provided many Scots men with experience of argument from theological principles and a belief in the principles of equality and community. Arguably the Scottish resistance to laws in the making of which they have had only a minor part or which seem to embody excessive individualism derives in part from this group experience. It certainly made natural

---

25 Stair Inst I, 1, 12: 'though it be not acknowledged as a law binding for its authority, yet being, as a rule, followed for its equity'.

26 See P Stein 'The influence of Roman law on the law of Scotland' 1963 JR 205. He concludes 'many parts (of Scots law) still bear an unmistakeably Roman stamp'.

and acceptable the theological slant to the work of Viscount Stair, the late 17th century consolidator of Scots law[27].

In the ten years before and after the Reformation Act of 1560 there was popular hostility to the French counsellors and soldiers who accompanied Mary of Lorraine, the Queen Regent, and later her daughter Queen Mary. This was more than equalled by hatred of the English, following the invasions of Scotland by the Earl of Hertford in 1544 and 1545 and by the Earl of Somerset in 1547, during which many churches and towns were destroyed. When the Reformation came it took a distinctively Scottish course which owed nothing to the example of England and arguably strengthened the Scots sense of nationhood, albeit as a branch of a reformed universal church.

UNION OF THE CROWNS

2.18   The first of the three major steps which brought about the present constitutional position of Scotland was the Union of the Crowns in 1603. Queen Mary of Scotland had one child, James. When she fled to England and was imprisoned there by her cousin, Queen Elizabeth, her son was educated by tutors, including George Buchanan, an intellectual of European renown. At the age of 12 James took up the powers of kingship and was an able and vigorous monarch in trying to pacify the more disorderly parts of his realm and play off the various political and religious factions. On the execution of Mary in 1587, James became heir to the English throne, a prospect he had long relished. When Elizabeth died in 1603, James immediately made a ceremonial procession to London, feted in every town. He returned to Scotland again only once, in 1617. None the less, during his reign James VI and I took as close an interest in the government of Scotland as that of England. The introduction of Justices of the Peace into Scotland in 1609 and the creation in 1617 of the still extant Register of Sasines, providing a register of all deeds concerning title to land (outside the burghs till 1681), were two of his lasting innovations. Above all, looking at his reign over Scotland as a whole, his government provided more rigorous state control than had been previously seen in the kingdom.

Throughout his reign over the two kingdoms James cherished a scheme for their union. He derived it from his belief in the Divine Right of Kings. Since God had appointed him to rule the two realms, they should be treated as one. In his first address to the English

27 See para **2.21**.

23

Parliament in 1603 he fancifully compared himself to a husband wedded to the whole island of Britain as his wife. In 1604, the two Parliaments at his request appointed Commissioners from Scotland and England to discuss the project of unification. One of the Scots, Thomas Craig, author of the *Jus Feudale*, wrote a treatise in 1605 arguing for union on mainly practical grounds[28]. In it he asserted 'that at the present day there are no nations whose laws and institutions more closely correspond than England and Scotland' (at p 304). Although the Commissioners reported in favour of a fuller union, the proposals were opposed by both Parliaments and nothing then came of them.

One of the issues driving the king to raise the question of unification in some form was the legal status of Scots in England. Nationality was by now such a strong force that Scots and English were treated as foreigners in each other's country, a handicap felt much more by Scots than English. Despairing of finding a solution through the English Parliament, James arranged a collusive case before the highest English judges called *Calvin's Case*[29]. Land in London was bought for an infant born in Edinburgh in 1606. Its seizure by others was challenged. The judges held that *post-nati*, ie persons born in Scotland since the accession of James to the throne of England, were entitled to hold land in England, since they owed allegiance to him as King of England and he owed them protection. This limited form of naturalisation removed one of the grievances of Scots in England.

THE 17TH CENTURY; RELIGIOUS FEUDS

2.19 Throughout most of the 17th century disputes about religion took precedence over nationhood. James following out his doctrine of the Divine Right of Kings (to rule) contemplated a single church in England and Scotland led by bishops appointed by him. This provoked resistance in Scotland in his reign and even more so in that of his successor, Charles I. Charles was about to introduce Episcopacy in Scotland. The Scots of all classes reacted in 1638 by signing a National Covenant, which echoed some of the arguments of the Declaration of Arbroath in portraying the Scots as a chosen people, like the Jews, covenanted to God. This elevated form of nationalism was not long persisted in as a matter of policy, but it led

---

28 *De Unione Regnorum Britanniae Tractatus*, with translation by CS Terry (Scottish History Society). See also BP Levack 'The Proposed Union of English and Scots in the 17th Century' 1975 JR 97.
29 (1608) 7 Co Rep 1a.

to the raising of a Scottish army, which gave a boost to the concept of Scottish identity. The Scots troops invaded the North of England and occupied Newcastle. In the face of this threat Charles gave way and in 1641 ratified laws of the Scots Parliament against Episcopacy. Emboldened by this success, the Scots Covenanters then sought to impose their Presbyterian form of church government on England. Commissioners of the English Parliament, by now in conflict with the king, sought the support of the Scots. In a Solemn League and Covenant signed in 1643 the Scots and English agreed that the Church of England should be reformed on the model of the reformed faith practised in Scotland, so that there would be one form of church government throughout Britain. The Scots took this as acceptance of Presbyterianism.

This incursion into English affairs was to lead to years of skirmishes and minor battles among the armed sectarians, as an off-shoot of the English Civil War. Most Scots, though rejecting the ecclesiastical claims of Charles and his son, were shocked at the English Parliament's execution of the king in 1649 and refused to accept the ensuing Republic under Oliver Cromwell. They also were concerned that Cromwell declined to endorse Presbyterianism and instead showed a tenderness to the consciences of most believers (except of course Catholics). The period of the Commonwealth from 1649 to 1659 was thus for Scotland one of military occupation and a forced union with England.

Some Scots welcomed that unity. But when the monarchy was restored in 1660 in the person of Charles II, it was a restoration of the status quo and the two Parliaments resumed their separate existence. The religious feuds continued, but no longer reinforced nationalism, for Scots were much divided as to whether Scotland was still covenanted to impose Presbyterianism on England. Constitutional issues then came to the surface. Charles ruled in Scotland through the Scottish Privy Council, which had more power than it had enjoyed since the Middle Ages. It exercised both legislative and judicial functions, thus challenging the Parliament and the Court of Session respectively, and purported to do so under the royal prerogative, the residual powers of the king as the fountain of justice.

Resentment against this autocratic style of government eventually led to the dethroning of Charles' successor, his brother James VII (in Scotland) and II (in England). His successor (and son-in-law), William of Orange, was invited to Britain by some English nobles, prompting James's precipitate flight. The question was thus posed: who was now the King of Scotland? The Estates of Scotland (or Parliament) answered by offering the Crown to William and his spouse Mary. In a long preamble they denounced the abuses by James, who was in any case disqualified as a 'papist'. He had thus 'invaded the fundamental constitution of the Kingdom, and altered it from a legal limited Monarchy, to an arbitrary despotic Power' leading to 'the violation of the laws and liberties of the Kingdom, inverting all the ends of Government'. The Estates then declared William and Mary to be King and Queen of Scotland, confident they would preserve the rights they had asserted. Thus, the Estates were appealing to a fundamental law, by which sovereignty resided in the people (represented by the Estates of Parliament), who conferred the Crown on one who would respect that fundamental law. Indeed, the whole document is styled the Claim of Right and is the Scottish equivalent of the English Bill of Rights[30].

For much of the 17th century men's energies were thus taken up with argument and warfare on essentially religious issues. Amid the clash of arms the laws were often silent. What did emerge from this epoch of legal significance was a constitutional settlement in which the autocratic powers claimed by the Stewart monarchs were rejected and parliamentary government put in place. From it by gradual extensions of the franchise the form of parliamentary democracy now in existence in the United Kingdom emerged.

THE 18TH CENTURY

Union of the Parliaments

2.20   The inconveniences of governing two kingdoms under one king became more obvious in the reign of William, who was often absent on the continent. Scots resented their exclusion from England's foreign trade and engaged in a disastrous attempt to establish a colony at Darien in Central America. When William was succeeded by Anne, who outlived all her many children, matters came to a head, for the English Parliament, without consulting the Scots, passed the Act of Settlement in 1701, declaring that the Electress Sophia of Hanover and her offspring should succeed to the English throne. So Scots who wished the Union of the Crowns to continue would have to accept the English choice. Those who did not would have to find an alternative. James VII and II and his descendants could provide one.

Faced with this deterioration in relations, Queen Anne took the initiative and instructed that commissioners should be chosen from

---

30 See RPS M 1689/3/20.

each country to negotiate a complete union. The Scots commissioners chosen were wholeheartedly in favour, their price being that Scots should have complete equality in trade with England. The English were luke-warm. Negotiations collapsed when the Scots demanded an 'equivalent' or compensation for taking on a share of the English national debt. The Scots Parliament reacted by passing in 1703 an Act of Security declaring that on Anne's death it would nominate a successor from the royal house of Scotland provided he or she was a Protestant. The English retaliated by passing the Alien Act 1705, making Scots aliens in England and restricting trade between the two countries.

It seemed as if the two countries were on a track leading to complete separation. But in 1706 Anne restarted negotiations, this time nominating the commissioners herself, with on each side a majority in favour of an incorporating union under one Parliament. Working on the drafts of the earlier meetings, a draft treaty was produced within a few months[31].

The resultant articles of union then had to be approved one by one by the Estates of Scotland in Parliament. They were unpopular with several groups, as well as with the ordinary people of the towns. The Presbyterians of various persuasions resented the lack of protection for that form of church government. They were placated by the passing of an Act for Securing the Protestant Religion and Presbyterian Church Government, which was declared to be 'a fundamental and essential condition of any Treaty or Union ... in all time coming'[32]. In the same Act the then four universities of Scotland were to 'continue within this Kingdom for ever'. The legal profession had already had many of its doubts met by articles preserving the private law of Scotland, with change to be only on grounds of 'evident utility', and forbidding Scottish cases to be heard in any court 'in Westminster Hall'. Noblemen who saw their offices of state about to disappear were won over with sinecures, pensions, arrears of salaries (paid out of the agreed equivalent) and the retention of their hereditary rights of dispensing justice on their own lands. But the greatest lure of the union was the promise of freedom of trade with England and its colonies, which could be presented as the means to raise living standards in Scotland to equal those enjoyed in England.

The articles of union were debated by the one-chamber Scots Parliament over several months and each was voted on separately

31 The Articles of Union are printed in G Donaldson *Scottish Historical Documents* (1970) p 268.
32 *Scots Statutes Revised*, 201.

by the nobles, barons and burgesses[33]. They were all approved, with minor amendments, on 16 January 1707, together with the Act on Presbyterian Church Government. The English Parliament, urged by Queen Anne, then with less deliberation ratified the Treaty and passed an Act of Union in terms corresponding to and incorporating the Scots Act[34]. The Scots Privy Council by a proclamation dissolved the Scots Parliament on 28 April 1707 and on 1 May the United Kingdom of Great Britain, as defined in Article II, came into being. There was no corresponding dissolution of the English Parliament, but the existing members of the English Parliament, unlike members of the Scots, automatically became members of the Parliament of Great Britain and it followed the procedure of the English Parliament.

The main features of the Treaty of Union are these. The two kingdoms were united under the name of Great Britain, the succession to the monarchy being conferred on the Electress Sophia of Hanover and her descendants, as the English Parliament had decreed. There was to be one Parliament of Great Britain, in the Commons of which there should be 45 elected Scots representatives, and in the Lords 16 peers elected by their fellows. All subjects of Great Britain were to have full freedom of trade and navigation in Britain and the Dominions. The same customs and duties were to apply throughout the kingdom and the same coinage and weights and measures. The Court of Session and Court of Justiciary were to remain in all time coming in Scotland. 'No causes in Scotland [were to] be cognisable by the Courts of Chancery, Queen's Bench, Common Pleas or any other Court in Westminster Hall', a sentence the meaning of which was to be later the subject of debate[35]. The Scots Privy Council was to continue until altered by Parliament (which promptly abolished it). Heritable jurisdictions and offices were reserved to their owners. Laws concerning 'Public Right, Policy and Civil Government may be made the same throughout the whole United Kingdom', but 'no alteration be made in Laws which concern private Right, except for the evident utility of the Subjects within Scotland' (Article XVIII). The rights and privileges of the royal burghs of Scotland were preserved. Laws and statutes of either kingdom so far as inconsistent with the Articles were void[36].

---

33 Minutes of the debates can be read from RPS M 1706/10/1.
34 Union with Scotland Act 1706 (6 Anne c 11). At this time Acts were dated by the first day of the session in which they were passed.
35 RPS 1706/10/257.
36 For text with subsequent amendments, see *Scots Statutes Revised* 203.

Rational exposition of the law

2.21   Apart from Craig's defence in Latin of feudal law, writing about the law as distinct from collections of laws in the 17th century had scarcely gone beyond the stage of *Digest-Practicks* (see para **2.14**). Sir George Mackenzie, Lord Advocate under Charles II and founder of the Advocates' Library (the precursor of the present National Library of Scotland), was a man of learning who wrote much on morality, religion and heraldry. But in writing his *Laws and Customs in Matters Criminal* he gathered together and analysed pieces of law from many varied sources under subject-headings. James Dalrymple, Viscount Stair, then with one massive and masterly work transformed the civil (ie non-criminal) law of Scotland from uncoordinated fragments of law from various sources of uncertain weight and priority into a coherent and rational system of law, expounded in magisterial style. This work was *The Institutions of the Law of Scotland* of 1681 (extensively revised and republished in 1693)[37].

Stair's achievement is summed up in the sub-title 'Deduced from its originals, and collated with the Civil [ie Roman] Canon and Feudal Laws, and with the Customs of Neighbouring Nations'. Stair had been a Regent (or Professor) of Philosophy at Glasgow University from 1641 before embarking on a legal career which carried him to the top post of Lord President of the Court of Session in 1671. In 1681 he refused to take an oath under the Scottish Test Act 1681, had to resign and retired in 1682 to Leiden in the Netherlands, where he remained until the deposition of James VII and II in 1688. He then returned to Britain in the company of the future King William of Orange who re-appointed him Lord President[38].

Stair's concept of a work expounding as a system the whole of a nation's civil law had no counter-part in England until William Blackstone's *Commentaries* of 1765, but he may have been inspired by the similar treatment of the civil law of the Netherlands by Hugo Grotius, who is celebrated as the founder of international law. Stair's achievement thus put Scots law in line with the major systems of law which took Roman law as their inspiration. In Scotland his example was followed by the *Institute of the Law of Scotland in Civil Rights* of Andrew McDouall, Lord Bankton, of 1751, the *Institute of the Law of Scotland* of John Erskine, Professor of Scots Law at Edinburgh, of 1773, and the *Commentaries on the Law of Scotland and the Principles of Mercantile Jurisprudence* of 1804 and the *Principles of the Law of*

---

37 The 1693 text was used in a new edition, edited by DM Walker in 1981.
38 For a fuller account of his life, see *Stair Tercentenary Studies*, edited by DM Walker (Stair Society, 1981).

Scotland of 1829 of George Joseph Bell. The relative weakness of legal literature on the criminal side was remedied by David Hume (nephew of the philosopher of the same name) in his *Commentaries on the Law of Scotland Respecting Crimes* of 1797, which performed the same organising role for criminal law as Stair had done for civil law a century earlier. Erskine, Bell and Hume were all holders of the Chair of Scots Law at Edinburgh University and evidence the contribution that the Universities of Edinburgh and, to a lesser extent, Glasgow (in William Forbes and others) were making to the development of Scots law, following the establishment of Chairs of Law there in the early 18th century.

As such they were part of the movement in scholarship called the Enlightenment in which Scotland played a leading role through the writings of men such as David Hume, the philosopher, Adam Smith, the economist and jurist, John Millar and Adam Ferguson, the forerunners of modern sociology. Stair, though founding his work on theological assumptions that were undermined by the philosopher Hume, had in common with the Enlightenment movement of the next century his claim that the constitution rested on rational foundations and his imposing order on the hitherto disorderly and incomplete civil law of Scotland. Within the 18th century the most prominent contributor from the legal profession to the Enlightenment movement was Henry Home, Lord Kames (1696–1782). Kames was an enthusiastic polymath, whose interests extended to agricultural improvement, transport, town planning, history, philosophy and literature, as well as law and its science, jurisprudence. His main work on the law is his *Principles of Equity* of 1760, in which in typical Enlightenment fashion he precedes his account of equitable procedures in Scots law and English law with a discussion of the principle of utility under which courts have a role to play in advancing the well-being of people[39].

THE 19TH CENTURY

2.22 The transformation of the social life of Scotland through the Industrial and Agricultural Revolutions could not fail to have an impact on its legal system and in several ways it adapted itself to meet the challenge. The upsurge of trade and manufacturing

---

39 For biographies of Kames, see Ian S Ross *Lord Kames and the Scotland of his Day* (1972) and William C Lehmann *Henry Home, Lord Kames, and the Scottish Enlightenment* (1971). On the Enlightenment as a whole see Arthur Herman *The Scottish Enlightenment* (2002).

made new demands on the legal concepts of contract and property. Innumerable daily deals for the supply and transformation and transport of commodities required an environment in which they could be entered into with confidence that they would be carried out. Insurance and bankruptcy laws had to be available to cope when they were not. But land law, still rooted in the feudal law handed down from the Middle Ages, was ill-adapted to industrial needs and in the hands of rapacious landlords could become an instrument of oppression in rural areas, most notoriously in the Highland Clearances. Police forces were rudimentary, until the Police (Scotland) Act 1857 required all counties and the larger burghs to maintain a local force. Thus, conditions of law and order in which industrial and commercial activity could flourish were secured.

At the start of the century the law could enable people to come together in business only by means of partnership and unincorporated joint stock companies. Their resources could be pooled in the enterprise, but each individual's own entire assets remained fully liable if it failed. From the creditor's point of view there was the handicap that each contributor to the enterprise had to be sued separately. By means of several statutes this brake on commercial enterprise was removed by 1862 through the creation of incorporated companies, which have an existence in law distinct from that of the individuals who as shareholders are their members. Their personal liability for the company's debts is limited to the value of their shares, including any unpaid ones. Banks, however, were excluded from incorporation until after the disastrous collapse of the City of Glasgow Bank in 1878 which brought ruin to many in the West of Scotland.

Restructuring of the courts

2.23   Early in the century the Court of Session was restructured and thus became better able to deal with the later upsurge of commercial litigation. It had sat since its inception in 1532 as a single court of fifteen judges, one of whom in turn sat in the 'Outer House' to take evidence, while the rest sat in the 'Inner House'. In 1808 the Inner House was made an appellate court, sitting in two divisions, each of four judges[40]. The remainder dealt alone with cases at first instance, that is, on first hearing. Procedure was also facilitated by cutting down the length of written pleadings. Later in the century, shorthand

---

40 On the reform of the Court of Session, see Nicholas Phillipson *The Scottish Whigs and the Reform of the Court of Session* (Stair Society, vol 37) ch V.

writers were admitted to record evidence. Appeals from the Court of Session to the House of Lords, which had begun immediately after the Union of 1707 and flourished in the 18th century, were curtailed by the Court of Session Act of 1808. Many of the sheriff courts had been poorly served since the abolition of heritable jurisdictions in 1747, for the sheriffs were Edinburgh advocates, who seldom attended, but acted through unqualified resident sheriff-substitutes. From 1825 this abuse was remedied in that sheriff-substitutes had to be advocates or solicitors of at least three years' standing.

Growth of case law

2.24 The smaller appellate courts led to the judges feeling an onus upon each of them to justify his decision; and as the century wore on these tended to become fuller and supported by the authority of past cases and, in their absence, of the class of authorities who became recognised as institutional writers. From 1821 the judgments, mainly of the Inner House, were collected and published in annual volumes which form part of the series now known as *Session Cases*. In this manner the essential requirement for the emergence of a practice of judicial precedent, namely accurate reports of litigation and reasoned judgments upon it, gathered by advocates in a standardised form, was met. Previously it had been left to the initiative of individuals, of whom two of the best qualified were Stair and Kames, to publish such decisions as they selected. Now the material was available and the structure was in place to operate a system of judicial precedent. In the 19th century the typical form of law was thus the published judgment. As more and more issues arose for decision from the industrial and commercial community, Scottish advocates cited and Scottish judges used English decisions more and more to justify their judgments and thereby gave the business users of the law a legal environment which was nearly uniform throughout Great Britain. Statutes such as the Mercantile Law Amendment Act of 1856 and the Sale of Goods Act of 1893, applying throughout Great Britain, accentuated this trend.

THE 20TH AND 21ST CENTURIES

2.25 While the decisions of judges still play a creative role, now in most of the law there is less scope for innovation and development than before. In part this is because more law is already settled. But chiefly it is because of the dominance of enacted law, both in changing existing areas of law such as family law, and in opening up new areas of legal regulation; for example, road traffic law, planning law, social security law, race and sex discrimination, employment protection, misuse of drugs and new forms of taxation. In these areas the role of the courts is a secondary one, clearing up ambiguities in the law that comes from Parliament. The courts too play a less dominant role than before, because much of the work of decision-making is entrusted to specialised tribunals, such as immigration tribunals, employment tribunals, and Commissioners of Income Tax. Road traffic law remains with the courts, but the volume of cases has been lessened by procedures allowing many minor criminal, including road traffic, offences to be dealt with by the acceptance of a penalty offer, recourse to the courts being at the option of the alleged offender.

Nearly all these new areas of statutory law are common to Great Britain or the United Kingdom and represent the notional will of the whole electorate as mediated through the United Kingdom Parliament. Thus, they diminish the proportion of the law prevailing in Scotland which is distinctively Scottish. Most of the tribunal systems operate on a British basis and so offer little or no scope for a distinctive Scottish contribution. Occasionally in road traffic and drug law the Scots courts will differ from their English counterparts, but such disagreements do not usually last long.

Parliaments are ill-equipped to deal with these demands for new and complex legal regulation. Much of such law calls for a response to changing circumstances; for instance, new drugs, new vehicles, new forms of disability. For this reason and the sheer volume of regulations required, most enacted law takes the form of regulations classed as statutory instruments and produced by government departments, under powers delegated by Parliaments, but with little or no parliamentary scrutiny. Often, as in the Social Security Act 1986, the Act itself is a mere framework, authorising the creation of benefits through easily amended statutory instruments such as in that example income support and housing benefit.

During the years of Conservative rule from 1979 to 1997 a ground-swell of discontent arose at the imposition of policies on Scotland which were opposed by the majority of MPs elected in Scottish constituencies. This first took the form of a pressure-group called the Campaign for a Scottish Assembly. This demand was taken up in a formal way by the formation of a Scottish Constitutional Convention composed of representatives of certain political parties, local authorities, trade unions and churches. It published a Claim of Right deliberately echoing that of the late 17th century and asserting the right of the Scottish people to determine the form of government that best suited their needs. The Labour government that returned to power on 1 May 1997 was, with the Liberal Democrats, pledged to create a Scottish Parliament. This commitment was fleshed out in a White Paper, *Scotland's Parliament*. Its terms were put to a referendum of voters registered in Scotland and supported by a large majority. The first Scottish Parliament was elected in May 1999 and exercises authority over all matters which are not specifically reserved to the United Kingdom Parliament. During its first fixed term of four years the Parliament passed over 62 Acts. The Parliaments elected in 1999 and 2003 produced governments that were coalitions of the Labour and Liberal Democrat parties, which together held a majority of the seats. But in 2007 the Scottish National Party, whose aim is the independence of Scotland, obtained the largest number of votes, but in seats won only one more than the Labour Party. It formed a ministry, acknowledging it would have to secure the approval of at least some of the other parties to any legislation it proposed. After a difficult four years, however, the Scottish National Party not only won a majority of votes but also took an overall majority of the seats in the Scottish Parliament in the 2011 election. This triumph gave it the mandate to put the question of independence or not to the Scottish people in a referendum, albeit the legislation to bring that about required the agreement of the United Kingdom government. That was achieved in the autumn of 2012 (the Edinburgh Agreement), and the referendum will be held in October 2014.

The continuing parts of the law of Scotland have the means of being kept up to date through the research and reports of the Scottish Law Commission, regardless of whether the issues involved have engendered appeals to the courts[41]. This has been supported by a resurgence of the academic study of law in the university law schools, substantial evidence of which is to be seen in the volumes of the Scottish Universities Law Institute (SULI) and *The Laws of Scotland: Stair Memorial Encyclopaedia*, both initiated by Sir Thomas Smith. But, as we shall see, there have been some difficulties in securing the enactment of the Commission's draft Bills, which should be remedied by the Scottish Parliament. Other changes to Scots law have sometimes been made as part of mainly English measures, such as the Unfair Contract Terms Act 1977 and the Criminal Justice Act 1988. Even today, Acts which apply throughout Britain and have special applications to Scotland, such as the Civil Partnership Act 2004, may be passed in the Westminster Parliament.

The United Kingdom's membership of the European Union creates a layer of legal regulation above that emanating from Parliament and

41 See ch 8 below

thus diminishes to some degree the identity of the Scots law[42]. The characteristics of the law produced by the European Commission have much in common with the statutory instruments produced by United Kingdom ministries. They are difficult to discover and to understand because of their technical expression and lack of a context. They are prone to frequent unannounced change. Any disadvantage emerging to the detriment of the issuing authority can quickly be corrected by amendment, sometimes with retrospective effect. The legal profession tends to be reluctant to become involved with regulations. Thus, this law is weighted in favour of its creators, who are also its enforcers, and any rights it appears to confer on individuals are purely theoretical. We may call this law bureaucratic law, and with its adjunct in tribunals it is the typical legal product of the second half of the 20th century.

However, just as the volume of law of all kinds seems to be in danger of collapsing under its own weight, computer technology has come to the rescue in the form of data retrieval bases. These have been in operation for over 20 years in the form of LexisNexis, Westlaw and others which give access to decisions (some unreported) and statutory materials in the United Kingdom, Commonwealth countries, USA, France and to a minor extent the European Union. *Statutes in Force* and the Land Register of Scotland can also be accessed by computer. A database of sentences passed on offenders in various circumstances has been provided for High Court judges to promote consistency in sentencing. Judgments of the Court of Session and High Court are now available on the Internet on the day of publication.

CONCLUSION

2.26   It is a far cry from the trading customs of Scottish burghs in the 12th century to a print-out of the latest statutory instrument in the early 21st. All they have in common is the capacity to change people's behaviour, at the behest of those who control them, from what it would otherwise be. But that is the tenuous essence of law. Scotland in its chequered but well-documented history has generated the full range of forms that law can take.

---

42 See para **3.6**.

3 Institutions – the constitutional background

CONSTITUTIONS AND CONSTITUTIONAL REFORM

3.1   Any legal system has to be understood against its constitutional background, a fact particularly true for any of the three legal systems of the United Kingdom. This is because the United Kingdom is most unusual in being a unitary rather than federal state[1], yet having within it three separate legal systems[2]. This situation clearly pre-dates devolution, being built into the constitution of the United Kingdom.

This chapter considers the relevant aspects of the constitutional background to the Scottish legal system, firstly in relation to the United Kingdom, including Scotland, and then in relation to 'Europe'[3], including the United Kingdom.

THE UNITED KINGDOM

3.2   The state is properly called 'the United Kingdom of Great Britain and Northern Ireland'. This title was assumed after what is now the Republic of Ireland seceded in 1922. It does not include the Channel Islands and the Isle of Man, which are technically dependencies of it. The preceding title, 'the United Kingdom of

---

1   Federal states are those containing a number of sub-units of varying, but considerable, degrees of autonomy. Thus in Germany, there are 16 'states' (*Länder*), such as Baden-Württemburg, Bavaria, and so on, each of which has its own Government, Parliament, court system and legal powers, and together they make up the Federal Republic of Germany (*Bundesrepublik Deutschland*), which has a federal Government, Parliament, court system and legal powers (thus arguably constituting 17 legal systems in all). Similarly, in the United States, there are 50 'states', such as Alabama, Alaska, Arizona, and so on, making up the (federal) United States of America (thus arguably constituting 51 legal systems in all). Such arrangements are to be distinguished from devolution.

2   This last fact more than any other distinguishes devolution from federalism. For a useful brief history of the devolution legislation, see CMG Himsworth & CR Munro *The Scotland Act 1998* (W Green/Sweet & Maxwell, 2nd edn, 2000).

3   Deliberately in quotation marks, to indicate an ambiguity discussed below.

Great Britain and Ireland', was created when Great Britain and Ireland were formally amalgamated by the Union of 1801.

'Great Britain' comprises Scotland, England and Wales. This title was adopted when the two previous states (Scotland, and England and Wales, respectively) were combined in 1707, after sharing monarchs since 1603 (when the failure of the Tudor dynasty to produce an heir brought the Stewart dynasty to England as well as Scotland). Wales had been conquered by England in the 13th century, and was legally and administratively combined with it in the 16th century[4].

The laws and legal institutions of Scotland and of England and Wales were not merged by the Union of 1707. Thus, they remain separate 'law areas', with separate court systems (as does Northern Ireland), and it is necessary to distinguish Scots law and English law (and Northern Irish law). However, a single legislature was created by the 1707 Union (and continued by the 1801 Union[5]). This legislature is common to all the law areas and much legislation is passed which applies to the whole of the United Kingdom, or of Great Britain. It makes sense, therefore, to speak of 'United Kingdom law' and 'Great Britain law' in fields such as tax and social security law which are common to the whole United Kingdom, or to Great Britain, as well as speaking of 'Scots law' and 'English law' (and 'Northern Ireland law')[6]. With the Welsh Assembly set up by the Government of Wales Act 1998 gaining legislative powers under the Government of Wales Act 2006, it is becoming possible also to speak of 'Welsh law', even though Wales is not (yet) a separate jurisdiction like the other constituent parts of the United Kingdom or Great Britain.[6a]

In 1973 the United Kingdom acceded to the European Community, which was itself incorporated into the European Union[7] in 1992. This has had considerable legal and governmental effects in the four

---

4   See Jones, Turnbull & Williams 'The Law of Wales or the Law of England and Wales?' (2005) 26 Stat LR 135–145.
5   Or rather, perhaps, created in 1801, out of the merger of the Parliaments of Great Britain and of Ireland.
6   'British' is a very ambiguous word in constitutional terms, and has no specific legal meaning, save in specific contexts, such as 'British citizenship', as created by the British Nationality Act 1981. On the Treaty and Acts of Union, see ch 2.
6a See *Local Government Byelaws (Wales) Bill 2012 – Reference by the Attorney General for England and Wales* [2012] UKSC 58, [2012] 3 WLR 1294, where Lord Hope of Craighead refers, in a significant case on Welsh devolution, to 'Welsh law' (para 71).
7   The European Union was considered as comprising the 'three pillars' of: the European Community; the 'Common Foreign and Security Policy' of EC Member States; and 'Police and Judicial Co-operation in Criminal Matters' (previously 'Justice and Home Affairs') among EC Member States. However, the 'three pillars' have now been integrated: this is discussed in more detail below.

decades of United Kingdom membership. The principal effect, so far as the legal system is concerned, is that there are institutions generating and judging the law created by the European Union ('European Union law' or 'EU law'), and this law can apply in the United Kingdom and, indeed, displace Scots or English law (or Northern Ireland law).

United Kingdom government and Parliament

The Crown and government

3.3 'The Crown' is a term used to mean, in effect, the state. It is a symbol of the power of the state, which was formerly vested in the monarch. Thus, for example, prosecution of crime is said to be on behalf of 'the Crown'. For very few purposes does 'the Crown' refer to the monarch personally. When reference is made to the Queen's formal powers and duties, the terms 'Sovereign' or 'Her Majesty' are often used.

Government is carried on in the name of 'the Crown', so the Crown often comes to mean the government of the United Kingdom. This comprises the Prime Minister and some 25 senior ministers (those in charge of departments usually being called 'Secretary of State'[8]) who form the Cabinet, and up to 100 or so junior ministers (usually called 'Minister of State' or 'Parliamentary Under-Secretary of State') and unpaid 'Parliamentary Private Secretaries'. By a 'convention of the constitution' (that is, an unwritten rule of the constitution[9]), members of the government must be members of one or other House of Parliament. The Prime Minister is appointed by the Sovereign. However, her discretion is extremely constrained, for there is another strong convention of the constitution that she appoint the person who can command a majority in a vote in the House of Commons. In practice this means the leader of the party which won the last general election[10]. The other ministers are also appointed by the Sovereign, but in practice on the nomination of the Prime Minister. It is the United Kingdom government which proposes most legislation in

---

8 Thus, eg, Secretary of State for Foreign and Commonwealth Affairs ('Foreign Secretary ') etc. There is no fixed number or identity of these offices.

9 And is not to be confused with the European Convention on Human Rights, discussed below.

10 Thus, when Mr Blair, Prime Minister by virtue of leading the Labour Party which had won the previous three elections, resigned in 2007, and Mr Brown was the only candidate for leadership of the Labour Party, it was clear that only Mr Brown could be appointed Prime Minister

the United Kingdom Parliament (including some which relates to Scotland, either because it relates to the whole United Kingdom or to Great Britain, or because it has been asked to by the Scottish Government, typically 'piggy-backing' upon similar legislation for England and Wales[11]). The United Kingdom government is sometimes referred to as 'Whitehall'[12], after the name of the street in which most central government offices are situated.

Secretary of State for Scotland. Before devolution, the Scottish Office, headed by a Secretary of State for Scotland, was the United Kingdom government ('Whitehall') department responsible for Scotland. Responsibility for most Scottish matters, including the legal system, is now, however, devolved to the Scottish Government (and Scottish Parliament). However, a Scotland Office[13] remains in Whitehall, under a Secretary of State for Scotland, despite the reduction in his functions, and he is able to participate in decisions on matters reserved to the United Kingdom government as they affect Scotland[14]. Under the devolution legislation, he can forbid any action proposed by a member of the Scottish Government which he believes would be incompatible with any international obligations, including Community law and rights under the European Convention of Human Rights, and likewise to order action to be taken to give effect to such obligations[15]. Similarly, he can also revoke Scottish delegated legislation which he believes to be incompatible with international obligations or with the interests of defence and national security or which purports to modify reserved matters[16]. Thus, he can be said to have a supervisory function to ensure that the Scottish authorities do not exceed their powers. However, while the Secretary of State may be said to have a number of roles (including representing Scotland in Westminster and Whitehall, and vice versa; resolving issues between the two; determining whether proposed Scottish legislation is within devolved powers and challenging legislation which is not; and being the channel of funds from the United Kingdom government to the Scottish Government and negotiating in relation to them), it has been doubted whether, with devolution, there is a real role for the office. The present incumbent, Michael Moore MP, is however full-

---

11 See the discussion of legislative process in Ch 7.
12 The phrase 'Westminster Government' is also commonly used.
13 Note the change of name.
14 See www.scotlandoffice.gov.uk/. The Secretary of State for Scotland at the time of writing is Michael Moore, Liberal Democrat MP for Berwickshire, Roxburgh and Selkirk.
15 Scotland Act 1998, s 58.
16 *Ibid.*

time and has played a prominent role in the debate about Scottish independence and the referendum on that question to be held in October 2014.

Law Officers of the Crown – Advocate-General for Scotland, Attorney General and the Solicitor General (for England and Wales). The Law Officers of the Crown are the chief Government legal advisers. The devolution settlement also made provision for a new Law Officer, the Advocate-General for Scotland, to advise the Westminster government on matters of Scots law[17]. This was necessary because the Lord Advocate, who provided such advice before devolution, was translated to the Scottish Government under the devolution settlement. There is no requirement that the Advocate-General be a Member of Parliament, nor even qualified in Scots law. Under the devolution legislation, he is one of those who can initiate court proceedings to determine any dispute or doubt that has arisen over the operation of that legislation[18], and can (as can the Attorney General for England and Wales) raise proceedings before the Supreme Court of the United Kingdom, which is the ultimate authority on the meaning of the Scotland Act, including the question of whether a Bill of the Scottish Parliament is one which it has power to pass[19].

The Attorney General and the Solicitor General are Law Officers for England and Wales[20] (and, to maintain the former of the two 'conventions of the constitution' referred to above, are invariably members of one or other House of Parliament, though not necessarily in Cabinet[21]). They may appear for the Crown in major litigation on behalf of the Crown, and provide legal advice on English law, but are

---

17 Scotland Act 1998, s 87: see www.oag.gov.uk/ The first Advocate-General for Scotland was Lynda Clark, QC, MP, who remained in that office as Lady Clark of Calton after the 2005 General Election, when her constituency was abolished. She became a judge in 2006 and was replaced by Neil Davidson, QC, who was not an MP, but was a former Solicitor-General for Scotland. Thus, the former of the two 'conventions of the constitution' referred to above does not appear to apply to this office. The current Advocate-General for Scotland is Lord Wallace of Tankerness QC. The Advocate-General for Scotland should not be confused with the Advocates General of the Court of Justice of the European Union (discussed below).

18 Scotland Act 1998, Sch 6, Pt II.

19 Scotland Act 1998, s 33: but note below, and in Ch 4, in relation to the Supreme Court.

20 There is also an Attorney General (but no Solicitor General) for Northern Ireland.

21 The Attorney General at the end of 2012 was Dominic Grieve QC and the Solicitor General for England & Wales was Oliver Heald QC.

likely to be asked to give legal advice on United Kingdom law, and indeed, international law, as well[22].

The other Law Officers, that is, the Lord Advocate and the Solicitor General for Scotland, are considered below.

Lord Chancellor and Secretary of State for Justice, and the Secretary of State for Home Affairs. In day-to-day terms, the Lord Chancellor and Secretary of State for Justice (two offices held by the same person) bears no responsibility for the Scottish legal system. He is the Cabinet minister responsible in England and Wales, firstly (as Lord Chancellor[23]), for appointments to the judiciary, and secondly (as Secretary of State for Justice), for courts, prisons, etc[24]. In addition to the Lord Chancellor and Secretary for Justice[25], the Ministry of Justice also contains several other ministers[26]. However, because the responsibility for appointments to the judiciary includes appointments to United Kingdom tribunals, and because the Lord Chancellor has a wide range of disparate statutory responsibilities, his functions may touch upon the machinery of justice in Scotland.

Reflecting the history of the Lord Chancellorship, and constitutional significance of responsibility for judicial appointments the Constitutional Reform Act 2005 requires certain qualifications of an appointee, imposes a responsibility upon him to uphold judicial independence, and obliges him to take an oath[27].

The Secretary of State for Home Affairs (the 'Home Secretary') and his Department (the residual Home Office), bear no day-to-day responsibility for the Scottish legal system either. They continue to have some responsibility relating to the English legal system in relation to criminal law and sentencing, which is less likely to impinge on the Scottish legal system than the responsibilities of the Lord Chancellor and Secretary of State for Justice. Their other functions in relation to immigration and anti-terrorism do impinge, however.

---

22 The advice of the then Attorney General (Lord Goldsmith) on the legality of the invasion of Iraq in 2003 became controversial, though remaining officially confidential.
23 Still, technically 'Lord High Chancellor of Great Britain', successor to the Lord Chancellors of Scotland and England & Wales. The former office of Lord Chancellor of Ireland was abolished upon Partition in 1922.
24 See also references to the Appellate Committee of the House of Lords and the Supreme Court of the United Kingdom below and in Ch 4.
25 At the end of 2012 the Lord Chancellor and Secretary of State for Justice was Chris Grayling MP.
26 See http://www.justice.gov.uk/.
27 Constitutional Reform Act 2005, ss 2, 3 & 17: see also the curious assertion of fact in s 1. The qualifications are, however, less than exiguous.

The United Kingdom Parliament[28]

3.4 The Parliament of the United Kingdom comprises the Sovereign, the House of Lords, and the House of Commons. In this, it reflects the traditions of the English Parliament rather than the Scots. It is sometimes referred to as 'Westminster', as the building it meets in is technically the Palace of Westminster.

The Sovereign is a ceremonial element of Parliament only. The House of Lords used to comprise all hereditary peers[29] (who latterly numbered some 750, though few sat regularly) and all life peers[30] (who number some 700). This had been regarded by many for a century or more as an indefensible anomaly, but several efforts to reform it over that period failed. As first stage of the most recent attempt, legislation[31] allowed all the life peers to continue to sit, but only 92 hereditary peers chosen by election from among themselves (giving an overall total of some 730), radically altering the composition of the House into a largely appointed one[32]. It also continued to contain certain Church of England bishops and the Lords of Appeal in Ordinary (for whom, see below). However, the matter has remained stalled since then – most recently in summer 2012, when the Coalition Government withdrew a reform Bill in the face of resolute opposition from backbench Tory MPs – as dispute between those who seek a House of Lords wholly or largely appointed by the government, and those who seek one wholly or largely elected by the electorate, remains unresolved.

The House of Commons comprises 650 MPs, elected in single-member constituencies of roughly equal population. There are 59 Scottish constituencies, a number reduced in 2005 from an

---

28 See www.parliament.uk/, also www.parliamentlive.tv.
29 From the Union until the Peerage Act 1963, while all holders of post-1707 peerages, and all holders of (pre-1707) English peerages, might sit in the House of Lords, only 16 elected 'representative' holders of (pre-1707) Scottish peerages could sit. The 1963 Act permitted all Scottish peers to sit.
30 Permitted by the Life Peerages Act 1958 (though there were some examples before that). Life peers are, in effect, nominated by the Prime Minister, typically as party political appointments from the major political parties, though not all are. In 2000, the government set up an extra-statutory House of Lords Appointments Commission to recommend non-political appointments ('people's peers').
31 House of Lords Act 1999.
32 *Lord Gray's Motion* 2000 SC(HL) 46 unsuccessfully challenged the change as a breach of the Treaty of Union. Peers may now, however, seek election to the House of Commons (and the Scottish Parliament).

admitted overprovision of 72, to reflect the existence of the Scottish Parliament[33].

The United Kingdom Parliament is (subject to EU legislation) the legislature, in which most law for the United Kingdom is made. It is also the forum in which government policy is discussed, and provides the means by which governments are created. The party which can command the largest number of votes in the House of Commons is, by a convention of the constitution, entitled to form the government[34]. The system of simple majority voting in general elections has had the effect that the party which receives most votes in total usually has a disproportionate number of members returned. Coalition governments were almost unknown, except in war-time, until the 2010 General Election, in which the Conservatives were the largest party, with 307 seats, but this was not enough for an overall majority in the House of Commons. There was accordingly a coalition agreement with the Liberal Democrats, whose 57 seats enabled the two parties together to command a majority and so form a government.

The United Kingdom constitution has usually been said to display 'parliamentary supremacy' (alias 'parliamentary sovereignty'), that is, that there are no legal boundaries to Parliament's legislative power: it may pass any law to any effect[35]. As governments almost invariably have a majority in the House of Commons (indeed, that is why they are the government), and a convention of the constitution requires that the House of Lords not veto legislation which the Commons insists upon, there has long been in practice 'executive dominance of the legislature', or more bluntly 'governmental supremacy'[36]. The

33 Devolution has created the anomaly whereby the Scottish MPs can vote on legislation relating to English law while English and Welsh MPs cannot vote on legislation relating to Scots law, responsibility for which has been devolved to the Scottish Parliament. This is commonly known as the 'West Lothian Question' after Tam Dalziel, for many years MP for West Lothian, who is credited with drawing attention to it. It is a constitutional problem (though no greater than the anomaly preceding devolution whereby English MPs could outvote Scottish ones on a matter of Scots law: a sort of 'West Sussex Question').

34 Hence the 'convention of the constitution' that the Sovereign appoint as Prime Minister the person who can command a majority in a vote in the House of Commons

35 It has been argued that this is an English principle, which the Scottish constitution never recognised (see *eg MacCormick v Lord Advocate* 1953 SC 396); also that it is a 19th-century invention. Be that as it may, it has been the UK constitutional orthodoxy for well over a century. Thus, the Scottish Parliament's power to make law derives from the Scotland Act which can be amended or repealed by the UK Parliament.

36 Lord Hailsham, a former Conservative Lord Chancellor, described it even more bluntly as 'elective dictatorship'.

Coalition Government formed in 2010 illustrates some political qualification of this dominance when the two constituent parties disagree – as, for example, in the case of House of Lords reform already mentioned.

Parliamentary supremacy as a constitutional principle is extremely unusual, for nearly all other states have a written constitution which, among other things, limits the powers of the legislature. In any case, accession to the European Union has required that Acts of Parliament be subordinate to EU legislation, apparently fatally compromising this 'supremacy'.

There is a House of Commons Scottish Grand Committee, comprising all Scottish MPs, which can debate government policy but, since devolution, has little to do[37]. There is also a Select Committee on Scottish Affairs, which consists of back-benchers, reflects party strengths, and scrutinises the policy and decisions of the Scotland Office, including its relationship with the Scottish Parliament. This will no doubt continue for as long as the office of Secretary of State for Scotland remains.

The Scottish Parliament and Government

3.5   Scotland now has a large measure of devolution[38]. There is a Scottish Parliament (sometimes referred to as 'Holyrood', as it is located is next to the Palace of Holyrood) and a Scottish Administration (in effect a Scottish government, a phrase it sometimes applies to itself, though it is not used in the legislation), led by a Scottish Government). The Acts grant to these devolved institutions the powers and responsibilities which used to be exercised by the United Kingdom Parliament and United Kingdom government.

There have been many legislative successes, such as the reform of landownership. Legislative procedures are interestingly different from those of Westminster; and policies at variance with those of Whitehall pursued (as devolution was intended to permit). However, the early years were overshadowed by a rapid turnover of First Ministers, and the lateness and expense of the new Scottish Parliament building[39].

More recently we have seen the Calman Commission's proposals for extension of the devolved powers to include new taxation powers in relation to land and income tax, drugs legislation, borrowing powers (under tight Treasury control) etc implemented by the

---

37 At the time of writing (December 2012), it has not met since November 2003.
38 See Scotland Act 1998 as amended by the Scotland Act 2012.
39 It was completed some three years late and some ten times over budget.

Scotland Act 2012 (although they will not come fully into force until 2015). The SNP's unprecedented overall majority in the 2011 Scottish Parliament election has also brought the question of independence to the forefront of Scottish politics[40]. A referendum on independence is expected to take place in October 2014. This could have major effects on the constitutions of both the United Kingdom as a whole and Scotland as a separate nation. It was disputed whether the Scottish Parliament had the legislative competence to pass legislation providing for the referendum; but that uncertainty was removed by the 'Edinburgh Agreement' of September 2012 between the UK and the Scottish Governments, under which the former agreed to promote an Order in Council under section 30(2) of the Scotland Act 1998, which would put beyond doubt the power of the Scottish Parliament to legislate on the matter and provide for a single-question referendum[41].

Devolved matters and reserved matters

3.6 The basic principle of Scottish devolution is that everything is devolved unless specifically reserved. The powers and responsibilities devolved are essentially domestic ones, but the division is not simple and unavoidably leaves a large number of 'debatable lands'. The legislation contains the detailed list of 'reserved matters'. They may be modified by Orders in Council, as in the case of the independence referendum just mentioned[42]. They are divided into 'General Reservations' and 'Specific Reservations'.

The **General Reservations** are the Constitution, Political Parties, Foreign Affairs, the Civil Service, Defence, and Treason. These are clearly United Kingdom responsibilities. Some of these have exceptions, however. An important one is that, while relations with the European Community are reserved, 'observing and implementing international obligations, obligations under the Human Rights Convention, and obligations under Community law' are not, and are therefore devolved so far as Scotland is concerned.

---

40 In the fourth Scottish Parliamentary election in 2011, the Scottish National Party, committed to independence, won an overall majority of seats in the Scottish Parliament (69).
41 Scotland Act 1998, s 30(2) allows the list of 'reserved matters' (for which see below) to be modified by 'Her Majesty in Council' (in effect, the Westminster Government), and it has been, for example, to enable the Scottish Parliament to pass a Referendum Bill.
42 Scotland Act 1998, Sch 5.

The **Specific Reservations** are set out under 11 subject-headings, often with reference to particular statutes and again with exceptions. These are cases where there is tension between the wide sweep of devolution on the one hand and the desire to reserve certain specific matters on the other. They are therefore much more complicated, and are as follows:

A – Financial and Economic Matters
Council tax and non-domestic rates are not reserved, but money laundering is. There is now a power to 'set' rather than 'vary' income tax for Scottish taxpayers (Scotland Act 2012, s 25 and Scotland Act 1998, s 80C) and for the removal of UK Stamp Duty Land Tax in relation to Scottish transfers of property with a few exceptions (Scotland Act 2012, ss 28 and 80I)

B – Home Affairs
A miscellaneous assortment is included here, reflecting the interests of the former Home Office (including the current Home Office and Ministry of Justice). The Misuse of Drugs Act 1971 and legislation on drug-trafficking and international control of substances used for manufacture of controlled drugs was reserved, but section 19 of the Scotland Act 2012 amends the 1971 Act to allow an 'appropriate authority' to make regulations for preventing misuse of controlled drugs (Misuse of Drugs Act 1971, s 10(2A)), with the Scottish Ministers being considered an appropriate authority (Misuse of Drugs Act 1971, s 10(2B)). Confiscation orders in relation to the misuse of drugs have never been reserved, nor are the prosecution of drug offences and police, social work and health involvement with controlled drugs.

Also reserved are the Data Protection Act 1998, elections, firearms, classification of films and video-recordings, immigration and nationality, the Animals (Scientific Procedures) Act 1986, most of the Official Secrets Acts, betting gaming and lotteries, emergency powers and extradition.

C – Trade and Industry
This is a lengthy list with many detailed exceptions. Among the reservations are business associations (covering limited liability companies, partnerships and unincorporated associations), but not charities; insolvency (including preferred or preferential debts under the Bankruptcy (Scotland) Act 1985, but not other aspects of Scots bankruptcy law); anti-competitive practices law (but not so far as it affects the legal profession); intellectual property; import and export control; sea fishing; consumer protection; product standards, safety and liability (but not as concerns food safety or

items used in agricultural and fisheries); weights and measures; telecommunications and wireless telegraphy (including the Internet); postal services; research councils; and industrial development.

D – Energy
Electricity, oil and gas, coal, nuclear energy and energy conservation are reserved.

E – Transport
Road transport (including the Road Traffic Act 1988 and Road Traffic Offenders Acts 1988, but not road safety), rail transport, marine transport (except ports and harbours), and air transport are reserved matters.

F – Social Security
Social security schemes, child support, occupational and personal pensions and war pensions are reserved matters.

G – Regulation of Professions
Regulation of architects, health professionals, as defined, and auditors is a reserved matter, but not that of the legal profession.

H – Employment
Employment and industrial relations (except the Agricultural Wages (Scotland) Act 1949), health and safety at work, and job search and support are reserved matters.

J – Health and Medicine
Abortion, xenotransplantation (ie from a non-human species to a human), embryology surrogacy and genetics, medicines, poisons and welfare foods are reserved matters.

K – Media and Culture
Broadcasting, and public lending rights are reserved matters, but the Scottish Arts Council (now replaced by Creative Scotland), National Galleries, Libraries and Museums are not.

L – Miscellaneous
Remuneration of judges, equal opportunities (including the Equal Pay Act 1970, Sex Discrimination Act 1976, Race Relations Act 1976 and Disability Discrimination Act 1975 – all now replaced by the Equality Act 2010), control of weapons of mass destruction, the Ordnance Survey, and finally (and perhaps unsurprisingly) Outer Space are reserved matters.

Thus, most obviously important for present purposes, responsibility for the legal system is devolved, save for the remuneration of judges (and also, in fact, responsibility for the appointment of the most senior judges: see below), as is regulation of the legal profession. Other noteworthy matters which are devolved are education and training at all levels, the National Health Service (though regulation of the health professions is not), housing, the environment, agriculture, forestry and fisheries, and the arts. Transport is reserved, but with numerous exceptions.

The practical significance of the list of 'reserved matters' is as follows: firstly, the list is the basis of the Scottish Parliament's 'legislative competence', that is, its ability to make law[43]. Secondly, this legislative competence is, in turn, the basis of the Scottish Government's 'devolved competence', that is, its ability to exercise any function (including making delegated legislation[44]). However, the list of reserved matters does not actually define the legislative and government devolved competencies, which are considered separately below.

It should also be remembered that 'power devolved is power retained' and the United Kingdom Parliament retains its powers to make laws for Scotland, as the devolution legislation expressly declares[45].

The constitution and role of the Scottish Parliament and Government (including their 'competences'), and the concept of 'devolution issues', are considered below in this Chapter, and Acts of the Scottish Parliament and 'Scottish Statutory Instruments' in later Chapters.

The Scottish Parliament[46]

3.7   Election of the Scottish Parliament. The Scottish Parliament, unlike theWestminster Parliament, has only one chamber. There are 129 Members of the Scottish Parliament ('MSPs')[47]. Also unlike MPs in the United Kingdom Parliament, MSPs are elected by two simultaneous ballots. The first ballot is by the 'first-past-the-post system' for 73 individual 'constituency members', on theWestminster model. But because 'first-past-the-post' tends to produce a result unrepresentative of the actual votes for each party, a further 56

---

43 *Ibid* 1998, ss 29, 30.
44 For which, see Ch 10.
45 Scotland Act 1998, s 28(7). The (UK) Housing Act 2004 inadvertently amended Scots law in a devolved area. However unfortunate, this amendment was effective.
46 See www.scottish.parliament.uk/ and http://www.scottish.parliament.uk/newsand mediacentre/3168.aspx/.
47 It was intended that the number be reduced when the number of Scottish MPs was reduced in 2005, but this did not happen.

'additional members' are elected by the somewhat complicated second ballot to remove this unrepresentativeness. For this ballot, there are eight 'regional' constituencies. Each political party draws up a list for each of these constituencies, and independent candidates may stand. The voters in each regional constituency vote for one of those lists, or for any independent candidate. Reflecting the voters' preferences between those lists (or independent candidates), the top-scoring names (selected on a mathematical formula designed to give each party about the same proportion of MSPs as their proportion of the total vote once the constituency member results are declared), provide seven 'additional' ('list' or 'regional') members for that constituency[48]. The relationship between 'constituency' and 'additional' MSPs has been a source of debate.

A person may be a member of both the House of Commons and the Scottish Parliament[49] and a member of the House of Lords may be elected to the Scottish Parliament[50].

The Parliament is elected for a fixed period of four years, the election being held on the first Thursday in May. The Parliament elected in May 2011 will sit for five years because otherwise there would be a clash between the Scottish Parliamentary election and the UK General election due in 2015. Exceptionally the Scottish Parliament may be dissolved if two-thirds of the membership vote for a resolution to that effect, or if it fails to nominate a First Minister.

48 The formula can be found in the Scotland Act 1998, ss 6–8. It is expressed more simply in Annex C of the White Paper, *Scotland's Parliament*. See also the hypothetical worked example in Page, Reid and Ross *A Guide to the Scotland Act 1998* (1999) App 1. This method is one very likely to produce coalition governments, since the largest party is unlikely to have an overall majority. This happened in all three of the elections by 2007. In the fourth election in 2011 however, the Scottish National Party achieved an overall majority of seats. In 2007, council elections were run at the same time as Scottish Parliamentary elections, producing two ballot papers with three votes, each based on a different system of voting. This in turn produced, in an election producing a very close outcome, a considerable number of spoiled papers, casting doubt on some individual results, though none was contested, in the event: see below. The council elections were held a year after the 2011 Scottish Parliamentary elections to avoid a repeat of this situation.

49 In 2007, Alex Salmond, who had been MP for Banff & Buchan since 1987, was elected as MSP for Gordon, for which he had also been MSP from 1999–2001 (and as leader of the Scottish National Party, which achieved the largest number of seats, became First Minister: see previous note and below). He remains First Minister at the time of writing.

50 In 2007, George Foulkes (who had been a Labour MP in Scottish constituencies for 25 years and member of the 'Westminster' Labour Government for several years), elevated to the peerage as Baron Foulkes of Cumnock in 2005, was elected as a 'list' MSP for the Lothian 'regional' constituency. He left the Scottish Parliament in 2011.

The law-making powers of the Scottish Parliament – 'legislative competence'. The devolution legislation declares that 'the Parliament may make laws, to be known as Acts of the Scottish Parliament'[51]. However, it limits this power by the concept of 'legislative competence', and any provision which is outside that competence is declared to be 'not law'[52]. The boundaries of legislative competence appear in what seems a simple list, but it requires some explanation. A provision is declared to be outside the legislative competence if it:

(i) purports to apply outwith Scotland – This is an obvious limitation, but raises interesting questions where legislation concerns personal status which may have effect abroad, such as in relation to marriage or to recognition of professional qualifications.

(ii) relates to 'reserved matters' – These are described above. The question of whether a provision of an Act of the Scottish Parliament relates to a reserved matter or not is to be determined from the purpose of that provision (having regard among other things, to its effects)[53]. This makes the boundaries of legislative competence a little elastic. Legislative competence is also potentially extended into reserved matters by providing that if the Scottish Parliament makes an incidental foray into a reserved matter in the course of making an Act modifying Scots private law[54] or Scots criminal law[55], the offending provision is not to be treated as dealing with a reserved matter if it makes 'the law in question apply consistently to reserved matters and otherwise'[56]. This somewhat obscure piece of drafting seems to mean that if the Scottish Parliament is legislating on, say, the law of contract (which is devolved), and its legislation carries implications for consumer law (which is not), then the

---

51 Scotland Act 1998, s 28.
52 *Ibid.* s 29.
53 *Ibid.* s29(3).
54 Defined as: the general principles of private law (including private international law); the law of persons (including natural persons and unincorporated bodies); the law of obligations (including those arising from contract, unilateral promise, delict, unjustified enrichment and *negotiorum gestio*); the law of property (including heritable and moveable property, trusts and succession); the law of actions (including jurisdiction, remedies, evidence, procedure, diligence, recognition and enforcement of court orders, limitation of actions and arbitration); and judicial review: *ibid.* s 126(4).
55 Defined as: criminal offences, jurisdiction, evidence, procedure and penalties and treatment of offenders: *ibid.* s 126(5).
56 *Ibid.* s 29(4).

legislation is nevertheless to be treated as not affecting reserved matters[57].

(iii) is in breach of certain further specific restrictions – In addition to the limit on reserved matters, there are further consequential restrictions[58]. These, in effect, protect the actual devolution settlement from amendment by the Scottish Parliament. The most important is that (subject to exceptions) an Act of the Scottish Parliament cannot modify (a) the Scotland Act itself, (b) certain other basic provisions of existing law (including the parts of the (English) Act of Union with Scotland 1706 and (Scottish) Act of Union with England 1707 which relate to freedom of trade; the essential parts of the European Communities Act 1972; or any part of the Human Rights Act 1998; and (c) 'the law on reserved matters'. This last, in drafting of quite outstanding complexity and some uncertainty, is a belt-and-braces provision preventing the Scottish Parliament from amending Acts of the United Kingdom on reserved matters, or altering the common law on reserved matters (subject to exceptions).

(iv) is incompatible with Convention rights or EU law. Another obvious limit to the legislative competence of the Scottish Parliament is the inability to pass Acts incompatible with Convention rights (that is, rights derived from the European Convention on Human Rights: see below) or EU law (that is, the law of the European Union: see below).

(v) would remove the Lord Advocate from his position as head of the systems of criminal prosecution and investigation of deaths – Finally, this curiously specific limit is designed to protect the Lord Advocate from improper pressure by the Scottish Government in exercising his prosecutorial and related functions.

However, note that, within that legislative competence, the Scottish Parliament may amend or repeal Acts of the United Kingdom Parliament, typically those concerned with devolved matters[59].

---

57 Thus, suppose that the Scottish Parliament sought to introduce the English law 'doctrine of consideration' into Scots contract law. It could do so in relation to contract, as such, under its ordinary devolved powers without reference to this provision, but not to consumer contracts, or any other contracts within reserved matters. This provision would allow it to do so even though it would affect consumer contracts and any other contracts within reserved matters.
58 Listed in Scotland Act 1998, Sch 4.
59 Acts of the United Kingdom may, of course, amend or repeal Acts of the Scottish Parliament, as its legislative omnicompetence (subject to EU law) is unaffected: Scotland Act 1998, s 27(8).

The policing of the boundaries of legislative competence is considered below in relation to 'devolution disputes' and 'devolution issues', and in Chapter 8 in relation to Acts of the Scottish Parliament.

Activities of the Scottish Parliament. The Scottish Parliament passed over 60 Acts in each of its first two sessions and over 40 in its third session, on a variety of topics. While many of these were uncontroversial 'house-keeping' measures, some were very controversial. In the first session, they ranged from the abolition of feudal land-holding and fox-hunting, to reform of the means of appointing judges and the Scottish Qualifications Agency: in the second, from the prohibition of anti-social behaviour and prostitution in public places, to support for the Gaelic language and breastfeeders. In the third session the controversial nature of the minority government's Bill on minimum pricing of alcohol meant that it did not pass. The Bill was however reinstated by the government after it won its overall majority in the 2011 election and it is now on the statute book, albeit subject to a court challenge as to competence that is unresolved at the time of writing. The government has promised a Bill on same sex marriage, which also seems likely to be the subject of controversy. However, a surprising amount of legislation for Scotland has been passed in Westminster (as discussed below and in Chapters 7 and 8).

But the Scottish Parliament is not only a legislature, it is also a forum for discussion of important matters, and it has oral and written questions to Scottish Ministers on a wide range of devolved topics, and debates on a yet wider range (including reserved matters, such as defence, topics for discussion are not limited to the Parliament's legislative competence).

The Parliament operates to a considerable extent through a committee structure, built in from the beginning as an improvement upon Westminster[60]. Some are mandatory (including Committees on European and External Relations, Finance and Subordinate Legislation), others concern the devolved areas (such as the Education, Culture and Sport, and Health Committee, the Community Care Committee, and Justice Committee[61]). It has made considerable efforts to involve the

---

60 In the 1999–2003 and 2003–2007 Parliaments, the Executive coalition parties had a majority in these Committees. This was no longer true in the 2007–2011 Parliament, as there was a minority Executive, so a minority on these Committees. As of the 2011–2016 Parliament, the Scottish National Party government has a majority in Parliament and thus in the committees.

61 During the 2003–2007 Parliament, there were two Justice Committees but only one was established in the 2007–2011 Parliament. There remains only one in the 2011–2016 Parliament.

public in its activities, including special procedures to permit petitions on almost any matter of public interest, and actively employing IT.

The Scottish Government[62]

3.8   Appointment of the Scottish Government. There is a Scottish Government (comprising 'the Scottish Ministers'), which is in effect the Scottish Cabinet[63].

The devolution legislation states that the First Minister, that is, the head of the Scottish Government, is 'appointed by Her Majesty from among' MSPs, following a nomination by the Scottish Parliament[64]. He appoints other Ministers to the Government from among the remaining MSPs 'with the approval of Her Majesty' and the agreement of the Scottish Parliament[65]. However, the Lord Advocate and the Solicitor-General for Scotland (see below), who are also members of the Scottish Government, and are also recommended by the First Minister to Her Majesty for appointment, need not be

---

62 See www.scotland.gov.uk.

63 Scotland Act 2012, s 12 renamed the Scottish Executive as the Scottish Government. The first two Scottish Executives (1999–2003 and 2003–2007, respectively) were Labour/Liberal Democrats coalitions, but the third was a Scottish National Party minority Executive (with limited support from Greens and even more limited from the Liberal Democrats). As noted above, the voting system makes coalitions very likely but the Scottish National Party achieved a majority of seats in Parliament in 2011 to form a single party government for the first time since devolution.

64 Scotland Act 1998, ss 45(1), 46. During the life of the first Scottish Executive, the First Minister changed twice. The initial appointment, Donald Dewar, architect of devolution, died in office: the second, Henry McLeish, resigned. The third, Jack McConnell also remained in office during the whole of the rest of the life of the second. All three were leaders of the Labour Party in Scotland, the senior party in the Labour/Liberal Democrats coalitions. In the third Scottish Executive, the First Minister was Alex Salmond, in a minority administration. Alex Salmond continued as First Minister in the fourth Scottish Government after the Scottish National Party's success in the 2011 elections.: see previous note.

65 *Ibid.* s 47(1), (2). In the first two Scottish Executives, there were about a dozen Scottish Ministers at one time, including a Deputy First Minister, who was leader of the junior coalition party (initially Jim Wallace, followed by Nicol Stephen). In the third, there were (at least initially) only six, known as 'Cabinet Secretaries', the number no doubt reflecting in part the smaller number of eligible MSPs supporting a minority Executive. In the fourth there continue to be six Cabinet Secretaries. The Cabinet Secretaries mostly have at least one Junior Minister (see further below).

MSPs, though they may speak in the Parliament[66]. The ministers can be given titles showing their functions[67].

'Junior ministers' can also be appointed by the First Minister from among MSPs, but they are not part of the Scottish Government[68].

The Scottish Ministers are supported by the staff of the Scottish Administration, who are civil servants of all levels. There is also a small number of non-career civil servant 'special advisers' ('spads'), who work to individual ministers or the Government as a whole, and are appointed by them and leave with them. The Civil Service is a reserved subject, and civil servants remain members of the United Kingdom Home Civil Service and subject to the same terms of service[69].

Functions of the Scottish Government – 'devolved competence'. The purpose of the Scottish Government is to run Scotland over broadly the same range of functions as the United Kingdom government's pre-devolution Scottish Office did. This apparently straightforward proposition needs clarification, however.

Firstly, where governmental functions were conferred before devolution upon the Secretary of State for Scotland or other members of the United Kingdom government, they are now conferred upon the Scottish Ministers, so far as they are to be exercised within the 'devolved competence'[70]. Thus, where a pre-devolution Act of the United Kingdom Parliament refers to 'the Secretary of State', in relation to devolved matters it is implicitly amended to read 'the Scottish Ministers' instead. This 'devolved competence' thus covers the same range of topics as permitted by the Scottish Parliament's 'legislative competence'.

Secondly, these functions now conferred upon the Scottish Government are exercised by them exclusively. However, there are

---

66 *Ibid.* ss 27(1), 48(1).
67 In the first two Scottish Executives, there were up to another dozen Junior Ministers at one time. In the third, there were (at least initially) a similar number, two attached to most 'Cabinet Secretaries', but one to the rest. Although officially 'Junior Ministers', and not 'Scottish Ministers', they have been referred to (presumably in distinction to the 'Cabinet Secretaries') simply as 'ministers'.
68 Scotland Act 1998, s 51.
69 *Ibid.* ss 52–54. For certain purposes the First Minister and the Lord Advocate (in the latter case, in order to preserve his independence as head of the criminal prosecution service) are in a special position. Also, in a belt-and-braces provision, by s 57(2), the Scottish Government is explicitly denied the power to do any act (including making delegated legislation) incompatible with Convention rights or EU law, although they are in any case outwith their delegated competence because they are outwith the Scottish Parliament's legislative competence.
70 *Ibid.* s 56.

two important exceptions to this. In the first place, there is a variety of disparate matters, from road safety information and training to the funding of scientific research *via* arrangements for employment and training, which are 'shared powers', and are therefore carried out on a shared basis by the Scottish Government and the United Kingdom government[71]. In the second place, although it is important to realise that the carrying out of EU law obligations is devolved, and they are therefore normally carried out in Scotland through the Scottish Ministers' functions, the United Kingdom government can also still act to carry them out in Scotland[72]. These two provisions further obscure the already complicated difference between reserved and devolved matters.

However, thirdly, although certain matters are clearly reserved to the United Kingdom government, there are powers enabling it to transfer reserved matters to the Scottish Government[73]. This process, which clearly enables the United Kingdom government without further legislation to extend the functions of the Scottish Ministers beyond the devolved competence (further blurring the reserved/devolved boundary), is sometimes referred to as 'executive devolution'.

Fourthly, the United Kingdom government can, in any case, make an 'agency arrangement' for the Scottish Ministers (and vice versa)[74]. This means that the Scottish Ministers carry out specified functions on behalf of the United Kingdom government; or concurrently with the United Kingdom government; or they are carried out by the United Kingdom government but only in agreement with, or after consultation with, the Scottish Ministers (and vice versa). This renders the reserved and devolved distinction yet more opaque.

Fifthly, in any case further Acts of United Kingdom and Scottish Parliaments may add further functions.

71 *Ibid.* s 57
72 *Ibid.* s 63. By the end of 2012, there had been more than a dozen 'Scotland Act 1998 (Transfer of Functions to the Scottish Ministers, etc) Orders' under s 63, transferring a variety of functions under legislation from the Small Landholders (Scotland) Act 1911 (SI 1999/1750) to the Fire Services Act 1947 (SI 2006/304). There are also powers to transfer functions from the Scottish Ministers to the United Kingdom government in s 108 which had not been exercised by mid-2007.
73 *Ibid.* s 93. By the end of 2012, there had been 13 'Scotland Act 1998 (Agency Arrangements) (Specification) Orders' under s 93, creating arrangements relating to functions ranging from the funding and conduct parliamentary elections (SI 1999/1512), to certificates for NHS charges for personal injuries (SI 2006/3338).
74 *Ibid.* s 58.

Finally, as an interesting long-stop measure, the Secretary of State (in effect, the United Kingdom government) may direct that a proposed action not be taken, if he has reasonable grounds to believe it would be incompatible with international obligations (which would include the European Convention on Human Rights, and obligations under the various treaties constituting the European Union), or to order that a particular action be taken in order to give effect to such obligations[75].

Thus, there is a good deal of latitude in working out at ministerial and Civil Service level the exact interface between Whitehall and the Scottish Administration, and the pattern of devolved executive powers is extremely complex[76]. Electricity provides a good example[77]. The generation and supply of electricity is a reserved matter, so is outwith the devolved competence of the Scottish Ministers. However, the power to grant consents for generating stations and overhead lines in Scotland has been transferred to the Scottish Ministers, though not as part of the general conferring of powers, but rather by an order transferring responsibility[78]. But the same order provides that powers to require certain statistical information are to be exercised concurrently by Scottish Ministers and the Secretary of State, though it also provides that the power to license suppliers of electricity remains a power of the Secretary of State, but only after consultation with the Scottish Ministers.

Interestingly, 'inter-governmental relations' within the United Kingdom have been concluded to have no statutory basis, resting in practice (at least during the first two Scottish Executives) on a Memorandum of Understanding, various 'concordats' and a Joint Ministerial Committee, and while these relations are intensive, they are in general highly informal, which may cause problems when

---

75 In addition to the functions of the Scottish Government, as such, the Scotland Act 1998, ss 88–90 creates a regime for 'cross border public authorities', that is, bodies which operate on a UK or GB basis and are concerned with reserved and devolved matters, such as the Council on Tribunals.

76 The original authors expressed gratitude to their colleague Colin Reid who supplied this example, fully explained in his 'Devolution and the Environment' in Ross (ed) *Environment and Regulation (Hume Papers on Public Policy vol 8, no 2)* (David Hume Institute, 2000) at 104.

77 Ie not under ss 52–54, but under s 63, of the Scotland Act 1998.

78 House of Lords Committee of the Constitution Second Report 2002–03, HL Paper (2002–03) no 28, (*House of Lords Constitution Report*). The Memorandum of Understanding was published as Cm 5240 (2001), and it and the concordats can be found on the Scottish Government website at http://www.scotland.gov.uk/About/Government/concordats.

different parties form the United Kingdom government and the Scottish Government.

Law Officers of the Crown – Lord Advocate and Solicitor-General for Scotland[79]**.** There are two specifically Scottish Law Officers[80], the Lord Advocate and the Solicitor-General for Scotland[81], both being ancient offices[82]. (The other Law Officers were considered above). They have two roles. Firstly, they are responsible for providing the government with legal advice on Scots law and may sue and be sued on its behalf. Secondly, they are head and depute head of the prosecution service and responsible for fatal accident enquiries. Until devolution, they were members of the United Kingdom government and the Lord Advocate, at least, was either an MP or peer.

They are now, as noted above, *ex officio* members of the Scottish Government, and may speak in the Scottish Parliament, but need not be MSPs. In their first role, they must be politically acceptable to the Government (before devolution, to the United Kingdom government). However, in their second, they hold quasi-judicial office and must be independent of the Government. Their position is therefore constitutionally odd.

---

79 See www.crownoffice.gov.uk/ (also http://www.scotland.gov.uk/About/People/ 14944/Scottish-Cabinet). In late 2012, the Lord Advocate was Frank Mulholland QC. The Solicitor-General for Scotland in late-2012 was Lesley Thomson QC.

80 In contradistinction to the Advocate-General for Scotland, who is part of the United Kingdom Government.

81 For the history of these offices, see *Laws of Scotland: Stair Memorial Encyclopaedia*, 'Constitutional Law' and 'Criminal Procedure'. For recent Scottish Law Officers, see White 'The Career Path of Recent Scottish Law Officers' 2006 SLT 144–147 and 'The Career Path of Recent Scottish Law Officers Revisited' 2007 SLT (News) 223: also next note.

82 The anomaly is less than it was, as the Lord Advocate's powers are more restricted than was once the case. In the 18th century, they were essentially Governors of Scotland on behalf of the Westminster government, and were for a long time party political appointments. In more recent times, they still had considerable powers in appointing judges (and not infrequently appointed themselves: on the appointment of judges now, see below). In 2007 the Lord Advocate (but not the Solicitor General) was retained by the incoming Scottish National Party minority administration, although appointed by the previous Labour/Liberal Democrat coalition. As also noted, this was the first occasion ever on which an incoming administration (whether during or before devolution) had not appointed a new Lord Advocate, thus marking an important stage in the de-politicisation of the offices. As further noted, the Lord Advocate was no longer in the 'Scottish Cabinet', noteworthy in that a non-nationalist Lord Advocate was advising a nationalist Executive on the boundaries of the Scottish Parliament's legislative competence and the Executive's own devolved competence.

Minister for Justice[83]. As legal powers generally have been devolved, one Scottish Minister has always been a Minister of Justice[84]. He is responsible for the Scottish legal system, both civil and criminal justice, including the courts (though prosecution is a matter for the Lord Advocate, as discussed above, and judicial appointments, discussed below, are a matter for the First Minister)[85].

Financial arrangements. Checks as to income and expenditure by the Scottish Administration follow the well-tried United Kingdom model. There is a Scottish Consolidated Fund[86], into which all Scottish Administration income is paid, and out of which all Scottish Administration expenditure is paid. Such payments must be authorised by some enactment and under Treasury rules, and there is an Auditor General for Scotland to check that all expenditure is properly authorised. The main source of income is the block grant from the Treasury, to be

---

83 In the first Scottish Executive, it was Jim Wallace (also Deputy First Minister), who was leader of the Liberal Democrats (the junior partner in the coalition), and an advocate. In the second, it was Cathy Jamieson, (of the Labour Party, the senior partner in the coalition), who was not a lawyer. In the third, Scottish National Party minority Executive, it was Kenny Macaskill, a solicitor, as 'Cabinet Secretary for Justice', and assisted by one (Junior) minister, Fergus Ewing, also a solicitor (but unlike some other Departments in that Executive, no other (Junior) minister). Kenny Macaskill remained as 'Cabinet Secretary for Justice' following the 2011 election with Roseanna Cunningham MSP as Minister for Community Safety and Legal Affairs.

84 The remit was expressed on the Scottish Government website in late 2012 as Police (overall responsibility for reform of police and fire and rescue), Joint Action Group, Prisons and Sentencing Policy, Reducing Reoffending, Life Sentence Prisoner Casework, Criminal Justice Social Work and System Reform, Youth Justice, Licensing Making Justice work (justice system improvement including implementation of the Civil Courts Review), Victims and Witnesses, Criminal Law and Procedure, Legal Aid, Judicial Appointments and High-Level Engagement with Judiciary, Resilience (dealing with emergencies), UK Supreme Court, EU Justice and Home Affairs, and International Law and Cashback Programme and Proceeds of Crime Act, while the Minister for Community Safety and Legal Affairs' remit was expressed as Community Safety and Anti-Social Behaviour, Sectarianism, Violence, Human Rights, Drugs, Civil Law, Charity Law, Fire and Rescue, Religious and Faith Organisations, Tribunals and Administrative Justice, Arbitration and Alternative Dispute Resolution, Law Reform, Engagement with the Legal Profession and Liaison with Parliamentary Committees: see http://www.scotland.gov.uk/About/People/14944/Scottish-Cabinet/Scottish-Cabinet/Justice.

85 Scotland Act 1998, s 64(1).

86 See Cm 5240 (2001) and http://www.scotland.gov.uk/About/Government/concordats.

spent as determined by the Government and authorised by the Parliament. It can be supplemented or reduced if the Parliament votes in favour of a tax-varying resolution moved by a member of the Scottish Government varying the basic rate of income tax payable by Scottish tax-payers by no more than 3 pence in the pound, up or down, for one assessment year[87]. The Scotland Act 2012 has extended the taxation powers of the Scottish Government and also introduced new borrowing powers, which will come into effect in 2015. Section 25 of the 2012 Act amends the 1998 Act and grants the Scottish Parliament, by way of a resolution, to set the Scottish rate of income tax for Scottish taxpayers. Tax on transactions involving estates and land in Scotland has also been devolved (save for a few exceptions) by section 28 of the 2012 Act as a replacement for the UK Stamp Duty Land Tax. These changes allow the Scottish Parliament to generate extra income by raising rates; but they may also choose to reduce rates. Section 32 provides Scottish Ministers with borrowing powers but with restrictions.

Devolution disputes and 'devolution issues'

3.9   Plainly, there is scope for a lot of questions to arise concerning the relative powers of the Scottish Government and Scottish Parliament and the United Kingdom Government and Parliament. To avoid such problems so far as possible, as noted above, an extra-statutory 'Memorandum of Understanding' and 'concordats' were devised, that is, working arrangements on such matters as relations with the European Union and application of EU law[88]. Also, problems in relation to making delegated legislation can be aired through the normal processes of approval of such legislation[89].

In any case, since any Act of the Scottish Parliament beyond its legislative competence is *ultra vires* (that is, 'beyond the powers'), it is void. Indeed, as noted, the devolution legislation expressly says that any such purported Act 'is not law'[90]. Any action of the Scottish Government beyond its devolved competence is in a similar

---

87 *Ibid.* ss 73–75. In late 2012, this power had never been exercised.
88 See Chs 7 & 8.
89 Scotland Act 1998, s 29.
90 Though there is no equivalent of s 29.

position[91]. Thus such matters may arise in the course of ordinary civil litigation (for example, answers in a claim for damages) or criminal prosecution (for example, a defence to a prosecution). They may also arise through a person directly challenging such Act or action through judicial review (for which, see below)[92]. Such cases may include challenges in terms of human rights (for which, see below)[93] or otherwise.

However, there are specific devices for dealing with devolution disputes. Firstly, there are various scrutiny devices in the process of enactment of Acts of the Scottish Parliament to try and ensure they are within its legislative competence. These are dealt with below, when such Acts are discussed[94].

Secondly, there are special procedures to deal with what are called 'devolution issues'. These are defined rather elaborately[95] and can take any one of six forms, that is, questions as to:

- whether or not an Act of the Scottish Parliament (or part of one) is in fact within its legislative competence (thus recognising the scrutiny in the enactment process might not have worked);
- whether or not a governmental function is one which is conferred on Scottish Ministers, the First Minister or the Lord Advocate (in other words, whether it is one which has been devolved);
- whether or not the actual exercise of a governmental function by a member of the Scottish Government is within its 'devolved competence' (for which, see above);
- whether or not such an actual exercise would be incompatible with Convention rights or EU law;
- whether or not a failure to act is incompatible with Convention rights or EU law; and

---

91 Attempts to subject Acts of the Scottish Parliament to judicial review have generally been unsuccessful: see *Adams v Scottish Ministers* 2003 SC 171 (OH), 2004 SC 665 (IH); *Friend v Lord Advocate* 2004 SC 78 (OH), 2006 SC 121 (IH); *Axa General Insurance v Lord Advocate* [2011] UKSC 46, 2012 SC (UKSC) 122; *Imperial Tobacco Ltd, Petitioner* 2012 SC 297, affirmed [2012] UKSC 61; *Pairc Crofters v Scottish Ministers* [2012] CSIH 96. But see *Salvesen v Riddells and Lord Advocate* [2012] CSIH 26, 2012 SLT 633. See also Winetrobe 'The Judge in the Scottish Parliament' 2005 PL 3–12.
92 The power to do this under the Scotland Act 1998 is expressly preserved by s 100: see *Adams v Scottish Ministers* and *Friend v Lord Advocate* (and previous note).
93 See Ch 9.
94 Scotland Act 1998, Sch 6.
95 Devolution issues have arisen in District Courts, for example: see *eg Kelly v Clark* 2003 SC(PC) 77.

- any other question about whether a function is within the devolved competence or relates to Scotland or which concerns reserved matters (for which, see above).

Where a 'devolution issue' thus defined arises in any court or tribunal of whatever level[96], then (provided it is not dismissed there as 'frivolous or vexatious'), it can be separated from the rest of the proceedings, and intimation made to the Lord Advocate and Advocate-General for Scotland in case they wish to participate. These separated proceedings are as elaborate as the definition of 'devolved issues'.

A court or tribunal faced with a devolution issue may decide the matter itself, or may refer it to the Inner House (in civil proceedings) or High Court acting as an appeal court (in criminal proceedings)[97]. At least in the early years of devolution, any such case was likely to be referred unless very straightforward[98]. The court to which reference is made must decide the matter itself, but its decision can be appealed in all cases to the Judicial Committee of the Privy Council. If the Inner House or High Court acting as a court of appeal are faced with a devolution issue directly, they may also either decide it themselves or refer it to the Supreme Court. If they decide it themselves, the matter can be appealed to the Supreme Court. Hundreds of devolution issues have been raised in this way, mostly in criminal cases concerning human rights, as discussed below.

In any case, the Lord Advocate[99] or the Advocate-General for Scotland may institute proceedings on a devolution issue on their own initiative (and the Lord Advocate may defend proceedings instituted by the Advocate-General[100]); they (and the law officers of England and Wales, and of Northern Ireland) may require any court or tribunal to refer such a case direct to the Supreme Court;

---

96 For these courts, see below.
97 Incidentally, a problem occurs where the devolution issue arises in the middle of a trial, for halting proceedings for some months for such a reference is impractical.
98 Given the Lord Advocate's membership of the Scottish Government, and the opportunities to challenge non-Government Bills before the Royal Assent (for which, see Ch 8), such occasions are likely to be rare.
99 Indicating, in effect, a disagreement between the UK government and the Scottish Government which has not been resolved by other means.
100 Scotland Act 1998, ss 29(2)(c),(d), 30, Schs 4, 5 (which define the 'legislative competence' of the Scottish Parliament) and ss 54 and 57(2) (which, read with s 53, define the 'devolved competence' and rule-making power of the Scottish Executive) respectively. (As noted, s 29(1) roundly declares the legislation outside the legislative competence 'is not law'.) There is no saving provision for those adversely affected by such a finding. Remedial action does not arise. Fresh legislation would have to be made.

and they (and those other law officers) may forestall a dispute by referring to the Supreme Court action proposed by a member of the Scottish Government before it happens.

Interlinking of 'human rights' with the concept of 'devolution issues'

3.10 'Human rights' are dealt with below. However, it is useful to recall here that, as noted above, the powers of the Scottish Parliament and Scottish Government are limited by the devolution legislation to, among other things, actions compatible with Convention rights, ie, rights derived from the European Convention on Human Rights[101]. Inevitably, some legislation passed by the Scottish Parliament will turn out to be incompatible, despite the scrutiny during the enactment process designed to weed it out[102]. Equally, some actions of the Scottish Government will too (including making delegated legislation and performing administrative acts whether by Ministers themselves or by their civil servants). These are thus *ultra vires*, ie 'beyond the powers' the Parliament and Government have, and may be dealt with as described above as 'devolution issues'.

And it is thus worth noting, that, while Convention rights came into full force throughout the whole United Kingdom in 2000, they were brought partly into force in Scotland in 1998, as part of the devolution arrangements. One result of this is that all the early human rights cases in United Kingdom law were Scottish ones, arising as 'devolution issues' under the devolution legislation. As noted above, some hundreds were initiated, though few made their way as far as the Judicial Committee of the Privy Council (which had jurisdiction in such matters before the arrival of the Supreme Court) The vast majority were challenges to actions of the Scottish Executive (as it then was), not the Scottish Parliament. In particular, they were challenges to decisions by the Lord Advocate to prosecute, and related decisions, so arose in criminal cases, relied on the right to a fair trial under Article 6 of the European Convention on Human Rights (see below), and were referred from, or via the High Court[103]. This is discussed further in relation to the human rights legislation, in Chapter 7.

---

101 As described in Ch 8.
102 Early examples included *Starrs v Ruxton* 2000 JC 208 (Temporary Sheriffs), *HM Advocate v McNab* 2000 JC 80 and *HM Advocate v McLean* 2000 JC 140 (both delays in prosecution), *HM Advocate v Montgomery and Coulter* 2000 JC 111 (pre-trial publicity), and *Brown v Stott* 2000 SLT 379 (self-incrimination).
103 See http://www.coe.int/.

'EUROPE' – THE COUNCIL OF EUROPE AND THE EUROPEAN CONVENTION ON HUMAN RIGHTS

3.11 'Europe', in quotation marks, is a useful, but ambiguous term. It is useful to refer to two separate institutions which have strongly modified, and continue to modify, the Scottish legal system. These two institutions are the Council of Europe (and its principal product, the European Convention on Human Rights), and the European Union (including the European Community, once referred to as 'the Common Market', and its principal product 'EU law').

It is ambiguous because these two separate institutions are frequently confused in public discussion. In particular: the Council of Europe's European Court of Human Rights is thought to be the same as the European Union's Court of Justice; and the European Convention on Human Rights is thought to be a product of the European Union, and part of EU law. Neither of these things is true. The ambiguity is therefore embraced here deliberately to draw attention to the necessity of distinguishing. Appendix 3 assists in this.

This section therefore deals with the Council of Europe and the European Convention on Human Rights, and the next deals with the European Union.

The Council of Europe and the European Convention on Human Rights

The Council of Europe and 'human rights'[104]

3.12 The Council of Europe has had a considerable effect upon the Scottish legal system, most noticeably since the passing of

---

104 'Human rights' has become a popular phrase to describe certain obligations considered by their exponents to be more fundamental than ordinary law, indeed perhaps more fundamental than law itself. There are important questions to be asked as to what makes a claim a 'human right', and who decides, which cannot be considered here. However, it should be noted that numerous international treaties assert a range of human rights, fundamental freedoms and the like, including the United Nations Universal Declaration of Human Rights (1948), and related documents like the International Covenant on Civil and Political Rights and International Covenant on Economic, Social and Cultural Rights (both 1966), not to mention a host of others on specific rights such as those concerned with the treatment of prisoners, the death penalty, torture, genocide, prisoners of war, children and so on. Further, the European Union is expanding into the field, by introducing legislation on race and gender discrimination; requiring Member States to adhere to respect for human rights, democracy and the rule of law; 'proclaiming' its own Charter of Fundamental Rights (though without any means of enforceability at present); and acceding, in its own right, to the European Convention on Human Rights and Fundamental Freedoms.

the Human Rights Act 1998. Like the European Union, but in a different way, it has introduced what amounts to a new source of law, requiring to be treated in a different fashion, and overriding existing Scots law.

The first thing to note is that the Council of Europe is not the same thing as the European Union which is dealt with below. Set up in 1948 in the aftermath of the Second World War by ten Western European states, it is a treaty organisation, intended to promote unity through democracy and human rights. The United Kingdom was a founder member[105]. Membership has now expanded to nearly 50 Western, Central and Eastern European states[106], and it has links with other states. Its decision-making body is a Committee of Ministers comprising the Foreign Ministers of the signatory states. It also has a representative deliberative Parliamentary Assembly[107]. In addition, there are a Secretary-General and a Commissioner for Human Rights, both elected by the Parliamentary Assembly. The Secretary-General has, among other things, the function of monitoring states' compliance with the European Convention on Human Rights (see below), and the Commissioner has the function of promoting observance of that Convention. Most importantly, it set up the European Court of Human Rights[108] to judge 'human rights' cases.

The Council of Europe has promoted the creation of treaties among its members. There are over 200 to date, and they cover a wide variety of subjects, ranging from terrorism to nationality, and from social security to cybercrime. However, the first and most important of these treaties is the European Convention for the Protection of Human Rights and Fundamental Freedoms (commonly called the 'European Convention on Human Rights', abbreviated to 'ECHR'). The United Kingdom was joint first signatory in 1950, the Convention came into force in 1953, and it has been signed by all Council of Europe members. The ECHR is an attempt to implement the United Nations Universal Declaration of Human Rights of 1948, and requires its signatories to 'secure' (that is, not to allow breach of) certain specified human rights, such as a right to life, freedom from torture or inhuman or degrading treatment, a right to liberty

---

105 See Appendix 3.
106 It extends eastwards far enough to include Azerbaijan, Georgia, the Russian Federation and Ukraine among its members.
107 See http://assembly.coe.int/. The Parliamentary Assembly of the Council of Europe some times refers to itself as 'PACE', which is slightly confusing as this acronym is used in England and Wales to refer to the Police and Criminal Evidence Act 1984.
108 See http://www.echr.coe.int/ECHR/homepage_en.

and security of person, and a right to family life. There are amending Protocols which add further rights, but the United Kingdom has not signed up for all of these.

The European Convention on Human Rights ('ECHR')

3.13 The ECHR is designed to limit the actions of government bodies and officials by declaring certain obligations which the signatories accept as binding. The United Kingdom has accepted (subject to certain derogations, that is, 'disapplications') the following obligations in the Convention itself[109]:

- Article 1 All signatory states agree to secure to everyone within their jurisdiction the rights and freedoms listed.
- Article 2 Everyone's life shall be protected by law, except where the death penalty is provided by law or where death results from defence from unlawful violence, to effect arrest, to prevent escape from detention, or in quelling a riot or insurrection.
- Article 3 'No one shall be subjected to torture or to inhuman or degrading treatment or punishment'.
- Article 4 'No one shall be held in slavery or servitude. No one shall be required to perform forced or compulsory labour'.
- Article 5 'Everyone has the right to liberty and security of person' except under lawful arrest or detention. In such cases he must be given reasons and must be brought promptly before a judge.
- Article 6 Everyone is entitled to a fair and public hearing in civil and criminal law. Everyone charged with a criminal offence is presumed innocent until proved guilty.
- Article 7 No one shall be guilty of an offence which was not one under national or international law when it was committed,

---

109 Those listed below in quotation marks are quoted verbatim. The full text, and details of derogations, etc, can be found through the Council of Europe website (see above). In particular, note that the United Kingdom has not ratified the Fourth Protocol (Art 1: 'No one shall be deprived of his liberty merely on the ground of inability to fulfil a contractual obligation'; Art 2: Freedom of movement within the state, and freedom to leave it; Art 3: No expulsion of nationals or deprivation of their right to enter the country) nor even signed the Seventh Protocol (Art 1: Expulsion of aliens only after a reasoned decision with appeal and representation; Art 2: Right to have criminal convictions reviewed by a higher tribunal governed by law; Art 3: Compensation for those wrongly convicted of a crime; Art 4: No one subjected to double jeopardy in criminal proceedings; Art 5: Equality of rights and responsibilities of spouses). This is because United Kingdom law is inconsistent with them.

except for an act which was criminal according to general principles of law recognised by civilised nations.

- Article 8 'Everyone has the right to respect for his private and family life, his home and correspondence' (subject to certain exceptions).
- Article 9 'Everyone has the right to freedom of thought, conscience and religion' (subject to certain exceptions).
- Article 10 'Everyone has the right to freedom of expression' and opinions (subject to certain exceptions).
- Article 11 'Everyone has the right to freedom of peaceful assembly and to freedom of association with others' (subject to certain exceptions).
- Article 12 'Men and women of marriageable age have the right to marry and to found a family'.
- Article 13 Everyone whose rights or freedoms have been violated to have an effective remedy before a national authority.
- Article 14 'The enjoyment of the rights and freedoms set forth in this Convention shall be secured without discrimination on any ground such as sex, race, colour, language, religion, political or other opinion, national or social origin'.
- Article 15 In time of war or other public emergency threatening the life of the nation, measures limiting the application of the rights may be taken, except from Article 2 (other than in respect of deaths from lawful acts of war), Article 3, Article 4 (in respect of slavery or servitude), and Article 7.
- Article 16 Restrictions may be imposed on the political activity of aliens.
- Article 17 Nothing must be done that is aimed at the destruction or limitation of the rights.
- Article 18 Permitted restrictions to the rights and freedoms must not be used except for the purposes for which they are prescribed.

In addition, the United Kingdom has agreed to secure the following additional rights and freedoms in the First Protocol to the Convention:

- Article 1 The peaceful enjoyment of possessions is protected. No one can be deprived of possessions, except in the public interest.
- Article 2 'No person shall be denied the right to education'. The right of parents shall be respected.
- Article 3 Free elections shall be held at reasonable intervals by secret ballot.

It has also agreed to secure the following additional right or freedom in the Sixth and Thirteenth Protocols to the Convention (which overlap):

- Article 1 'The death penalty shall be abolished. No one shall be condemned to such penalty or executed'.

Certain of the Articles and Protocols are subject to qualifications. Thus, the right to peaceful enjoyment of possessions is subject to the right of the state to control the use of property and to secure the payment of taxes. They are also subject to possible derogations and reservations (that is, *ad hoc* exceptions and exclusions[110]).

However, the underlying message is clear, and the United Kingdom, its government and Parliament, the Scottish Government and Scottish Parliament, and all other 'official' institutions, are bound by its terms.

Thus, the United Kingdom has, for over fifty years, committed itself to promoting a number of rights and freedoms, commonly enumerated as: 'the right to life (including abolition of the death penalty)', 'freedom from torture', 'protection from slavery', 'liberty and the security of persons', 'a fair trial', 'the principle of legality', 'respect for private and family life', 'freedom of expression', 'a right to peaceful assembly', 'the right to marry and to found a family', 'peaceful enjoyment of possessions', 'the right to education', the 'right to free elections' and the right to an effective remedy for any breach, and non-discrimination in the application, of the law. Some of these can be derogated from 'in time of war or other public

---

110 In the early days of the ECHR, the United Kingdom derogated from obligations in relation to colonies. However, the two most important derogations, resulting from terrorist activities, were from Art 5. During the 'Troubles' in Northern Ireland, the United Kingdom entered a derogation from Art 5(3) concerning judicial control over arrest and detention powers there under the Prevention of Terrorism (Temporary Provisions) Act 1984, after an adverse ECtHR decision (*Brogan v UK* (A 145–B) (1989) 11 EHRR 117), in order to continue using those powers (finally repealed by the Terrorism Act 2000). It also entered a derogation from Art 5(1)(f) concerning detention in any part of the United Kingdom through the Human Rights (Designated Derogation) Order 2001, SI 2001/3644 to allow ss 21–23 of the Anti-terrorism, Crime and Security Act 2001 (passed in the wake of '9/11') which permitted those subject to deportation as 'suspected international terrorists' to be detained indefinitely if they could not be deported because it would subject them to the risk of torture (thus breaching Art 3) or it was impossible because no state will take them, or like reason. However, in *A & Others v Secretary of State* [2004] UKHL 56, [2005] 2 AC 68 the Appellate Committee of the House of Lords declared that those powers were disproportionate and discriminatory, so could not justify derogation, rendering the legislation incompatible with the ECHR, and the derogation was withdrawn.

emergency threatening the life of the nation, and reservations can be entered to some.

Some of the rights and freedoms are defined with a degree of explicitness (for instance the 'right to a fair trial'), while others are not (for instance the 'right to private and family life'). This means courts are required to interpret them, and certainly, some such interpretations have been surprising. However, a considerable case law has grown up in the different signatory states and, most importantly, from the European Court of Human Rights itself, and it is important to realise that these are a set of rights and freedoms held against the organs of the state, rather than against other people.

Enforceability of the ECHR

3.14   But what does the agreement to 'secure' these rights mean?

Enforceability of the ECHR by states and by individual petition. All signatory states, including the United Kingdom, agree to secure to everyone within its jurisdiction the rights and freedoms declared in the ECHR[111]. That agreement, being a matter of international law, did not make the Convention part of the law of the United Kingdom. It merely allowed states to refer to cases the Court of Human Rights ('ECtHR') in Strasbourg (and which is discussed below in Chapter 7).

Inter-state cases have been rare however[112], and much more important is the 'right of individual petition', which allows individuals claiming that they have been treated in a manner which contravened one or more Articles of the Convention, and who have exhausted possible remedies in their local courts, to petition the ECtHR[113].

There have been a considerable number of petitions from Scotland, concerning trials, prisoners' rights, and other matters, and there are a number of examples of enforcement by individual petition following a judgement of the ECtHR. *Campbell and Cosans*[114] concerned corporal punishment in schools. The parents of Campbell, who went to school in Bishopbriggs, objected to the use of corporal punishment and sought assurance from Strathclyde Regional Council (then the relevant local authority) that it would not be inflicted upon their

---

111 Art 1, ECHR.
112 One of significance, nevertheless, was *Ireland v UK* (1979–80) 2 EHRR 25, which concerned treatment of detainees in Northern Ireland.
113 Art 34, ECHR: the United Kingdom accepted this right from 1966.
114 (1982) 4 EHRR 293.

son. This was refused. Cosans, who went to school in Cowdenbeath, refused to submit to corporal punishment, a form of punishment which Fife Regional Council (then the relevant local authority) permitted. He was suspended. The petitioners claimed corporal punishment breached Article 3 of the ECHR (inhuman or degrading punishment) and Article 2 of the First Protocol (requirement for respect for parents' right to ensure education is in conformity with their religious and philosophical beliefs). The matter eventually went to the ECtHR, which held that Article 3 had not been breached, but (though by a majority only) that Article 2 of the Protocol had been.

The case was adjourned on the question of compensation, with a view to the parties agreeing a sum. More importantly, after this case, the law on corporal punishment in state schools was abolished[115], indicating that the United Kingdom was 'securing' the right generally, and not simply compensating the applicants. However, the process from petition to judgment took seven years, and from petition to the change of law, a decade.

It is important to remember that the implementation of the content of the ECHR by the United Kingdom Human Rights Act 1998 (discussed below) does not remove a victim's right of individual petition. It merely requires the victim, when exhausting possible remedies for their grievances in the courts of the United Kingdom before petitioning, to invoke any remedies under that Act. However, the existence of the legislation is likely to reduce considerably the number of individual petitions.

Enforceability of the ECHR through EU law. Although the ECHR and its institutions are separate from the European Union and its institutions, and although the European Union has its own Charter of Fundamental Rights, the ECHR may be enforceable through EU law. This is discussed in Chapter 6 in relation to EU law. The EU is negotiating accession to the ECHR in its own right at the time of writing (January 2013).

Enforceability of the ECHR through United Kingdom law – 'embedding'. Before the Human Rights Act 1998, the Scottish courts had, over time, changed from the view that the ECHR was not legislation, so could be ignored, to the view that it should be used, at least by way of requiring statutes to be interpreted in conformity with it. However, the position has been further changed radically by the Human Rights Act 1998. It is sometimes said that this 'incorporates' the ECHR into United Kingdom law. This is misleading terminology,

---

115 Education (No 2) Act 1986, s 48.

for it implies that its terms have 'direct effect', as EU law has (for which see Chapter 6). However, instead it may be said to 'embed' it[116], by cutting and pasting most of the contents of the ECHR, and its First and Sixth Protocols, into the United Kingdom Act, calling them 'Convention rights', with a unique status, and putting them into a somewhat unusual United Kingdom Act[117].

These Convention rights have nevertheless become part of United Kingdom law and, broadly speaking, United Kingdom law is intended to be 'compatible' with them (though, as we shall see, the United Kingdom still retains a 'let out' clause, by which its law may remain incompatible).

This compatibility is sought in various ways. The legislation imposes requirements firstly in relation to parliamentary scrutiny during the process of legislation of all subsequent Acts of the United Kingdom, secondly in relation to statutory interpretation, and thirdly in relation to legislation by devolved bodies. These are dealt with in the relevant sections in Chapter 7.

The legislation also creates rights for victims of breaches of Convention rights, which are dealt with here. It makes it 'unlawful for a public authority to act in a way which is incompatible with a Convention right' (subject to exceptions)[118] and allows a 'victim' to 'bring proceedings against the authority ... in the appropriate court or tribunal' or to 'rely on the convention right ... concerned in any proceedings' (within certain time limits)[119]. Thus, he can both sue and defend himself on the basis of Convention rights. 'Public authority' is defined so as to include any court or tribunal (including the Appellate Committee of the House of Lords), and 'any person certain of whose functions are of a public nature' (other than the Westminster Parliament or a person exercising functions on its

---

116 The distinction is not obvious, but crucial. If the terms were 'incorporated' and had 'direct effect', then the United Kingdom could not alter them, but they could be altered by agreement of the other members states of the Council of Europe. But they are 'embedded', and have no 'direct effect', so the United Kingdom can alter them unilaterally, and does not have to accept alterations agreed by the other member states.

117 Human Rights Act 1998, s 1 and Sch 1. The Act omits Arts 1, 13 and 15 of the Convention, and all other Protocols. Arts 1 and 15 are omitted because it was thought that they do not add anything to the obligations listed in the Schedule. Omission of Art 13 is more controversial. It can be seen, like Arts 1 and 15, as adding nothing. However, another view is that it was omitted because judges might use it to extend the range of remedies available. The Act also omits the other Protocols because either they are purely procedural, or because, in the case of Protocols 4 & 7, because the United Kingdom has not ratified them.

118 Human Rights Act 1998, s 6.

119 *Ibid.* s 7.

behalf)[120]. This is clearly very wide and 'public authority' includes the Scottish Parliament, all government departments (including the Scottish Government), local authorities, quangos, universities etc (and including the Law Society of Scotland and the Faculty of Advocates). 'Victim' is also defined widely as 'any person, non-governmental organisation or group of individuals'[121]. Such challenges have been attempted even against Acts of the Scottish Parliament[122].

Where a court or tribunal finds an act of a public authority unlawful, it can 'grant such relief or remedy, or make such order' as it considers 'just and appropriate', subject to certain limitations[123].

Human Rights Act cases in Scotland. The immediate effect of the Human Rights Act 1998 was considerable. A large amount of litigation arose, mostly by way of devolution issues (because the cases were initiated in the period between the coming into force of the Scotland Act 1998 and the complete coming into force of the Human Rights Act, as noted above) and mostly concerning the criminal law. As much publicity has been given to the notion that embedding of the ECHR has thrown the legal system into turmoil, and produced ridiculous results, it is worth noting that many of these decisions affirmed the law as fulfilling the requirements of the Convention rights, such as *Brown v Stott*[124] and *Clark v Kelly*[125]. In the former, despite doubts in courts below, the Judicial Committee of the Privy Council concluded that requiring a driver to take a breath test did not breach the privilege against self-incrimination and therefore prejudice the right to a fair trial[126]. In the latter, it decided that the position of the clerk of court and legal adviser (a local authority employee with limited security of tenure) in the

---

120 *Ibid.* s 6(3),(4).
121 *Ibid,* s7(7) (echoing Art 34 ECHR).
122 But by the end of 2012, only unsuccessfully with one exception: see eg *A v Scottish Ministers* 2002 SC (PC) 63 (judicial review of Mental Health (Public Safety and Appeals) (Scotland) Act 1999 sought for incompatibility with Convention right Art 5), *Adams v Scottish Ministers* 2002 SCLR 881 (judicial review of Protection of Wild Mammals (Scotland) Act 2002 sought for incompatibility with Convention right Arts 8 and 14 and Protocol 1, Art 1); *Axa General Insurance v Lord Advocate* [2011] UKSC 46, 2012 SC (UKSC) 122; *Imperial Tobacco Ltd, Petitioner* 2012 SC 297, affirmed [2012] UKSC 61, 2013 SLT 2. For the exception, see *Salvesen v Riddells and Lord Advocate* [2012] CSIH 26, 2012 SLT 633.
123 Human Rights Act 1998, s 8.
124 2001 SC(PC) 43.
125 [2003] UKPC D1, 2003 SC(PC) 77.
126 Human Rights Act 1998, Sch 11 (embodying Article 6, ECHR).

District Court did not compromise the right to an independent and impartial tribunal[127].

However, some did have far-reaching effects. The best-known example in the early years was *Starrs v Ruxton*[128], which illustrated the considerable power of the Act. The case concerned Temporary Sheriffs, that is, advocates or solicitors appointed to serve part-time, and who undertook some 25% of the criminal work of the court. As they were appointed by the Lord Advocate, a member of the Scottish Executive and (of more immediate relevance) the head of the prosecution service, their appointments were clearly acts of a public authority. On an appeal from a decision by a Temporary Sheriff, the High Court of Justiciary decided that, because their appointments were short term, and they could be sidelined by being given no work, or dismissed at will, Temporary Sheriffs lacked security of tenure. This breached the Convention right to an independent and impartial tribunal[129]. As a result, Temporary Sheriffs ceased to be appointed or used, and the office was abolished, and replaced by that of 'Part-time Sheriff' with greater security of tenure[130]. More recently we have seen *Cadder v HM Advocate*[131], in which the Supreme Court held that a person detained by the police for questioning had an immediate right to legal advice, rather than having to wait for a period unadvised, as provided for in the Criminal Procedure (Scotland) Act 1995. Since the material obtained during these unadvised interviews was often vital to successful subsequent prosecutions, the decision forced a re-consideration of several elements of criminal procedure and evidence. Legislation was passed almost immediately to deal with what were seen as the readily soluble issues; in the longer term, *Cadder* has also raised the possibility that the long-cherished requirement of corroboration in criminal evidence will be replaced.

Scottish Human Rights Commission. Following lengthy consultation[132], the Scottish Parliament passed the Scottish Commission for Human Rights Act 2006, creating such a Commission

---

127 See previous note.
128 2000 JC 208.
129 Human Rights Act 1998, Sch 1 (embodying Art 6, ECHR). The decision had an incidental effect on the District Court, where it was concluded, without litigation, that the reasoning excluded councillors from sitting as JPs because District Courts were run by local authorities. It did not have effect on the Court of Session, however: see *Clancy v Caird* 2000 SC 441.
130 Bail, Judicial Appointments, Etc (Scotland) Act 2000.
131 [2010] UKSC 43, 2011 SC (UKSC) 13.
132 See *Protecting Our Rights; a Human Rights Commission for Scotland* (Scottish Executive 2001) and *Scottish Human Rights* (Scottish Executive 2003).

comprising a Chairman and not more than four other members[133]. Its job is not, however, to enforce, or assist in enforcing the Human Rights Act 1998, or other legislation, but to 'promote human rights and ... to encourage best practice in relation to human rights', by publication and dissemination of information, conducting research, providing training, monitoring practice, conducting enquiries, etc[134]. This role is designed to mesh with that of the (Great Britain) Commission for Equality and Human Rights (a merger of the former Commission for Racial Equality, Equal Opportunities Commission and Disability Rights Commission), set up by the Equality Act 2006, with its functions in relation to Scotland somewhat restricted to take account of devolution.

'EUROPE' – THE EUROPEAN UNION

The European Union[135]

3.15   The European Union has had a considerable effect upon the Scottish legal system since United Kingdom accession in 1973. Like the Council of Europe, though in a different way, it has introduced what amounts to a new source of law, requiring to be treated in a different fashion, and overriding existing Scots law.

The European Union is only readily understood by considering its evolution from the original treaties to the present day, firstly in terms of institutional origins and changes, and secondly in terms of original membership and changes to it (although these two sets of changes have affected each other). After that, the institutions of the European Union require to be considered.

Evolution from the original treaties to the present day

3.16   Institutional origins and changes: In the 1950s, six European states[136] set up three 'communities', that is, the European Coal and Steel Community ('ECSC'), the European Atomic Energy Community ('Euratom'), the European Economic Community

---

133 Scottish Commission for Human Rights Act 2006, s 1 and Sch 1. There are currently three members working with the Chair of the Commission, Professor Alan Miller.
134 *Ibid.*, ss 2–4.
135 See Appendix 3. The European Union website is at http://europa.eu.int/.
136 *Ie* Belgium, France, Germany, Italy, Luxembourg and the Netherlands.

('EEC'). They were set up under three separate treaties[137], the main one of which was the EEC Treaty, sometimes referred to as the 'Treaty of Rome'. Each community had its own separate institutions to carry out its purposes of promoting economic and political integration (to a degree still disputed among the Member States).

After a Preamble reciting that the Member States are 'Determined to lay the foundations of an ever closer union among the peoples of Europe' and similar sentiments, and Article 1, actually establishing the Community, the EEC Treaty continued:

Article 2 'The Community shall have as its task, by establishing a common market and an economic and monetary union and by implementing common policies or activities referred to in Articles 3 and 4, to promote throughout the Community a harmonious, balanced and sustainable development of economic activities, a high level of employment and of social protection, equality between men and women, sustainable and non-inflationary growth, a high degree of competitiveness and convergence of economic performance, a high level of protection and improvement of the quality of the environment, the raising of the standard of living and quality of life, and economic and social cohesion and solidarity among Member States'.

Article 3 refers to prohibition of customs duties, a common commercial policy, an internal market with free movement of goods, persons, services and capital, etc, and Article 4 to adoption of a common economic policy and a single currency.

Thus, in the words of the EEC Treaty[138], the EEC sought 'ever closer union' through 'a common market and an economic and monetary union', requiring 'prohibition of customs duties, a common commercial policy, an internal market with free movement of goods, persons, services and capital, etc,' and not least 'a common economic policy and a single currency'.

In 1965, the 'Merger Treaty' merged the institutions of the three communities, while leaving them technically separate, but under the new collective title of 'the European Communities'.

In 1986, the 'Single European Act' altered significantly some internal procedures (for instance, introducing qualified majority voting of Member States in some matters, instead of unanimity) and

---

137 These can be found at http://eur-lex.europa.eu/en/treaties/index.htm: click on 'Founding Treaties'.

138 For the current version, see also http://eur-lex.europa.eu/LexUriServ/LexUriServ.do?uri=OJ:C:2010:083:0013:0046:en:PDF.

sought to extend co-operation over a new area of 'justice and home affairs' under the title 'European political co-operation'.

In 1993, the Treaty on European Union[139] (the 'Maastricht Treaty') created the European Union ('EU'). It is important to note how this was done, and what it means (and not least the difference between 'EEC', 'EC' and 'EU'). After a Preamble reciting that the Member States 'Resolved to mark a new stage in the process of European integration undertaken with the establishment of the European Communities', and similar sentiments, Article 1 established the European Union and continues:

> 'This Treaty marks a new stage on the process of creating an ever closer union among the peoples of Europe, in which decisions are taken as openly as possible and as closely as possible to the citizen.
>
> The Union shall be founded on the European Communities, supplemented by the policies and forms of co-operation established by this Treaty. Its task shall be to organize, in a manner demonstrating consistency and solidarity, relations between the Member States and their peoples'.

Article 2 set the objectives of economic and social progress, high employment and balanced and sustainable development through the creation of an area without internal frontiers; to assert an identity on the international scene through a common foreign and security policy; to maintain and develop an area of freedom, security and justice etc.

Thus, firstly, this Treaty sought to re-emphasise the aim of 'closer union' of Member States by renaming the three communities ('the European Communities') as simply 'the European Community' ('EC') and by institutional changes within the Community. Secondly, it sought to embed co-operation between member states outwith the Community in the justice and home affairs area and extend co-operation over another such area, that is, foreign and security policy. Joint action in these areas was to be by 'intergovernmental co-operation', that is by agreement among governments as such, involving the Community institutions to only a limited degree, and thus without the degree of integration achieved in the Community. These two areas were described as second and third 'pillars', respectively, being added to the first pillar, the EC itself. The EU was the resulting edifice, comprising all three pillars. In addition to these changes the Treaty sought to include the principle of subsidiarity,

---

139 For the current version, see previous note.

whereby, in areas in which either Member States or the Community might act, it is the Member States which should do so.

In 1997, the Treaty of Amsterdam amended the aims of the EC and EU in a number of ways, extending the EU competence, creating some new 'social' rights, such as a right against discrimination, and transferring questions of 'external borders' (that is, immigration, visas and asylum) from 'third pillar' to 'first', allowing there to be Community law on the subject[140]. It also renumbered the Articles of the EC Treaty (as amended). However, a principal result was to blur the distinction between the pillars. It also encouraged different Member States to integrate at different speeds (known as 'variable geometry') and assisted non-member states associated with the EC/EU and likely to become members.

In 2000, the Treaty of Nice, largely concerned with recent and impending expansion of the EU, extended majority voting in the EC, further encouraged 'variable geometry', and made alterations to the European Court of Justice. However, from the point of view of the legal system, it was principally concerned with two matters. Firstly, as an alternative to acceding to the ECHR (discussed above), the EU adopted a 'Charter of Fundamental Rights'. This contained provisions similar to those in the ECHR, but went beyond it to include 'social rights' in relation to education, employment, asylum, data protection and the freedom to conduct business. Nevertheless, this Charter did not have legal force, although it could influence decision-making, and was intended by some Member States to have some such force in the future. Secondly, the Treaty of Nice prepared the way for enlargement of the EU, by the accession of ten states with effect from 2004.

In 2003, a 'Draft Treaty establishing a Constitution for Europe' was published, to introduce further institutional change, in general involving closer integration, but seeking to involve Member States' Parliaments into the EC law-making process and adopting the 'Charter of Fundamental Rights'. However, following rejection of this by referendums in the Netherlands and France, it was put into abeyance.

The Member States signed up to the Treaty of Lisbon in December 2007 in a renewed attempt to bring about institutional change making the EU more effective in the light of its constant evolution. The Treaty came into force in December 2009 and greatly enhanced the powers of the European Parliament with regard to legislation. The European Parliament is now placed on an equal footing with the Council of the Union for legislating in several policy areas.

---

140 The United Kingdom, however, opted out of much of this transfer.

Legislation is passed by co-decision of these institutions. Unanimity is not required in so many policy areas for voting in the Council of the Union, with qualified majority voting now more frequently used. A new 'double majority' system will be used to calculate a qualified majority in the voting procedure from 2014 onwards. The double majority system will require a decision to be accepted by at least 55% of Member States who, together, represent 65% of the EU's population. The provisions of the Charter of Fundamental Rights and Freedoms now have a binding legal force following the Treaty.

Original membership and changes to it: As noted, the EEC started with six original Member States in the 1950s. At the same time as all the institutional changes indicated above, there were considerable changes of membership. By means of a number of 'Accession Treaties' coming into force in 1973 (when the United Kingdom acceded), 1981, 1986, 1995 and 2007, the original Member States were successively joined by groups of others[141], and more accessions are likely[142].

Further, in the midst of this, with effect from 1994, the EC also created the 'European Economic Area' ('EEA') with the remaining members of a rival organisation, the European Free Trade Area ('EFTA')[143]. This arrangement allowed the EFTA members to participate in benefits of EC membership, such as the free movement of workers, goods and services within the EC, but without participating in the EC institutions.

In 2002, Switzerland, though not a member of EFTA, also joined the EEA, by a bilateral agreement.

The current European Union: These institutional and membership changes affected each other in various ways, most particularly in that institutional change was required by changes in membership, for institutions designed for six very similar Member States had difficulty in coping with 27 much less similar ones. As a result, however, for some years, the EU has appeared to be in a state of continuous revolution, and the whole enterprise is becoming more complex and difficult to understand.

---

141 *Ie* Denmark, Ireland and the United Kingdom (1972), Greece (1981), Spain & Portugal (1986) and Austria, Finland & Sweden (1995), Cyprus, Czech Republic, Estonia, Hungary, Latvia, Lithuania, Malta & Poland (2004) and Bulgaria & Romania (2007). Thus, by 2007, membership had more than quadrupled, and totalled 27.

142 Croatia, Former Yugoslav Republic of Macedonia, Iceland, Montenegro, Serbia and Turkey are 'candidate countries'.

143 Iceland, Liechtenstein & Norway.

The most important effect of all this as far as the Scottish legal system is concerned is that some EU law has 'direct effect'. The meaning of this term is discussed below in Chapter 6. For the moment, it can simply be described as the process whereby EU law becomes part of the law of Scotland without the intervention of either Westminster, or Holyrood, Parliaments (and is thus incapable of being changed unilaterally by the United Kingdom, but is possibly capable of being changed by agreement of the other Member States).

The Institutions of the European Union

3.17   The European Commission[144]**:** The Commission, which sits in Brussels, exists to further the interests of the EU. Sometimes described as the 'Executive' of the EU, it is better regarded as the top grade of its civil service. It initiates and implements EU policy (including legislation), but can legislate under powers delegated by the Council of the Union. This legislative power is only to allow laws to be updated when necessary and all legislation is scrutinised by both the Council of the Union and the Parliament. EU citizens now have the ability to ask the European Commission to propose laws through the European Citizens Initiative. The deliberations of the Commission, however, are confidential.

There are 27 Commissioners, one from each Member State, nominated by the Member States. They are appointed by the Council of the Union subject to the approval of the European Parliament[145]. Nevertheless, Commissioners are required to owe their political allegiance to the Community, not the nominating government.

One Commissioner is President, others may be Vice-Presidents, and each has responsibility for an area of Community policy[146]. The Commission is accountable to the European Parliament, insofar as Commissioners can be removed by a no confidence vote of that body[147]. Each has a small personal 'Cabinet', and they are supported

---

144 See http://ec.europa.eu/index_en.htm. See also Appendix 3.
145 Change to the size, and means of appointment to, the Commission is one of the matters which increased membership necessitates.
146 In late 2012, the UK Commissioner was Catherine Ashton who is the Vice-President under Jose Manuel Barroso.
147 In 1999, the entire Commission resigned to avoid being dismissed by the Parliament, after allegations of fraud and mismanagement, though most were re-appointed. In 2004, the Parliament objected to a nominee as Commissioner for Freedom, Security and Justice as his views were thought incompatible with fundamental human rights, so blocked appointment of all Commissioners until he was replaced.

by a Civil Service with some 25 directorates-general and other agencies such as the Legal Service and the Translating Service.

The European Commission is responsible for the EU's budget and allocation of funding as well as enforcing EU law. It checks that Member States are implementing EU law correctly and can take action where it sees a Member State failing to do so.

The European Commission should not be confused with the European Commission on Human Rights (discussed above).

The Council of the Union (sometimes referred to as 'the Council of the European Union' and formerly called the 'Council of Ministers')[148]**:** The Council of the Union, which also sits in Brussels, exists to represent the Member States, and co-ordinate their views. It is responsible, along with the European Parliament, for giving final approval on all EU legislation. Voting in the Council of the Union may require unanimity, but can be by 'qualified majority voting' ('QMV'), a complicated weighted system for legislative measures. As noted above, QMV is now involved in far more decisions following the Treaty of Lisbon. 'Double majority' QMV (see above) will be used from 2014 onwards. The Council of the Union's deliberations are also generally secret but it must meet in public when legislation is to be adopted[149].

The Council of the Union is made up of one minister from each Member State. There are ten different configurations within the Council of the Union, each responsible a different policy area, eg Foreign Affairs. The minister from the Member States will be different depending on which configuration of the Council of the Union is meeting. If the Agriculture and Fisheries configuration was to meet the Council of the Union would be comprised of the agriculture and fisheries ministers of the Member States and so on.

Presidency of the Council of the Union has become quite complex under the Treaty of Lisbon. Presidency is held by groups of three of Member States who hold the Presidency for a period of 18 months. During those 18 months each of the three Member States will have a six month spell as chair of the group. The groups of three have been set and the group holding the Presidency will rotate after each 18-month period. There is one exception to this which is in the area of Foreign Affairs. A High Representative of Foreign Affairs and Security Policy sits as President for the Foreign Affairs configuration.

The EU Member States decided they wanted a common European economic policy in the wake of the current financial crisis and it is

---

148 See http://www.consilium.europa.eu/homepage.aspx?lang=en.
149 Article 2 (189) Treaty of Lisbon, introducing Article 201b TFEU.

the Council of Europe that has been given responsibility for this. The respective Economics and Finance Ministers from each Member State are responsible for the discussions. There is also a joint foreign and defence policy being developed which will likely be overseen by the Council of Europe.

The Council of the Union, as well as suffering from a variety of names itself, is easily confused with the European Council, which is now an EU institution in its own right (see below). It is also easily confused with the Council of Europe which is, of course, nothing to do with the EU (as discussed above).

COREPER (the 'Comité de réprésantants permanents' or 'Committee of Permanent Represetnatives)[150]: COREPER is the French acronym usually used for the Committee of Permanent Representatives and is not, strictly speaking, one of the EU institutions, but a name given to the regular meetings of top civil servants of Member States. Because meetings of the Council of the Union are infrequent, involve different ministers on different occasions, and because ministers have other responsibilities, Council of the Union work is carried on between meetings by Permanent Representatives (sometimes referred to as 'Ambassadors') from each Member State, who are national civil servants, and their staff[151].

The significance of COREPER is great. It deals with all business going to the Council of the Union and, if it is unanimous, the Council will rubber-stamp its decision.

The European Parliament[152]: The European Parliament, despite its name, is not the sole legislature of the EU. It works together with the Council to pass legislation on a number of areas in a co-decision capacity. There remain areas where it only plays a consultative role but is directly involved in a greater number of policy areas following the Treaty of Lisbon. The Treaty of Lisbon also gave the European Parliament far greater rights than it had previously regarding the EU budget. Previously, the Council of the Union had the final say in areas of compulsory expenditure, while the European Parliament could only give an opinion on these areas. Now, the European Parliament has an equal say in the final decision on budgetary matters with the Council of the Union.

---

150 There is no COREPER website.
151 In mid 2012, the UK Permanent Representative was Sir Jon Cunliffe CB, described as 'Ambassador Extraordinary and Plenipotentiary Permanent Representative of the United Kingdom'.
152 See http://www.europarl.europa.eu/portal/en

The Parliament exists to represent the population at large of the Member States, and is directly elected every five years[153], thus providing the EU with some democratic legitimacy. MEPs sit in political groupings[154], but there are no 'government party' and 'opposition parties'.

The European Parliament also plays an important supervisory role over the other EU institutions. As noted, appointment of the European Commission must be approved by the European Parliament. The Commission must also report to the European Parliament and answer its questions, and it could be dismissed by the European Parliament in a vote of censure[155]. The Council of the Union must also make certain other reports to the European Parliament, which also has powers in relation to the Community budget. The European Parliament may also review the activities of other EU institutions, and appoints a European Ombudsman.

The European Parliament sits for only a short part of the year, and most of its work is done by committees. It has a secretariat, with five directorates-general. As a result of a compromise, the European Parliament itself sits in Strasbourg, the committees in Brussels, and the secretariat in Luxembourg.

The European Council[156]: The European Council is now officially an institution of the EU following the coming into force of the Treaty of Lisbon. Formerly it existed as a semi-formal institution. It is comprised of the Member State heads of government and the President of the European Commission and meets quarterly. The European Council sets the overall EU policy but is not responsible for adopting legislation.

---

153 There are 754 MEPs, 72 from the United Kingdom, which is divided into 12 constituencies of which Scotland is one. Scotland has 6 MEPs

154 Such as the 'Group of the European People's Party' (Christian Democrats) and 'European Conservatives and Reformists Group' (to which the United Kingdom Conservative Party MEPs belong), Group of the Progressive Alliance of Socialists & Democrats in the European Parliament (to which the United Kingdom Labour Party MEPs belong), 'Group of the Alliance of Liberals and Democrats for Europe' (to which the United Kingdom Liberal Democrats belong) and 'Group of the Greens/European Free Alliance' (to which the United Kingdom Green Party and Plaid Cymru and Scottish National Party MEPs belong).

155 As noted above in relation to the Commission, this power to dismiss has been exercised, in effect if not technically, in both 1999 and 2004.

156 See http://www.european-council.europa.eu/the-institution?lang=en.

A President is appointed for two-and-a-half years[157] who is tasked with: chairing the European Council and driving forward its work; ensuring the preparation and continuity of the work of the European Council in cooperation with the President of the Commission, and on the basis of the work of the General Affairs Council; endeavouring to facilitate cohesion and consensus within the European Council; and presenting a report to the European Parliament after each of the meetings of the European Council[158].

The 'Court of Justice of the European Union': The Court of Justice of the European Union ('CJEU') exists to ensure that EU law is correctly interpreted, and is observed. It is split into three parts: the Court of Justice which is the main court; the 'General Court', from which, appeal to the Court of Justice is possible in certain circumstances; and the specialised courts (of which, in late 2012, there was only one)

The Court of Justice of the European Union, which sits in Luxembourg, is not to be confused with the European Court of Human Rights ('ECtHR'), which sits in Strasbourg. Both are discussed below in Chapter 4.

The European Central Bank[159]**:** The European Central Bank is an institution set up under the Treaty of Lisbon. It is responsible, together with the national banks of the Member States whose currency is the euro, for conducting the EU's monetary policy. Its main task is to maintain the purchasing power of the euro and keep prices stable[160].

Other EU bodies: There is also a Court of Auditors, which is a formal EU institution, and two advisory important bodies, the Economic and Social Committee ('ECOSOC') and the Committee of the Regions. ECOSOC represents functional interests, that is, 'the various economic and social components of civil society, and in particular producers, farmers, carriers, workers, dealers, craftsmen, professional occupations, consumers and the general interest'[161]. It gives its opinion on draft legislation and under the Treaty of Amsterdam can be consulted by the European Parliament. The

157 In late 2012, Herman van Rompuy was serving his second term in office.
158 Article 15(6) TEU.
159 See http://www.ecb.int/home/html/index.en.html.
160 Article 127(1) TFEU.
161 See http://www.eesc.europa.eu/.

Committee of the Regions, created under the Treaty on European Union, is a consultative body representing regional and national bodies[162]. It operates through 'Commissions' on a variety of topics such as 'territorial adhesion' and 'economic and social policy'.

---

162 See http://www.cor.europa.eu/.

4 Institutions – courts, tribunals, judges and procedure

UNITED KINGDOM COURTS, TRIBUNALS AND RELATED INSTITUTIONS

4.1   This Chapter (supplemented by Appendix 2) examines in detail the courts and tribunals which apply, or may make, Scots law; their judges (including questions of judicial appointments and judicial training and competence); and the procedures they follow (at least in outline). It is also useful in this Chapter at least to glance over the border and consider in outline courts in the other parts of the United Kingdom.

Courts in general

4.2   The courts are a major set of institutions in any legal system. So are the judges who sit in them and the procedures they follow, for the courts' operation is only comprehensible in the light of these aspects. This is particularly true in a common law, or hybrid, system in which the courts not only apply the law, but also make it[1].

It is to be noticed that courts in any jurisdiction, and their relationship, are commonly represented in diagrams (as in Appendix 2). These diagrams are two dimensional, and these dimensions represent something important. The vertical dimension is the more obvious. It indicates that courts are in a hierarchy. Thus some courts are 'higher', that is, more powerful than other, 'lower' ones. This is most obvious in the simple sense that ('higher') appeal courts may overturn the decisions of ('lower') 'courts of first instance', as courts which are not appeal courts are sometimes called, though the picture is more complicated in that, for instance, there may be more than

---

1   A matter discussed in Ch 5.

one level of appeal. It is also to be noted that courts of first instance usually have only one judge, while appeal courts usually have more, though there are important exceptions to this.

The horizontal dimension is less obvious, but indicates that at any level within the hierarchy, there may be several courts. At its simplest, by definition, there can only be one final court of appeal in any hierarchy, but there may be a large number of 'courts of first instance', typically because they are local courts, spread out across the land. (Thus, in Scotland, for instance, there is room for confusion with reference to 'the Sheriff Court', as there are 49 separate locations in which there is a Sheriff Court).

The vertical dimension has a further significance in a common law, or hybrid, legal system, in that it is the appeal courts, broadly speaking, which may make the law[2].

Scottish, United Kingdom and European courts and tribunals

4.3   There are two hierarchies of courts in Scotland: the civil and the criminal[3]. England and Wales and Northern Ireland have their own civil and criminal hierarchies, somewhat similar to the Scottish ones, but separate.

Nevertheless, five of the resulting six hierarchies are connected at the top in the final court of appeal. The normal Scottish civil hierarchy of courts ends with final appeal to a court called the Supreme Court, as do both civil and criminal courts of England and Wales, and Northern Ireland. This, incidentally, sits in London. However, the sixth hierarchy, normal Scottish criminal hierarchy, does not, as it ends within Scotland in the High Court of Justiciary. However, to complicate the position further, certain specialised questions concerning devolution and arising in either civil or criminal proceedings, also can go to the Supreme Court.

Further, from all courts in the United Kingdom there is the possibility of a 'preliminary reference' to the Court of Justice of the European Union in relation to European Union law (as also discussed in Chapter 3 and below). Also, again, a person who considers that his rights under the European Convention on Human Rights have not

---

2   See Ch 5.
3   It is sometimes suggested that there are three, that is, civil, criminal and 'administrative', the last-mentioned dealing with legal disputes involving government. However, the administrative is regarded here as a sub-set of the civil.

been protected, and who has taken the matter through the relevant United Kingdom courts unsuccessfully, may petition the European Court of Human Rights for a remedy (as again discussed in Chapter 3 and below). Neither of these types of proceeding is an appeal.

All these courts, whether in other parts of the United Kingdom, or of Europe, apply, or make, Scots law, so must be regarded as Scottish courts, even if they are not within Scotland.

In addition to the courts, as such, there are a number of 'tribunals', generally organised on a United Kingdom basis. These deal with certain types of legal dispute, but are not regarded as courts. Well-known examples are the Employment Tribunals and tribunals dealing with social security. Tribunals vary considerably in structure and personnel, but in general are less formal than courts, and litigants are often unrepresented by lawyers. There may be appeal from them to the courts.

There has been considerable dissatisfaction with the administration of both civil and criminal justice in Scotland recently. In 2007 a comprehensive review of Scotland's civil courts was undertaken by the then Lord Justice-Clerk, Lord Gill[4]. The Scottish Ministers accepted the majority of the review's recommendations in November 2010 and committed to bringing forward legislation implementing reform. Legislation had not been introduced by the end of 2012[5], although the Scottish Government introduced the Scottish Civil Justice Council and Criminal Legal Assistance Bill in May 2012 which aims, among other things to establish a Scottish Civil Justice Council to assist the Lord President in reviewing and making changes to civil procedure in Scotland.

A review[6] of Scottish criminal procedure was launched following the Supreme Court's decision in *Cadder v HMAdvocate*[7]. In July 2012, the Scottish Government signalled its intention to accept the 'broad reasoning' of the review and launched a further consultation paper on other issues that would arise from its implementation[8]. In December 2012, the Scottish Government published a further consultation canvassing change in such matters as the abolition of

---

4 See the *Civil Courts Review* under Lord Gill, the Lord Justice-Clerk: see http://www.scotcourts.gov.uk/civilcourtsreview/index.asp.
5 Although with Lord Gill being appointed Lord President in June 2012 this may soon change.
6 See The Carloway Review: http://www.scotland.gov.uk/About/Review/CarlowayReview.
7 2011 SC (UKSC) 13.
8 Reforming Scots Criminal Law and Practice: The Carloway Report: http://www.scotland.gov.uk/Publications/2012/07/4794.

the Not Proven verdict, and the size of majority in a jury required for conviction[9].

Judicial appointments and judicial independence

4.4   The appointment of judges raises important issues. In brief, who is to appoint them, and by what means? In some countries, at least some judges are elected. This raises interesting questions which cannot be pursued here. In most countries, they are all appointed by the Government. But if they are appointed by the Government, what is to make it appoint judges who are impartial, and in particular, what is to stop it appointing judges who are favourable towards it (a question of very considerable importance in a final court of appeal where, by definition, bias cannot be corrected on further appeal)? In short, how is 'judicial independence' to be preserved? These questions have become more obvious with the embedding of human rights into United Kingdom law through the Human Rights Act 1998 (discussed in Chapter 3). Courts with an international dimension raise further difficulties in that, for instance, all states accepting their jurisdiction are likely to want to be represented on the bench.

There are also three particularities about the appointment of judges in common law or hybrid countries (for the meaning of which, see Chapter 5). Firstly, in such jurisdictions, there is usually heavy reliance upon 'lay' (that is, non-professional) judges, at least in the criminal courts. This fact is less evident in Scotland than in some other jurisdictions. Nevertheless, lay justices in the Justice of the Peace Court ('JP Court') take about a third of all criminal proceedings[10]. Secondly, there is a major difference in relation to professional judges. In civil law countries, the judiciary is a distinct branch of the legal profession (so law graduates may opt for that choice upon graduation). In common law or hybrid countries, however, judges are usually only appointed after having pursued a successful career, typically as a court lawyer (so are invariably of a much maturer age and with the perspective of a participant). Thirdly, there is a further, consequential, major difference in relation to professional judges. In civil law countries, there is likely to be a career path within the judicial hierarchy, from minor courts to major ones. In common

---

9 Reforming Scots Criminal Law and Practice: Additional Safeguards Following the Removal of the Requirement for Corroboration: http://www.scotland.gov.uk/Publications/2012/12/4628.

10 In 2010/11 there were 40,783 summary disposals in JP Courts, while there were 65,209 in the Sheriff Court. There were around 5,000 solemn disposals in the same period.

law or hybrid countries, however, there are usually few prospects of promotion within the judicial hierarchy. Thus, for example, a Sheriff cannot expect to reach the Court of Session bench (though it has happened), and within the Court of Session, while all Outer House judges may have some expectation of becoming Inner House judges, not all will, and in any case, it remains a 'collegiate court'.

All three of these particularities have a bearing upon the underlying tension between Judiciary and Government, in that all three may be seen in practice as limiting the power of the Government over the Judiciary. In short, they can be seen as helping to preserve judicial independence, and such considerations explain a considerable emphasis upon the adequacy of arrangements to protect this independence in recent years. Such fears certainly generated United Kingdom legislation[11] which requires 'the Lord Chancellor, other Ministers of the Crown, and all with responsibility for matters relating to the judiciary or otherwise to the administration of justice' to 'uphold the continued independence of the judiciary', and which allows the 'chief justice of any part of the United Kingdom' (which in Scotland is the Lord President of the Court of Session) to 'lay before Parliament written representations on matters that appear to him to be matters of importance relating to the judiciary, or otherwise the administration of justice'[12]. In Scotland the Judiciary and Courts (Scotland) Act 2008 enshrined judicial independence in law, introducing a duty on Scottish Ministers, the Lord Advocate and MSPs to uphold the continued independence of the judiciary, and barring them from trying to exert influence through any special access to judges.

Several methods of appointment are used in Scotland though, to a large extent, these are variations upon the themes adumbrated above. There are different methods employed for the Supreme Court, for the senior Judges (and for appointment to the Inner House of the Court of Session) and for other Judges, for Sheriffs, and for Justices of the Peace. These are discussed below, in relation to each court. However, one important recent innovation deserves mention here, because it introduced radical change, rendered the process more uniform and more reliable, and demonstrates well some of the tensions in the appointment process. This is the Judicial Appointments Board for Scotland ('JABS').

JABS was set up in 2001, and placed on a statutory footing by the Judiciary and Courts (Scotland) Act 2008. It receives guidance

---

11 Constitutional Reform Act 2005, s 3.
12 *Ibid*, s 5. This does apply to Scotland, but 'matters within the competence of the Scottish Parliament' are excepted.

from ministers, but decides its own procedure. Its function is to provide the First Minister with a list of candidates recommended for appointment as Judge of the Court of Session, Sheriff Principal, Sheriff or Part-Time Sheriff (but not as Justice of the Peace) and to do so on merit, while considering ways of making representative recommendations. The Board comprises a mixture of lay members (including the Chairman), Judges, Sheriff Principals and Sheriffs, advocates and solicitors[13].

Judicial training and judicial competence

4.5   As noted in relation to judicial appointments, in common law and hybrid jurisdictions, being a judge cannot be embarked upon as a career path, and most of those appointed must have achieved some success in another, albeit related, job. Unsurprisingly, therefore, traditionally, there was no training and professional development for Judges or Sheriffs (though there has been for JPs for some time).

Since 1997, however, for Judges and Sheriffs, there has been a Judicial Studies Committee ('JSC')[14] to provide this. The JSC comprises a mixture of Judges (one being Chairman), Sheriff Principals and Sheriffs (one of whom is 'Director of Judicial Studies'), lay members and a civil servant from the Justice Department of the Scottish Government[15]. It organises induction courses for Sheriffs and Judges, refresher courses and seminars on specific topics, and publishes annual reports.

The JSC is continually looking to improve the training offered to the judiciary in Scotland and a new Head of Education post was created in 2011[16]. The Head of Education will 'help develop training modules and apply the principles of adult education and training to the work of the judiciary' and 'oversee educational content, working

---

13 The Chair at the end of 2012 was Sir Muir Russell KCB FRSE; the lay members were Professor Andrew Coyle CMG, Ms Elspeth MacArthur, Dr Michael Ewart and Ms Jeane Freeman; the judge was The Honorable Lady Dorrian; the Sheriff Principal, Sheriff Principal Bruce Kerr; the Sheriff, Sheriff Kenneth Ross; and the solicitor Martin McAllister.

14 See http://scotland-judiciary.org.uk/59/0/Judicial-Training (the Judicial College was set up in 2011 to train the judiciary in England and Wales, see http://www.judiciary.gov.uk/).

15 At the end of 2012, they were Lords Hamilton (President), Brodie (Chairman) and Malcolm (vice-Chairman), Sheriff Principal Stephen, Sheriffs Welsh QC (Director of Judicial Studies), Duff, Foulis, Fletcher and Fleming, Dr McClure (lay member), Rev. R Neilson (vice-Chairman of the justices association), Ms B Campbell (Director of criminal justice) and Mr A Clasper.

16 In mid-2012 the post was held by Ms Jessica Henderson.

closely with the Director of Judicial Studies to constantly evaluate the training needs of the judiciary'[17]. The JSC was rebranded as the Judicial Institute for Scotland in January 2013 and is now based in Parliament House in Edinburgh.

For JPs, training is described below in relation to the JP Court.

The Scottish courts

The Justice of the Peace Court[18]

4.6   JP Courts are local courts dealing with minor crime (and no civil matters), staffed by justices of the peace ('JPs') who are not qualified lawyers[19]. (In Glasgow, there are also salaried stipendiary magistrates, who are full time and legally qualified). The JP Courts were set up in 2007[20] to replace the old District Courts. The JP Courts deal with about a third of all criminal proceedings in Scotland, although these proceedings all concern minor crime.

The court. The JP Courts are managed by the Scottish Courts Service (an Executive Agency of the Scottish Government Justice Department[21]), as the Sheriff Courts are[22]. They are organised according to Sheriffdoms, normally with one JP Court in each Sheriff Court District[23], and Sheriff Principals are to administer them[24]. Each Sheriffdom has a Sheriffdom Legal Adviser, and deputes, for the JP Courts, and each JP Court only sits with a clerk of court who (save where there is a stipendiary magistrate) will act as Legal Adviser[25]. Prosecutions are undertaken by the Procurator Fiscal Service.

17 See Judicial Studies Committee Annual Report For Year to March 2011, available online at http://www.scotland-judiciary.org.uk/Upload/Documents/JSCAnnualReport2011.pdf.
18 The law on Justice of the Peace Courts is chiefly in the Criminal Proceedings (etc) (Scotland) Act 2007, Pt 4.
19 As noted, such 'lay' involvement, also manifested in juries, has been seen as a particular feature, and strength, of the administration of justice in common law and hybrid jurisdictions, but is a good deal more prominent in England & Wales.
20 Criminal Proceedings etc. (Reform) (Scotland) Act 2007.
21 See http://www.scotcourts.gov.uk/courtsadmin/scs.asp
22 Criminal Proceedings (etc) (Scotland) Act 2007, ss 59–61.
23 *Ibid.* s 59. For Sheriffdoms and Sheriff Court Districts, see below. The location of all JP Courts appears on the Scottish Courts website at www.scotcourts.gov. uk, and in the White Book (see above).
24 *Ibid.* s 61: For Sheriff Principals, see below.
25 *Ibid.* s 63: the clerks may also have such other functions as the Scottish Ministers confer.

Justices. Under the JP Court regime, lay JPs are appointed to a Sheriffdom 'in the name of Her Majesty' by the Scottish Ministers for a renewable period of five years, until reaching the age of 70[26]. The Scottish Ministers may make provision concerning the appointment process and residence[27], and have set up a Justice of the Peace Advisory Committee ('JPAC') for each Sheriffdom, appointed and convened by the Sheriff Principal, but with a specified membership, and no JP may be appointed unless recommended by a JPAC. The Judicial Appointments Board is not responsible for recommending JPs but the procedures for JPAC's recommendations to be made must be approved by the Judicial Appointments Board.

The Judicial Studies Committee took control of training for JPs in 2007[28].

The work of the JP Court. The JP Court may hear cases concerning offences which a statute has declared competent to it, and which occur within its area. The relevant area for each JP Court is the Sheriffdom[29] in which it sits.

All cases are prosecuted by summary procedure. As all such cases are competent in the Sheriff Court as well, it is the procurator fiscal who decides which cases go to which court in the light, among other things, of the limits to the JP Court's sentencing powers. A justice may impose up to 60 days' imprisonment and/or a fine of up to £2,500.

Appeal is possible, against conviction and/or sentence, to the High Court of Justiciary, sitting as an appeal court. It is available both to the person convicted, and (on a point of law only) to the prosecutor.

The Sheriff Court[30]

4.7 Sheriff Courts are local courts with very wide jurisdiction, both civil and criminal, and legally qualified judges. There is a Sheriff Court in every city and most towns[31]. Thus, for many purposes it is

---

26 Criminal Proceedings (etc) (Scotland) Act 2007, s 67.
27 *Ibid.* s 67. This power was exercised in the Justice of the Peace (Scotland) Order 2007 (SSI 2007/210).
28 See Justice of the Peace (Scotland) Order 2007.
29 Criminal Proceedings (etc) (Scotland) Act 2007, s 62.
30 Much of the relevant law is to be found in the Sheriff Courts (Scotland) Acts 1907 and 1971, as amended. Information on Sheriff Courts is available at www.scotcourts.gov.uk.
31 Their location is given at www.scotcourts.gov.uk and in the 'White Book' (see above).

the most important court in the land. In its civil jurisdiction (largely overlapping that of the Court of Session) it deals mostly with debt and divorce. However, many of these cases are simple, and much of a Sheriff's time may be taken up with the small proportion of difficult and important cases which may be debt or divorce or some other matter. In its criminal jurisdiction (largely overlapping that of the High Court of Justiciary on the one hand, and that of JP Court, on the other), it deals with about two-thirds of all criminal proceedings[32].

The court. Sheriff Courts are organised into six Sheriffdoms, based on the former local government regions[33]. Each Sheriffdom (except Glasgow and Strathkelvin) is divided into several Sheriff Court Districts, giving 49 Sheriff Courts in all[34]. The First Minister decides how many Sheriffs there shall be in each Sheriffdom, and Sheriff Courts often have more than one. Sheriffs are appointed to a Sheriffdom[35], and usually sit in only one Sheriff Court District, but may sit in more in areas with little business. There are also, however, 'floating' Sheriffs, part-time Sheriffs and honorary Sheriffs.

The First Minister has overall responsibility for the efficient organisation and administration of the courts[36], which he discharges through the Scottish Courts Service, an Executive Agency of the Scottish Government Justice Department[37]. It is responsible for provision of staff, court-houses etc. However, each of the six Sheriffdoms has a Sheriff Principal who is responsible for the speedy and efficient disposal of business[38], and each Sheriffdom has a

---

32 The Sheriffdoms of Glasgow and Strathkelvin; Grampian, Highland and Islands; Lothian and Borders; North Strathclyde; South Strathclyde; Dumfries and Galloway; and Tayside, Central and Fife.
33 For instance, the Sheriffdom of Tayside, Central and Fife is divided into the Sheriff Court Districts of Alloa, Arbroath, Cupar, Dundee, Dunfermline, Falkirk, Forfar, Kirkcaldy, Perth and Stirling. For locations, see www.scotcourts. gov.uk which gives addresses and maps, and for a complete list, the 'White Book' (see above).
34 Sheriff Courts (Scotland) Act 1971, s 14 (as amended), read with Scotland Act 1998, s 53. Glasgow and Strathkelvin Sheriffdom (and Sheriff Court District) has 22 Sheriffs.
35 *Ibid*, ss 7, 9 (as amended).
36 *Ibid*, ss 1, 24, 25 read with Scotland Act 1998, s 53.
37 See www.scotcourts.gov.uk/courtsadmin/scs.asp.
38 Sheriff Courts (Scotland) Act 1971, ss 15–17 (as amended). For the identities of Sheriff Principals, see http://www.scotland-judiciary.org.uk/35/0/Sheriffs-Principal.

regional sheriff clerk, and a sheriff clerk (and deputes if necessary) for each court, who run it day-to-day[39].

Sheriffs. The office of Sheriff is ancient, and Sheriffs were long a principal part of local law and administration. The office became largely hereditary in the Middle Ages, but Sheriffs appointed 'Deputes' to do the work, and they in turn appointed 'Substitutes', a sort of three rank system. Heritability was finally abolished after the 1745 rebellion[40]. No-one was thereafter appointed to the office of Sheriff (the top rank), but the office of Sheriff Depute (the second rank) was continued, and its holders were called by that title until the 19th century, when they became known simply as Sheriffs (or as 'Sheriffs Principal'). The appointment was part-time, and held by advocates[41]. In 1971 they became formally entitled Sheriffs Principal, and the post became full-time[42].

The Sheriff Deputes continued to appoint Substitutes (the third rank) after the heritable jurisdictions were abolished. These Substitutes became the full-time Sheriffs, with the title 'Sheriff Substitute', salaried and legally qualified from the early 19th century, but appointed by the Crown only later. In 1971 the Sheriff Substitutes finally fell heir to the title Sheriff[43]. The actual means of appointment, clear in formal terms, was somewhat obscure in practical ones, involving consultations with the Dean of the Faculty of Advocates and Sheriffs Principal, until the Judicial Appointments Board for Scotland was set up in 2002.

Today, the 'right of appointing' Sheriffs, including Sheriffs Principal (but excluding part-time and honorary Sheriffs), 'is vested in [Her] Majesty and shall be exercised by [the Scottish Ministers]'[44], after consultation with the Lord President and recommendation by the Judicial Appointments Board[45]. Those who have been advocates

---

39 The identities and addresses of sheriff clerks are given at www.scotcourts.gov. uk, and in the 'White Book' (see above).

40 Heritable Jurisdictions (Scotland) Act 1746.

41 Undoubtedly the most famous Sheriff was Sir Walter Scott, appointed Sheriff-Depute of Selkirk in 1799.

42 Sheriff Courts (Scotland) Act 1971, ss 4, 6 (as amended).

43 *Ibid*, s 4.

44 Sheriff Courts (Scotland) Act 1907, s 11 (as amended). In late-2012, there were some 142 full-time Sheriffs (including some 27 'floating Sheriffs'), some 30 of them women. A list of their identities, Sheriffdoms and Sheriff Court Districts is found at http://www.scotland-judiciary.org.uk/36/0/Sheriffs and in the 'White Book' (see above).

45 Sheriff Ian Macphail, appointed Sheriff Principal of Lothian and Borders in 2002 (but later Lord Macphail in the Court of Session), was the first to be so appointed.

or solicitors for at least ten years are eligible to be appointed Sheriff[46], but few are appointed with less than a couple of decades of experience, or more in the case of Sheriff Principals (who are usually appointed from among QCs and those who are Sheriffs already). Vacancies are now publicly advertised. Sheriffs may hold office until the age of 70[47]. They are salaried[48].

In addition to ordinary Sheriffs, full-time salaried 'floating Sheriffs'[49], appointed to a particular Sheriffdom or as 'all-Scotland floating Sheriffs', may be directed to sit anywhere to relieve pressure of business. There are also up to 85 part-time Sheriffs[50], appointed by the Scottish Ministers from those qualified to be Sheriffs, for five-year terms[51] (and are normally to be re-appointed), who may sit in any Sheriff Court District, and are expected to sit for between 20 and 100 days a year. If solicitors, they would not normally be used in the Sheriff Court District in which they practise. Like the floating Sheriffs, they add flexibility to the system, and a part-time appointment provides judicial experience for possible appointees to a full-time post.

Honorary Sheriffs are appointed by the Sheriff Principal[52]. They require no legal qualification (although many are senior solicitors). The office is honorary but may involve some judicial duties. In that role Honorary Sheriffs have the same powers as other Sheriffs.

Sheriffs can be removed from office if they are considered unfit for office by reason of inability, neglect of duty or misbehaviour[53]. The First Minister, on request from the Lord President of the Court of

---

46 Sheriff Courts (Scotland) Act 1971, s 5 (as amended).
47 *Ibid*, s 65A (as inserted by Judicial Pensions and Retirement Act 1993, Sch 6, para 10).
48 In 2012, Sheriff Principals received £138,548 and Sheriffs, £128,296.
49 In 2012, there were some 27 floating Sheriffs.
50 See Judicial Studies Committee Annual Report For Year to March 2011, available online at http://www.scotland-judiciary.org.uk/Upload/Documents/JSCAnnualReport2011.pdf.
51 Sheriff Courts (Scotland) Act 1971, ss 11A–11D (as inserted by the Bail, Judicial Appointments etc. (Scotland) Act, s7). Part-time Sheriffs replaced the former 'Temporary Sheriffs' after it was decided in *Starrs v Ruxton* 2000 JC 208 that the latter did not provide the 'independent and impartial tribunal' required by Art 6 of the ECHR, because of their lack of tenure. The method of appointing, terms of office and means of removal of part-time Sheriffs are laid down in the Bail, Judicial Appointments, Etc (Scotland) Act 2000. For the full list of their names, see: http://www.scotland-judiciary.org.uk/37/0/Part-Time-Sheriffs
52 The identities of Honorary Sheriffs are given in the entry for the relevant Sheriffdom in the White Book (see above).
53 Sheriff Courts (Scotland) Act 1971, s 12A(1), as inserted by the Judiciary and Courts (Scotland) Act 2008.

Session, must constitute a tribunal to investigate whether the person is unfit for office for the reasons above[54]. The First Minister may also constitute such a tribunal if the First Minister believes there are other circumstances he thinks fit to do so[55]. The Lord President must still be consulted in this latter case[56]. The tribunal must consist of a qualifying member of the Judicial Committee of the Privy Council, a Sheriff or Sheriff Principal depending on which position the person subject to the tribunal holds, a person who has been a solicitor or advocate for at least ten years and a person who is none of the preceding types of person[57]. The First Minister selects the members with the agreement of the Lord President of the Court of Session[58]. The tribunal produces a written report which must contain reasons for its conclusions and submits it to the First Minister[59]. The First Minister then must lay the report before the Scottish Parliament. In the situation where the tribunal concludes a person is unfit for office, the First Minister may remove that person from their office. The First Minister may only remove a person by making a statutory instrument[60,61] (subject to annulment by the Scottish Parliament[62]) removing the person as a sheriff. This has only been done twice and never since the new rules came into force in 2008. In 1977, a Sheriff was removed for having organised local political plebiscites, and in 1992 another was removed for inability[63]. Honorary Sheriffs are appointed by the Sheriff Principal, so may be removed by him.

The Judicial Institute for Scotland[64] provides training and professional development for Sheriffs.

The work of the Sheriff Court. In civil proceedings, the basic principle is that a pursuer must bring his case in the Sheriffdom of the defender's domicile. This is much broadened, however, to include

---

54 *Ibid.* s 12(1) (a).
55 *Ibid.* s 12(1)(b).
56 *Ibid.* s 12(3).
57 *Ibid.* s 12(4).
58 *Ibid.* s 12(7)
59 *Ibid.* s 12D.
60 *Ibid.* s 12E(3).
61 For the nature of statutory instruments, see Chs 9 and 10.
62 *Ibid.* s 12E(4)(a).
63 See the Sheriff (Removal from Office) Order 1992, SI 1992/1677 and *Stewart v Secretary of State* 1995 SLT 895, 1996 SLT 1203, 1998 SLT 385.
64 See: http://scotland-judiciary.org.uk/59/0/Judicial-Training.

other connections with the Sheriffdom, such as that the relevant contract was performed there, or the relevant delict occurred there[65].

Within these limits, a Sheriff Court may take almost any kind of civil case, including contract, delict, property and divorce (though that has its own grounds of jurisdiction). It also hears appeals from, or review of, a large number of local authority and other administrative decisions, such as licensing appeals. There are some types of case it cannot hear[66]. On the other hand, it has 'privative' (ie exclusive) jurisdiction in relation to actions for sums of £5,000 or less[67], and to many statutory applications and appeals. As a civil court, it employs 'small claims', 'summary cause' and 'ordinary cause' procedures[68] for cases of different levels of complexity and value, and also summary application procedure for the great variety of emergency and administrative applications under common law and legislation.

Appeal in civil cases depends upon the procedure used. In small claims, appeal is to the Sheriff Principal on a point of law only, and no further. In summary causes, it is to the Sheriff Principal on a point of law only and thence (by leave only) to the Inner House of the Court of Session and thereafter to the Supreme Court. In ordinary causes, it is to the Sheriff Principal and then (generally as of right) to the Inner House, or direct to the Inner House, and thereafter in either case, on a point of law only, to the Supreme Court. The number of appeals is small compared with the number of cases dealt with.

In criminal proceedings, in broad terms, the Sheriff Court has jurisdiction only over offences occurring within the Sheriffdom. Also, there are certain offences, the main ones being murder and rape, which cannot be tried in a Sheriff Court. There are limits too on a Sheriff's sentencing powers. In summary proceedings, a Sheriff can impose up to twelve months' imprisonment and/or a fine at level five of the standard scale (currently £5,000)[69], and in solemn proceedings (used in serious cases with a jury), five years'

---

65 Sheriff Courts (Scotland) Act 1971, s 7, Civil Jurisdiction and Judgments Act 1982, Pt II & Sch 8 (as substituted by Civil Jurisdiction and Judgments Order 2001 (SI 2001.2929) Sch 2 para 6).

66 For instance, by virtue of the Insolvency Act 1986, s 120(3), the Sheriff Court cannot hear petitions to wind up a company with fully paid up share capital of greater than £120,000.

67 The Sheriff Courts (Scotland) Act 1971 (Privative Jurisdiction and Summary Cause) Order 2007 (SSI 2007/507), art 2.

68 Sheriff Courts (Scotland) Act 1907, s 7 (as amended).

69 See *ibid*, ss 35–38, 41–42.

imprisonment (or in some cases more[70]) and/or an unlimited fine[71] (and may remit to the High Court for heavier sentence[72]). Within these limits, however, a Sheriff can try any criminal case, and by summary or solemn procedure, as appropriate[73]. Prosecution is by the Procurator Fiscal Service, and the fiscal chooses between summary or solemn procedure where a choice is available.

Appeals in criminal cases may be against conviction and/or sentence, and are to the High Court of Justiciary. In summary proceedings, the person convicted can appeal against conviction and sentence or other disposal. The prosecutor may appeal, but only on a point of law, against conviction or sentence. In solemn procedure, only the person convicted may appeal. Appeals are a small proportion of cases heard.

The High Court of Justiciary[74]

4.8 The High Court of Justiciary is the trial court for major crime, and the final appeal court for all crime, in Scotland. As a trial court, it goes on circuit to a number of towns and cities, with a single judge. It deals with a very small proportion of all crime, although all that it does deal with is serious[75]. As an appeal court (called the Court of Criminal Appeal in appeals under 'solemn procedure'[76]), it sits only in Parliament House in Edinburgh[77], usually with a bench of three judges, although a larger bench can be convened to review precedents[78] which are doubted. The judges are the same as those who staff the Court of Session. It is the supreme criminal court for Scotland, but is significantly affected by the Supreme Court of the United Kingdom in that under the Scotland Act 2012 there may be

---

70 But, for instance, six months for a second or subsequent offence of dishonest appropriation or personal violence: Criminal Procedure (Scotland) Act 1995, s 5.
71 Particular statutes may impose different sentencing powers *ad hoc*.
72 Criminal Procedure (Scotland) Act 1995, s 3(3) (as amended).
73 *Ibid*, s 219(8).
74 For 'summary' and 'solemn' proceedings, see below.
75 Much of the relevant law is found in the Criminal Procedure (Scotland) Act 1995.
76 For 'solemn' proceedings, see below. See also Shiels 'The Origins of the Court of Criminal Appeal' 2006 SLT 215–218.
77 That is, the building erected in 1639 for the Scottish Parliament, in the Edinburgh High Street, behind St Giles, and vacated upon the Union of Parliaments in 1707, now with an annexe across the road in the Lawnmarket.
78 For the meaning and significance of 'precedent', see Ch 12.

appeals to that court from the High Court on issues of EU law and Convention (that is, ECHR) rights[79].

The court. In 1672, the High Court of Justiciary was set up to replace the previous system of lay 'Justices-General' (earlier called 'Justiciars') appointed to tour the country dealing with crime (and other matters) of particular concern to the Sovereign. The sovereign might directly interfere in the business, and the system was ineffective even by the standards of the day. The High Court originally comprised the Lord Justice-General (a layman who often did not sit[80]), the Lord Justice-Clerk (originally the clerk of court to the lay Justiciars), and five Lords Commissioners of Justiciary from among the Court of Session judges.

In 1837, the office of Lord Justice-General was passed to the Lord President of the Court of Session, and in 1887 all Court of Session judges became Lords Commissioners of Justiciary and the court took its present form.

The court may sit anywhere in Scotland. It used to go on four fixed circuits, but now sits where the Lord Justice-General determines after consultation with the Lord Advocate. Half a dozen Lords Commissioners will be on circuit much of the time (but with a permanent presence in Glasgow), sitting singly with a jury, and three more sitting in Edinburgh hearing appeals.

The Lord Justice-General is responsible for the administration of the court, acting through the Principal Clerk of Session and Justiciary and his staff, who may act as clerks of court on circuit.

High Court of Justiciary judges ('Lords Commissioners of Justiciary'). The Lord President of the Court of Session is the Lord Justice-General, and all Court of Session judges ('Senators of the College of Justice') are also High Court judges ('Lords Commissioners of Justiciary') *ex officio*[81]. Temporary Judges of the Court of Session are also Temporary Judges of the High Court[82].

As with Court of Session judges (and Sheriffs) the Judicial Institute for Scotland[83] provides training and professional development.

---

79 Thus preserving the anomaly that civil appeals from Scotland can go on a further appeal, but criminal cases generally cannot, creating the further anomaly that the Supreme Court of the United Kingdom is thus a misnomer.

80 The office became hereditary in the Dukes of Argyll.

81 For their identities, see http://scotland-judiciary.org.uk/34/0/Senators-of-the-College-of-Justice, the 'White Book' (see above), or the bound volumes of Session Cases and Scots Law Times.

82 See previous note.

83 See http://scotland-judiciary.org.uk/59/0/Judicial-Training

The work of the High Court. As a trial court, the High Court of Justiciary has jurisdiction over all offences in Scotland (unless excluded by statute). Thus, its jurisdiction overlaps that of other criminal courts, and it is the prosecutor's decision in most cases whether a case goes to the High Court or elsewhere. However, no other court may try certain offences, principally murder and rape, and the High Court also wields the *nobile officium* (see Chapter 12) and, possibly, a 'declaratory power' to create new offences (see also Chapter 12), although this is very constrained if indeed it still exists. On the other hand, it does not deal with offences triable by summary proceedings, so trials are always by solemn procedure, before a single judge and a jury of 15. Prosecution is by one of some 20 Advocates-Depute in the name of the Lord Advocate[84], but occasionally by the Lord Advocate or the Solicitor-General in person[85].

Appeal from the High Court sitting as a trial court is to the High Court sitting as a court of appeal, which usually comprises three judges, but may comprise only two, and is often called 'the Court of Criminal Appeal'. It also sits as the appeal court from all summary proceedings in the JP Court and the summary and solemn proceedings in the Sheriff Court. In practice, one or other of the Divisions of the Inner House of the Court of Session, under their presiding judges, almost always provides the criminal appeal court. There is no further appeal save in a devolution case (as discussed below).

The Court of Session[86]

4.9   The Court of Session has jurisdiction over most civil matters in Scotland, but sits only in Parliament House[87] in Edinburgh. It comprises the 'Outer House' and the 'Inner House'. Judges of the former (known as 'Lords Ordinary') sit singly, and deal with cases at first instance. Judges of the latter sit on one or other of two 'Divisions' (though there may be an 'Extra Division'), normally with three judges, and chiefly hear appeals (although they also hear petitions in which one party seeks some special permission, usually without opposition). Also, as with the High Court of Justiciary, a larger bench can be convened to review precedents[88]. The Court of

---

84 For the identities of Advocates-Depute, see the 'White Book' (see above).
85 For example, the Lord Advocate, Colin Boyd QC, led the prosecution of the Lockerbie bombers.
86 Much of the relevant law is found in the Court of Session Act 1988.
87 See above in relation to the High Court of Justiciary.
88 For the meaning and significance of 'precedent', see Ch 12.

Session is the supreme civil court in Scotland, although there is an appeal from it to the Supreme Court of the United Kingdom.

The court. The date traditionally taken to be the year of the court's foundation is 1532. Since the late 15th century the King's Council had been sitting intermittently to dispense civil justice. Its lack of funding, and the limited availability of the nobility around the time of the Kings James IV and V, impeded its efficiency. An Act of 1532 (later called the College of Justice Act) made arrangements for a central royal court under the name of the 'College of Justice' to be set up[89]. It comprised fifteen men (eight, including the Lord President, being clerics) appointed as 'Lords of Council and Session' to be professional judges, supported financially by church endowments and exhorted to sit daily. But it was not until an Act of Parliament of 1541, confirming that of 1532 and a Bull of Pope Paul III of 1535, that the court began to function regularly with some semblance of sufficient funding.

At first it dealt only with cases at first instance, with possible appeal to the Privy Council, and it had no jurisdiction over marriage and some other matters, which were then dealt with by ecclesiastical courts. It rapidly expanded its jurisdiction, however, and became an appeal court as well. The leading writer on Scots law, Viscount Stair, referred to the court in his *Institutions* of 1681[90] as 'the Session' or 'the College of Justice'. By the time of the Union of 1707, it was called the 'Court of Session'.

Until the Union rendered Parliament House vacant[91], 'the Haill Fifteen' usually sat in an inner room in the Edinburgh Tolbooth[92],

---

89 On this complex subject, see AM Godfrey, *Civil Justice in Renaissance Scotland* (2009).

90 *Institutions*, IV, 1, 22.

91 See above in relation to the High Court of Justiciary.

92 Or rather, it sat in the Tolbooth itself till 1560, but from 1564 to 1640 in an upstairs room in an annexe to St Giles church, referred to as the 'Over' or 'Upper Tolbooth' (the High Court of Justiciary sitting in a lower room). MacQueen 'Two Visitors in the Session, 1629 and 1639' in MacQueen (ed) *Miscellany IV* (Stair Society, 2002) reproduces two 17th-century accounts by English visitors, including a sketch map of the lay-out of the 'Upper Tolbooth'. One of the visitors (Sir C Lowther) recorded (p163) that in the Outer House 'is allway grete noyse and confusion, but the Inner House very orderly ... it onely medleth with things not determined or where his [*scil* the Outer House judge's] judgment is disliked'. The other visitor (Sir W Brereton) also recorded (at p166) that 'I observed the gretest rudeness, disorder and confusion that ever I saw in any court of justice, no, not the like disorder in any of our sessions, for here two or three plead and speak together, and that with such a forced, strained voice as the strongest only caries it ...'.

save for one or two judges dealing with witnesses and preliminary matters outside, reporting back to them. This practice persisted when the court moved into the adjacent Parliament Hall within Parliament House. They would send one of their number in turn to hear evidence on the other side of a partition and report back to them. Thus the titles 'Inner' and 'Outer House' arose. In 1808 and 1825 a number of reforms resulted in the court taking its present form. It is still 'collegiate' in that decisions are given in the name of the whole court, judges from one House may sit in the other, and all are said to be of equal status (although Inner House judges are paid slightly more, and the Lord President most of all).

There is provision for 34 Court of Session judges[93] and also additional temporary judges. One judge is always seconded to the Scottish Law Commission as whole- or part-time chairman[94]. The more junior Court of Session judges (that is, those who are not members of the Inner House) sit as Lords Ordinary in the Outer House. But they will not do so every working day. Some may be sitting as Lords Commissioners of Justiciary in the High Court of Justiciary, usually away from Edinburgh on circuit. Others may be sitting in other judicial capacities, such as Chairman of the Employment Appeal Tribunal, and yet others may be undertaking other functions, such as judicial inquiries[95].

The Inner House comprises the 'First' and 'Second' Divisions, which are, despite their titles, of equal status. The First is composed of the Lord President of the Court of Session and four senior judges, and the Second, the Lord Justice-Clerk and four other senior judges. Both have a quorum, and normal complement, of three (for the others may be performing other tasks). An Extra Division may also be convened. Also, occasionally, a Court of Seven (or more) Judges is convened for a point of special difficulty, or where overruling a precedent[96] of a Division is in contemplation.

The Lord President is responsible for administration of the court, acting through the Principal Clerk of Session and Justiciary and his staff.

---

93 Court of Session Act 1988, s 1(1) (as amended by the Maximum Number of Judges (Scotland) Order 2004 (SSI 2004/499), Art 2).

94 In late-2012, Lady Clark of Calton.

95 Lord Cullen of Whitekirk, Lord President 2001–5, while a judge, had conducted the Public Inquiry into the Piper Alpha disaster between 1988 and 1990, the Public Inquiry into the Dunblane Primary School shootings in 1996, and the Ladbroke Grove Rail Inquiry in 1999, for instance.

96 For the meaning and significance of 'precedent', see Ch 12.

Court of Session judges (Senators of the College of Justice).
The judges of the Court of Session, the senior permanent Scottish judges, are technically 'Senators of the College of Justice'[97]. The power of appointment lies with Her Majesty, and under arrangements introduced upon devolution, on the recommendation of the First Minister and after consulting the Lord President[98] and receiving recommendations from the Judicial Appointments Board for Scotland. Those eligible are Sheriffs and Sheriffs Principal of five years' standing, and advocates and solicitors with five years' right of audience in the Court of Session[99]. Vacancies are now advertised. On appointment judges take the courtesy title 'Lord' or 'Lady'[100]. They are not thereby members of the House of Lords[101]. Some follow a tradition of taking a territorial or family title instead of

97 For their identities, see http://scotland-judiciary.org.uk/34/0/Senators-of-the-College-of-Justice, the 'White Book' (see above), or the bound volumes of Session Cases and Scots Law Times. In late-2012, the Lord President was Lord Gill, and the Lord Justice Clerk, Lord Carloway.

98 Scotland Act 1998, s 95(4). See also, Judiciary and Courts (Scotland) Act 2008 Chapter 3.

99 Until the Law Reform (Miscellaneous Provisions) (Scotland) Act 1990, s 35, it was not clear who was eligible. There was no legislation on this matter, but Art 19 of the Treaty of Union permitted (on various conditions) advocates, Writers to the Signet and Principal Clerks of Session to be appointed. Only senior advocates who were not Sheriffs had been appointed for many years, so the 1990 Act broadened eligibility considerably. However, advocates as such are not mentioned in the 1990 Act, so while they are undoubtedly still considered eligible, it is presumably on the basis of the Treaty of Union, Art 19

100 In late-2012, there had been seven women judges (six of whom were still sitting): Lady Cosgrove (appointed 1996, having been a Sheriff and Temporary Judge, and the first woman judge, also becoming the first woman to serve in the Inner House, in 2003: retired 2006); Lady Paton (appointed 2000, direct from the Bar, having been an advocate-depute and standing counsel to various Government departments); Lady Smith (appointed 2001, direct from the Bar, having been a Temporary Sheriff and an advocate-depute: she was appointed by a temporary formal selection process which briefly preceded the Judicial Appointments Board); Lady Dorrian (appointed 2005, direct from the bar having also been an advocate-depute and standing counsel to Government departments); Lady Clark of Calton (appointed 2006, having been standing counsel to Government departments and Advocate-General for Scotland); Lady Stacey (appointed 2009, direct from the bar having also been an advocate-depute); and, most recently, Lady Scott who took up her seat in November 2012. Morag Wise QC was appointed to the bench in January 2013.

101 Nor are they knighted, as are their equivalents in England & Wales. However, several judges were already life peers for other reasons, typically as law officers required to sit in the House of Lords (not being MPs), such as Lord McCluskey, Lord Cameron of Lochbroom, Lord Rodger of Earlsferry and Lady Clark of Calton. Also, recent Lord Presidents not previously ennobled have received peerages, ie Lord Hope of Craighead and Lord Cullen of Whitekirk.

their surname, which may some times be justified as avoiding the surname of another judge[102]. In addition, Temporary Judges may now be appointed by the First Minister from among retired judges for a year at a time up to the age of 75 and also from those eligible to be appointed as full-time judges (usually senior Sheriffs or practising advocates)[103]. The latter do not have the title of 'Lord' or 'Lady'.

Appointment to the Inner House is by the Lord President and Lord Justice-Clerk, with the consent of the Scottish Ministers and 'after such consultation with judges as appears to them to be appropriate in the particular circumstances'[104]. However, the Lord President of the Court of Session and the Lord Justice-Clerk 'continue to be' appointed by Her Majesty on the recommendation of the Prime Minister, after consulting the Lord President and the Lord Justice-Clerk, unless the office is vacant[105]. Occasionally they are appointed straight from the Bar, but otherwise from among existing judges[106].

102 The practice may be increasing in popularity, for among judges sitting recently, many have taken advantage of it: eg Lord Kingarth was Derek Emslie, Lord Abernethy was John Cameron, Lord Eassie is Ronald Mackay, Lord Carloway is Colin Sutherland, Lord Bracadale is Alistair Campbell, Lord Kinclaven is Alexander Wylie, Lord Uist is Roderick Macdonald, and Lord Malcolm is Colin Campbell. This practice incidentally raises the subject of Scottish judicial dynasties. Lord Clyde (appointed 1985, Lord of Appeal in Ordinary 1996–2001) was son of the late Lord Clyde (Lord President 1954–72) and grandson of another late Lord Clyde (Lord President 1928–35). Lord Kingarth (appointed 1997) and Lord Emslie (appointed 2001) are both sons of the late Lord Emslie (appointed 1970, Lord President 1972–89). Lord Wheatley (appointed 2000) is the son of the late Lord Wheatley (appointed 1954, Lord Justice Clerk 1972–85).
103 Judicial Pensions and Retirement Act 1993, s 26(4)–(7); Law Reform (Miscellaneous Provisions) (Scotland) Act 1990, s 35(3). For a list of their identities see, http://www.scotland-judiciary.org.uk/55/0/Temporary-Judges.
104 Court of Session Act 1988, s 2(6) (as amended).
105 Scotland Act 1998, s 95.
106 The current (from June 2012) Lord President (Lord Gill) was previously Lord Justice Clerk; his immediate predecessor (Lord Hamilton) was appointed from the First Division; his predecessor (Lord Cullen) was previously Lord Justice-Clerk; his predecessor in turn (Lord Rodger, who later became a House of Lords judge) was appointed from the Outer House, but his further predecessor (Lord Hope, now also a Justice of the Supreme Court), was appointed from the Bar where he was Dean of the Faculty of Advocates. The current Lord Justice-Clerk (Lord Carloway) was appointed from the Inner House; his immediate predecessor (Lord Gill) was an Outer House judge, and Chairman of the Scottish Law Commission; his predecessor was Lord Cullen (see above), whose predecessor (Lord Ross) was appointed from the Inner House.

Senators are paid[107]. They are required to retire at 70 and when they do so they retain their title. Provision is now made for the removal of a judge of the Court of Session. If the removal of a judge is contemplated, the First Minister must convene a tribunal of two individuals who have held high judicial office (eg a judge from the Supreme Court or Court of Session), an individual who is, and has been for at least ten years, an advocate or solicitor and an individual who does not hold (and never has) high judicial office and is not (and never has been) an advocate or solicitor[108]. At least one of the individuals must be a member of the Judicial Committee of the Privy Council[109] and at least one must hold, or have held, office as a judge in the Court of Session[110]. The tribunal must be chaired by a member of the Judicial Committee of the Privy Council[111]. This tribunal is to report whether the judge is unfit for office 'by reason of inability, neglect of duty or misbehaviour'. If such a report is made, the First Minister may recommend to the Scottish Parliament that the judge be removed and if it so resolves he shall make a recommendation to Her Majesty to that effect. The procedure is similar to that for the removal of a Sheriff.

The Judicial Institute for Scotland[112] provides training and career development of judges.

The work of the Court of Session. The Outer House of the Court of Session is a court of first instance, and can hear most types of civil case. Therefore many cases can be brought either there or in the Sheriff Court, and pursuers choose on the basis of cost, importance, convenience etc. Some cases, however, such as judicial review over certain administrative bodies, and exercise of the *nobile officium* (for which, see Chapter 12), are reserved to the Court. Some others though, such as actions for £5,000 or less and a number of appeals from administrative decisions, are reserved for Sheriffs. There is a limited degree of specialisation among the Court of Session judges, for instance, in judicial review cases and in intellectual property, commercial and patent cases there are special

---

107 In 2012, the Lord President received £214,165; the Lord Justice-Clerk, £206,857; Inner House judges £196,707; and other Senators, £172,753.
108 Judiciary and Courts (Scotland) Act 2008, s 35(4).
109 *Ibid.* s 35(6).
110 *Ibid.* s 35(7).
111 *Ibid.* ss 35(9) and (10).
112 See: http://scotland-judiciary.org.uk/59/0/Judicial-Training.

provisions to enable them to be dealt with quickly[113]. The Inner House of the Court of Session is primarily a court of appeal from the Outer House, Sheriffs Principal and Sheriffs, certain specialised courts (such as the Scottish Land Court), and a variety of tribunals (such as the Employment Appeal Tribunal and the Social Security Commissioners). As a court of first instance, it hears 'special cases', that is, certain ones in which the facts are agreed, and only the law is disputed (for example, on the interpretation of a will), and certain petitions, generally purely formal (such as to appoint solicitors as notaries public), but also including those seeking variation of trusts.

Appeal from the Outer House to the Inner House is as of right and is called a 'reclaiming motion', as one part of the collegiate court is reviewing the decision of another part. Thereafter it is to the Supreme Court, provided it is from a final judgment, or the judges were not unanimous, or the Inner House gives leave. Where the appeal originated in the Sheriff Court, there are restrictions on appeal to the Inner House. It may go thereafter to the Supreme Court on a point of law.

The Court of Session has the power of judicial review over the decisions of lower courts and tribunals and of government, on grounds of procedural impropriety, such as *ultra vires* (acting beyond one's powers), or lack of 'natural justice' (for instance, not hearing both sides of the case). This process is considered further below in relation to civil procedure.

It can also exercise the *nobile officium* (see Chapter 12).

Supreme Court of the United Kingdom[114]

4.10 Subject always to the decisions of the Court of Justice on the European Union on EU law matters, the final court of appeal from civil courts (but not from criminal courts, except in England and Wales and Northern Ireland) is the Supreme Court of the United

---

113 At the end of 2012, the 'Commercial Judges' were Lords Hodge, Malcolm and Woolman.
114 The relevant law on the Supreme Court is found in the Constitutional Reform Act 2005, Part 3.

Kingdom[115.] It sits in the former Middlesex Guildhall, opposite the United Kingdom Parliament, in Parliament Square[116].

The court. The Supreme Court was set up to replace the former Appellate Committee of the House of Lords ('ACHL'). That particular institution descended from the House of Lords of Great Britain, set up in 1707, but followed the traditions of the English House, which heard appeals from the courts. There was dispute as to whether the new House could hear appeals from Scottish courts, but quickly after 1707 it assumed jurisdiction[117], and there were many Scottish appeals until the twentieth century. The House of Lords only grew into a professional court in the 19th century, when a convention grew up that lay peers should not sit on appeals, judges were ennobled in order to hear such appeals, and finally the ACHL was set up in 1876[118].

The Supreme Court of the United Kingdom is the successor body to this arrangement. It was set up by legislation in 2005 and began operating in 2009. To a certain extent, the move was driven by a felt need to separate the judicial arm of government clearly from its legislative and executive branches; but the result has been something rather more than a moving of the furniture across Parliament Square.

Judges of the Supreme Court of the United Kingdom. There are twelve judges in the Supreme Court of the United Kingdom with one taking the position of President of the Supreme Court[119]

---

115 Constitutional Reform Act 2005, Part 3. (Part 1 of the Act oddly asserts that, *int. al.* it "does not adversely affect … the constitutional principle of the rule of law"; Part 2 deals with the position of the Lord Chancellor (and was referred to in Ch 3 in that regard); Part 4 with appointment to, and discipline of, the judiciary, chiefly in England & Wales; Part 5 with judicial appointments and removals in Northern Ireland; Part 6 with other matters, including the Judicial Committee of the Privy Council; and Part 7 with general matters.

116 The other two sides, interestingly, are formed by Westminster Abbey (God) and the Treasury (Mammon).

117 The first reported case, *Greenshields v Magistrates of Edinburgh* (1710–11) Rob 12, was in 1710. An Episcopalian minister was imprisoned by the magistrates, at the behest of the Presbytery, for using the Anglican form of service. The Court of Session upheld their decision, but the House of Lords set its stamp on the matter by overturning it.

118 Appellate Jurisdiction Act 1876.

119 Lord Phillips of Worth Matravers was the first President, holding office until the end of September 2012, when he retired and was succeeded by Lord Neuberger of Abbotsbury.

and another taking the position of Deputy President[120]. The other ten judges are known as Justices of the Supreme Court[121]; all enjoy the courtesy title 'Lord' or 'Lady' unless (as will decreasingly be the case in future as new appointees replace former Lords of Appeal in Ordinary) they are already peers and so have a title in their own right.

Those who have held 'high judicial office' for at least two years or been a 'qualifying practitioner' for at least fifteen years, are eligible for appointment as a Justice of the Supreme Court[122]. So far the appointees have all previously held judicial office, with the exception of Lord Sumption, who was appointed directly from practice at the English Bar in 2011 (he took office at the beginning of 2012 to enable him to complete unfinished business at the Bar). There is a formal selection procedure, whereby the Lord Chancellor convenes a 'Selection Commission' comprising the President (as chair) and Deputy President of the Supreme Court, and one representative each from the Judicial Appointments Board for Scotland, the Judicial Appointments Commission (for England and Wales) and the Northern Ireland Judicial Appointments Commission, nominated by that Board or Commission itself (one of whom must be non-legally qualified)[123]. The Selection Commission determines its own procedure, but must consult such other 'senior judges'[124] as are ineligible for appointment (failing which, the most senior of the relevant court), the Lord Chancellor, the First Minister of Scotland and the Secretary of State for Northern Ireland, and must select on the basis of merit, though also ensuring knowledge among the Supreme Court of the legal system of each of the constituent parts of the United Kingdom, and having regard to any guidance given by the Lord Chancellor[125]. The Commission reports to the Lord Chancellor in a form which he approves[126]. The Lord Chancellor may

---

120 In late 2012 this position was held by one of the two Scottish Justices, Lord Hope of Craighead.
121 Constitutional Reform Act 2005, s 23(6).
122 Constitutional Reform Act 2005, s 25(1). 'High judicial office' is defined (with presently irrelevant exceptions) as being a judge of the Court of Session, or its equivalents in England and Wales, and Northern Ireland: s 60; 'qualifying practitioner' means an advocate or solicitor-advocate, or their equivalents in England and Wales, and Northern Ireland: s 25(2).
123 *Ibid*, s 26(5)-(8) and Sch 8.
124 That is, the Lord President of the Court of Session, the Lord Justice-Clerk, and their equivalents in England & Wales and Northern Ireland: s 60(1).
125 Constitutional Reform Act 2006, s 27.
126 *Ibid*, s 28.

accept or (on grounds of 'suitability') either reject the selection or require the Commission to reconsider it and, following any rejection or reconsideration, the Commission has effectively the same choices (though cannot re-nominate a rejected recommendation), but after any third nomination by the Commission, the Lord Chancellor must accept it[127]. His acceptance is indicated by notifying the Prime Minister[128], who must 'recommend' such person[129]. Recommendation is presumably to Her Majesty (though the legislation does not actually say so), as it is she who appoints the judges[130].

The work of the Supreme Court of the United Kingdom. The Supreme Court is the final court of appeal from the Scottish civil courts (and their equivalents, and from the criminal courts, in England and Wales and Northern Ireland). Appeals to it from Scotland are relatively few but this does not make them unimportant, as they usually lay down broad principles which other courts must follow[131].

The Supreme Court has also taken jurisdiction on 'devolution matters'[132]. This jurisdiction used to lie with the Judicial Committee of the Privy Council[133]. Under the Scotland Act 2012, as already noted, it may hear appeals from the High Court of Justiciary on issues of EU law and Convention rights.

The Judicial Committee of the Privy Council[134]

4.11   The Privy Council is the surviving remnant of the former English Privy Council, the Privy Council of Scotland having been abolished in 1707[135]. It was an advisory body to the sovereign at

---

127 *Ibid*, ss 29–31: 'suitability' means lack of evidence of suitability, evidence that the candidate is not the best person, or lack of evidence that the Court will have knowledge of all three United Kingdom jurisdictions (in all cases, in the opinion of the Lord Chancellor): s 30.

128 *Ibid*, s 29.

129 *Ibid*, s 26.

130 *Ibid*, s 23.

131 See Ch 12.

132 Constitutional Reform Act 2005. s 41 and Scotland Act 1998, s 33.

133 See below.

134 The most important legislation in relation to the Privy Council is the Judicial Committee Act 1833, the Appellate Jurisdiction Act 1887, the Judicial Committee (Amendment) Act 1895 and the Appellate Jurisdiction Acts 1908.

135 See www.privy-council.org.uk.

a time when sovereigns wielded real political power. The Privy Council, as such, still has a shadowy existence as a dignified, rather than useful, part of the United Kingdom constitution. Membership is a form of honour for certain ministers of the Crown, senior opposition politicians, senior judges and others. 'Prerogative Orders in Council' (for which, see Chapter 5) which are used for some constitutional legislation are technically Orders of the Sovereign in Privy Council. It does, however, have various committees which do have important functions. One, for instance, exercises certain regulatory powers over Scottish Universities. Another is the Judicial Committee.

The court. The Judicial Committee of the Privy Council ('JCPC'), set up in 1833 is, in effect, a court. As such, it has a very miscellaneous jurisdiction.

In part this is 'imperial'. At one time, the colonies of the British Empire, and later the Commonwealth countries (other than the United Kingdom itself), had a final right of appeal to the Judicial Committee, which was thus a sort of central imperial court. A couple of dozen small Commonwealth countries retain a possibility of appeal on a variety of different conditions, as it is useful for such jurisdictions, with few judges and few cases, to have an 'external' appeal court. These include Antigua, the Bahamas, the Falkland Islands and Gibraltar, as well as the Channel Islands and the Isle of Man (which technically are not part of the United Kingdom).

In part, the jurisdiction is in relation to professional discipline, as it acts as a final court of appeal from certain professional disciplinary bodies, such as the Disciplinary Committee of the Royal College of Veterinary Surgeons.

In part the jurisdiction is ecclesiastical, as it deals with appeals against certain actions of the (Church of England) Church Commissioners (and in principle, of the Church of England itself, though this jurisdiction has not been exercised for many years).

As, strictly speaking, it is a committee of an advisory body rather than a court, the judgments of the JCPC used to conclude with words tendering advice to the Sovereign in Council. By the same token, traditionally, there was a single 'judgment', but occasionally the right to give a dissenting judgment is exercised.

Members of the Judicial Committee of the Privy Council. Membership of the Judicial Committee comprises the President and Deputy President of the Supreme Court as well as the other ten Justices, the Lord Chancellor, Lord Justices of Appeal and any members of the Privy Council who hold or have held high judicial office in the United Kingdom[136] or have been judges in the highest courts of those Commonwealth territories from which appeals still go to the JCPC[137]. Appeals are in practice nearly always heard by three or five of the Justices; so it is effectively the same court as the Supreme Court and can therefore include those trained in Scots law. Court of Session judges may also be Privy Councillors and sit on the Judicial Committee.

The work of the Judicial Committee of the Privy Council. The number and size of countries using it as their final court of appeal has diminished and this work has therefore declined. As the law of these countries is based on English law, such appeals have in fact clarified some points of English law, chiefly criminal law (as several such countries retain the death penalty against which appeal to the JCPC is very likely[138]).

Other courts in Scotland

4.12 There are several specialised courts of special jurisdiction, most of which are rarely convened.

There are the closely associated **Scottish Land Court**[139] and **Lands Tribunal for Scotland**[140] (which, despite its name, is really a court). The former deals with disputes over agricultural tenancies and crofting lands, has a legally qualified chairman who is not, but has the same status as, a Court of Session judge[141], and three lay members with agricultural experience, including at least one Gaelic speaker, and there is appeal on a point of law to the Inner House. The latter is concerned with disputes over tenants' 'right to buy', compensation for compulsory purchase, and other such matters, and also has a legally qualified President[142], and three lay members. In

---

136 Given the same meaning as under Part 3 of the Constitutional Reform Act 2005.
137 Judicial Committee Act 1833 (as amended).
138 For example, the law of provocation was reviewed in *A-G for Jersey v Holley* [2005] JCPC 23, an appeal from Jersey. This has caused difficulties, however, considered in Ch 12 in relation to the system of precedent in practice in the criminal courts.
139 See www.scottish-land-court.org.uk/ and the court's centenary history *No Ordinary Court: 100 Years of the Scottish Land Court* (2012).
140 See www.lands-tribunal-scotland.org.uk/.
141 In late-2012, it was Lord McGhie.
142 In late-2012, it was also Lord McGhie.

addition, there are a **Lands Valuation Appeal Court**[143], concerned with disputes arising out of local rates, comprising three Court of Session judges, and there is no appeal, and **Court of Teinds**[144], concerned with disputes over teinds (or 'tithes'), comprising five Court of Session judges.

Further, there are the **Registration of Voters Appeal Court**[145], comprising three Court of Session judges, and the **Election Petition Court**[146], comprising two Court of Session judges, not to mention the **Court of the Lord Lyon**[147], concerned with heraldic issues.

European Court of Human Rights[148]

4.13 The relevant meaning of 'human rights', and the role of the Council of Europe, are dealt with in Chapter 3. It was observed there that the most important treaty the Council of Europe has generated is the European Convention on Human Rights and Fundamental Freedoms ('ECHR'). The content of the ECHR was also discussed., and the fact that thereby, the United Kingdom has committed itself to promoting a number of rights and freedoms, commonly enumerated as: 'the right to life (including abolition of the death penalty)', 'freedom from torture', 'protection from slavery', 'liberty and the security of persons', 'a fair trial', 'the principle of legality', 'respect for private and family life', 'freedom of expression', 'a right to peaceful assembly', 'the right to marry and to found a family', 'peaceful enjoyment of possessions', 'the right to education', the 'right to free elections'. It has also committed itself to ensuring a right to an effective remedy for any breach, and non-discrimination in the application, of the law.

The primary means of so doing is now through the ordinary courts of the land, by relying on the Human Rights Act 1998 (as discussed further in Chapter 7). However, before that came into effect (apart from the rare inter-state actions), the only method an individual could employ was a petition to the European Court of Human Rights ('ECtHR'), which is thus the principal institution set up under the ECHR. This right of individual petition, however, continues to exist (provided the applicant has exhausted all national remedies), and in any case, the judgments of the ECtHR on the

143 The Lands Valuation Appeal Court has no website.
144 The Court of Teinds has no website.
145 The Registration of Voters Appeal Court has no website.
146 The Election Petition Court has no website.
147 See: http://www.lyon-court.com.
148 See www.echr.coe.int/echr/.

interpretation of the ECHR remain the most authoritative, and the powerful guide to national courts.

The court. A chief means of enforceability of the ECHR, whether by inter-state actions or individual petitions, is thus through the ECtHR, which sits in Strasbourg (so is occasionally referred to as 'the Strasbourg Court'). It is not to be confused with the Court of Justice of the European Union, which is considered below.

Judges of the European Court of Human Rights. The European Court of Human Rights has one judge from each of the signatory states[149]. However, they are not representatives of their states, though they will be familiar with its legal system. They are appointed by the Parliamentary Assembly of the Council of Europe (for which, see Chapter 3) for a period of six years, and sit full-time[150]. The full Court elects its President and two Vice-Presidents for a period of three years[151]. The Court is divided into five 'Sections', each led by a Vice-President or a 'Section President'. Within each Section, Committees of three judges are set up for 12-month periods. However, in cases of major importance, or where a respondent state requests, it is possible for the case to be referred to a Grand Chamber of 17 judges[152]. The official languages of the Court are French and English only.

The work of the European Court of Human Rights[153]. After a preliminary sifting, a three-judge Committee considers the 'admissibility' of an application, that is, whether the applicant had

---

149 At the end of 2012, there were 45 judges with the seats of the judges elected from Bosnia and Herzegovina and the Republic of Moldova vacant.
150 At the end of 2012, the United Kingdom judge was Paul Mahoney.
151 At the end of 2012, the President was from Luxembourg (Dean Spielmann) and the Vice-Presidents Italian (Guido Raimondi) and Andorran (Josep Casadevall).
152 Art 43, ECHR.
153 Until Protocol 11 to the ECHR in 1998, a petition was considered first by another body, the European Commission on Human Rights ('EComHR') which, having decided whether or not the petition was admissible, would seek a friendly settlement. If it failed to achieve a settlement, it considered whether or not to pass the matter to the ECtHR, or to the Committee of Ministers. If it did so, the ECtHR might proceed to a judgment, or the Committee to a decision, respectively. In all of this complicated procedure, enforceability depended upon the state in question agreeing to comply with the conclusion of Commission, Court or Committee. This is important to know, because reports of pre-1998 ECtHR cases carry opinions by the Commission as well as the Court.

exhausted remedies in his own state and whether a violation of one or more Articles had been validly raised, etc[154]. A high proportion of applications fail at this stage.

If the application against a state is admitted (or the Committee is divided), it goes before a seven-judge 'Chamber' (formed of the members of a Section), which includes a judge from the respondent state (unless it is referred to a Grand Chamber). This considers written submissions, may hear evidence, and formally decides on admissibility, and on the merits of the case. Decisions in a Chamber are by majority, and dissenting judgments can be issued (as in the United Kingdom, but contrary to the practice in most countries of Continental Europe).

States agree to abide by the judgment of the ECtHR, though enforcement remains a matter of the state honouring its obligation to abide by the judgment, a process supervised by the Committee of Ministers (for which, see Chapter 3) which thus ensures that the judgments of the Court are complied with and corrective measures introduced where necessary, as there is no other enforcement machinery[155].

The Court of Justice of the European Union[156]

4.14 The European Union was discussed in Chapter 3. As noted there, it has had a considerable effect upon the Scottish legal system since United Kingdom accession, and has introduced what amounts to a new source of law, requiring to be treated in a different fashion than, and overriding, existing Scots law.

The court. The Court of Justice of the European Union sits in Luxembourg, and is not to be confused with the European Court of Human Rights ('ECtHR'), considered above, which sits in Strasbourg. As noted in Chapter 3, it exists to ensure that EU law is correctly interpreted, and is observed. The court is split into three categories of judicial tribunal by the Treaty on the Functioning of the European Union ('TFEU'). These are the 'Court of Justice', the 'General Court' and 'specialised courts'.

154 Art 35, ECHR.
155 Art 46, ECHR
156 See http://curia.europa.eu/.

The judges of the 'Court of Justice of the European Union'. Currently, the Court of Justice has 27 judges, one nominated by each Member State[157] for a renewable six-year term, and one is elected President[158].

The Court of Justice normally sits in 'Chambers' of three or five judges under an elected President, but may form a 'Grand Chamber' of 13, for a case of great significance, or where a Member State requests it, or may even sit as a 'Full Court'. Nevertheless, it is, like the Court of Session, a 'collegiate court'.

There are also eight Advocates General, an office for which there is no United Kingdom equivalent[159]. They present to the judges a fully reasoned preliminary judgment after hearing the parties' arguments. The Court of Justice's judgment, given thereafter, is by no means bound to follow the Advocate General's view, but is likely to[160]. The difference between the two styles of judgment has importance for judicial reasoning and the operation of precedent. This is discussed in Chapter 3 but, for the moment, it may be noticed that Advocate General's judgments, being the work of one person, are frequently more clearly reasoned and comprehensible, while those of the Court of Justice, although flowing from a draft prepared by one judge as '*rapporteur*', are ultimately a compromise between the several judges, and may be a good deal less clear.

The 'General Court' has 27 further judges, each also nominated for six years by a Member State[161], with another elected President[162], but no separate Advocates General (though a judge may act as Advocate General).

Specialised courts can be established by the European Parliament and the Council. These courts can hear certain classes of action or proceedings brought in specific areas. They are established by regulations which determine the organisation and jurisdiction of the court[163].

---

157 At the end of 2012, the UK CJ judge was Christopher Vajda QC who replaced Sir Konrad Schiemann (formerly a Court of Appeal judge in England) in October 2012,.

158 At the end of 2012, the President was the Greek nomination, Vassilios Skouris. For some years in the 1980s, the President was a Scottish judge, Lord Mackenzie-Stuart.

159 Advocates-General of the CJEU should not be confused with the Advocate-General for Scotland (see Ch 3). At the end of 2012, one of the Advocates-General was Eleanor Sharpston QC, an English barrister and legal academic.

160 The difference between the two styles of judgment has importance for judicial reasoning and the operation of precedent. This is discussed in Ch 12.

161 The Statute of the Court of Justice of the European Union, Art 48.

162 In late-2012, it was the Luxembourg nomination, Mark Jaeger.

163 Art 257 TFEU.

The work of the 'Court of Justice of the European Union'. Between them the 'Court of Justice' and the 'General Court' decide several classes of case.

Firstly, there are various types of 'direct action', in which the Court of Justice or General Court hears the whole proceedings. These include actions against EU institutions (for instance, where an institution is accused of acting *ultra vires* or otherwise improperly; appeals against penalties imposed by EU institutions; actions for damages against EU institutions for wrongful acts; and 'enforcement actions' brought by EU institutions against member states alleged to have failed to carry out their Treaty obligations[164]. Secondly, and of much more importance in the context of the Scottish legal system, the Court of Justice hears preliminary references under Article 267 of the TFEU. Here the proceedings neither start nor finish in the Court, but in ordinary national courts and tribunals. To explain this, it must be recalled that EU law may have 'direct effect'. This is discussed in more detail in Chapter 3, but means, among other things, that it is to be applied by the usual national courts. As these courts stretch from Shetland to the Peloponnese, the possibility of conflicting decisions is great. Article 267 therefore permits any national court hearing a case involving the validity or interpretation of EU law to send that question (but not the rest of the dispute) to the ECJ for an authoritative ruling, which binds that national court. The national court nevertheless decides all questions of fact, and any questions of national law, and gives the final judgment. Final courts of appeal in Member States are required to make preliminary references, subject however, to the *acte clair* doctrine, which dispenses with it where the law is clear (whether because it is inherently clear or because there is already a clear ruling).

Only one specialised court had been set up by the end of 2012, hearing actions from civil servants or employees of the EU in matters regarding their employment under the staff regulations.

Procedure in both the Court of Justice and the General Court follows civil law rather than common law patterns (for example, relying heavily upon written submissions, with very limited oral argument), and the language of the case is usually that of the applicant, although both use French as their working language.

---

164 For example, Art 157 (numbered 141 before the Treaty of Lisbon) requires sexual equality in employment, and the EC Equal Pay Directive (75/117) furthering that policy, was made in 1976. The European Commission considered that the relevant United Kingdom legislation, the Equal Pay Act 1970, did not fulfil the requirements of EU law and successfully brought enforcement proceedings against the United Kingdom (Case 51/81 *Commission v UK* [1982] ICR 578).

COURT PROCEDURE

4.15   In broad terms, both civil and criminal procedure in Scotland are 'adversarial' (or 'accusatorial'). In other words, the judge does not actively seek to discover what happened and what the law is on the subject, but leaves it to the parties to put their best case before him. This is to be contrasted with 'inquisitorial' proceedings, in which the judge does undertake such enquiries. While Scots law generally follows the 'adversarial' path, some proceedings are certainly 'inquisitorial', and there has been a general trend towards more 'inquisitorial' proceedings for some years (as also in England and Wales), largely through a desire for 'case management' by the judge, with a view to speeding up proceedings.

Usually, parties are represented by a lawyer. In the Court of Session, and the High Court of Justiciary, these must be advocates, or solicitor-advocates. In other courts, they may be advocates, but are much more likely to be solicitors[165]. To support litigants with limited funds, there is both civil and criminal 'legal aid'[166].

With few exceptions, all court proceedings are public, and may even be televised[167], though this has rarely happened.

Civil procedure[168]

4.16   Most civil disputes, that is, disputes concerning contract, delict, succession, and the like, are settled out of court, because litigation is slow, expensive and uncertain (though a private settlement may be adopted by the court at the request of the parties). Decisions

---

165 For the difference between advocates and solicitors (and solicitor-advocates), see Ch 14.

166 For which, see Ch 14. In criminal cases, it is interesting to note that the prosecution is funded by the state, and the accused is usually assisted by legal aid also provided by the state.

167 The Lord President and Sheriff Principals have given permission for television cameras to be used in court if, broadly speaking, the programme is educational or documentary, the proceedings do not show witnesses or juries, proceedings are not disrupted, the presiding judge approves (and he may set further conditions), and the parties approve: see 1992 SLT (News) 249 and 332. However, it has hardly ever been done (though see White 'Small Earthquake in Peru – not many killed' 1994 *Scolag* 59–60).

168 Most of the relevant law is in the Sheriff Courts (Scotland) Act 1907, Act of Sederunt (Small Claim Rules) 2002, SI 2002/133, Act of Sederunt (Summary Cause Rules) 2002, SI 2002/132, Ordinary Cause Rules 1993, SI 1993/1956, Court of Session Act 1988 and Rules of the Court of Session 1994, SI 1994/1443 (all as amended).

of courts affect such settlements, as they show how the dispute might be determined if it were litigated, and litigation may be started as a threat to induce settlement.

Civil procedure is (as noted) usually adversarial. Thus, the person who initiates the case (the pursuer), bears the burden of proof (which is on the balance of probabilities) and puts before the court the evidence and arguments he considers appropriate to support his case, and to entitle him to a remedy. The person called upon to answer the claim (the defender), may put his evidence and arguments to show why a remedy should not be granted. In principle, the judge is referee, intervenes little, and decides if the pursuer has proved his case.

The precise procedure depends upon the remedy sought and the court used. In most forms, the pursuer initiates matters by issue of a 'summons' or an 'initial writ', specifying the parties and the remedy sought. The defender must reply to this or risk judgment against him by default. In practice, most proceedings are undefended, so the pursuer may not have to prove his case.

Where proceedings are defended, there may be 'written pleadings', that is, answers by the defender to the pursuer's claims, and possibly further interchanges, to specify more closely the facts and law in dispute. When these are complete, the proceedings continue in court in order to determine the result. These proceedings may be a 'proof' in the case of disputed facts (or possibly, in the Court of Session, a jury trial with a jury of 12), or a 'debate' in the case of disputed law.

Proof depends upon witnesses and other evidence. Witnesses are 'examined in chief' by the side which calls them, and 'cross-examined' by the other side. Examination in chief is designed to bring out the witness's story in his own words. Cross-examination is designed to cast doubt upon it, and may do so by asking leading questions, that is, questions suggesting an answer. In legal debate, the parties' lawyers argue as to what the applicable law is, which requires them to refer to relevant sources of law such as Acts of Parliament and precedents.

There may be 'proof before answer', whereby facts are determined before legal debate, and 'pleas to the relevancy', in which the defender argues that even if the facts are true, they do not entitle the pursuer to the remedy sought[169]. Commonly, a judge will not give an

---

169 Thus, in the celebrated *Donoghue v Stevenson* 1932 SC(HL) 31, the presence of the snail in the bottle was never admitted or proved. Stevenson's argument was that, even if there were a snail, it did not entitle Mrs Donoghue to any remedy from him.

ex tempore judgment, but 'take it to *avizandum*', that is take time for consideration.

Decisions by the judge on matters which arise as the case proceeds are called 'interlocutors'. At the end of the proceedings the judge states his findings of fact and law, and expresses, in greater or lesser detail, the arguments which he considers justify his decision. (This process, discussed more fully in Chapter 12, characterises legal reasoning, and thus the nature and importance of law reports, in a common law or hybrid system). This in turn leads to the final interlocutor in which, if he upholds the pursuer's claim, the judge grants decree against the defender and authorises enforcement.

The principal forms of civil procedure for disputes are small claims, summary cause, and ordinary procedure in the Sheriff Court, and Court of Session procedure[170].

Small claims procedure, an attempt at a truly simple and cheap procedure, is for sums less than £3,000 (excluding aliment claims, that is, claims for financial support by family members usually arising out of matrimonial proceedings). A *pro forma* summons initiates procedure, but thereafter it is largely at the Sheriff's discretion, and intended to be informal. It may not be in practice, as complicated questions of law may arise and be dealt with by Sheriffs in strict legal fashion.

Summary cause procedure, an earlier attempt at simplicity, is for sums between £3,000 and £5,000. It is more formal (and the actual rules are lengthy and complicated). Nevertheless, many summary causes are straightforward, and the Sheriff has a large discretion over procedure.

Ordinary cause procedure and Court of Session procedure are similar. They are much more formal, and there are full written pleadings. The summons must state the remedy sought (called 'craves' in Sheriff Court procedure and 'conclusions' in Court of Session procedure), the facts averred (called the 'condescendence'), and the rules and principles which, applied to those facts, in the pursuer's view entitle him to a remedy (called the 'pleas-in-law'). The defender enters formal defences, and these claims and counterclaims form the 'open record', which is 'adjusted' (that is, amended) by the parties to identify the points of agreement and, as closely as possible, the issue between them, resulting in the 'closed record', upon which any proofs or debate proceed. This process may take months.

---

170 These are found in updated form in the '*Parliament House Book*' (Parliament House book: statutes and regulations for Scottish lawyers: 5 volumes, loose-leaf) and at www.scotcourts.gov.uk/library/rules/index.asp .

In addition to these procedures, since 1994, three specialist judges[171] using a simplified commercial procedure with an 'inquisitorial', and informal, approach, have sat as 'commercial court' judges. In addition there are judges designated for intellectual property (that is, copyright, patents, etc) cases[172]. However, in 2007, a major review of the civil courts was set up under the Lord Justice-Clerk, to look specifically and costs of litigation, use of mediation and other methods of dispute resolution, better 'case-management' and further specialisation. The review was completed in 2009[173]. The Scottish Government accepted most of the review's recommendations in principle[174] and the Scottish Civil Justice Council and Criminal Legal Assistance Bill was before the Scottish Parliament in late 2012 as a first step towards implementing some of the recommendations.

In addition to these proceedings of an adversarial nature, which are usually contentious[175], there are also the usually non-contentious petition procedures[176]. There is a large number of types of petition. Very many are of a formal nature, such as those to the Court of Session seeking appointment of a trustee where a trust lacks one, or to the Sheriff Court for confirmation as executor of a will[177]. Others concern the dissolution of companies and sequestration of bankrupts. Others yet, involving contentious issues, include seeking interdict, an order forbidding a person or persons from acting in an unlawful way.

One form of petition (noted above in relation to the Court of Session) that deserves particular mention is 'judicial review'. In a nutshell, judicial review is a procedure whereby the Court of Session exercises its 'supervisory jurisdiction' over government departments and local authorities and other 'official' decision-takers. These have become common in many areas, such as environmental and planning law, and immigration law. It is not an appeal, but a procedure

---

171 At the end of 2012, Lords Hodge, Malcolm and Woolman (part-time).

172 At the end of 2012, Lords Glennie, Malcolm, Woolman and Pentland.

173 See, Report and Recommendations of the Scottish Civil Courts Review (2009): http://www.scotcourts.gov.uk/civilcourtsreview/.

174 See, Scottish Government Response to the Report and Recommendations of the Scottish Civil Courts Review (November 2011): http://www.scotland.gov.uk/Publications/2010/11/09114610/0.

175 Not all actions between parties are contentious. Many divorces are, for example, in effect by agreement.

176 But petition procedure may be contentious, as with judicial review, for instance, on which, see below.

177 Admission to the Law Society of Scotland requires petition to the Court of Session, which is organised as a 'block petition' with a large number of names, from time to time.

whereby the court is asked to quash an official's decision because it was taken in a wrong fashion. Typical ways in which the decision was wrongly taken those taken are *ultra vires* (acting beyond one's powers), or with a lack of 'natural justice' (for instance, not hearing both sides of the case). It has become a powerful remedy against improper government action, no less since the embedding of human rights into Scots law.

Remedies

4.17 The most common remedies are an order to pay a sum owed (such as the price under a contract); specific implement (an order requiring a person to carry out a legal obligation other than payment of money, for example, delivering goods contracted for); damages (an order to pay compensation, for example for injury done); declarator (a declaration that an individual or corporate body has a specific right or duty, for example that a local authority is obliged to house a homeless person); interdict (an order forbidding the commission of a wrong, for example publishing a defamatory statement); reduction (an order nullifying a document, for example an invalid will); aliment (an order to give financial support to dependants); divorce; and adoption.

There is also a large number of specific remedies under statute for specific circumstances. The Court of Session may provide a remedy in exceptional and unforeseen circumstances (the *nobile officium*).

Appeal

4.18 It is possible to appeal against almost every decision taken at first instance, and often thereafter further appeal is possible. Appeals are nevertheless a small proportion of cases heard[178].

Appeals may be on both law and fact, but are often limited to points of law, in part because of the difficulty of reopening the facts, for appeal is never by way of a complete rehearing (although appeal from a jury trial might result in a new trial).

An appeal court can usually affirm the decision below, substitute its own judgment, or remit the case to the lower court for further procedure (such as proof) or final decision in the light of the appeal court's judgment.

---

178 See relevant references in relation to individual courts.

Diligence and expenses

4.19   A court's order is usually obeyed. If it is not, the pursuer can 'do diligence', that is, enforce it. There are several forms of diligence. Most common are charges (formally requiring payment) and arrestment (impounding a debtor's funds held by a third party, such as a bank). The former method of 'warrant sale', technically 'poinding' (pronounced 'pinding') and sale, whereby sheriff-officers, or (if decree is from the Court of Session) messengers-at-arms, removed and might sell the debtor's moveable property, has been repealed and replaced by 'debt arrangement and attachment'[179]. Diligence is also possible against heritable property by 'inhibition' (forbidding sale of it), followed by 'adjudication', that is, its transfer to the creditor. Exceptionally there can even be diligence against the person, that is, imprisonment for debt, although this is available only for aliment, and is very rare.

Courts generally have discretion to award expenses, and usually the losing party is required to pay the 'judicial expenses' of the winning party (that is, those in connection with the action), although that sum is usually less than the actual expenditure.

Criminal procedure[180]

4.20   Criminal proceedings are held in public, but the judge is entitled to exclude all those not immediately involved in cases of rape and the like[181].

The public prosecution system[182]

4.21   Criminal proceedings are almost always brought by the Crown through the public prosecution system. Private prosecutions are possible with the consent of the Lord Advocate, failing which, if brought by someone with a direct interest, with the consent of the court, but are extremely rare.

179 Debt Arrangement and Attachment (Scotland) Act 2002
180 The relevant law is largely found in the Criminal Procedure (Scotland) Act 1995 and the Act of Adjournal (Criminal Procedure Rules) 1998, SI 1998/513.
181 Criminal Procedure (Scotland) Act 1995, s 92(3).
182 See www.crownoffice.gov.uk/.

The Lord Advocate, assisted by the Solicitor-General for Scotland[183], is in charge of public prosecutions, through the Crown Office[184], which is effectively the headquarters of the Procurator Fiscal Service (the whole being called the Crown Office and Procurator Fiscal Service (COPFS)). There is also an Inspectorate of Prosecutions in Scotland ('IPIS')[185].

In JP and Sheriff Courts, prosecutions are brought by COPFS. The Procurator Fiscal Service is organised on the basis of eleven areas[186]. Each of these has an area procurator fiscal who administers the service within that area and is the procurator fiscal for the Sheriff Court District in which he is. Prosecution is carried normally out by depute procurators fiscal[187].

In the High Court of Justiciary, prosecutions are brought by Advocates-Depute (*alias* 'Crown counsel') or, on occasion, the Lord Advocate or the Solicitor-General for Scotland in person. Advocates-Depute are advocates employed (temporarily and part-time) to prosecute on the Crown's behalf[188].

Public Defence Solicitors' Office[189]

4.22　In 1998, in response to the rising cost of criminal legal aid, the Scottish Legal Aid Board was given powers to employ solicitors, on a limited basis, and as a five year pilot scheme, to provide criminal legal assistance instead of paying solicitors in private practice for

---

183 These offices are discussed in Ch 3.
184 The Crown Office is situated in Chambers Street, Edinburgh. It produces annual 'reviews', and a Prosecution Code explaining how it exercises its discretion. These are available from www.crownoffice.gov.uk/, though not always easy to find.
185 See www.scotland.gov.uk/Topics/Justice/ipis. The members are all former employees of COPFS. IPIS also produces annual reports, 'office inspection reports' on individual procurator fiscal offices, and 'thematic reports' on general issues, all available from the website.
186 Ie, Argyll & Clyde, Ayrshire, Central, Dumfries & Galloway, Fife, Glasgow, Grampian, Highlands & Islands, Lanarkshire, Lothian & Borders and Tayside.
187 The identity of procurator fiscals can be found in the 'White Book', and on www.crownoffice.gov.uk/ (though it is not easy to find).
188 At the end of 2012, there were some 20 Advocates-Depute. Their identities are given in the 'White Book'. They are now divided into the categories of Senior Advocate-Depute, Advocate-Depute and Ad Hoc Advocate-Depute. This provides something of a career path for prosecutors.
189 See www.pdso.org.uk/.

criminal cases in the, then, District and Sheriff Courts[190]. This scheme was set up as a 'Public Defence Solicitor's Office' ('PDSO') in Edinburgh, and considered a sufficient success to expand to cover a large proportion of the country[191]. Initially, a proportion of cases (randomly selected) was directed to PDSO. However, it now relies on word of mouth, so offers essentially the same services to those accused of criminal offences, on the same terms, as do private solicitors (including the duty solicitor rota to provide initial assistance to those taken into custody)[192] but, effectively, in competition with them. The PDSO is fully discussed in Chapter 14.

Procedure

4.23 Criminal proceedings are (like civil) generally adversarial. Thus, it is not the judge who seeks to discover if there has been a crime or not[193]. It is for the prosecution to decide what crime it considers may have been committed, and it bears the burden of proof (which is beyond reasonable doubt). It therefore seeks and presents to the court the evidence it considers sufficient to prove it. The defence generally need prove nothing, but is entitled to have the case against it proved, to cast doubt on prosecution evidence, and to bring evidence if it chooses. Indeed, it may move that 'there is no case to answer' at the end of the prosecution evidence, seeking to have the case dismissed for want of proper evidence. Traditionally, the judge is a referee or umpire who intervenes little. He charges the jury if there is one, that is, reminds them of the main evidence presented and instructs them on the applicable law. It is, however, entirely for the jury to decide what conclusions they draw from the facts, and thus whether the prosecution has proved its case.

The two forms of criminal procedure are summary and solemn. Most common law offences are triable by either procedure. Statutory

---

190 Legal Aid (Scotland) Act 1986, s 28A (inserted by Crime and Punishment (Scotland) Act 1997, and as subsequently amended).

191 At the end of 2012, there were seven offices, in Ayr, Dundee, Edinburgh, Falkirk, Glasgow, Inverness & Kirkwall: the addresses of each office are to found on www.pdso.org.uk/.

192 As employees of the Scottish Legal Aid Board, PDSO's salaried solicitors are answerable to it, but they are operationally independent, and normal professional ethics apply to them, though in addition, there is a 'Code of Conduct for Public Defence Solicitors in Scotland', available on www.pdso. org.uk/.

193 Civil law systems tend to use inquisitorial procedure, whereby a judge (other than the judge at any resulting trial) actively pursues the investigation.

offences are declared by statute to be triable by one or both. The JP Court uses only summary procedure, the Sheriff Court both, and the High Court only solemn. It is for the prosecution to decide which procedure and which venue is appropriate[194].

In both forms the prosecution must serve on the accused a precise accusation, to which he pleads guilty or not guilty. If he pleads not guilty, a later date is fixed for trial. The trial may require facts to be proved, and law to be determined. These are done in essentially the same way as in civil proceedings, although the burden of proof, which is on the prosecutor, is higher ('beyond reasonable doubt'), and the accused must generally be present. Facts are proved by evidence, from witnesses and otherwise, and the law is determined by argument. After evidence has been given, the prosecution and defence address the court. At the end of the trial, the accused may be found guilty, not guilty, or the charge be found not proven[195]. A verdict of not proven is equivalent to an acquittal, and an acquitted person may not be retried. If found guilty, before sentence is passed, a list of previous convictions (if any) is produced by the prosecutor, and any plea in mitigation (that is, information tending to suggest a lenient sentence should be passed) is made by the defence.

In summary proceedings, the procurator fiscal details the charge in a complaint. The accused may appear in court to plead to this, but in many cases will plead by letter or be represented by a solicitor instead of appearing. If he pleads not guilty, a later date is fixed for trial, which is conducted before a Sheriff, JP or Stipendiary Magistrate, without a jury. If found guilty, the court sentences him.

In solemn procedure, the procurator fiscal drafts a petition alleging a named person committed a specified crime, and requesting authority to arrest him. The accused appears before the Sheriff in private for a brief first examination. Usually no plea or declaration is made and the accused is released on bail or committed in custody for trial (in which case, the trial must begin within 140 days[196]). There may be further judicial examination before the Sheriff in which the

---

194 England & Wales and Northern Ireland are markedly different, in that, albeit to an increasingly limited extent, in the case of an 'either way' offence (that is, one which may be tried by either procedure) the accused may be able to choose a jury trial: this is the so-called 'right to trial by jury', which has never existed in Scotland.

195 The Scottish Government initiated a consultation in December 2012 on whether the Not Proven verdict should be abolished: see para **4.3**.

196 Until the Criminal Procedure (Amendment) (Scotland) Act 2004, s 6(5)(b), the limit was 110 days. This remains remarkably speedy compared with many systems.

prosecutor may put a limited range of questions to the accused, to discover if he is going to use certain defences, or concerning any alleged confession. The accused is not on oath, and can decline to reply. The prosecutor then drafts the indictment detailing the charges upon which the accused will be tried (which is served upon the accused) and decides if the case is to go to a Sheriff or the High Court. In either case there will be a jury. There must then be a 'preliminary hearing', to deal with issues of 'competency' or of 'relevancy' of the indictment (for example, arguing that the facts alleged in the indictment disclose no crime known to the law[197]), and for 'case management' (that is, for the judge to assure himself that proper progress towards the trial has taken place).

The trial diet follows on similar principles to that in summary proceedings, but after the evidence and the addresses by the prosecution and defence, the judge charges the jury (as described above) before they retire to consider their verdict.

Guilty pleas

4.24   However, the great majority of those charged, whether under summary or solemn procedure, are not tried, because they plead guilty, usually at an early stage. (Indeed, if this were not so, the courts could not cope.) This plea may result from 'plea negotiation', an informal procedure whereby the accused, through his agent, agrees with the Crown to plead guilty (so there is a conviction), but only to some charges, amended charges, or lesser charges (so he may expect a lesser sentence). The court takes no part in this negotiation[198]. In any case, early guilty pleas are now encouraged by an obligation upon sentencers to consider a reduction of sentence for a guilty plea, with a greater reduction the earlier the plea[199].

Diversion schemes

4.25   The pressure upon the criminal courts has led to 'diversion from prosecution' schemes. The police may make a conditional

---

197 As happened in *Khaliq v HM Advocate* 1984 JC 23, where the accused were charged with supplying glue-sniffing kits to children.
198 The position is somewhat different in England & Wales, where he may do so in certain circumstances.
199 Criminal Procedure (Scotland) Act 1995, s 196 (as amended).

offer of a fixed penalty to the accused in certain minor road traffic offences[200], and a procurator fiscal may do so in certain other offences triable in the JP court[201]. Accepting it avoids going to court and risking a higher penalty on conviction. However, it may be declined, and the accused may be summoned to court and there seek acquittal. These are popularly referred to as 'fiscal fines'. They are separate from other diversion schemes, such as the fixed penalty notice for parking and similar offences, whereby a traffic warden affixes a notice to an illegally parked car, rendering the owner liable to a fine. In addition, somewhat controversially, a variety of new variations are to be introduced (as well as 'fines enforcement officers')[202].

In any case, it has long been accepted that fiscals are able to issue directly, or through the police, a formal warning, which is not recorded as a conviction. Fiscals may also divert cases to social work or psychiatric services. Further, a fiscal is always entitled to decide not to prosecute although there appears to be sufficient evidence, if the offence is trivial, or it is otherwise not in the public interest to prosecute.

Penalties

4.26   The principal penalties are: a fine (unlimited, or to a maximum permitted by statute); admonition (a warning); imprisonment or detention in a young offenders' institution; a community service order; probation; and a compensation order in favour of the victim, which may be combined with another penalty. Imprisonment or a supervised attendance order (requiring attendance at a certain place for some form of training) can be imposed to replace an unpaid fine.

Sentence is often deferred. This may be a brief deferral of, normally, some three weeks for social background, psychiatric, or other reports, or a lengthy one (such as six months) for good behaviour or restitution to a victim. In the latter case, it is in effect a sentence in itself, as the penalty is likely to be reduced if there has been good behaviour or restitution of property stolen or damaged.

---

200 These vary, depending upon the offence, from £30 to £200: Fixed Penalty Order 2000, SI 2000/2792 (as amended).
201 Criminal Procedure (Scotland) Act 1995, ss 302, 303 (as amended by the Criminal Proceedings, etc (Reform) (Scotland) Act 2007, s 50).
202 See Criminal Proceedings, etc (Reform) (Scotland) Act 2007, ss 50–54

Appeals and the Scottish Criminal Cases Review Commission[203]

4.27   A person convicted after summary procedure may appeal as of right to the High Court of Justiciary sitting as an appeal court by 'stated case'[204] on the ground of 'miscarriage of justice'. If convicted after trial, he may appeal against conviction and/or sentence; if after a guilty plea, against sentence only. He may seek to introduce new evidence unavailable at trial, but this is rare. He may also appeal by way of a 'bill of suspension' on the ground of procedural irregularity.

The prosecutor may also appeal, on a point of law only, against conviction or sentence by stated case or, on the ground of procedural irregularity, by 'bill of advocation'.

A person convicted after solemn procedure (again whether by guilty plea or trial) may appeal in like terms, save that the appeal is usually by 'note of appeal'. The prosecutor may not appeal at all against conviction, but after conviction, the Lord Advocate may appeal against sentence on the grounds of undue leniency.

The High Court is entitled to dismiss an appeal and affirm the verdict and sentence, quash a conviction, substitute conviction of a lesser offence, or impose a lesser or (unless appeal was against conviction only) a heavier sentence. It may authorise a retrial but is unlikely to do so if there was any fault on the part of the prosecution or the evidence was weak. It is for the Crown within two months to decide whether to prosecute again.

Three other procedures exist which are related to appeals. Both have been used, but rarely. Firstly, the Lord Advocate may refer any question of law which has arisen in a trial by solemn procedure resulting in an acquittal to the High Court for an opinion. This 'Lord Advocate's Reference' is not an appeal, so cannot overturn the acquittal, but the person acquitted may appear, and the High Court can give an authoritative view on the point of law.

Secondly, the Scottish Criminal Cases Review Commission[205] has powers to refer a case to the High Court for re-consideration after

203 See www.sccrc.org.uk/home.aspx.
204 In a stated case, the charges are listed and procedure outlined, and the judge lists the facts he found, or were admitted, indicates the reasons for his decision, and asks a question such as 'On the facts admitted or proved, was I entitled to convict the accused?'.
205 Set up under the Criminal Procedure (Scotland) Act 1995, s 194A & Sch 9A (inserted by the Crime and Punishment (Scotland) Act s 25), and sitting in Glasgow with eight members (in late-2012, Mrs Jean Couper CBE; Professor Brian Caddy; Mr Stewart Campbell; Mr Gerard McClay; Professor George Irving CBE; Mr Gerrard Bann; Miss Frances Jane McMenamin QC; Mr Peter Ferguson QC; Mr Gerard Sinclair; Mr Chris Reddick CMIIA; Mr Michael Walker; and Mr Gordon Newall) and support staff.

the appeal process has been exhausted (or, exceptionally, where it was not invoked). A person concerned may refer a conviction or sentence to the Commission, and it decides whether or not to accept such application. If it does accept it, the Commission receives any representations, and may make its own inquiries through its staff (and this may involve interviewing witnesses and taking evidence on oath, and using the services of expert advisers) as well as examining the trial and appeal papers. It only refers the matter to the High Court if it believes a miscarriage of justice has occurred and that it is in the interests of justice to make the reference. This might be because of new evidence which has emerged since the appeal. If the Commission does not refer the case, it gives its reasons to the applicant. If it does refer the case, it gives its reasons to the High Court, copied to the applicant and Crown Office. However, the Commission does not represent the applicant in the High Court re-consideration, which is conducted much as an ordinary appeal. Thus the applicant requires to obtain representation (for which legal aid will be available) or conduct it himself. The Commission publishes an annual report.

Thirdly, sections 73–76 of the Criminal Justice and Licensing (Scotland) Act 2010 make provision for a right for the Crown to appeal certain decisions in solemn criminal cases. The Crown now has a right to appeal against judicial decisions that end a trial without a verdict of a jury. These are:

(a) a ruling of no case to answer – where the judge rules at the close of the Crown case that the evidence led by the prosecution is insufficient in law to justify a conviction;

(b) a direction, after all evidence has been led, that the jury should not convict on a particular charge, or should consider only a reduced charge; and

(c) a ruling during a trial that an important item of prosecution evidence is inadmissible, leaving the Crown with no option but to abandon the case.

These provisions were introduced in response to the collapse of the trial of Angus Sinclair in the 2007 case sometimes referred to as the 'World's End' murders because that was the name of the pub where the two unfortunate victims were last seen alive. The judge ruled at the end of the prosecution evidence that Sinclair had no case to answer. The issues raised were referred to the Scottish Law Commission, and the new rights of the Crown to appeal in such cases are the result. The Commission also recommended that the rule against 'double jeopardy' – the possibility that an acquitted person be retried in relation to the same matter – be modified to allow a new trial where fresh evidence emerges after the acquittal. The recommendation was given effect in the Double Jeopardy (Scotland) Act 2011. In December 2012 it was announced that the Crown was seeking to bring a further prosecution against Angus Sinclair in connection with the 'World's End' murders, which will be the first use of the 2011 Act.

Expenses

4.28 Generally speaking, criminal courts cannot award expenses. The expenses of prosecution are paid by the prosecution. Those of the defence are usually paid from criminal legal aid (including *via* PDSO).

TRIBUNALS, OTHER RELATED INSTITUTIONS, ENGLISH AND WELSH AND NORTHERN IRELAND COURTS

Tribunals[206]

4.29 In modern times the state has entered into, or extended, numerous legal relationships with its citizens. Personal taxation and social security are two obvious examples. These give rise to legal rights and duties, on which disputes may arise. These disputes might have been entrusted to the courts, like any other justiciable issues. But courts would have been swamped by the number of such disputes and arguably forced to change in character to cope. They might have been left to the government departments concerned to decide internally at a higher level. But that would have contravened the principle of 'natural justice', that no-one should be judge in his own cause. So a new type of decision-making body was devised. They are independent and impartial like the courts, but less formal and more accessible. These are the tribunals. Tribunals underwent major reform as a result of the Tribunals, Courts and Enforcement Act 2007.

Tribunals were split into two tiers; the First Tier, which generally hears appeals from individuals against decisions of government

---

206 The Council on Tribunals' (see below) website is at www.council-on-tribunals. gov.uk.

or government bodies, and the Upper Tier, which generally hears appeals from the First Tier. Each of these consists of judges and members and a Senior President presides over both Tiers[207]. The Tiers are split into Chambers which specialise in certain areas of law such as the Tax Chamber which deals with disputes on matters of personal taxation. There is one, or sometimes two persons, presiding over each of the Chambers. The Tax Chamber is also an example of a UK-wide Chamber. Her Majesty's Court and Tribunal Service ('HMCTS') administer the tribunal systems throughout the UK except those which are in areas of devolved competence in Scotland, Northern Ireland and Wales. The Upper Tribunal enjoys the power to judicially review cases sent to it by the Court of Session in Scotland and the Court of Appeal in England. It has the same powers as the Court of Session or Court of Appeal would have over the matter so referred. There is a limited right of appeal to the Court of Appeal in England under the legislation[208]. There are areas which have a specifically Scottish tribunal system. This Scottish tribunal system covers areas which were not specifically reserved to Westminster under the Scotland Act 1998 but which was developed in an ad hoc and unplanned manner much like the old UK-wide system. A Scottish Tribunals Service was created in 2010 which provides administrative support to a number of devolved tribunals but more change is due. During 2012, the Scottish Government began the reform process with the aim of providing a more coherent and efficient tribunals system. A consultation paper was produced, on which a report was published in August 2012.

The Scottish system looks set to take a similar path to the UK as a whole: a two-tier system comprising a First Tier Tribunal to hear decision cases and an Upper Tribunal for appeals from the First Tier. These will be split into various Chambers which will have responsibility for administering hearings in particular areas of law.

The system will be led by the Lord President (in respect of the judicial leadership) and a new President of Scottish Tribunals (with regard the efficient disposal of business in the new system). Each Chamber will have a president to oversee its running.

The Tribunals Bill is part of the Scottish Government's Programme for Scotland 2012–13 and is due to be debated in the Scottish Parliament.

---

207 At the end of 2012 the position was held by Sir Jeremy Sullivan who succeeded Lord Carnwath of Notting Hill in June 2012.
208 Tribunals, Courts and Enforcement Act 2007, s 13.

Tribunals are enormously varied in subject-matter, extent and degree of formality. Some affect only people in special occupations and capacities, such as the Police Appeals Tribunal for Scotland which handles appeals by constables against dismissal and other penalties, and the Immigration Tribunal Chambers which hear appeals from individuals refused entry into the United Kingdom and related decisions. Although most tribunals stem from central government functions, a few relate to local authority activities. Housing Benefit Review Boards deal with questions about entitlement to or the amount of housing benefit, and Education Appeal Committees were set up to hear complaints arising out of parents' requests that their children be placed in a certain school.

The tribunal format has been extended to situations where private citizens are in dispute with each other or with a company or other corporate body. Industrial Tribunals were set up under the Industrial Training Act 1964 to handle questions arising from the imposition of levies on employers to help finance schemes of training in particular industries such as haulage contracting. In this and other roles they were so successful that in 1971 they were extended to claims for compensation for unfair dismissal brought by ex-employees against employers. This remains their largest type of business but, under various Acts of Parliament, and now called Employment Tribunals, they have various kinds of jurisdiction, including complaints of discrimination on grounds of gender or marital status, of failure to give equal pay, to supply written particulars of a contract of employment, to make a redundancy payment and to give time off work to safety representatives. Another private relationship in which tribunals are involved, though now less so than in the past, is that between landlord and tenant. Rent Assessment Committees establish fair rents when the parties cannot agree on them.

Characteristics

4.30   Since tribunals have such diverse functions it is not easy to generalise about their characteristics. Moreover, the strengths of some of them have been somewhat weakened with the passage of time. However, there would be general agreement that the following features are among the advantages of most kinds of tribunal and are in fact exhibited in most of them.

Informality. In comparison with courts all tribunals are informal. At some, such as Children's Hearings and those dealing with benefits, all the participants sit round a table and a relaxed discussion is encouraged, though not always achieved. Employment Tribunals, have become increasingly formal. The chairman and members sit on a raised dais, and evidence by the parties and witnesses they have summoned is usually given on oath and always subject to cross-examination. The Lands Tribunal for Scotland is also formal in its layout and presided over by a judge of Court of Session rank.

Representation. Informality tends to be eroded by the participation of lawyers accustomed to the procedure of courts. Employers in Employment Tribunal cases usually find it worthwhile to employ a lawyer; and appeals to the Employment Appeal Tribunal, which is chaired by a Court of Session judge, and from there to the Court of Session, are not infrequent. This means that judgments by Employment Tribunal chairmen have to be fully supported in law and in facts established in evidence. It also means that case law from the courts and Employment Appeal Tribunal feeds back into the tribunals and will be invoked by lawyers there.

On the other hand, lawyers scarcely ever appear before Children's Hearings, which have remained relatively informal. But people appearing before them are allowed and encouraged to bring a friend or relative to help them bring out the points they wish to make. More formal representation is given by appropriate non-lawyers before some tribunals, such as a trade union official at an Employment Tribunal. A guidance teacher might accompany a child at a Children's Hearing. Some Citizens Advice Bureaux also offer help at the less formal tribunals.

Cheapness. Unlike civil courts, where a fee usually has to be paid to initiate proceedings, tribunals are almost entirely free. Unlike courts again, the loser does not have to pay the winner's expenses. A minor exception is in Employment Tribunal procedure. If a party has acted frivolously, vexatiously or otherwise unreasonably (on which there may have been a finding at a pre-hearing assessment of the case) then he may be ordered to pay the other side's expenses, which might include the fees of the employer's lawyer.

Speed. Tribunals are intended to provide a rapid settlement of disputes. Unfortunately, for a variety of reasons, they do not always fulfil that expectation. As in courts, one side may use delaying tactics in the hope that the opponent will give up or evidence may be lost. In tribunals dealing with social security benefits, upsurges in claims and cuts in staffing can produce long delays. Thus, claims for the disability living allowance introduced in 1992 far exceeded expectations and led to the operation of disability appeal tribunals being held up and thus decisions being subject to long delay.

Specialisation. All tribunals are specialised to some extent, some highly so. The creation of Chambers in which specialist judges and other members hear cases on particular areas of law is an acknowledgement that specialisation is an important part of the tribunal system. The Scottish Government is insistent in its proposals for reform that tribunal judges will only be appointed to one Chamber but may, if they meet certain criteria, be able to appear in other Chambers. This is only when they have a certain degree of experience in certain areas. This point has caused some controversy in the consultation process with some respondents concerned about amalgamation of all the Chambers under the system, and the possible loss of specialisation in the composition of tribunals which really require it. Specialisation is an important characteristic of the tribunal system.

Legal authority

4.31   Despite the appearance of informality of many of them, tribunals are vested with legal powers, just as much as courts. The rules of law which they apply can be very complex, especially in the social security area. Their decisions are just as enforceable as court decrees and sentences. Appeal to the courts on a point of law is usually possible, as is judicial review by the Court of Session, that is, an inquiry on the adequacy of the procedure, but both are uncommon. In their conduct of cases, tribunals are bound to observe the same broad standards of fairness to all parties as courts. They must clearly state their decisions in writing, usually amplified by their findings on the facts and the reasons for the decision (in the case of Children's Hearings, only if requested to do so).

For all these reasons nearly all tribunals are now presided over by a legally qualified chairman. (A conspicuous exception is Children's Hearings.) For example, Employment Tribunal chairmen must be solicitors or advocates of at least seven years' standing. There is a danger that lawyer-chairmen may come to dominate the proceedings, unless the lay members have the confidence to make their own distinctive contribution.

The Tribunals, Courts and Enforcement Act 2007 has given extended enforcement powers to the tribunals under its jurisdiction. The powers are very similar to those of the courts.

Supervision

4.32   In their early days each tribunal was set up on an *ad hoc* basis, usually on the initiative of a government department. It could thus come under the influence of the department and conform to its expectations. The department's ascendancy could be exacerbated when it appointed the chairman and members, as was the case with the now extinct National Insurance Appeal Tribunals and Supplementary Benefit Appeal Tribunals. In 1957, the Franks Committee[209] urged that common standards of openness, fairness and impartiality should be observed by all tribunals. It scrutinised the mode of appointment and procedure of all the then tribunals and made recommendations for improvement. To provide a permanent form of supervision the Committee proposed a Council on Tribunals.

Such a Council, with a Scottish Committee, was set up and operated under the Tribunals and Inquiries Act 1992[210]. It has since been replaced by the Administrative Justice and Tribunals Council ('AJTC')[211]. The AJTC is an advisory, non-departmental government body which aims to help make tribunals more accessible, fair and effective. It plays a part in developing the principles of good practice in the tribunal system.

It would seem that some formality is inseparable from any system which expresses entitlements in legal form and thus makes them open to disputed interpretation.

Other related institutions

Arbitration and alternative dispute resolution

4.33   A popular alternative to litigation in some areas of industry and the professions is arbitration. Indeed, a number of trade and professional bodies have arbitration schemes for their members, including the building and engineering industries, the Scottish

---

209 *Report of the Committee on Administrative Tribunals and Enquiries* (1957) (Cmnd 218).
210 Its Statement of Purposes included ensuring that tribunals and inquiries are: open, fair and impartial; accessible to users; have the needs of users as their primary focus; offer cost effective procedures; are properly resourced and organised; and are responsive to the needs of all sectors of society: see *Council on Tribunals Annual Report 2001–02*. (The Scottish Committee seems more generous: see *Council on Tribunals Scottish Committee Annual Report 2001–02*.)
211 See: http://ajtc.justice.gov.uk/index.htm.

Motor Traders' Association, and the Association of British Travel Agents. The Law Society of Scotland also offers an arbitration scheme. Arbitration may also be international, between companies in different countries.

Essentially, arbitration is the submission of a dispute to a private judge (now called an arbitrator), whose decision is final. The courts are thus largely excluded. Arbitration may have advantages for those in dispute. The matter is disposed of privately and probably more rapidly than in the courts. The award may be a compromise acceptable to all parties, rather than (as commonly occurs in litigation) finding a winner, and thus a loser. No precedent is set for later disputes. The dispute may be on technical matters, so the arbitrator can be someone technically qualified. Arbitration may also be cheaper than litigation, although this depends upon the procedure used, which may be quite formal, with the parties legally represented, and a lawyer as arbitrator.

Commonly, arbitration is contractual; that is, the parties to a contract have agreed that any dispute arising out of the contract shall be dealt with thus. Probably the contract will be a standard form contract used in such cases, incorporating an arbitration scheme. The arbitrator is likely to be identified by office (for example, the president for the time being of a professional association), but may be nominated by the parties. The parties may be able to nominate an arbiter each, in which case there may also be appointed an 'oversman' to determine the matter if the arbitrators cannot agree. What disputes can be arbitrated, what procedure followed, and what awards made, are matters for the parties.

Although the aim is to exclude the courts, the courts do have a carefully limited role under the Arbitration (Scotland) Act 2010, which came into effect in June 2010. The Act is effectively a codification of the law on arbitration in Scotland and provides a statutory framework for the conduct of arbitrations. It applies to domestic, UK and international arbitrations which are 'seated' in Scotland. The Scottish Arbitration Rules govern any disputes so 'seated'[212] and these are set out in Schedule 1 to the Act. Under the Rules, the Outer House of the Court of Session may, on an application by any party, determine any point of Scots law arising in the course of the arbitration. But such an application is valid only if the parties have agreed that it may be made, or the tribunal has consented to it being made, and the court is satisfied that: (i) determining the question is likely to produce substantial savings

---

212 Arbitration (Scotland) Act 2010, s 7.

in expenses; (ii) the application was made without delay; and (iii) there is a good reason why the question should be determined by the court. The tribunal may continue with the arbitration pending determination of the application. The Outer House's determination of the question is final (as is any decision by the Outer House as to whether an application is valid), ie there is no appeal to the higher tiers of the court structure. Also, any award by the arbitrator may be open to challenge on grounds of 'serious irregularity' such as want of impartiality or 'legal error' on the part of the arbitrator. The challenge is to the Outer House, with an appeal to the Inner House only, ie the matter cannot be taken to the Supreme Court. An arbitrator's award may, if necessary, be enforced through the courts. There are also statutory arbitration schemes, for example under the Agricultural Holdings (Scotland) Act 1991.

While arbitration is as old as litigation, recently 'alternative dispute resolution' has come to prominence. 'ADR' is said to be widely used in many countries for many types of issue, from commercial to family disputes. Because of this wide usage, however, it is difficult to give exact meaning to the term. It refers to a variety of means of settlement alternative to litigation. These means include a repertoire of processes such as arbitration, conciliation, mediation and negotiation, all of which have semi-technical definitions. The means may also include variations upon, and combinations of, that repertoire (and indeed of litigation as well). Thus, for example, one ADR method is described as 'med-arb' or 'concilio-arb', in which mediation is used, failing which, arbitration[213]. In Scotland the Law Society keeps a Register of Accredited Mediators called ACCORD. There is also a Group called CALM (Comprehensive Accredited Lawyer Mediators). Family Mediation Scotland supports branches in some parts of Scotland where trained lay volunteers try to bring about agreement mainly on the relationships of divorcing or separated parents with their children.

Because ADR is argued for in such a variety of disputes, it is a matter for discussion which means or combinations of means are appropriate for each dispute. This in turn depends upon the perceived disadvantages of litigation, but these are not the same in all disputes. For example, in a commercial dispute between trading partners of roughly equal power, confidentiality may be all-important to both, and be a reason to avoid litigation, while cost is irrelevant. In one between a consumer and a supplier, however, firstly, the perspectives

---

213 For a review of ADR, see the memoranda prepared for the English Law Society called 'Alternative Dispute Resolution' (1991) and 'Alternative Dispute Resolution: Second Report' (1992).

of the two disputants may be very different from each other, and secondly, from the consumer's point of view, it is cost that may be all-important and a reason to avoid litigation, and confidentiality may be irrelevant. Considerations are different again in, say, family disputes where privacy may be predominant. In all cases the possibility of greater speed, however, is usually an advantage.

The significance of ADR probably does not lie in the novelty of the means of dispute resolution that it offers. Arbitration, conciliation and mediation have long been widely used in the United Kingdom in industrial disputes, for example, and were a strongly preferred alternative to litigation until legislation in the 1980s. The Advisory, Conciliation and Arbitration Service (ACAS) is well known and active in the field, and is the descendant of government services set up for this purpose as long ago as the late 19th century.

The significance lies rather in the existence of a conscious search for alternatives to litigation, premised upon a dissatisfaction with litigation, perhaps parallel to that which caused the enormous growth in tribunals a generation ago. This is important to the study of a legal system for it may indicate a declining relevance and use of courts, and the growth of alternative quasi-legal institutions. This particularly affects a legal system reliant upon precedent. It may also have importance in relation to civil liberties, in questions as to how far individuals may seek to use private means of dispute settlement, and whether stronger disputants may be enabled to force weaker ones into unsatisfactory arrangements.

Ombudsmen[214]

4.34   A method of redressing grievances imported from Scandinavia (via New Zealand) in the last few decades is the ombudsman, that is, an official who is not a judge, but who can examine critically the conduct of officials in a more effective way than could a court or tribunal (though usually only after the complainant has exhausted all other remedies). The first ombudsman, technically called the Parliamentary Commissioner for Administration (PCA), was appointed in 1967 under the Parliamentary Commissioner Act of that year[215].

---

214 A directory of Ombudsmen can be found on the Ombudsman Association website at http://www.ombudsmanassociation.org/.
215 The PCA website is at www.ombudsman.org.uk. The PCA in 2012 was Dame Julie Mellor DBE. She is simultaneously Health Service Ombudsman for England and Wales.

The PCA is appointed by the Crown, and may be removed only by an address of both Houses of the UK Parliament, so has protection of tenure similar to that of a judge, though most appointees have been civil servants. The PCA is entitled to investigate complaints of injustice resulting from 'maladministration' (a term given a technical meaning) by government departments in the exercise of their administrative functions. Various areas are specifically excluded from oversight, including foreign relations, the investigation of crime, and appointment and discipline within the Civil Service. Nor may the PCA investigate where the complainant has a legal remedy which could reasonably be pursued (such as an appeal against refusal of a benefit). On the other hand, the PCA has powers equivalent to those of the Court of Session to require production of papers and the attendance of witnesses (save in relation to Cabinet proceedings).

A complainant cannot approach the PCA directly, however, but only via an MP, who is not required to pass the complaint on. The PCA's conclusions after investigation are passed back to the MP, though he may also make a special report to Parliament. This indirect approach was the result of MPs' jealousy of Parliament's role as the place where grievances against government are dealt with. Thus, also, the PCA cannot order any remedy where maladministration is found, and it is up to the department concerned what it does. There is a Public Administration Select Committee which reports to the House of Commons, and which in practice assists in obtaining a remedy. The PCA issues an annual report and reports on specific issues.

There is also a Scottish Public Services Ombudsman[216], an office set up by the Scottish Public Services Ombudsman Act 2002 to replace the Scottish Parliamentary Ombudsman, the Health Service Ombudsman for Scotland, the Local Government Ombudsman for Scotland, and the Housing Association Ombudsman for Scotland. Consequently, the office covers a very wide range of organisations, including the Scottish Government, health service bodies, local authorities, further and higher education, and a variety of other governmental bodies from the Audit Commission for Scotland to the Water Industry Commissioner for Scotland (via the Crofters' Commission, the Parole Board for Scotland and the Scottish Arts Council). It also includes a large number of 'cross-border public authorities', that is, Great Britain or United Kingdom ones, some of whose activities relate to devolved matters, such as the Criminal

---

216 The website of the Scottish Public Services Ombudsman is at www.scottish ombudsman.org.uk. The SPSO is Jim Martin.

Injuries Compensation Authority, the National Consumer Council and the Unrelated Live Transplant Regulatory Authority. There is also a Scottish Legal Services Ombudsman (discussed in Chapter 7).

In addition, there is a UK-wide Financial Ombudsman Service (replacing the former Banking, Building Society, Insurance and Investment Ombudsmen) and Pensions Ombudsman, and several other ombudsmen whose jurisdiction relates to England and Wales only. Some of these schemes are closer to arbitration than to the usual role of an ombudsman.

Principal English and Welsh courts

Civil courts

4.35   Magistrates' courts are organised on a county basis, with lay justices of the peace ('JPs') assisted by a legally qualified clerk, but also in many urban areas with full-time District Judges. There are some 700 JPs in all and some 100 District Judges. They deal with certain family law matters including adoption proceedings (when they are termed 'Family Proceedings Courts'), recovery of charges from public utilities, and act as a licensing court for alcohol licensing. They are not equivalent to any Scottish Court.

County Courts, of which there are some 300, are found in all major towns. They are roughly equivalent to Sheriff Courts, and take a wide variety of civil cases within their areas, subject to certain limitations. District Judges may hear cases up to a limited figure, Circuit Judges hear above that limit, and there are small claims procedures. Many County Courts (though not all) deal with divorce.

The High Court of Justice is roughly equivalent to the Outer House of the Court of Session (and not to be confused with the Scottish High Court of Justiciary). However, it sits not only in London, but also in a number of provincial centres. It comprises three Divisions, but these are not like the Divisions of the Inner House, as they are distinguished in terms of jurisdiction. They are called, respectively, Queen's Bench (which includes the Commercial Court, the Admiralty Court and the Administrative Court), with some 73 judges, headed by the President of the Queen's Bench Division'[217]; Chancery, with some 18 judges headed by the 'Chancellor of the

217 At the end of 2012, Sir (Roger) John Laugharne Thomas

High Court'[218]; and Family (once known as the Probate, Divorce and Admiralty Division), also with about 19 judges, headed by the President of the Family Division[219].

The judges without titles are styled 'Mr Justice' ('J', after the surname; 'JJ' in the plural: thus, for instance, 'Collins J', and 'Collins and Butterfield, JJ'[220]). The High Court takes important civil litigation at first instance, and each Division has a small appeal jurisdiction. This is exercised by two or more judges and, confusingly, is known as the 'Divisional Court' (thus 'the Divisional Court of Queen's Bench' rather than 'Queen's Bench Division').

The Court of Appeal (Civil Division) chiefly takes appeals from the County Courts, a number of tribunals, and the three Divisions of the High Court, and is roughly equivalent to the Inner House of the Court of Session. It has some 40 judges, called Lords Justices of Appeal (abbreviated to 'LJ' after the surname; 'LJJ' in the plural), and is headed by the 'Master of the Rolls' ('MR': thus, as of 1 October 2012, 'Sir John Dyson, MR'). They sit in threes, usually.

The Supreme Court of the United Kingdom hears further appeals from the Court of Appeal, but also occasionally, with the consent of the parties, on questions of statutory interpretation of general public importance, direct from the High Court (for which there is no Scottish equivalent procedure).

Criminal courts

4.36   Magistrates' courts, essentially the same courts as for civil purposes, try minor offences, which constitute the overwhelming majority of all criminal cases, with restricted sentencing powers. Their nearest equivalent in Scotland is the JP Court but they take a much greater proportion of cases, so overlap with Sheriff Summary Courts. As the 'Youth Court', they try those aged between 14 and 17 years (as there is no equivalent to the Children's Hearings).

They also act as a 'Court of Committal', for which there is no Scottish equivalent. Any serious crime is tried 'on indictment' (roughly similar to solemn procedure) before the Crown Court, but traditionally, the person had first to appear before examining magistrates whose function was to decide if there were a prima facie

---

218 At the end of 2012, Sir Andrew Morrit.
219 At the end of 2012, Sir Nicholas Wall.
220 Though English High Court judges are made knights or dames, as appropriate, on appointment. Thus Collins J is Sir Andrew David Collins.

case against the accused. If they decided there was, the case was committed to the Crown Court for trial. If not, the accused was discharged. However, the unwieldiness of the proceedings means that they are now considerably watered down, and the process has lost much of its purpose.

Crown Courts (descended from the old 'Assizes' and 'Quarter Sessions'), which sit in some 90 locations, hear more serious criminal cases, including all trials on indictment, and are organised on a circuit basis so are the rough equivalent of the Sheriff Solemn Court, and High Court of Justiciary in Scotland. However, there are several levels of judge (High Court judges, Circuit Judges and Recorders), as the courts are organised into three tiers, reflected in the seriousness of the cases they may try. The 'Old Bailey' is the popular name for London Crown Court, technically known as the Central Criminal Court (which is situated in a street called 'Old Bailey'). Crown Courts also hear appeals from Magistrates' Courts.

The Court of Appeal (Criminal Division), headed by the Lord Chief Justice ('LCJ': thus 'Lord Judge, LCJ'), hears appeals against conviction and sentence, and other matters, from the Crown Court (so is the rough equivalent of the High Court of Justiciary acting as the Court of Criminal Appeal), and the Supreme Court of the United Kingdom is the final court of criminal appeal (though not in Scotland).

Judicial offices

4.37 Recent changes, in part flowing from the change in status of the Lord Chancellor[221], have created new judicial offices.

The Lord Chief Justice is now also the 'President of the Courts of England & Wales' and as such, responsible for conveying the views of the England and Wales judiciary to the Government, for training of this judiciary ('within the resources made available by the Lord Chancellor') and for 'maintenance of appropriate arrangements for the deployment of the judiciary in England and Wales. The Lord Chief Justice is also now 'Head of Criminal Justice' in England and Wales (or appoints a Court of Appeal judge to hold that office, after consultation with the Lord Chancellor)[222].

---

221 For which, see Chs 3 and 4, and above.
222 Constitutional Reform Act 2005, s 7.

The President of the Family Division is now also 'Head of Family Justice', and has a Deputy appointed by the Lord Chief Justice[223].

Principal Northern Ireland Courts[224]

Civil Courts

4.38   Magistrates Courts, County Courts and the High Court and the Court of Appeal operate in a similar fashion to their equivalents in England and Wales.

Magistrates Courts were originally staffed by lay Justices of the Peace. However, for two hundred years or more, there have been professional 'Resident Magistrates' who largely, but not completely, replaced them over time. Magistrates Courts deal with maintenance proceedings between husband and wife and related matters, small debts, land disputes and licensing within their area. Appeal is either to the County Court or the Court of Appeal (on a point of law only).

County Courts deal with the general range of civil matters including contract, delict and divorce (as well as appeals from Magistrates Courts) within their area. Appeal from County Courts is by way of a re-hearing to the High Court or by case stated to the Court of Appeal (on a point of law only).

The High Court, with three Divisions (as in England and Wales) hears the broad range of important civil matters from anywhere in Northern Ireland. Appeal is to the Court of Appeal or in some cases, direct to the Supreme Court of the United Kingdom.

The Court of Appeal hears appeals, as described above, with appeal to the Supreme Court of the United Kingdom.

Criminal Courts

4.39   Magistrates Courts, the Crown Court and the Court of Appeal also operate in a similar fashion to their equivalents in England and Wales

Magistrates Courts (usually staffed by 'Resident Magistrates', as noted above in relation to civil matters) undertake committal

---

223 *Ibid*, s 8.
224 For further detail, see eg Dickson *The Legal System of Northern Ireland* (SLS Publications, 5th ed 2005)

proceedings in respect of major crime, acting as a sieve for the Crown Court, but try summarily (that is, without a jury), the vast majority of criminal cases themselves, within their area. Appeal is either to the County Court (by way of a re-hearing) or to the Court of Appeal (on a point of law only).

County Courts hear the appeals just noted, but have no original jurisdiction in criminal matters.

The Crown Court hears major criminal cases on indictment (that is, with a jury) after the committal proceedings in the Magistrates Court. Appeal is the Court of Appeal and, thereafter to the Supreme Court of the United Kingdom.

5 Sources of law

THE MEANINGS OF 'SOURCES OF LAW'

5.1 'Sources of law' is a widely used phrase. It has several meanings, all of which have their importance, and each of which must be distinguished.

Historical sources

5.2 Legal rules and principles do not spring into existence, fully formed. They have their origins in political, moral and social ideas. Specific pieces of legislation (for example, the Equality Act 2010), and fundamental organising legal principles (such as contract), encapsulate such ideas. Thus, any legal provision has historical sources. Chapters 1, 2 and 15 look further at the process by which such ideas become law.

Formal sources

5.3 The most common use of the phrase 'sources of law', however, relates to the form in which the law appears. The formal sources of any legal system will be specific to it. Thus, the formal sources of Scots law are not identical to those of English law, and a good deal more different from those of, say, French law. The formal sources of Scots law can be divided into major and minor, reflecting their relative importance.

The major formal sources are:

(a) legislation, including:
 – Acts of the United Kingdom Parliament, two of which, the Human Rights Act 1998 and the European Communities Act 1972, have special status;
 – laws made by Ministers of the Crown and others under powers delegated to them by the United Kingdom Parliament;

- Acts of the Scottish Parliament also made under powers delegated by the United Kingdom Parliament;
- laws made by the Scottish Ministers and other, again under powers delegated by the United Kingdom Parliament;
- laws made by the Scottish Ministers and others, but under powers delegated by the Scottish Parliament; and
- European Union legislation of various types;

(b) precedent, that is, rules of law produced by courts without reference to the UK Parliament or any other legislature.

The minor formal sources can be said to be:

(a) prerogative legislation (that is, remnants of the former power of the Crown before the rise of Parliament in the 17th century, now exercised by the government, most of them being executive in form, but some being undeniably legislative);

(b) 'Institutional Works' (that is, certain writings on the law by individual authors who have won respect in the courts and elsewhere, their writings therefore being treated as authoritative); and

(c) custom (that is, practices observed by certain groups of people, or by people generally).

This typology of formal sources is the basis upon which, broadly speaking, most of the rest of this Chapter, and Chapters 6 to 13 proceed. Its importance is, incidentally, reflected in the most significant feature of a law library, which is visible at a glance. Half the books are textbooks, monographs, commentaries and other books about the law. The other half is the law itself, that is, collections of legislation, reports of cases etc. It is the most characteristic part of a law student's work that the law must be 'looked up', that is, find not just summaries of the law and comments on it but the actual legal provisions themselves.

Other uses of the term 'sources of law'

5.4   Before considering the various sorts of 'formal source' in detail, it should be noted that the term 'sources of law' can be used in yet other senses. For example, it is sometimes used to indicate that a rule is to be found in a specific piece of legislation or a particular precedent (that is, a particular decided case), as when the legal rules on how a valid marriage is contracted are said to have as their source the Marriage (Scotland) Act 1977, and the legal rules on what constitutes a contract to have as their source a large number of identifiable cases in which they were laid down. This usage, which does not have a conventional name, might be termed the 'locational source'.

Quasi-sources

5.5   Also before considering the various sorts of 'formal source' in detail, it should be further noted that some rules, although not actually rules of law, are similar to rules of law in some important ways. These require examination, if only to distinguish them, and can be described as 'quasi-sources'.

RANKING OF SOURCES

5.6   If there is more than one source of law, they might contradict each other. This would be, quite literally, intolerable, for it would be impossible to discover what the law was on any topic. So to prevent contradiction, the sources must be ranked in an order of precedence, the higher 'trumping' the lower.

Unfortunately, the details of how this ranking works are now very complicated. Nevertheless, ten principles broadly express this ranking:

1 Legislation – 'Convention rights'

5.7   'Convention rights' is the name given to the rights and freedoms contained within the European Convention on Human Rights (for which, see Chapter 3), which have been cut and pasted into the Human Rights Act 1998 (an Act of the United Kingdom Parliament) and made enforceable in United Kingdom courts. Their special significance is expressed in the first principle, that is, that courts, government and other public authorities must interpret all other laws, both existing and future, so far as possible consistently with them. There is an important exception to this, however, in that, if other Acts of the United Kingdom Parliament (but not other laws) cannot be interpreted consistently with them, the Convention rights are overridden (albeit that this might then give rise to a claim in the European Court of Human Rights).

147

2 Legislation – 'Community law'

5.8   This is the law created by the European Union (for which, see Chapters 3 and 6 and Appendix 3). The second principle is that all other existing and future law is valid only in so far as it is consistent with European Union (EU) law. This is required by the European Communities Act 1972. (However, EU law is still to be interpreted consistently with the European Convention on Human Rights in conformity with the first principle).

3 Legislation – United Kingdom Parliamentary legislation

5.9   This is the law passed by the United Kingdom Parliament, in Acts of Parliament. The third principle is that, subject to the first two, the United Kingdom Parliament may pass any Act, to any effect, that it wishes, and this legislation is therefore more powerful than the law created by any of the following means.

4 Legislation – Scottish Parliamentary legislation

5.10   This is law passed by the Scottish Parliament in Acts of the Scottish Parliament. The fourth principle is that, as the Scottish Parliament has law-making power only by virtue of the United Kingdom Parliament delegating such powers in the Scotland Act 1998 (as well as the extra powers delegated in the Scotland Act 2012), Acts of the Scottish Parliament are valid only in so far as permitted by the delegation in that Act. (It should be noted, however, that the Scotland Acts proceed on the basis that all powers are devolved unless specifically reserved.)

5 Legislation – other delegated legislation

5.11   This is law made by members of the United Kingdom government, or the Scottish Government, or other governmental bodies such as local authorities, in the form of Statutory Instruments (and Scottish Statutory Instruments), by-laws etc. It also is possible only by virtue of the United Kingdom Parliament (or, in the case of the Scottish Government and Scottish local authorities, the Scottish Parliament) delegating appropriate powers. The fifth principle is that, as with the fourth, such legislation is thus valid only in so far as it is permitted by the delegation in the relevant legislation.

6 Legislation – earlier and later legislation

5.12   The sixth principle is that, within any of the above classes of legislation, later legislation may repeal or amend earlier inconsistent legislation implicitly, even if it does not do so explicitly.

7 Judicial precedent – precedent and legislation

5.13   This is the law made by judges in deciding cases in courts, in the absence of legislation. The seventh principle is that such law is valid only in so far as it is compatible with legislation, in any of its forms.

8 Judicial precedent – higher and lower courts

5.14   Precedents can be laid down, in general, by any court. However, in general, it is those created by courts relatively high in the hierarchy, that is, appeal courts, which are significant in terms of law-making. Thus, the eighth principle is that higher courts can, despite the seventh principle, overturn the law created by judicial precedent in lower courts. (Note, incidentally, that a form of judicial precedent operates in cases interpreting legislation, that is, working out a meaning where the legislation is unclear, for such interpretations become embedded as precedents, and this principle applies in such cases.)

8 Judicial precedent – earlier and later judicial precedent

5.15   Those operating the system of judicial precedent, from whatever time, assume that no precedent contradicts any other, so are reconcilable until proved otherwise. The ninth principle is, therefore, to strive to maintain the whole body of judicial precedent as a coherent and consistent whole.

9 Minor sources

5.16   This is law made by a variety of disparate bodies (as described above). The tenth principle is therefore that law made by the minor sources may be drawn on in default of any of the above. Recourse to minor sources is so rare that there is no need for a principle to rank between them.

THE MAJOR FORMAL SOURCES OF LAW

Legislation and precedent: civil law, common law and mixed systems

5.17 It may be useful to start consideration of the major formal sources of law with the distinction between the 'civil' and 'common law' families of legal systems, for this throws light upon the relationship between legislation and precedent.

Civil law systems are the intellectual heirs of Roman law, and many of their legal rules are descended from it. 'Civil law' is a translation of the Latin *ius civile*, the name given by Roman lawyers to the bulk of their law. In general, civil law systems are codified systems, in the sense that much law is set out in logical, reasoned and encyclopaedic form in legislative 'codes'. In such a system, in principle, not only do all legal rules derive from legislation (principally the codes), but also the underlying principles of the system are set forth there. In such systems, precedent is not recognised as a source of law at all, or at least only as a minor, supplementary one. The legal systems of most of Continental Europe, such as Belgium, France, Germany, Italy and Spain, and to a large extent those parts of the rest of the world which were colonised by these European powers, such as the countries of South America, are civil law.

Common law systems are the heirs of English law. English law itself never adopted Roman law as other European countries did. The native law it developed depended heavily upon precedent. Indeed, only in the 19th century did legislation become a significant source of law. The name given to the kind of law created by precedent, 'the common law', is the very name identifying this type of legal system. Thus the rules, and the principles underlying them, are found in precedent. For example, the organising concepts of law such as contract, and the basic rules on the creation of contracts, the effect upon them of error by a party, and on performance or non-performance of contracts, and so on, are found in precedent. Legislation merely alters the application of those principles, to a greater or lesser extent, in respect of specific contracts (such as sale of goods, consumer credit or insurance contracts). Even great new areas of law such as company law, which were created by legislation, depend upon underlying common law rules and principles. English law was exported to British colonies, and thus became the type of law found in much of the rest of the world, including most of the countries of North America, and the British Commonwealth.

Scots law forms one of a small group of 'mixed' or 'hybrid' systems, which partake of both civil and common law. Other mixed or hybrid systems are, because of the vagaries of their colonial history, the state of Louisiana in the USA, South Africa, the province of Quebec in Canada, and Sri Lanka. Scots law is said to be a civil law system, in so far as Roman law, and the law of civil law countries, has influenced it, through the works of the Institutional Writers and the fact that, when law teaching in Scottish universities was less than lively, law students commonly repaired to France (before the Reformation) and the Netherlands (after it) for their instruction. However, Scots law is not codified and since the 19th century, but especially since the mid-20th century, it has accepted precedent as a source of law on the common law model.

Legislation

5.18 'Legislation' is surprisingly hard to define. It is both a process and a product. As a product, it is easiest to say that, so far as Scotland is concerned, legislation is the law created by certain European Union institutions, by the United Kingdom and Scottish Parliaments and by those to whom the United Kingdom and Scottish Parliaments have delegated legislative power. This, however, begs the question of what these bodies have in common.

It is better therefore to say that legislation is deliberately and formally created law. Acts of the United Kingdom Parliament have commonly been regarded as the standard example, in as much as throughout the United Kingdom, they prevailed over all other forms of law until the coming of European Union law (and still formally prevail over the European Convention on Human Rights). Legislation is produced by a process. It is thus commonly, but not necessarily, produced by a deliberative body (sometimes referred to as a legislature, and sometimes elected). It nearly always deals in general rules rather than specific cases. While in civil law countries the whole law can be presumed to be the result of legislation (often in the form of encyclopaedic codes), in common law countries, which admit precedent as a formal source of law, this is not so, for the purpose of legislation is to change (or sometimes restate) the law. Legislation in common law countries is thus essentially *ad hoc*.

The various types of legislation applying in the United Kingdom are discussed in Chapters 6–10.

Precedent

5.19 Precedent is law created incidentally, by an adjudicative body (usually a court), in the course of judging disputes. It is to be found, therefore, in specific cases dealing with specific facts, and the actual rules of law applied must necessarily be inferred from those facts, typically by other judges in other cases appealing to precedent, as further described in Chapters 12 & 13 and Appendix 1. Acceptance of precedent as a means of creating law effectively defines common law legal systems. These inferred rules purport to express timeless principles inherent in the system, rather than specific contemporary policy. While it is possible for the law to be changed through precedent, the process is usually slow, limited and uncertain, so legislation is usually sought for this purpose. Thus, the underlying principles of the legal system are to be found in the common law, that is the law created by precedent, rather than in legislation, which merely modifies or adds to it. Indeed, common law can be put into abeyance by legislation, but not wholly destroyed, for it takes force again if the legislation replacing it is repealed. Precedent can even determine the meaning of legislation.

THE MINOR FORMAL SOURCES OF LAW

5.20 The minor sources are prerogative legislation, the Institutional Writings, and custom.

Prerogative legislation

5.21 Generally speaking, the Crown (that is, in practice, the government of the day) has no power to create law, for under the 'doctrine of the separation of the powers', creating law is the job of another body, that is, Parliament. However, it does have some limited residual powers, dating from a time before the separation of the powers was thought sound theory, and when monarchs could thus legislate without reference to Parliament. These powers are part of the 'royal prerogative', which is the name given to the ill-defined bundle of legal powers enjoyed by the Crown[1].

These powers are chiefly executive rather than legislative, and include the Sovereign's power to appoint ministers to form a government, and the powers of the government (in the name of the

---

1 In *Laker Airways v Department of Trade* [1977] QB 643, Lord Denning described the royal prerogative as 'a discretionary power to be exercised for the public good' and so it was examinable by the courts.

Crown) to conduct foreign affairs including, for example, the power to sign treaties and declare war[2].

But among these prerogative powers, certain residual legislative ones exist. Although they are undoubtedly legislative, they are minor, so are dealt with here, rather than in Chapters 6–10. They are residual in that, as noted above, they are the remains of the broad legislative powers claimed by the Crown before the 'Glorious Revolution', that is, the constitutional settlement of 1688–89 in both England and Scotland (which had shared a king from 1603). In this settlement, Parliament took most of these powers away from the Crown, and what remains could also be removed by Parliament. The prerogative powers therefore continue to exist on sufferance[3], and there remains no general right on the part of the Crown to legislate[4], only a limited right to do so in relation to certain topics. These topics include the colonies, internal governmental matters, and possibly certain emergencies and otherwise.

Examples of its use are therefore few and disparate. One, concerned with colonial legislation, was the constitution of Hong Kong from its acquisition by the United Kingdom until it was handed back to China in 1997. This constitution was latterly contained in certain acts of prerogative legislation (called 'Letters Patent')[5]. All legislation made in Hong Kong by the Governor in the Legislative Council (Hong Kong's Parliament) was therefore valid by virtue of the fact that the Letters Patent created the post of Governor, set up the Legislative Council and provided for its composition, and gave legislative powers to the Governor in Legislative Council.

A second example, concerned with internal governmental matters, is the principal regulations for the internal operation of the Civil Service[6]. A third, concerned with emergencies, is certain legislation

---

2 Section 20 of the Constitutional and Governance Reform Act 2010 transferred some powers to Parliament to object to the ratification of a treaty. Ministers may still press ahead with the treaty but must lay before Parliament a statement indicating that the minister is of the opinion that the treaty should nevertheless be ratified and explaining why (see sections 20 (4) and 20 (8).

3 See, for example, the English case of *Re de Keyser's Royal Hotel* [1920] AC 508.

4 Claim of Right 1689; *Grieve v Edinburgh and District Water Trustees* 1918 SC 700, 1918 2 SLT 72; also the English *Case of Proclamations* (1611) Co Rep 74.

5 Letters Patent of 14 February 1917 (as amended); also Royal Instructions of 14 February 1917 (as amended) etc; see Wesley-Smith *Constitutional and Administrative Law in Hong Kong* (1987) vol 1, ch 4.

6 For example, the Civil Service Orders 1982, 1991 and 1995. It has been suggested that these ought to be replaced by a 'Civil Service Act', *ie* an Act of Parliament. Note also the Diplomatic Service Orders in Council of 1991, 1994 (two), 1995 & 204.

made on the outbreak of war in 1914, when no standing emergency legislation existed[7], and somewhat more recently at the time of the Falklands emergency[8].

A fourth example was the former Criminal Injuries Compensation Scheme. When the government decided in 1964 that persons suffering injuries as a result of criminal acts should receive some compensation from the state (being unlikely to obtain it from the criminal) it used the prerogative to set up a scheme of awards, based on the level of damages that the courts in Scotland or in England would grant. The justifications for circumventing Parliament were that the scheme was experimental and the costs to the state uncertain. In fact, dissatisfaction with this arrangement led eventually to the Criminal Injuries Compensation Act 1995, under which schemes are now authorised, the most recent at the end of 2012[9].

While acts of prerogative legislation answer to a variety of names[10], such as 'Letters Patent', 'Royal Instructions', 'Proclamations' and 'Royal Warrants', they are usually issued in the form of (prerogative) 'Orders in Council', that is, Orders purportedly made by the Sovereign on the advice of the Privy Council[11]. The title 'Order in Council' is misleading. Firstly, the involvement of the Sovereign and the advice of the Privy Council are fictional as the content is dictated by the government of the day. Secondly, the same name is used for another much more common type of legislation, that is (delegated) Orders in Council, a form of delegated legislation (see Chapter 9).

---

7 For example, the Trading with the Enemy Proclamation 1914.

8 Requisitioning of Ships Order of 4 April 1982.

9 The story is in fact more complicated, and instructive on the relationship of prerogative and legislation. A statutory scheme to replace the non-statutory one was introduced by the Criminal Justice Act 1988, ss 108–117. However, it was not brought into effect, and some time later, the Secretary of State announced that he was not going to bring it into force, but would introduce a new non-statutory scheme. In *R v Secretary of State for the Home Department ex parte Fire Brigades Union* [1995] 2 AC 513, the Appellate Committee of the House of Lords held that, while he was not obliged to bring the statutory scheme into force, it was an abuse of the prerogative power to introduce an inconsistent non-statutory scheme under the royal prerogative. The Criminal Injuries Compensation Act 1995 therefore repealed the relevant portions of the Criminal Justice Act 1988, and introduced the scheme as a statutory one. For the present rules see the Criminal Injuries Compensation Scheme 2012.

10 Acts of prerogative legislation are cited by name and date, as the examples above show. Some are bound in the annual volumes of *Statutory Instruments*, so can be cited by that reference. They do not appear on Westlaw or LexisNexis.

11 The Privy Council, originally a sort of forerunner of the Cabinet, is almost fictional in that it never meets as a whole, and the title 'Privy Councillor' is a sort of honour bestowed upon leading politicians, judges and bishops.

The Institutional Writings

5.22   In the 17th century, Scots law was an amalgam derived from various sources. It included old unwritten custom, written custom and other rules recorded in medieval writings, such as that called *Regiam Majestatem*[12], which were considered authoritative, *ad hoc* Acts of Parliament of various vintages, and decisions of the Court of Session, at least in so far as available in the collections known as '*Practicks*'.

Scots law was not the only system with such characteristics. But the advantages of a systematic treatment were clear to lawyers and others across Europe at this time. A widely known model for systematising native law was the *Corpus Iuris Civilis* (which can be roughly translated as 'the Body of the Civil Law'). This was a codification of late Roman law, produced in the 6th century AD in Constantinople (which was by then the capital of the Eastern part of the Roman Empire, known today as Istanbul) under the auspices of the Emperor Justinian. It comprised four parts, two of which were of greater importance than the rest. The '*Pandects*' (or '*Digest*') was a reconciliation of the commentaries of the major Roman legal writers of previous centuries. The '*Institutiones*' was a general introductory book on Roman law, dedicated to law students, and based around the idea that the objects of law were Persons (the actors recognised by law), Things (persons' rights against other persons (family, contract, delict), and to other things (property)), and Actions (the means by which rights could be made good in law).

In Scotland such attempts to produce a systematic treatment took place from the mid-17th to the early 19th centuries. The writers of these works have become known as 'Institutional Writers', as several of their works adopted the title '*Institutes*' or '*Institutions*' in imitation of the title and structure of Justinian's '*Institutiones*'. Their work remade Scots law.

It can be debated whether a particular writer or work is institutional. However, undoubtedly Stair's *Institutions of the Law of Scotland* is the greatest of them all, while certain other works are in all lists of authoritative writings. They are[13]:

---

12 See Ch 2. It appears that *Regiam Majestatem* was heavily based upon an earlier English work, called *Glanvil* after the name of its presumed author. '*Regiam majestatem ...*', meaning 'Royal Majesty ...', are its opening words.

13 All dates given are of the first edition. Later editions may be more authoritative. The first edition of Stair's *Institutions* was defective, for example, and the second, published in 1693, is more reliable. In any case, later editions of all the works are usually preferred.

- Thomas Craig's *Jus Feudale* (1655);
- Sir George Mackenzie's *Laws and Customs of Scotland in Matters Criminal* (1678);
- James Dalrymple, Viscount Stair's *The Institutions of the Law of Scotland* (1681);
- Andrew McDouall, Lord Bankton's *An Institute of the Laws of Scotland* (1751–53);
- Professor John Erskine's *An Institute of the Law of Scotland* (1772);
- Baron David Hume's *Commentaries on the Law of Scotland Respecting the Description and Punishment of Crimes* (1797);
- Professor George Joseph Bell's *Commentaries on the Law of Scotland and Principles of Mercantile Jurisprudence* (1804) and *Principles of the Law of Scotland* (1829);
- Archibald Alison's *Principles of the Criminal Law of Scotland* (1833) and *Practice of the Criminal Law of Scotland* (1833)[14].

Sometimes also included are Mackenzie's *The Institutions of the Law of Scotland* (1684); Erskine's *Principles of the Law of Scotland* (1759); and Henry Home, Lord Kames' *Principles of Equity* (1760).

The current significance of these works is that, at least since the middle of the 19th century, they have been accorded a special status. That is, they are regarded not as commentaries upon, illustrations of, opinions about, or textbooks concerning, the law, but as in themselves actually constituting the law[15]. Thus, in effect, the Institutional Writers have been regarded as akin to legislators.

While it is undeniable that the Institutional Writers are sources of law, explicit recognition of the position is limited to a small number of 19th-century cases, decided at a time when attitudes to the nature of law were different from today's, buttressed by a few authoritative,

---

14 References to Stair are usually cited by name, book, title and section, for example, 'Stair I, 1, 22' (or, more traditionally 'I, i, 22'), but sometimes in the form 'Stair *Institutions* I, 1, 22'. Bankton (commonly abbreviated to Bankt) and Erskine's (often abbreviated to Ersk) '*Institute*' are cited in essentially the same way, for example, 'Bankt I, 5, 28' and 'Ersk III, 1, 2' (and Erskine's '*Principles*' similarly, but with '*Prin*' inserted). Bell's '*Commentaries*' are cited as, for example, 'Bell *Comm* I, 343', but his '*Principles*' (which has continuous paragraphing throughout), as 'Bell *Prin* 267'. Hume is cited as, for example, '*Hume* 1, 52'.

15 It is unusual for legal systems to regard such writers as sources of law. South African law appears to be the only other system which does so. There, rules may be regarded as legal rules simply by virtue of having been written by one of the 'old authorities', chiefly internationally renowned Dutch writers on law, such as Grotius (Hugo de Groot 1583–1645): see *The Laws of Scotland: Stair Memorial Encyclopedia* vol 22, para 435, and Cairns 'Institutional Writings' in Kiralfy and MacQueen *New Perspectives in Scottish Legal History* (1983).

but less than comprehensive, 20th-century cases[16]. No works have been added to the canon since the middle of the 19th century and none deleted, although, so far as institutional authority depends upon judicial recognition, in principle either event could occur.

When an Institutional Writing is cited, the question of its weight in comparison with other sources arises. There is little guidance on the answer. Lord Normand, a distinguished Scottish judge, observed in an often quoted[17] published lecture of 1941 that they were as respected in court as decisions of the Appellate Committee of the House of Lords (now the Supreme Court of the United Kingdom). However, there are few cases explicitly dealing with the authority of the Institutional Writers and judges have rarely discussed the matter. Clearly, the Institutional Writings carry less weight than any legislation and, given their status, it is unlikely that any judicial decision will flatly contradict them, but in many areas, such as family law and employment law, social and moral changes have been so substantial as to reduce their persuasiveness considerably, or justify use of the maxim *cessante ratione legis, cessat ipsa lex*[18]. The deference suggested by Lord Normand now seems exaggerated[19]. Thus, an Institutional work may be regarded as potentially decisive, but only where no legislation or clear precedent exists, and in areas of law in which the principles have not altered significantly since the Institutional Writers were at work.

In any case, although Institutional Writings were of enormous importance in the past, it would be very unusual for any court today to justify its decision solely by reference to one. Indeed, although the High Court refers to Hume's works from time to time in relation to major common law criminal offences[20], it is rare for Institutional Writers even to be cited in court, in part because the tide of precedent and statute has washed over so much law in the

---

16 For example, *Sugden v HM Advocate* 1934 JC 103, 1934 SLT 465; *Fortington v Lord Kinnaird* 1942 SC 239, 1943 SLT 24.

17 For example, in *The Laws of Scotland: Stair Memorial Encyclopedia* vol 22, 'Sources of Law (Formal)', para 437.

18 *Ie*, approximately, 'if the reason for the law ceases, so does the law'.

19 See *HM Advocate v Stallard* 1989 SCCR 248, 1989 SLT 469. The learned commentator on the SCCR report of that case observed that 'it is not necessary to convene a Full Bench [*ie* an enlarged bench of judges, capable of giving more authoritative decisions] to depart from a proposition of Hume, which was repeated by later authorities and has been unchallenged by any authority for almost two centuries'.

20 As in *Khaliq v HM Advocate* 1984 JC 23, where Hume was relied upon, and *HM Advocate v Stallard* (see note above), where he was mentioned only to reject him.

last hundred years (although those precedents may themselves be built on the Institutional Writers' views, which are thus embedded in the law through a different route). Their primary role today is thus, perhaps, to supply a moral and intellectual sheet anchor for the law, providing stability while not excluding change.

Other, non-institutional, works may be referred to in argument or decision in court, and increasingly are. Indeed, some highly respected but non-institutional works, such as Gloag's *Law of Contract* (2nd edn, 1929) and McBryde *The Law of Contract in Scotland* (3rd edn, 2007), are cited more frequently than Institutional Works. But in such cases, if the judge adopts the rule described, he is not accepting it as the actual law, but making it law by his decision. Thus, in *Black v Carmichael* 1992 SLT 897, the judges accepted a statement in Gordon's *Criminal Law* (2nd ed 1978[21]) at para 14–63 that in theft it is the owner's loss, not the thief's gain, that is important. In *Morgan Guaranty Trust Co v Lothian Regional Council* 1995 SC 151, Lord President Hope acknowledged 'the work of academic lawyers whose detailed research and vigorous criticism has already had a marked influence on debate among the judiciary'.

Custom

5.23   The common law (in the sense of law not created by Parliament) emerged from unwritten custom. Institutional Writers digested it in their works, and judges adopted it in their judgments, which clearly made it law which was common to the whole country. However, local custom might also be recognised. For example, some Institutional Writers recognised 'udal tenure', a form of land-holding found only in Orkney and Shetland, as custom enforceable through the courts[22].

It remains possible for custom to be a source of law. Nevertheless, because most rules once referred to as customs, such as 'legitim' (rights held by a deceased person's children to his moveable property), have now been enshrined in precedent, and thus incorporated into the common law, even that possibility exists only in limited circumstances. It is thus very rare today to assert the existence of a custom, and the leading case, *Bruce v Smith* (1890) 17 R 1000 (which concerns the rejection of a claim by the owner of land abutting the shore in Shetland, by virtue of owning the land,

---

21 See now 3rd edn, 2000 & 2001 (2 vols).
22 Stair IV, 22, 2.

to one third of the value of pilot whales driven onto that shore and slaughtered), is well over a century old.

In so far as a custom might still be declared enforceable in the courts, it must pass certain tests. The custom must not contradict the general law[23], it must be certain[24], it must be generally accepted or acquiesced in as being obligatory[25], it must be reasonable (although what this means is not clear and might be difficult to decide), and it must have continued for a long time, although no particular period is required and interruption is not fatal. But a custom may be regarded as falling into desuetude, or as losing authority by contrary usage[26]. Any enforceable custom is likely to be restricted to a locality or trade, because any more general custom will either have been absorbed into the common law by judicial precedent, or be regarded as contrary to the general law.

Although the test of an enforceable custom has been laid down by precedent, it is of the essence of the idea of custom that it can be binding without judicial recognition. Explicit recognition of a custom is very rare, but one modern example is *Stirling Park & Co v Digby Brown and Co* 1996 SLT (Sh Ct) 17. A firm of solicitors, as agents for a client, instructed sheriff officers to serve a charge and carry out a 'poinding' (that is, impounding a debtor's goods) in order to recover a debt. The solicitors did not pay the sheriff officers' fees and expenses, and were sued. On appeal a Sheriff Principal held there was a custom to that effect 'so certain, uniform, notorious and reasonable' as to be binding on the solicitors, as if it were part of a contract.

Legislation may implicitly or explicitly delegate to custom, as when a statute uses words such as 'reasonable', which give judges a wide interpretive discretion. For example, by virtue of s 8(4)(a) of the Employment Rights Act 1996, part of the test of whether an employee was unfairly dismissed is that the employer 'in the circumstances ... acted reasonably ...'. In applying this test, judges have regard to what is commonly called 'custom and practice', that is, what is commonly regarded as acceptable in that employment.

In addition, custom-like rights may be recognised in other ways. Rights of way, for example, may arise from prescription, that is,

---

23 *Anderson v McCall* (1866) 4 M 765.
24 Erskine I, 1, 44.
25 *Bruce v Smith* (1890) 17 R 1000.
26 *Bruce v Smith* (1890) 17 R 1000; *McAra v Edinburgh Magistrates* 1913 SC 1059, (1913) 2 SLT 110; *Royal Four Towns Fishing Association v Dumfriesshire Assessor* 1956 SC 379, 1956 SLT 217.

continuous use over a period, now fixed by statute at 20 years[27]. Also, trade practices may be incorporated into a contract.

Most important of all, however, as a 'historical source', custom may affect the law in a major fashion without being explicitly recognised. Judges' views of what people, generally or within a particular milieu, consider acceptable will influence the way they take their decisions, both in applying and developing precedent, and in statutory interpretation. An example may be Lord Atkin's implicit, but clear, adoption of Christian morality in his 'neighbour test'[28] in *Donoghue v Stevenson* 1932 SC(HL) 31.

QUASI-SOURCES

5.24 As well as the major and minor sources of law, there are also what are called here 'quasi-sources'. This term refers to a great and amorphous variety of rules and principles which are not unequivocally law, which therefore do not fit into the generally accepted categories of formal sources of law, but which are nevertheless connected to law, look like law, or are treated much as if they were law.

Constitutional conventions

5.25 One of the most important types of quasi-source is constitutional conventions. The United Kingdom has no single document called 'the constitution'. Constitutional laws, therefore, are found in the same sources as other laws, chiefly legislation (such as the Scotland Act 1998) and precedent. There are no fundamental laws such as exist in, for example, Germany and the United States[29]. Unwritten rules affect the way in which the constitution operates in practice in all states, no doubt. Because of the unwritten nature of the United Kingdom constitution, these unwritten rules, usually

---

27 Prescription and Limitation (Scotland) Act 1973, s 3.
28 See Matthew xix, 19 and the Catechism in the (English) Book of Common Prayer.
29 But it has been argued that various documents, such as the Acts of Union of the two Parliaments which created Great Britain in 1707, in fact form at least part of a constitution, and are fundamental law. Also, accession to the European Community has considerably altered the constitutional map, and the EC and EU Treaties bear to be the constitution of the United Kingdom as well as any other document. Further, the embedded position of the Human Rights Act (see Ch 7) was intended to make it, in some sense, fundamental.

termed 'conventions of the constitution', have assumed special significance.

For example, there is no law requiring there to be a Prime Minister, let alone stipulating how a person is to be appointed to the office. In law there is simply a power on the part of the Sovereign to appoint ministers. Nevertheless, there is an unwritten rule, a constitutional convention, that the Sovereign will appoint the person who can command a majority of the votes on an issue of confidence in the House of Commons[30]. Indeed, it is only by convention that members of the government must normally have a seat in one or other House of Parliament[31] and that the Speaker of the House of Commons is an impartial chairman once elected to that office by the House, although invariably an MP who is a member of a political party. Another important convention is that the Sovereign should not refuse assent to a Bill which has passed both Houses of Parliament. Indeed, the role of the Sovereign as one who 'reigns but does not rule', that is, one who acts in accordance with the basic constitutional conventions, has grown up by convention only.

Conventions are created by behaviour which becomes strictly observed because thought to be right, but by the same token can be tacitly altered by simple non-observation. For example, until the beginning of the 20th century, the convention was that a Prime Minister might be a member of either House, as long as his party had a majority in the House of Commons. Thus, the Marquess of Salisbury was Prime Minister from 1895 to 1902 because the Conservative Party had a majority in the Commons. However, at some time in the 20th century, it became accepted that the Prime Minister must be a member of the elected House, and the convention altered, so no peer has been thought eligible since at least the middle of that century. Indeed, the Earl of Home renounced his peerage in 1963 and successfully sought election for Kinross and West Perthshire solely in order to be eligible to become Prime Minister (an aim he achieved shortly thereafter).

The Scottish Parliament and Government may be expected to develop practices which will be observed with a sense of duty and so become constitutional conventions. The relationship between them and the United Kingdom Parliament and government will, if it is to

---

30 To command a majority in the House of Commons requires in practice that one be an MP, and leader of the party which won the last general election. As party leaders are elected by party members according to various rules, it is an interesting question as to whether such party rules are part of the constitution of the United Kingdom, and thus quasi-sources.

31 This convention has occasionally not been observed for brief periods, and the ease of creating life peers provides a means of avoiding embarrassment.

be harmonious, require to be regulated by fresh conventions. The 'Sewel Convention', discussed in Chapter 7, provides one example of such a development.

Constitutional conventions are certainly not enforceable by courts, but can be argued to be law in so far as they are respected and acted upon and thus, like laws, have a certain obligatory character. Like a jigsaw, they interlock with one another and so give a certain coherence to the public life of a society. They are part of the political morality of the state. Indeed, 'unconstitutional' in the United Kingdom more readily fits a breach of convention than one of ordinary law.

Administrative quasi-legislation

5.26 Governments produce among other things, guidance, guidelines, advice, plans, information upon their intentions, and so on. Various regulatory agencies set up by government do likewise. Within this mass of communications there are rules and principles, not contained in legislation, but intended to be acted upon, and often directed to officials. Indeed, the process is sometimes referred to as administrative rule-making or (somewhat misleadingly, insofar as the point is that it is not law) 'soft law'[32]. To some extent, its growth parallels that of delegated legislation, for it has increased through an increase in the activities of government and regulatory agencies, but it may also have grown through a desire to influence activities through self-regulation rather than directly.

On the other hand, some of this guidance etc reflects a need for comprehensibility, which the United Kingdom style of legislative drafting does not promote, and is aimed at the general public, or those engaging in particular occupations or activities.

There are concerns over the growth of administrative quasi-legislation. While legislation comes under Parliamentary and other scrutiny (albeit sometimes of a limited kind), quasi-legislation may come under less or none. Indeed, it may actually be secret, and in any case may be seen as reflecting too cosy a relationship between government and some interest-groups. Although any government must be entitled to produce internal rules for its civil servants, some quasi-legislation may appear to be legislation by government, outside the royal prerogative and without recourse to Parliament.

---

32 The learned editor of the entry on Legislation in *The Laws of Scotland: Stair Memorial Encyclopaedia of the Laws of Scotland* vol 22, paras 233ff used the phrase 'ersatz legislation' ('Ersatz, *m.* substitute ...' Chambers New German Dictionary).

This quasi-legislation includes many types of communication, including codes of practice, professional codes of conduct, government circulars, and perhaps the Citizen's Charter.

Codes of practice

5.27 The Highway Code is a well-known example, though not necessarily typical, of a code of practice, one form of administrative quasi-legislation which is increasingly common. Such codes are in general relatively brief, but systematic and reasonably comprehensive sets of precepts, produced by government or a regulatory agency, and addressed to the public. They are produced in order to allow a particular activity to be carried out more safely, or better in some other way, so are written in standard English for the layman rather than in watertight drafting for the lawyer and judge.

Usually they are required or permitted by an Act of Parliament, and may require parliamentary approval. They are not, however, legislation, but paraphrases or interpretations of it, or embellishments upon it. They have varying legal force. Some offer only guidance, and are wholly unenforceable, as, for example, the Secretary of State's 'guidance' to be issued under the Transport Act 1985, s 125 in relation to the transport needs of disabled persons. Others are indirectly enforceable, for example, the Highway Code. The Road Traffic Act 1988, s 38 (7) stipulates that a breach of the Highway Code renders no-one liable to criminal proceedings, but may be relied upon in civil or criminal proceedings to assist in establishing liability. In short, failure to signal a right turn, for example, is not an offence, but if an accident occurs in the course of such a manoeuvre, it can be used to help prove the offence of careless driving or negligence creating liability to compensate somebody injured. Other examples of codes, breach of which may result in some form of liability, are the code of practice on the employment of the disabled under the Equality Act 2010, and the ACAS Code of Practice on Disciplinary and Grievance Procedures, which under s 207A of the Trade Union and Labour Relations (Consolidation) Act 1992 courts and tribunals are bound to 'take into account'.

Professional codes of conduct

5.28 Suppliers of services organised as a profession often have a registration procedure as a precondition of practice, and a code of conduct, breach of which may be punished, and may even result in deregistration. It is part of the orthodox notion of a profession that the code of conduct is produced and enforced by the profession itself. This is modified in some cases by legislation requiring and otherwise controlling such a code.

For example, under ss 34, 35 and 53 of the Solicitors (Scotland) Act 1980 (as amended), the Law Society of Scotland is required to make such rules, usually called practice rules and accounts rules. Breach, judged by the independent Scottish Solicitors' Discipline Tribunal, may constitute professional misconduct, attracting one of a range of penalties, including 'striking off the roll', that is deregistration. (This procedure is more fully dealt with in Chapter 14.)

Government circulars

5.29 Government circulars form a miscellaneous category of quasi-legislation, comprising a variety of advice and guidance, diversely titled, issued as a formal letter to officials in central or local government, or in the National Health Service, or to police, or otherwise. Some are very important, for example, Crown Office Circulars to procurators fiscal are presumed (for they are secret) to detail procedures to be followed and how discretion is to be exercised in prosecuting offences. At the other extreme, Scottish Home and Health Department Circular 6/1992 (ref: CPF/2/7) dated 30 April 1992 to chief executives of islands and district councils informed them of rates of travelling and subsistence allowances to be paid to justices of the peace.

Circulars are not legislation, so cannot vary the enacted law. Thus, in *Inglis v British Airports Authority* 1978 SLT (Lands Tr) 30, a woman claimed compensation for depreciation in the value of her house by reason of the construction of a new runway at Edinburgh Airport. The Airports Authority resisted her claim, relying on advice as to its obligations contained in the Scottish Development Department Memorandum No 85/1973. The Lands Tribunal described the memorandum as 'an administrative circular', and decided it was mere guidance to public authorities as to the scope of the relevant legislation on compensation, and could not be used as an aid to construe the wording of a statute. So compensation was awarded.

There are few other cases directly in point, but some decisions from the Appellate Committee of the House of Lords (now the Supreme Court of the United Kingdom) in English cases broadly support the conclusion. In *Gillick v West Norfolk and Wisbech Area*

Health Authority [1986] AC 112, the health authority, following advice from the Department of Health and Social Security in Circular HSC(IS)32 (memorandum of guidance on family planning), gave contraceptive advice to young people, including those under 16. Mrs Gillick (who had five children under 16) sought a declaration that this was unlawful. Although this point was not the main issue in the case, the Appellate Committee of the House of Lords concluded that it could issue a declaration correcting erroneous advice on the law issued by government departments in a public, non-statutory document such as a circular. This clearly involved concluding that such legal advice could be wrong, and that a circular could not alter the law.

However, it is certainly the case that some circulars can be enforced indirectly. For example, if local planning authorities ignore planning circulars, their decisions can be overturned on appeal.

Also, circulars addressed by central government to civil servants are from the Crown to Crown servants, and from employers to employees, and may be enforced through disciplinary proceedings[33]. Thus, in *Palmer v Inverness Hospitals Board* 1963 SC 311 a circular of the Department of Health concerning hospital disciplinary proceedings was held to create a right to a hearing, which could be read as part of the contract of employment of a dismissed house surgeon. In *Tehrani v Argyll and Clyde Health Board (No 1)* 1989 SLT 851 the suspension of a hospital consultant on full pay in accordance with a Scottish Home and Health Department circular was not disputed, but in the absence of reasons and the brief duration of the suspension beyond that envisaged in the circular were held to be not unreasonable.

Chartermarks and benchmarks

5.30 One interesting example of quasi-legislation emerged through the 'Citizens' Charters', an idea produced by the Conservative Government of the early 1990s, and adopted by the Labour Government of the late 1990s, designed as a means of setting and raising standards in the provision of public sector services by mechanisms such as performance targets, publication of information, and encouragement of means of complaint and redress. There are

---

33 See *R v Ponting* [1985] Crim LR 318.

now some hundreds of 'national charters', from HM Revenue and Customs 'Travellers [*sic*] Charter' for travellers entering the United Kingdom, to Scotrail's 'Passengers' Charter' for customers on its train services.

Such charters, while indicating good practice, and how to complain about service, do not create legal rights or new means of redress in themselves, however. Nor do they have any parliamentary approval.

6 Legislation – European Union law

THE INSTITUTIONAL BACKGROUND

6.1   The institutional background of European Union institutions is discussed in Chapter 3 (among other things, distinguishing them from the Council of Europe and the European Convention on Human Rights). This Chapter deals with the meaning and types of European Union ('EU') law, the EU legislative processes, the relationship between EU law and national systems in general and with United Kingdom law in particular, and with the publication and citation of EU law.

THE MEANING, TYPES AND STYLE OF EU LAW

The meaning of 'EU law'

6.2   As discussed in Chapter 3, the European Community was set up by various Treaties in order to promote certain aims. The most important aims were explicitly stated in the opening Articles of the original European Economic Community Treaty of 1957, which, as amended and now called the Treaty on the Functioning of the European Union ('TFEU'), remain in force. The Preamble speaks of the intention 'to lay the foundations of an ever closer union among the peoples of Europe', and the Treaty Articles specify numerous policies to that end, including free movement between Member States of goods, persons, capital and services, and non-discrimination against their nationals on the ground of nationality or sex.

In order to fulfil these aims, the Treaties do something of enormous significance, that is, they give the EU the power to make its own law. EU law is thus a 'separate legal order' from those of the Member States. However, EU law exists only for the purpose of achieving the aims specified, so any piece of EU legislation might be *ultra vires*, that is, beyond the powers granted to the EU's institutions by the various Treaties, and thereby invalid[1]. It is important to realise that anything done within the EU must be justified by reference to a Treaty provision. Nevertheless, the EU's aims are so broad, and so broadly interpreted by the Court of Justice of the European Union ('CJEU'), that this is not a major limitation in practice. The remit of the EU with regard to law making has expanded greatly and will most likely continue to do so in years to come.

EU law and the European Convention on Human Rights

6.3   The European Convention on Human Rights ('ECHR') is fully considered in Chapters 3 and 4. However, here it should be noted that, although the ECHR and its institutions are separate from the EU and its institutions (and the EU has its own 'Charter of Fundamental Rights'), the former may be enforceable through the latter.

In Case 11/70 *Internationale Handelsgesellschaft* [1970] ECR 1125, the European Court of Justice ('ECJ') (not the European Court of Human Rights) held, in a creative decision, that respect for the fundamental freedoms enshrined in the ECHR was an integral part of the general principles of law which it had to uphold. In Case 4/73 *Nold* [1974] ECR 491, the Court went further and declared that international Treaties for the protection of human rights to which Member States were signatory could supply guidelines to be followed within the framework of Community law (now known as EU law). A United Kingdom case, Case C-63/83 *R v Kirk* [1984] ECR 2689, concerned penalties for illegal fishing. Regulation 170/83 appeared to permit a retrospective penalty, but the court interpreted the Regulation to exclude this, expressly by reference to Article 7 (non-retroactivity of criminal law) of the ECHR.

---

1   Articles 263 and 264 TFEU (ex Articles 230 and 231) allow the CJEU to review the legality of acts of the Commission, the Council and the European Central Bank on specified grounds including *ultra vires*, and to declare them void. For example, the UK sought to have the 'Working Time Directive' (EC) 93/104 (which imposes regulation of working hours, rest breaks, night work and annual leave) set aside as *ultra vires* because it was based on Art 118a of the Treaty (now Art 154: which concerned health and safety at work and required only a qualified majority vote, from which the United Kingdom in fact abstained), when it should have been based on Art 100 or Art 235 (now Arts 115 and 352 post-Lisbon) which allow legislation to fulfil the purposes of the Treaty in areas not specifically covered, and requires unanimity, and thus could be vetoed by the United Kingdom). In Case C–84/95 *UK v EU Council (working time)* [1996] 3 CMLR 671, the ECJ rejected the argument on the facts, however, as health and safety were the essential objectives of the Directive.

Therefore, EU law will be applied by the CJEU subject to the ECHR. As such decisions are binding on the courts of Member States, Scots courts must loyally apply the same principle when deciding EU law cases. The EU is negotiating accession to the ECHR in its own right at the time of writing (January 2013).

Types of EU legislation and their forms

6.4 Four types of EU legislation can be said to exist: Treaties; Regulations; Directives; and Decisions.

Treaties

6.5 The Treaties, sometimes referred to as the EU's 'primary legislation', form its constitution (although some parts concern very detailed provisions of other sorts, for instance on customs duties). They have lengthy names, but are often referred to by abbreviations, such as 'the TFEU'. The principal ones[2] are:

- the European Economic Community Treaty of 1957 (the EEC Treaty, once often referred to as the Treaty of Rome, but now, after many amendments, referred to as the Treaty on the Functioning of the European Union ('TFEU'));
- the Merger Treaty of 1965;
- the First Accession Treaty of 1972, and subsequent Accession Treaties;
- the Single European Act ('SEA') of 1986;
- the Treaty on European Union ('TEU', often referred to as 'the Maastricht Treaty') of 1992;
- the Treaty of Amsterdam ('ToA') of 1997;
- the Treaty of Nice ('ToN') of 2000; and
- the Treaty of Lisbon ('ToL') of 2007.

The original EEC Treaty was drawn up in the four languages of the original six Member States. More recent Treaties are drawn up in the official language of each Member State. Each version has to

---

2 For the purpose and significance of these Treaties, see Ch 3. Other Treaties entered into by the Community (such as the Lomé Convention, with West African states), and possibly some entered into between Member States (such as the Convention on Jurisdiction and Enforcement of Judgments) are also relevant. Other agreements, such as the 'Luxembourg Accord', by which Member States promised informally not to exercise majority voting where one of them claims its vital national interests are involved, are not Treaties.

be equally authentic, which has caused problems where there are discrepancies.

The form of all the principal Treaties is broadly similar. They start with a series of statements of purposes[3]. They may be divided into Parts, subdivided into 'Titles' and 'Chapters'[4], but the basic unit is the Article. Articles are usually numbered sequentially throughout, ignoring the parts, titles etc. The Treaty of Lisbon renumbered the Articles of the principal Treaties as well as renaming the former EC Treaty. This means that commonly Articles are referred to by both pre- and post- Lisbon numbers, as, for example, 'Article 28 TFEU (formerly Article 23)' or 'Article 267 TFEU (ex Article 234). To avoid confusion between Treaties, Articles may be referred to as, for example, 'Article 25 TEU' or 'Article 25 TFEU' to identify the Treaty in question.

The Articles may be brief or lengthy[5], and may be divided into paragraphs and sub-paragraphs. These in turn may be identified by number and letter in the United Kingdom fashion (for example, Article 45(3)(b) TFEU (ex Article 39(3)(b)) or otherwise (for example, Article 49 TFEU (ex Article 43) which has two paragraphs identified by neither number nor letter, while Article 46 TFEU (ex Article 40) has no numbered paragraphs, but four lettered ones expanding upon the first). This can make citation of specific passages difficult[6]. Commonly the Treaties also have numbered 'Annexes' and unnumbered 'Protocols'. These are essentially Schedules, containing material too detailed or too specific for the body of a Treaty, though they may reflect the fact that unanimity was not achieved on a matter, but the majority are going ahead anyway as between themselves[7].

---

3 The TFEU Preamble commences 'Determined to lay the foundations of an ever closer union among the peoples of Europe ... ', and the opening Articles specify the establishment of a common market, and a variety of specific policies to that and other ends, such as the elimination of customs duties, and the approximation of the laws of Member States

4 The TFEU is divided into seven numbered and named 'Parts', 'PART ONE – Principles', 'PART TWO – Non-discrimination and Citizenship of the Union' etc. Parts One, Three, Five and Six are divided into 'Titles', several of which are divided into 'Chapters', and some of those even further into 'Sections'.

5 The TFEU has over 350 articles.

6 Thus, there may be circumlocutions such as 'point (1)(b) of the first sub-paragraph of Article 63'.

7 The TFEU and TEU jointly have 37 Protocols, including specific material such as the Statute of the Court of Justice of the European Union (Third Protocol), but also others recording the special position of the United Kingdom, Ireland and Denmark who declined to accept certain aspects of freedom of movement of persons (Twentieth to Twenty-fifth Protocols).

As is common with Treaties generally, some Articles are simple exhortation. Others are specific enough to be applied by courts, and may therefore have 'direct effect' (for which, see below).

Article 288 (ex Article 249) specifically permits the institutions (see Chapter 3), under various powers elsewhere in the Treaty, to make Regulations, Directives and Decisions, which are collectively referred to as 'acts', but sometimes colloquially as 'secondary legislation'. The difference between each type is significant for the legal effect they have in Member States, which is dealt with below.

Regulations

6.6 Regulations[8] are the principal means by which the EU legislates, and there are thousands made every year[9].

Regulations start with a title in a form exemplified in the following: 'COMMISSION REGULATION (EEC) No 417/85 of 19 December 1985 on the application of Article 85(3) of the Treaty to categories of specialization agreements'. There follows a preamble opening with the name of the initiating institution and closing with the formula indicating enactment, for example, 'THE COMMISSION OF THE EUROPEAN COMMUNITIES ... HAS ADOPTED THIS REGULATION'. These two items are separated by a recital of the Treaty provisions giving authority for the Regulation to be made, the consultative procedure followed, and the reasoning which has produced the proposal, in a series of statements, possibly covering more than a page, and beginning 'Having regard to ... ' or 'Whereas ... '.

This lengthy preliminary exists because Article 296 (ex Article 253) requires legislative acts of the EU to state the reasons on which they are based and to refer to any proposals or opinions required by the relevant Treaty to be obtained. This in turn allows the CJEU to review the validity of them[10].

---

8 The name 'Regulation' is also given to one type of UK delegated legislation (for which, see Ch 9). The two should not be confused.

9 In 2012 there were over 1,000 Regulations.

10 Regulation (EC) 3595/85 concerned tariff preferences for developed countries. In Case 45/86 *Council v Commission* [1987] ECR 1493 (the 'Generalised Tariffs case'), the ECJ annulled the Regulation because the recital was insufficiently concise, clear and relevant on the relevant issues of law and fact. Directive (EC) 86/113 concerned minimum sizes for battery hens' cages. Community officials altered the reasons recited after the Council of Ministers had approved it. The United Kingdom successfully challenged the validity of this Directive on this ground in Case 131/86 *United Kingdom v EC Council* [1988] 2 CMLR 364.

The actual provisions of the regulation follow in numbered Articles, often grouped into 'sections' or 'titles', in much the same fashion as in the Treaties. The last Article usually declares the date on which the regulation comes into force, but if there is no declaration, then by virtue of Article 297 (ex Article 254) it comes into force on the twentieth day following publication in the *Official Journal*. Unless a Regulation stipulates that it is to cease having effect on a certain date, it continues in force until amended or repealed.

After the body of the text, a Regulation has the formula: 'This Regulation shall be binding in its entirety and directly applicable in all Member States', which reproduces part of Article 288 (ex Article 249), and indicates its 'direct effect'. Regulations terminate with a statement of the place and date of its making, and the name of the Commissioner responsible.

Directives

6.7   Directives are much less frequent than Regulations[11], but no less important. They were originally intended to be policy statements delivered by former Community institutions to a particular Member State government or to Member State governments generally. However, they may be drafted to leave little discretion to the Member State and, as a result of creative adjudication by the CJEU, the distinction between Regulations and Directives is now blurred.

The form of a Directive is much the same as that of a Regulation[12]. By virtue of Article 288 (ex Article 249), Directives take effect from the date of notification to Member States, but because they may require action on the part of Member States, a period for implementation, often two years, is allowed. Directives also finish with a different formula from Regulations, reflecting their different original purpose, as follows: 'This Directive is addressed to the Member States'.

Decisions

6.8   Decisions of which there are hundreds made each year[13], were originally intended to be individualised executive decisions,

---

11 In 2012 there were over 50.
12 For example, 'EIGHTH COUNCIL DIRECTIVE of 10 April 1984 based on article 54(3)(g) of the Treaty on the approval of persons responsible for carrying out the statutory audits of accounting documents (85/253/EEC)'. They are sometimes given more memorable colloquial names, such as 'the Equal Treatment Directive' (76/207).
13 In 2012 there were just under 800.

addressed by EU institutions to Member States, companies or individuals. Most are of limited scope and importance, but some have laid down rules rather like Regulations so, as with Directives, the distinction between them and Regulations may be blurred.

The form of Decisions is essentially the same as Regulations. As with Directives, a Decision applies only to its addressees, and takes effect upon notification to them. They usually end with the words 'This Decision is addressed to ... ', followed by the words 'Member States', or a particular addressee or addressees, such as 'the Federal Republic of Germany and the United Kingdom'.

Other Community documents

6.9 The institutions may also, by virtue of Article 288 (ex Article 249) make Recommendations and deliver Opinions but these are not legally binding.

Some other types of document have exceptionally been held to be legislative when the ECJ has sought to further EU aims at the expense of legal exactitude[14].

The content of such documents is sometimes referred to as 'soft law' which is a misleading term since they are not law at all.

THE EU LEGISLATIVE PROCESSES

Legislative powers of the EU and the EU legislative process

6.10 Authority to make EU legislation, and the method of legislation, must be found in the Treaties. Some Articles of the Treaties give specific powers to the Commission and the Council of Ministers to legislate. However, since the Treaty of Lisbon there

---

14 For example, a Resolution of the Council of Ministers in Case 22/70 *Commission v Council (the ERTA case)* [1971] ECR 263, [1971] CMLR 335. An interesting example is the United Kingdom 'Declaration' as to who are 'United Kingdom nationals' for the purpose of free movement of workers within the old Community. This was appended to the United Kingdom Treaty of Accession. The definition, like the title, was different from any existing form of United Kingdom nationality. The declaration was amended in 1982 to take account of the British Nationality Act 1981 (see OJ C23, 28.1.1983: also Cmnd 9062). It is a unilateral declaration, and not a Treaty, nor a United Kingdom statute, nor had Parliamentary approval, nor was a decision of a court. However, the ECJ accepted it in *R v Secretary of State for the Home Department, ex parte Manjit Kaur* [2001] ECR I–1237.

is now a far greater role for the European Parliament within the legislative process of the EU. This has been done deliberately with the aim of providing more popular accountability and legitimacy to EU legislation. The Parliament is the only EU institution to be directly elected by the public and it was felt that this should be recognised.

Ordinary legislative procedure (formerly co-decision procedure)[15]

6.11   The co-decision procedure was introduced by the Maastricht Treaty on European Union, and extended by the Amsterdam Treaty. The Treaty of Lisbon renamed co-decision procedure, 'ordinary legislative procedure'. This is now the main legislative procedure of the EU.

The procedure puts the European Parliament and the Council of the European Union on an equal footing for decision-making on a wide range of areas including economic governance, immigration, energy, transport, the environment and consumer protection. Nowadays, the vast majority of European laws are adopted following this procedure.

The Commission still comes up with legislative proposals and passes these to the European Parliament and the Council of the European Union. From there, the proposal is considered and discussed twice by the European Parliament and the Council of the European Union. If no agreement is reached on the proposal it is brought before a Conciliation Committee made up of an equal number of representatives of the European Parliament and the Council of the European Union. Representatives of the Commission also attend the meetings of the Conciliation Committee and contribute to the discussions.

Once agreement is reached, the proposed legislation is sent back to the European Parliament and the Council of the European Union for a third reading, so that the legislation can be adopted. Parliament now has the power to reject the proposed legislation if the majority vote against the proposed legislation on the third reading.

'Co-operation procedure'

6.12   The Amsterdam Treaty introduced the co-operation procedure which allows Member States to establish closer co-operation with one

15 Article 294 TFEU (ex Article 251).

another in areas covered by the Treaties. Areas of exclusive European Union competence cannot be subject to a proposal of Member States for co-operation. The Commission is tasked with assessing proposals and taking them to the Council of the European Union for authorisation to proceed. The Commission can choose not to present a proposal but must explain its reasons to the Member States concerned. If the Commission presents a proposal to the Council of the European Union, the European Parliament's consent must be obtained for the proposal to be approved.

The situation is somewhat different for the common foreign and security policy. Co-operation requests are sent to the Council of the European Union who must seek the opinion of the High Representative for Foreign Affairs and Security Policy and the Commission. The European Parliament is kept informed throughout the process.

Consultation procedure

6.13 Article 289 TFEU (ex Article 249) provides for a consultation procedure for passing legislation in the EU. The Council of the European Union will ask the European Parliament for its opinion on proposed legislation before it can be adopted. The European Parliament's opinion does not bind the Council of the European Union but the latter cannot act without having taken this step. This procedure is used in legislative areas such as internal market exemptions and competition law. The European Parliament's opinion must also be sought, where international agreements are being adopted under the Common Foreign and Security Policy ('CFSP').

Consent

6.14 A further legislative procedure is the consent procedure (formerly known as the assent procedure). The Council of the European Union must request the European Parliament's consent under Article 289(2) TFEU (ex Article 249) for certain non-legislative agreements and also legislative proposals regarding combating discrimination. The European Parliament can approve or reject the legislative proposal and the Council of the European Union cannot act if the European Parliament rejects the proposal. Consent is also required as a non-legislative procedure when the Council of the European Union is adopting certain international agreements or for accession and withdrawal of Member States.

The role of the Court of Justice of the European Union ('CJEU')

6.15 The CJEU may hear an enforcement action brought by the Commission against a Member State appearing not to be fulfilling its EU obligations (for example, by failing to implement a Directive). It may also hear a preliminary reference under Article 267 (ex Article 234) from a national court or tribunal with a view to ensuring consistent decisions on validity and interpretation throughout the EU and some other types of action.

The full importance of Article 267 (ex Article 234) depends upon the principle of 'direct effect' of EU law.

THE RELATIONSHIP OF EU LAW TO NATIONAL SYSTEMS IN GENERAL, AND UNITED KINGDOM LAW IN PARTICULAR

The relationship between EU law and national systems in general

6.16 The Treaties give remarkably little explicit guidance on the effect EU legislation is to have on Member States' own law.

Direct applicability, primacy and direct effect

6.17 Regulations are said in Article 288 (ex Article 249) to be 'binding' and 'directly applicable'. This was intended to mean that they should be incorporated into national law without national legislation, unlike Directives (which though 'binding upon Member States' were intended to be incorporated by way of national legislation), and also unlike Decisions (which are 'binding upon those to whom [they] are addressed').

However, certain ideas were implicit in the structure of EU law, and the ECJ ingeniously built upon them in various decisions[16]. 'Primacy' is thus regarded as a basic principle, that is, that EU law is intended to supersede national law where the two conflict.

Further, EU legislation is intended, provided that certain conditions are fulfilled, to have 'direct effect'. This term does not

---

16 Chiefly Case 26/62 *Van Gend en Loos* [1963] ECR ; Case 6/64 *Costa v ENEL* [1964] ECR 585; Case 11/70 *Internationale Handelsgesellschaft* [1970] ECR 1125; and Case 106/77 *Simmenthal (No 2)* [1978] ECR 629.

appear in any of the Treaties, but is hallowed by usage. It means that individuals may bring and defend cases in court on the basis of legislation if it has that characteristic.

These ideas taken together involve that, at least in EU law terms:

(a) EU legislation can be law in every Member State;
(b) it may be so without the need for national legislation;
(c) it may therefore be so against the wishes of the national legislature;
(d) such EU legislation supersedes any existing contrary national law;
(e) the existence of such EU legislation prevents a national legislature from passing valid contrary legislation in future;
(f) EU legislation is applied by the ordinary courts and tribunals of the Member State;
(g) the ordinary courts of the Member State must apply such EU legislation even if there is contrary national law;
(h) such EU legislation may, under appropriate circumstances, be invoked before ordinary national courts by individuals and companies against other individuals and companies, and against Member States.

These conclusions can be exemplified by Case 26/62 *Van Gend en Loos* [1963] ECR 1. Community law (as it was then), in the form of the then Article 25 (now Article 30) obliged Member States not to raise existing customs duties. However, the Dutch government altered the law to raise them in respect of certain chemicals. Van Gend en Loos was a company which had to pay the higher rate. It therefore sued the Dutch government. On a then Article 234 (now Article 267) preliminary reference, the question of the relationship of national law (here Dutch) and Community law went to the ECJ (now CJEU). It decided that Article 25 (now Article 30), being clear and unconditional, had 'direct effect' and that the Treaty provision took precedence over Dutch law. Thus, the Dutch tax tribunal hearing the case had to ignore Dutch law, and apply Community law instead.

In practice, national courts may apply EU law without the rigour the CJEU would like. On the other hand, the Court has not yet exhausted its ingenuity, as *Francovich* and other decisions (discussed below) show.

Vertical and horizontal direct effect

6.18   Direct effect is complicated by a division into 'vertical' and 'horizontal', worked out by the Court in relation to Directives.

EU law may place an obligation with direct effect upon a Member State. If it does, but the obligation is not fulfilled, a person or company which suffers as a result can sue the Member State. This (on the assumption that the Member State is 'above' the person or company) is described as 'vertical direct effect', and *Van Gend en Loos* is an example.

EU law may place an obligation with direct effect upon a person or company. If it does, but the obligation is not fulfilled, another person or company which suffers as a result can sue the first one. This is referred to as 'horizontal direct effect' (on the assumption that the individuals or companies are on the same level). An example is Case 43/75 *Defrenne v Sabena* [1976] ECR 455. Article 141 (now Article 157) requires equal pay between the sexes. Defrenne was an air stewardess employed by Sabena, a Belgian airline. She discovered she was being paid less than the male stewards, so sued Sabena. On an Article 234 (now Article 267) preliminary reference, the ECJ (now the CJEU) held that Article 141 (now Article 157) (as well as being vertically directly effective) was directly effective as between persons and companies (that is, horizontally directly effective).

Direct effect and different types of EU legislation

6.19   The conditions under which EU legislation has direct effect are not explicitly laid down in the Treaties (nor whether it be vertical, horizontal, or both), but must be inferred from the decisions of the CJEU.

Broadly, there are two conditions necessary to create direct effect. Firstly, the legislation must be clearly and specifically enough drafted for a court to be able to apply it[17]. Secondly, it must create an unqualified right or duty and not require action by some other body before a court can apply it.

Direct effect and the Treaties. The Treaties are binding upon the signatory Member States. However, certain articles of the Treaties also have direct effect. The *Van Gend en Loos* case decided that Article 25 (now Article 30) had direct effect, although the EEC Treaty itself made no mention of its effect, and Article 25 (now Article 30) itself certainly did not say that an aggrieved person could sue a Member

17 Thus, for example, in Case C-126/86 *Gimenez Zaera* [1987] ECR 3697, Article 2 (which remains Article 2) was found to impose insufficiently precise obligations to create direct effect.

State for breach of it. Where a Treaty Article has direct effect, it is likely to be both vertical and horizontal.

Direct effect and Regulations. Regulations were undoubtedly intended to have direct effect (at least if the conditions were fulfilled). Article 288 (ex Article 249) describes a Regulation as having 'general application' and 'being binding in its entirety and directly applicable in all Member States'. Occasionally, however, a Regulation is drafted in unspecific language, or requires action by another body before a court could apply it, so is not directly effective[18].

Direct effect and Directives. Directives are in a more complicated and uncertain position. Article 288 (ex Article 249) says they are 'binding as to the result to be achieved, upon each Member State to which [they] are addressed, but shall leave to the national authorities the choice of form and methods', and time for implementation (perhaps two years) is given. As this implies, originally they were not intended to be directly effective, for they apparently require action by some other body (the national authorities) before a court could apply them.

However, Member States have a poor record of compliance with them, and the ECJ (now the CJEU), in a number of major cases in the 1970s such as Case 41/74 *Van Duyn* [1974] ECR 1337[19], inventively reinterpreted the law to give them direct effect in certain circumstances. Directives are now regarded as directly effective provided they are sufficiently clear and specific, require no specific action by another body, and their time limit for implementation has expired.

But because Directives are addressed to Member States, they have been held only vertically directly effective, and not horizontally. This was settled in Case 152/84 *Marshall v Southampton and South West*

18 Case C–403/98 *Azienda Agricola Monte Arcosu Srl v Regione Autonoma della Sardegna* [2001] ECR I–103.
19 Free movement of workers between member states is a fundamental principle of the EU, enshrined in Articles 45–47 (ex Articles 30–41), and given flesh by Regulations and Directives. Directive 64/221 allowed a Member State to limit this free movement on grounds of public policy if the personal conduct of the individual warranted it. Van Duyn was a Dutch Scientologist. Scientology is a quasi-religious cult employing pseudo-scientific learning, invented by L Ron Hubbard, an American science-fiction writer. The Home Office wished to discourage Scientology without banning it, and refused van Duyn leave to enter. She sued the United Kingdom government to vindicate her right to free movement. The ECJ (on an Article 267 (ex Article 234) preliminary reference) upheld her argument, declaring the Directive directly effective, and therefore nullifying any contrary UK law.

Area Health Authority [1986] ECR 723. Marshall was a dietician employed by the health authority. She was required to retire at the age of 62, although men were not required to do so until the age of 65. National legislation, the Sex Discrimination Act 1975 s 6(2), expressly permitted this discrimination. A Directive, the 'Equal Treatment Directive' (76/207), did not. The ECJ, on an Article 234 (now Article 267) preliminary reference, held the differential breached the Directive, and that where the employee was employed by a public body, she was employed by the Member State (to which the Directive was addressed). It was therefore in breach of EU law and the public body employer could be sued. However, a private employer cannot breach a Directive, because it is addressed to, and therefore binding only upon, Member States[20]. Thus, in general terms, an individual or ordinary commercial company cannot be sued for breach of a Directive.

However, in Cases C–6/90 and C–9/90 *Francovich v Italy* [1991] ECR I–5357, the Court was again inventive and decided that where a Member State has failed to implement a Directive, it may be liable to pay compensation to individuals harmed by non-implementation. Directive 80/987 required Member States to approximate laws guaranteeing the protection of employees' unpaid remuneration upon insolvency of the employer. The ECJ held that the Directive was unspecific as to who was responsible for fulfilling the guarantees, therefore it was not directly effective. However, it also decided that the TEC (now the TFEU), in particular ex Article 10[21], made Member States liable for injury caused by their own infringements of Community law, provided that three conditions are fulfilled. They are: that the Directive gives rights to the individual; that the content of those rights can be identified from the Directive; and that it was the non-implementation which caused the harm complained of. This reduces the importance of the vertical/horizontal distinction, and provides possible enforcement even where a Directive has no direct effect. Indeed, yet further cases have blurred the very distinction between 'vertical' and 'horizontal' direct effect.

In addition, in another line of cases including Case C-14/83 *Von*

---

20 A question remains as to what organisations are part of the Member State for this purpose. In Case C–188/89 *Foster v British Gas* [1991] 1 QB 405, the ECJ decided (and the old House of Lords therefore held) that British Gas, when still nationalised, was so. The English Court of Appeal, applying the test laid down by the ECJ in *Doughty v Rolls-Royce plc* [1992] 1 CMLR 1045, CA, held that Rolls-Royce, when in form a commercial company, but wholly owned by the government, was not.

21 'Member States shall take all appropriate measures, whether general or particular, to ensure fulfilment of the obligations arising out of this Treaty ...'.

Colson & Kamann v Land Nordrhein-Westfalen [1984] ECR 1891 ('Van Colson') and Case C–106/89 *Marleasing SA v La Comercial Internacionale de Alimentacion SA* [1990] ECR I–4135 ('*Marleasing*'), the ECJ was developing another principle. This is that, because Directives were addressed to Member States, they were addressed to all organs of the Member State. Courts, as one such organ, should therefore decide cases 'in the light of directives', even if the Directives were unimplemented. This is sometimes called 'indirect effect' because it falls between having direct effect and not having direct effect.

Direct effect and decisions. Decisions were originally intended to be essentially executive decisions. Article 288 (ex Article 249) declares a Decision to be 'binding in its entirety upon those to whom it is addressed'. Nevertheless, in Case 9/70 *Grad v Finanzamt Traunstein* [1970] ECR 825, the ECJ declared a Decision directly effective. The position of Decisions is probably the same as that of Directives.

The relationship between EU legislation and United Kingdom law in particular

6.20 The issues in the relationship of EU legislation and national systems described above operate in relation to all Member States. Their operation raises particular questions in the case of the United Kingdom, however. These are described below, save for the way in which statutory interpretation is affected, which is dealt with in Chapter 11.

EU legislation with direct effect and United Kingdom law

6.21 Community law (now EU law) did not become directly effective (let alone achieve primacy) in the United Kingdom as a result of the United Kingdom joining the Community by signing the Treaty of Accession in 1972. In United Kingdom law, Treaties have no effect in national law[22]. Legislation was required to change it.

That legislation was supplied by the European Communities Act 1972 (now as amended). The most important provision is s 2(1),

---

22 *The Parlement Belge* (1879) 4 PD 129; *Attorney-General for Canada v Attorney-General for Ontario* [1937] AC 326; *British Airways v Laker Airways* [1984] 3 All ER 39. For the special position of the European Convention on Human Rights, see Chs 3 & 7.

which is unfortunately drafted in turgid and dense language. The gist of it is, however, clear. It provides that all directly effective EU legislation (whether already made or to be made, and whether in Treaty, Regulation, Directive or Decision form), creates 'enforceable Community rights' (now 'enforceable EU rights'), that is, it has direct effect in the United Kingdom, and will be enforced by courts and tribunals, and that United Kingdom law is to be applied subject to it. Devolution to Scotland and elsewhere has made no difference to this.

These central provisions are supported by s 3(1) and (2). These provide firstly that judges are to be presumed to know the content and significance of the Treaties, of the *Official Journal of the European Union*[23] (in which the other legislation is published), and of decisions of the CJEU. Secondly, they provide that questions of the validity and interpretation of EU law, if not actually sent to the CJEU for an Article 267 (ex Article 234) preliminary reference, must be decided in accordance with the decisions of the court and the principles laid down by it.

In a long series of cases over the following years United Kingdom courts, chiefly the English Court of Appeal, struggled to take on board the full implications of the legislation[24].

Full acceptance of the implications of s 2(1) of the European Communities Act 1972 seems to be shown in the *Factortame* cases[25]. These cases concerned 'quota-hopping' under the old Community's fisheries policy. Spanish vessels were registered in the United Kingdom to enable them to fish the United Kingdom national quota. Parliament passed legislation introduced by the government (the Merchant Shipping Act 1988) which, together with delegated legislation under it (the Merchant Shipping (Registration of Fishing Vessels) Regulations 1988, SI 1988/1926), imposed a nationality condition upon registration. The Spanish companies adversely

---

23 Previously *Official Journal of the European Community*.
24 See, for example, *Bulmer (HP) Ltd v Bollinger (J) SA* [1974] Ch 401; *Schorsch Meier GmbH v Hennin* [1975] QB 416; *Felixstowe Docks v BT Docks Board* [1976] 2 CMLR 655; *Shields v E Coomes (Holdings) Ltd* [1979] 1 All ER 456; *Macarthys v Smith* [1979] ICR 785. The various postures of Lord Denning (who as Master of the Rolls, president of the Court of Appeal, had a pivotal role) are interesting.
25 *R v Secretary of State for Transport, ex parte Factortame* [1990] 2 AC 85 (HL); Case C-213/89 *R v Secretary of State for Transport, ex parte Factortame (No 2)* [1991] 1 AC 603 (ECJ); Case C-48/93 *R v Secretary of State, ex parte Factortame (No 4)* joined with *Brasserie du Pêcheur SA v Federal Republic of Germany* [1996] QB 404 (ECJ); and *R v Secretary of State for Transport, ex parte Factortame (No 5)* [2000] 1 AC 524 (HL).

affected sued the United Kingdom government for breach of Articles 12 (now Article 18: non-discrimination on grounds of nationality) and 48 (now Article 54: right to establish a business) of the EEC Treaty. Proceedings were lengthy and complicated, involving two preliminary references under Article 234 (now Article 267), and appeals as far as the Appellate Committee of the House of Lords (now the Supreme Court). There were also separate enforcement proceedings by the Commission[26].

The outcome, however, was that the House of Lords accepted that an Act of Parliament contradicting, and passed after, certain Community legislation, could not be enforced by United Kingdom courts. Moreover, because Community law had to be enforced, courts were entitled to issue orders carrying it out, even though national law gave no such right. This was revolutionary in that it appears to have abandoned the principle of parliamentary supremacy. Nevertheless, if Parliament decided to withdraw the United Kingdom from the EU, or explicitly and clearly passed legislation in defiance of EU law, the judges would probably still apply Parliament's expressed will in preference to EU law.

Article 267 (ex Article 234) references. United Kingdom courts have the same power and obligation as courts in any Member State to refer questions of the validity or interpretation of Community law to the CJEU under Article 267 (ex Article 234), and reference is usually discretionary. Scottish devolution has made no difference to this. When the choice exists, there is no clear authority from any United Kingdom court on when it is appropriate to refer. In an English case on Great Britain legislation, *Garland v British Rail Engineering Ltd* [1983] 2 AC 751, the Appellate Committee of the House of Lords suggested there should be reference where a novel point of law arose, or where there is no constant series of decisions from the Court.

There have been few references from Scotland. In *Walkingshaw v Marshall* 1992 SLT 1167, concerning illegal fishing, the High Court of Justiciary, on appeal from the sheriff court, made a reference. In *Westwater v Thomson* 1993 SCCR 624, also concerning illegal fishing, the High Court of Justiciary held that the point at issue was too plain to require a reference to the ECJ. In *Brown v Rentokil Ltd* 1996 SLT 839 a previous decision of the Court made a reference unnecessary.

---

26 Case C–246/89 *Commission v UK* [1991] ECR I–4585).

EU legislation without direct effect and United Kingdom law

6.22   Not all EU legislation has direct effect, but it is nevertheless intended to apply within all Member States. Directives, for example, are intended to be implemented by the Member State (although they may acquire direct effect if they are not).

Implementation may be by Act of the United Kingdom Parliament or of the Scottish Parliament. For instance, the Consumer Protection Act 1987 implements Directive 85/347, the Products Liability Directive. However, the European Communities Act 1972 (as amended), in addition to providing that direct effect should operate in the United Kingdom, also provides in s 2(2) a short-cut method of implementation of legislation which does not have direct effect. The provision is almost as difficult to understand as s 2(1). However, again, the gist is clear, for s 2(2) delegated from the United Kingdom Parliament to the United Kingdom government the power to implement any Community right (now EU right) or obligation by delegated legislation[27]. Thus, the United Kingdom government can implement a Directive without an Act of Parliament and the statutory instrument is the 'form and method' chosen to implement the Directive. This power has been widely used. An example is the Equal Pay (Amendment) Regulations 1983, SI 1983/1794, which were designed to amend the Equal Pay Act 1970 to conform to the Equal Pay Directive 75/117, after the enforcement proceedings in Case C-61/81 *Commission v United Kingdom* [1982] ICR 578.

The restrictions upon the use of s 2(2), found in s 2(4) and Sch 2, are that the power may not be used to: impose or increase taxation; make retrospective legislation; allow further delegation (unless for the making of procedural rules for courts and tribunals); or create criminal offences carrying greater than a certain penalty. Thus, any Directive requiring any of these things to be done would necessitate an Act.

The Scotland Act 1998, by s 53, transfers to the Scottish Ministers functions in relation to observing and implementing obligations under EU law, with respect to devolved functions. However, there is a reserve power in s 57(1) enabling ministers of the United Kingdom government to exercise these functions too, presumably to avoid the possibility that a failure of the Scottish Ministers to act would put the United Kingdom in breach of its EU obligations.

---

27 Commonly by Statutory Instrument (for the meaning and significance of which see, see Ch 9), but also through the Legislative and Regulatory Reform Act 2006 (for which see Ch 9).

THE RELATIONSHIP OF EU LAW TO NATIONAL SYSTEMS IN GENERAL **6.23**

Direct effect, parliamentary supremacy and the role of the United Kingdom Parliament

6.23   The primacy and direct effect of EU legislation appear irreconcilable with the parliamentary supremacy traditionally professed by the United Kingdom Parliament. (No such problem arises with the Scottish Parliament which does not profess parliamentary supremacy.) In EU law terms the United Kingdom Parliament irrevocably gave up parliamentary supremacy in the 1972 Act (if not by signing the Treaty of Accession), and the United Kingdom judges' reaction in the *Factortame* cases appears to acknowledge that fact. In United Kingdom constitutional terms it is less clear for, despite *Factortame*, there can be little doubt that the United Kingdom judges would give effect to conscious and explicit repeal of the European Communities Act 1972, and thus to the removal of direct effect, whatever the EU law position.

In respect of legislation with direct effect, neither the United Kingdom Parliament nor the Scottish Parliament has in formal terms any role, for all national legislatures are bypassed in such cases.

In respect of legislation without direct effect, the United Kingdom Parliament and, in relation to devolved functions, the Scottish Parliament, have roles in that either a statute or a piece of subordinate legislation may be required to implement the obligation under the European Communities Act 1972. However, 'executive dominance of the legislature' means that the government or Scottish Government can normally get through the legislation it wants.

There are two committees of the United Kingdom Parliament directly concerned with EU matters. Both produce reports prolifically. The House of Commons European Scrutiny Committee[28] looks at Community documents (including legislation and legislative proposals), seeks to monitor the activities of United Kingdom ministers in the Council of the European Union, and keeps EU developments under review generally. It can form sub-committees, take evidence, and it has a number of expert advisers. It can recommend a proposal be debated on the grounds of its legal or political significance, in which case it normally will be, and the government will not normally assent to the proposal in the Council of the Union until it has been. However, while the Committee

---

28 Formerly called the House of Commons Select Committee on European Legislation.

produces reports on a wide variety of subjects (such as the mobile phone 'roaming' costs, fisheries 'by-catches' and discards, and the transfer of sentenced persons[29]) and generates discussion, it is not clear that it makes much difference, given the quantity of documents and the secrecy of Commission and Council of the European Union proceedings, the fact that its views are not part of the input into EU legislation, and related reasons.

The House of Lords Select Committee on the European Union[30] has broader terms of reference, and is more powerful. It has six sub-committees examining different aspects of the EU[31]. Its reports[32] are useful and robust, but again are not part of the formal input into EU legislation.

Other Committees may consider such questions as they arise during consideration of other matters.

In respect of EU legislation, the United Kingdom Parliament is thus primarily in the position of a well-informed pressure group upon the United Kingdom government and European Commission.

The Scottish Parliament has a European and External Relations Committee. Its terms of reference are: to consider and report on proposals for EU legislation, the implementation of such legislation, and any other EU issue (as well as questions of other links the Scottish Government has with other countries and territories). It has produced reports such as those on the European Union Trafficking Directive[33]. It also produces 'Brussels Bulletin', an electronic newsletter available on its website[34].

---

29 See http://www.parliament.uk/business/committees/committees-archive/european-scrutiny/. By late 2012, it had produced 24 Reports in that year alone.

30 Formerly called the House of Lords Select Committee on the European Communities.

31 These change from time to time, but in late 2012 were on: Economic and Financial Affairs; the Internal Market, Infrastructure and Employment; External Affairs; Agriculture, Fisheries, Environment and Energy; Justice, Institutions and Consumer Protection; and Home Affairs, Health and Education.

32 See http://www.parliament.uk/business/committees/committees-a-z/lords-select/eu-select-committee-/.

33 See http://www.scottish.parliament.uk/parliamentarybusiness/CurrentCommittees/29814.aspx

34 See http://www.scottish.parliament.uk/parliamentarybusiness/CurrentCommittees/31755.aspx.

PUBLICATION AND CITATION OF EU LAW

Publication and citation of EU legislation in general

6.24   The EU publishes the *Official Journal of the European Union*[35]. Certain legislative material must be published in it, and it is the main means of publishing all official information. The *Official Journal* appears in three parallel series.

The first of these series is the 'L' (for 'Legislation') series, and itself now[36] contains up to four sections, that is: 'Acts adopted under the EC Treaty/Euratom Treaty whose [*sic*] publication is obligatory'[37] (for material required to be promulgated through the *Official Journal*); 'Acts adopted under the EC Treaty/Euratom Treaty whose [*sic*] publication is not obligatory'[38]; 'Acts adopted under the EU Treaty'; and, occasionally, 'Other Acts'.

The second of these series is the 'C' (for 'Communication') series, and contains, among other things CJ and General Court judgments[39]. The C series has an electronic section called the 'C E' series which contains documents only published electronically, and which contains European Parliament minutes and resolutions, and Council of the European Union 'Common Positions'.

The third of these series is the 'S' (for 'Supplement') series, which contains tenders and awards for public works and supply contracts. Debates of the European Parliament are published as an Annex to the *Official Journal* up to May 1999, after which they appear online and on CD-ROM (see below).

The *Official Journal* is officially distributed, on subscription, by EUR-OP, the Publications Office of the European Union[40]. The *Official Journal* 'L' and 'C' series appear daily on paper in numbered issues, and are also available on a hybrid CD-ROM/Internet version monthly, with an annual cumulative version from 1999. There is a hard copy monthly and annual (cumulative) alphabetical and methodological index published in arrears. It is accompanied by a twice-yearly, two-volume, *Directory of European Union Legislation in Force*. The monthly and annual index, and the *Directory*, are included

---

35 Formerly *Official Journal of the European Communities*.
36 There was a simpler subdivision in the past.
37 Formerly 'Acts whose publication is obligatory'.
38 Formerly 'Acts whose publication is not obligatory'
39 Until September 2006 it also contained European Parliament minutes and resolutions.
40 See http://publications.europa.eu.

in the subscription to the *Official Journal*. The 'S' series is available in a twice-weekly CD-ROM format, or online on the TED (Tenders Electronic Daily) database[41] and no longer on paper.

Single copies of the *Official Journal* can be purchased from The Stationery Office ('TSO'), the United Kingdom government's publishing agency. Two multi-volume 'Special Edition' series of the *Official Journal* (one for 'Acts whose publication is obligatory', one for the rest) were produced upon United Kingdom accession, containing an authentic English language text of the legislation then in force. Much of this is still in force.

However, EU legislation and related documents are readily available online through EUR-lex[42]. EUR-lex gives access to draft legislative texts from the Prelex[43] and OEIL[44] databases, which help track the legislative progress of proposals. (The legislative sites of most Member States[45] are also accessible through another database, N-lex[46]).

An item in the *Official Journal* 'L' series is conventionally cited in the following form: 'OJ L180, 13.7.90, p 26', (or occasionally [1990] OJ L180, 13.7.90) that is, 'the item on page 26 of the 180th issue of the L series, which was published on 13 July 1990'. This is in fact the citation of a directive on the rights of workers exercising their rights of free movement within the EU. The 'C' series is commonly referred to by a different convention, for example 'OJ C80/1, 10.3.01', that is, series/issue/page/date (or even the more ambiguous '01/C 80/01', that is, year/series/issue/page number). This is the Treaty of Nice. Citations of items in the Special Edition include the abbreviation 'S Edn'.

The *Official Journal* and commercial derivatives, can be found in any of the 44 European Documentation Centres in universities throughout the United Kingdom, or in the European Information Points in the Public Information Relays (PIRs) within public libraries.

---

41 See http://ted.europa.eu/TED/main/HomePage.do

42 See http://eur-lex.europa.eu/en/index.htm.

43 See http://ec.europa.eu/prelex/apcnet.cfm?CL=en.

44 See http://www.europarl.europa.eu/oeil/home/home.do.

45 Ie Austria, Belgium, Bulgaria, Cyprus, Czech Republic, Denmark, Estonia, Finland, Germany, Greece, France, Hungary, Ireland, Italy, Latvia, Lithuania, Luxembourg, Malta, Netherlands, Poland, Portugal, Romania, Slovakia, Slovenia, Spain, Sweden and the UK.

46 See http://n-lex.europa.eu.

Publication and citation of Treaties

6.25   Treaties often bear a long official title, but an abbreviated form is usually used[47]. References to the Treaty on the Functioning of the European Union ('TFEU') are commonly given in the form 'Article 294 TFEU'. Because of the numbering of articles in the TFEU and TEC affected by the Treaty of Rome, the form is now commonly 'Article 294 TFEU (ex Article 251 TEC)'.

EU publication

6.26   The Treaties are published by the EU. New Treaties are published in the *Official Journal* 'C' series. Consolidated versions of the TFEU and TEU, incorporating amendments to date, are also published in the 'C' series[48], and on the official EU website, EUR-lex[49]. Treaties are also likely to be published as a separate document by EUR-OP[50].

United Kingdom official publication

6.27   The United Kingdom government, through TSO, publishes the Treaties as Command Papers[51]. These include, for example, the *Treaty concerning the Accession of ... the United Kingdom ... to the European Economic Community* (Brussels, 22 January 1972; Cmnd 7460–7463, 1979) (UKTS Nos 15–18). It also produced *European Communities Treaties and Related Documents* in ten volumes up to date

---

47 For example, the Treaty Establishing the European Economic Community (Rome, 25 March 1957) is usually referred to as the 'EEC Treaty', and by some as the 'Treaty of Rome'. It is now amended to become the Treaty on the Functioning of the European Union, which is usually referred to as the 'TFEU'.
48 OJ C325/E/1 (*et seq*), 29/02/06.
49 See http://eur-lex.europa.eu/en/index.htm.
50 For example, the Treaty on European Union was so originally published in 1992.
51 Command Papers are formal government policy documents and the like, produced 'by Command of Her Majesty'. They are numbered up to 9,999, so new series are commenced every few years. Different series are distinguished by preceding initials. Currently these are 'Cm'; for the previous series they were 'Cmnd'; before that 'Cmd'. Some sets of Command Papers are published or republished in subordinate series, such as the United Kingdom Treaty Series (UKTS).

to 1972. Although reliable, these are not authoritative in EU law terms and are outdated.

United Kingdom commercial publication

6.28 Some commercial publishers produce compilations of the Treaties, which, although not authoritative, are in practice more useful, as they may be consolidated and annotated (that is, showing the current version, as amended, and comment). These include the multi-volume loose-leaf and CD-ROM *European Union Law Library* (Sweet & Maxwell), which contains the Treaties and many associated documents. Foster *Blackstone's EU Treaties and Legislation* (Oxford UP, 23rd edn, 2012) also gives the texts up to date of publication. Texts of relevant parts of the Treaties may be found in encyclopaedias and textbooks on subjects with a significant EU law dimension[52] and extracts in 'cases and materials' books, such as Craig and de Búrca *EU Law: texts, cases and materials* (Oxford University Press, 5th edn, 2011).

There are also several online subscription services such as Westlaw.

Publication and citation of Regulations, Directives and Decisions – 'secondary legislation'

EU publication

6.29 Regulations bear a title, but are usually cited in the following form: 'Council Regulation 1251/70/EEC', or simply 'Regulation 1251/70/EEC'[53], which refers to the 1,251st Regulation of 1970, initiated by the Council of Ministers of the EEC (now 'Council of the European Union'). It is useful to cite them by the Official Journal reference as well (in this case 'OJ L124, 30.6.70, p 24 (S Edn 1970 (II), p 402)').

Directives and Decisions also bear little-used titles and are cited with the abbreviated year preceding the sequential number, for example 'Council Directive 90/364/EEC (OJ L180, 13.7.90, p26)'.

---

52 For example, *Butterworths Immigration Law Service*, a looseleaf encyclopaedia on immigration law, contains EU legislation relevant to the subject, and is continuously updated. Macdonald and Webber (eds) *Macdonald's Immigration Law and Practice* (8th edn, 2010), a textbook, contains similar material, updated to the date of publication.

53 The form '1251/70' is too ambiguous and unhelpful.

Because the series are now published in separate sequences, with the same 'year/number' citation, the simple form '90/364' is ambiguous, making the correct *Official Journal* citation vital. Directives are sometimes given semi-official names, such as 'First Directive on Company Law Harmonisation' (Cl Dir 68/151/EEC); popular names, such as 'the Equal Pay Directive' (Cl Dir 75/117/EEC); or at least abbreviated names, for example 'the Directive on Animal Semen' (Cl Dir 87/328/EEC). Commonly, however, indication of the initiating body is dropped, as in 'Dir 64/221' (which contains the 'public policy proviso' exception to the free movement of workers), giving no hint that it was initiated by the Council of the European Union.

Regulations must be published in the *Official Journal*, as 'Acts adopted under the EC Treaty/Euratom Treaty whose publication is obligatory'. Although Article 296 (ex Article 253) TFEU only requires Directives and Decisions to be notified to their addressees, in practice they appear in the section 'Acts adopted under the EC Treaty/Euratom Treaty whose publication is not obligatory', so are available generally. Up-to-date texts, containing amendments and excluding repeals, are not officially produced, unless there is consolidating legislation, but the EUR-OP *Directory of European Union Legislation in Force* also provides the means of updating.

Again, however, secondary legislation is readily found online through EUR-lex (see above).

United Kingdom commercial publication

6.30 Commercial publications are therefore, as with the Treaties, in practice the most useful compilations. These include the multi-volume loose-leaf *Encyclopaedia of European Union Law* (Sweet & Maxwell) which contains most EU legislation, gives annotations and is continually updated, and works such as Foster *Blackstone's EU Treaties and Legislation* (Oxford UP, 23rd edn, 2012). Also, as in the case of the Treaties, encyclopaedias and textbooks on subjects with a significant EU law dimension may contain texts of relevant Regulations etc, as may 'cases and materials' books.

The online subscription services such as Westlaw also contain the secondary legislation.

Publication and citation of other related materials published by the EU

6.31 The EU also publishes an enormous quantity of information relating to its legislative and other activities. This includes the annual

General Report on the Activities of the Union and monthly *Bulletin of the European Union*. The latter (published on-line since 2006) contains an account of current proposals and other matetial. The 'COM' series of Commission documents includes proposals and discussion papers from the European Commission on EUR-lex, and there are very many regular and *ad hoc* publications. The European Parliament also published its Working Documents in paper form to 1990 and on microfiche to 1997, since when they can be found only online.

7 Legislation – United Kingdom Parliamentary Legislation (including the Human Rights Act 1998)

THE INSTITUTIONAL BACKGROUND

7.1 The institutional background of United Kingdom Government and Parliament (and of the Council of Europe and the European Convention on Human Rights) were dealt with in Chapter 3. This Chapter deals with the nature and style of United Kingdom legislation (including the Human Rights Act 1998), the United Kingdom Parliament legislative process, and the publication and citation of United Kingdom legislation.

THE NATURE AND STYLE OF UNITED KINGDOM PARLIAMENTARY LEGISLATION (INCLUDING HUMAN RIGHTS LEGISLATION)

Parliamentary legislation, human rights, Community law and devolution

7.2 Acts of Parliament, often referred to as 'statutes', are usually regarded as the normal form of legislation in the United Kingdom[1]. The United Kingdom is a state, and does not exist in order to fulfil certain specified policies but, rather, to run its territory and population in all their complexity. Thus, Acts of Parliament range over many subjects and touch on almost every aspect of life. On the other hand, such Acts rarely deal in fundamental principle, for the underlying principles of the legal system are found in the

---

1 In terms of sheer quantity, however, delegated legislation is much greater: see Chs 9 & 10 below.

common law[2]. The lack of a written constitution underlines the point. Legislation is thus principally a means of changing the law, and of stating new law in detail, and such changes and detail may vary widely and rapidly with changing political priorities of different governments. As noted in Chapters 3 and 6, traditionally, there has been argued to be 'parliamentary supremacy', that is, that there are no legal boundaries to Parliament's legislative power, only boundaries created by the political prudence and the morality of its members[3]. In law, it may pass any Act to any effect. In practice, the position is more complicated.

Firstly, 'parliamentary supremacy' means that the United Kingdom Parliament may legislate on 'human rights' issues, and it has. However, 'human rights' has come to be seen as a means of limiting the ability of legislatures to enact laws, thus at least touching upon parliamentary supremacy (as well as limiting the ability of government to take decisions). The European Convention on Human Rights (ECHR) is thus such a limit, indeed is one of the two principal sources of such limits in the United Kingdom context. The nature of the ECHR and its institutions are discussed in Chapter 3, and the relationship between the ECHR, the Human Rights Act 1998 and Acts of Parliament sketched in Chapter 4, but is considered in detail below. It should be recalled that the Human Rights Act 1998 may limit, but certainly in fact preserves, parliamentary supremacy.

Secondly, 'parliamentary supremacy' means that the United Kingdom Parliament may legislate on matters within the remit of the European Union. However, the idea of the 'direct effect' of EU law is specifically designed to limit the powers of the legislatures of Member States on matters within the Union competences, and thus, in the United Kingdom case, to limit parliamentary supremacy in those areas. It should be noted that, unlike any state, the European Union exists for relatively specific (albeit evolving) purposes. The Treaties therefore include statements of underlying principles and relatively constant (if also evolving) policies. On the other hand, such relative constancy is in part because EU institutions are much less answerable to any electorate. Also, because it exists for relatively specific purposes, the range of EU legislation is narrower than that of parliamentary legislation. The nature of the European Union

2   For which, see Chs 4 & 12.
3   The Legislative and Regulatory Reform Act 2006, discussed in Chapter 9, shows the breadth of this power in a paradoxical fashion.

and its institutions was also discussed in Chapter 3, its relationship with Acts of Parliament sketched in Chapter 5, but is considered in detail in Chapter 6 (including how far parliamentary supremacy is compromised).

Thirdly, the introduction of devolution means that the devolved legislatures are taking over responsibilities within their competences, and thus removing from the United Kingdom the need to legislate on those matters, though not the right to do so[4]. Thus, in relation to Scotland, Acts of the Scottish Parliament are gradually taking over the role of normal legislation in those areas not reserved to Westminster. The nature of devolution and its institutions was also discussed in Chapter 3, with the relationship with Acts of Parliament again sketched in Chapter 5, and they will be considered in detail in Chapter 8 (including that parliamentary supremacy is clearly preserved).

United Kingdom Acts of Parliament, their types and form

7.3   Most statutes are technically 'public, general' statutes, and discussion in this chapter relates exclusively to such statutes unless otherwise stated. 'Local', 'personal', 'private' and 'hybrid' legislation (which are not 'public, general') and particular types of public general Acts are discussed below as 'Special cases'.

In the last ten years there has been an average of 39 Acts of Parliament passed each year[5]. Many Acts repeal or amend existing legislation, so the annual increase is not as great as this rate of production suggests. Acts also vary enormously in length. Effectively, the shortest possible is two sections. Recent examples include the Census (Amendment) Scotland Act 2001, the Criminal Defence Service (Advice and Assistance) Act 2001 and the Civil Defence (Grants) Act 2002. There is no theoretical maximum, and many have hundreds of sections, for example the Enterprise Act 2001 with 281 sections, the Capital Allowances Act 2001 with 581 sections, though by far the longest so far is the Income and Corporation Taxes Act 1988, which approaches 1,500 sections (though, as a Consolidating statute – for the meaning of which,

---

4   The United Kingdom Parliament may, of course, continue to legislate in devolved areas if it chooses: Scotland Act 1998, s 28(7).

5   In 2006 there were 55 and in 2011 only 24. These represent the extremes in recent years.

see below – it is not typical). The Companies Act 2006, at exactly 1,300 sections and 16 Schedules, is another, more recent, monster, again the result of a Consolidation exercise. The average length of statutes is increasing.

Statutes also vary enormously in age. The great majority of Acts in force are relatively modern, but there are still many older ones, and even a few dating from the Parliaments of Scotland and England, which ceased to exist in 1707[6], and the Parliament of Great Britain which lasted from 1707 to 1801.

There is a conventional structure to a modern UK Act of Parliament, described in the following paragraphs[7].

Short Title, Chapter Number and Arrangement of Sections

7.4 United Kingdom Acts commence with a 'Short Title', for example the 'Scotland Act 1998'. The Short Title is a 19th-century invention, but all earlier statutes still in force have been given them retrospectively by the Short Titles Act 1896 and the Statute Law Revision (Scotland) Act 1964. It is the relatively brief name almost invariably used to identify the Act. Short Titles include the year of enactment, which may be important as Acts of similar Short Title may be passed in different years and may be in force at the same time[8]. (Nevertheless, when there can be no doubt which Act is being referred to, a form such as 'the 1971 Act' is common, and an example of this usage is noted below in relation to Marginal Notes). However, sometimes, when a series of related Acts exists, the last may give a

6   See below in relation to Acts of the original, pre-1707, Parliament of Scotland.
7   The Human Rights Act 1998, s 19, requires a minister introducing a Bill into Parliament to state whether or not it conforms to the requirements of that Act (for which, see below). However, there is no requirement that this statement, or an amended form of it, appear on the face of the Act.
8   For example, the British Nationality Acts of 1948, 1958, 1964, 1964 (No 2) and 1965 were all in force at the same time, and required reference to the British Nationality and Status of Aliens Act 1914 (itself amended by similarly entitled Acts in 1918, 1922, 1933 and 1943, which were all in force at the same time, too). All were repealed by the British Nationality Act 1981 (itself now amended, though by, *int al*, the British Nationality (Falkland Islands) Act 1983, the British Nationality (Hong Kong) Act 1997, and the Immigration, Asylum and Nationality Act 2006.

collective title, for example the 'Official Secrets Acts 1911–89'[9] or simply 'the Immigration Acts'[10].

On the other hand, reflecting the *ad hoc* nature of legislation in a common law or mixed system, Acts on similar topics may have dissimilar names, for example, those concerned with statute law[11]. Short Titles often incorporate brackets, and almost all pre-devolution Acts applying only to Scotland are indicated in this way[12], though there are exceptions[13]. Other common uses of brackets are '(Amendment)', and '(Miscellaneous Provisions)'. An Act's Short Title is officially given to it by a Short Title provision (for which, see below) in a section towards the end of the Act (often in the 'Supplementary' or 'Miscellaneous and Supplemental' sections, for which, see below).

As well as a Short Title, Acts of the United Kingdom Parliament have a 'chapter number' which denotes the sequential number of that Act in the year. They are rendered variously as, for example, 'chapter 15', 'chap 15' 'ch 15' or 'cap 15'[14]. Taken with the year of enactment, it provides a unique reference number of that Act, known as the 'citation'. Thus, the citation '1998 c46' refers uniquely to the Scotland Act 1998[15].

An Act of greater length than a couple of sections is officially printed with an 'Arrangement of Sections', which is a contents list

---

9 See Official Secrets Act 1989, s 16(2).

10 *Ie* the Immigration Act 1971, Immigration Act 1988, Asylum and Immigration Appeals Acts 1993, Asylum and Immigration Act 1996, Immigration and Asylum Act 1999, Nationality, Immigration and Asylum Act 2002 and Asylum and Immigration (Treatment of Claimants, etc) Act, 2004 and Immigration, Asylum and Nationality Act 2006 (but not the Special Immigration Appeals Commission Act 1997): see Immigration, Asylum and Nationality Act 2006, s 64(2), UK Borders Act 2007 and the Borders, Citizenship and Immigration Act 2009.

11 The principal ones include the Acts of Parliament (Commencement) Act 1793; Short Titles Act 1896; Parliament Act 1911; Consolidation of Enactments (Procedure) Act 1949; Acts of Parliament Numbering and Citation Act 1962; Royal Assent Act 1967; and Interpretation Act 1978.

12 *Eg* Criminal Procedure (Scotland) Act 1995. For transitional examples, see the Scottish Enterprise Act 1999 and the Mental Health (Scotland) Act 1999. A parallel convention applies to Northern Ireland legislation. Curiously, none applies to legislation applying only in England.

13 Modern examples include the Scotland Acts 1978, 1998 and 2012 (and there is the transitional example of the Scottish Enterprise Act 1999).

14 In medieval English constitutional theory, a parliament passed only one statute, so, if it covered different topics, each was distinguished as a 'chapter' (in Latin '*caput*').

15 But see below 'Publication and citation of parliamentary legislation: Acts of the Parliaments of Great Britain and the United Kingdom'.

of Sections and Schedules and their Marginal Notes (for which, see below).

Long Title, Date of Royal Assent and Preamble

7.5   In addition to Short Titles, United Kingdom Acts also have 'Long Titles'. These were used well before Short Titles. In practice they may be brief or lengthy[16]. Their function is to indicate and delimit the subject matter of the Bill when first introduced into Parliament, and they may be an aid to interpretation of a statute. At the end of the Long Title is given, in square brackets, the 'Date of Royal Assent', that is, the date on which the Act is actually formally enacted[17]. However, while this is the date of enactment, confusingly, it is not necessarily (or indeed, generally) the date or dates on which the Act actually comes into force, for which, see below in relation to 'Commencement'.

Preambles to Acts were formerly used to show their purpose. Very occasionally, a modern Act may have a preamble, commencing with the word 'Whereas ... ', and outlining the reasons for it[18]. This precedes the Long Title.

The Enacting Formula

7.6   United Kingdom Acts of Parliament do not have lengthy recitals of their origins at the beginning, as EU legislation does. They do, however, have an 'Enacting Formula' immediately before the actual substantive provisions. It is a validating incantation, recording enactment. There are four forms of it: one is the basic, the others are

---

16 The long title of the Official Secrets Act 1989 runs to 20 words and reads 'An Act to replace section 2 of the Official Secrets Act 1911 by provisions protecting more limited classes of official information'. That of the Water Act 1989 runs to some 200 words.

17 Thus, for example, after the Long Titles of the Official Secrets Act 1989 and Water Act 1989 appear '[11th May 1989]' and '[6th July 1989]' respectively.

18 The Welsh Language Act 1967 has the following: 'Whereas it is proper that the Welsh language should be freely used by those who so desire in the hearing of legal proceedings in Wales and Monmouthshire; that further provision should be made for the use of that language, with like effect as English, in the conduct of other official or public business there; and that Wales should be distinguished from England in the interpretation of future Acts of Parliament ... '. Private Bills (for which, see below) always have a Preamble, however: see, for example, the British Railways Act 1992.

used in taxation legislation, government expenditure legislation, and legislation under the Parliament Act 1911, respectively[19].

Sections, Marginal Notes and Marginal References

7.7   The basic unit of a United Kingdom Act is the 'Section', and Sections are numbered sequentially throughout the Act. Draftsmen aim at exactitude (in 'fixed verbal form': see Appendix 1). They break down the content into 'Sub-sections', 'Paragraphs' and 'Sub-paragraphs' as necessary[20], and use typographical devices to express grammatical, and thus logical, structure. This use of numbers, letters and indentation thus typifies statutory language. The principal convention on nomenclature and labelling is as follows (although the sub-section level is sometimes omitted in a short but sub-divided Section, so that the draftsman goes straight from Section to Paragraph):

section	1	**(emboldened)**
sub-section	(1)	(unemboldened)
paragraph	(a)	(unemboldened)
sub-paragraph	(i)	(unemboldened)

As well as assisting in exact expression of meaning, this convention allows precise identification of provisions, for example, 'Consumer Credit Act 1974, s 10 (3)(b)(i)', that is, 'section 10, sub-section 3, paragraph b, sub-paragraph i of that Act' (or, where the draftsman has gone straight to paragraphs, 'Nationality, Immigration and Asylum Act 2002, s 5(b)', that is, 'section 5, paragraph b' of that Act).

Where an amending Act inserts a whole new Section, it is identified by a capital letter after the preceding number. A new section after

---

19 Its basic form, reflecting the relationship of the three parts of Parliament until the 19th century, reads 'Be it enacted by the Queen's most Excellent Majesty, by and with the advice and consent of the Lords Spiritual and Temporal, and Commons, in this Parliament assembled, and by authority of the same as follows … '. Amusingly, the Finance Acts, which permit taxation, refer to taxes 'freely and voluntarily given', and the Consolidated Fund and Appropriation Acts, which permit government expenditure, to funds 'cheerfully granted'. Legislation under the Parliament Acts omits reference to the Lords but inserts 'in accordance with the provisions of the Parliament Act 1911'.

20 In grammatical terms, the sentence contained in the Section is broken into its constituent clauses and phrases. The main clause is likely to start or finish the section. The subordinate clauses form the various Sub-sections etc, reflecting their relationship with the main clause. Much of the skill of drafting is finding a suitable means of expressing visually the internal and grammatical logic of the intended provision.

's 1' is thus 's 1A', and its Sub-sections would be rendered 's 1A(1), 1(A)(2)' and so on[21]. Thus, ss 128–139 of the Immigration and Asylum Act 1999 inserted 11 new sections between ss 28 and 29 of the Immigration Act 1971, which therefore appear as 'ss 28A–29K' of that Act. A similar principle applies to inserted Sub-sections etc. Thus, s 140(3) of the Nationality, Immigration and Asylum Act 2002 inserted a new paragraph between s 87(3)(e) and (f) of the Immigration and Asylum Act 1999, which therefore appears as 's 87(3)(ea)' of that Act.

Every section has a Marginal Note. This is a signpost rather than a description, and is the form of words used in the relevant entry in the Arrangement of Sections.

Where a section in one Act refers to another Act, for instance to amend it, an abbreviated citation to that other Act may given in the margin. For example, s 22 of the Immigration and Asylum Act 1999 affects the Asylum and Immigration Act 1996, so, in the margin of the former, next to s 22, appears '1996 c49', the citation of the earlier Act. However, the practice also exists of giving short title, year and chapter number in the text itself.

These conventions are used in official editions of United Kingdom Acts. Usage may vary somewhat in commercially produced ones or in textbooks. For example, Marginal Notes may not be in the margin, but follow the section number; Marginal References may not appear at all; 'section' is usually abbreviated to 's' ('ss' in the plural); and the brackets round the sub-section number removed.

Headings

7.8   A variety of Headings may be used in the text of an Act. Groups of sections may be collectively labelled as Parts, with capital roman numerals and centred capitalised names. For example, ss 1–31 and ss 32–43 of the Immigration and Asylum Act 1999 are labelled as, respectively:

'Part I: IMMIGRATION: GENERAL'
Part II: CARRIERS' LIABILITY'

Occasionally, Parts are divided into 'Titles' or even 'Chapters'[22].

---

21 It follows that a 's 1(a)' and 's 1A' in any statute are entirely separate provisions. Indeed, there might be a 's1(a)' and a 's 1A(a)' which are equally separate. Obviously, this can be a source of confusion.
22 An extreme example is the Capital Allowances Act 2001, which has 12 Parts, divided into 10, 20, 12, 6, 7, 5, 3, 5, 0, 8, 2 and 6 Chapters respectively.

Whether or not an Act has Parts, smaller groups of Sections are likely to be labelled by a 'Cross-heading', centred and italicised. For example, within Part 1 of the Immigration and Asylum Act 1999, ss 1–5, 6–8 and ss 9–15 are cross-headed as, respectively:

> *'Leave to enter, or remain in, the United Kingdom'*
> *'Exemption from immigration control'*
> *'Removal from the United Kingdom'*

A common usage is to label (whether as a separate Part or, more usually, under a Cross heading) 'Supplementary' or 'Miscellaneous and Supplemental' the last few Sections which contain a number of operating instructions for the Act, such as the Interpretation Section, Repeals and Amendment Provisions, and others described below.

Interpretation Sections

7.9   Interpretation Sections (usually identified by the Marginal Note), may appear anywhere in a United Kingdom Act, but are commonly found towards the end (often in the 'Supplementary' or 'Miscellaneous and Supplemental' sections)[23]. They specify meanings of words and phrases for the purposes of the Act. This may be necessary because the words are inherently vague, because they are used in an unusual sense, or because they have been invented for the purpose. For example, s 33 of the Immigration Act 1971 stipulates that '"aircraft" includes hovercraft', '"airport" includes hoverport', and '"port" includes airport', and also that '"Convention adoption" has the same meaning as in the Adoption Act 1976 and the Adoption (Scotland) Act 1978'. The meanings assigned may not actually be definitions, for sometimes the Section stipulates that one term 'means' something, sometimes that it 'includes' something, and occasionally that it 'does not include' something. The opening words of an Interpretation Section commonly, but unhelpfully, assign meanings 'unless the context otherwise requires'. Section 127 of the Scotland Act 1998 usefully gives a list of some 60 expressions used in the Act (such as 'cross-border authority', 'open power' and 'Scots private law') and in which sections their definition can be found[24].

---

23 See Simamba, B 'The Placing and Other Handling of Definitions' (2006) 27 Stat LR 73–82.

24 A similar provision in Sch 1, Part 2 to the Capital Allowances Act 2001 lists 130 such expressions.

Repeals and Amendments

7.10   United Kingdom Acts of Parliament continue in force unless repealed or amended, subject to an exception. Firstly, a provision in the Act may specify a terminal date (a 'sunset clause'), as did s 27 of the Prevention of Terrorism (Temporary Provisions) Act 1989 (and its predecessors). However, this is rare[25].

United Kingdom Acts, therefore, commonly repeal or amend earlier Acts, and no special process is required (and amendment does not only occur in Acts with '(Amendment)' in the short title). This follows from the doctrine of parliamentary supremacy, although the direct effect of EU law would appear to have limited this freedom.

Moreover, Delegated Legislation (for which, see Chapters 9 and 10) may repeal or amend an Act of Parliament, provided that Parliament has delegated the power to do so.

Two methods of amendment may be employed[26]. The 'textual' or 'direct' method simply substitutes a new provision for the old, a 'scissors and paste' process. It is generally preferred by the users of statutes as it shows the final form clearly. The 'referential' or 'indirect' method leaves the original text, but describes how it should be changed. It is preferred by Parliament as it shows what changes are proposed.

Repealing and Amending Provisions may appear anywhere in an Act, but commonly do so in a specific Section or Sections at the end of the Act (often in the 'Supplementary' or 'Miscellaneous and Supplemental' sections). Where there are numerous repeals and amendments, they are usually detailed in a Schedule, for example Sch 9 to the Social Security Act 1989 lists 18 Acts which it repeals to varying degrees. Indeed, where chiefly one Act is amended, and there are many amendments to other Acts, there may be two Schedules, as in Schs 4 ('Amendments of the Immigration Act 1981') and 7 ('Consequential Amendments') of the British Nationality Act 1981.

Occasionally, 'Statute Law Revision Acts' and 'Statute Law (Repeal) Acts' have been passed, which remove from the statute book obsolete and unnecessary legislation, which inevitably accumulates in

---

25 The Murder (Abolition of Death Penalty) Act 1965, most unusually, provided that 'This Act shall continue in force until the thirty first day of July nineteen hundred and seventy, and shall then expire unless Parliament by affirmative resolution of both Houses otherwise determines'. Such an affirmative resolution was forthcoming. Note also that an Act of the (pre-1707) Parliament of Scotland may fall into 'desuetude', that is, lapse through the growth of contrary practice: see *The Laws of Scotland: Stair Memorial Encyclopaedia* vol 22, para 129 and Ch 8.

26 Miers and Page *Legislation* (2nd edn, 1990) p 195, n 6 suggests that ss 60 and 61 of the Wildlife and Countryside Act 1981 are paradigm cases.

a system in which legislation is generally *ad hoc*. These are discussed under 'Special cases' below.

Transitional Provisions

7.11   When a United Kingdom Act is repealed or amended, transitional difficulties may arise, for instance in relation to litigation which is in progress. Transitional Provisions, usually found at the end of an Act (often in the 'Supplementary' or 'Miscellaneous and Supplemental' sections), provide a solution, and the detail is often put in a Schedule. For example, s 169(2) of the Immigration and Asylum Act 1999 reads 'Schedule 15 contains transitional provisions and savings'.

Commencement Provisions

7.12   By virtue of the Acts of Parliament (Commencement) Act 1793, a United Kingdom Act comes into force on the Date of Royal Assent, unless it specifies otherwise[27]. They often so specify in a Commencement Section normally found at the end of the Act (often in the 'Supplementary' or 'Miscellaneous and Supplemental' sections). The simplest form of Commencement Section gives a specific date for commencement[28]. A rare variant is to declare that the Act comes into force at the same time as another Act[29], and a common one that it does so at a specific period after the Date of Royal Assent, typically three months[30]. A very common method nowadays is to delegate the power to the government to bring the Act into force, to be exercised through a Statutory Instrument (for which, see Chapter 9) known as a 'Commencement Order'. An Act may have different sections brought into force on different days, and use a mixture of commencement methods[31], and more

---

27 Thus the British Nationality Act 1958 (not specifying otherwise) came into force on the Date of Royal Assent (20 February 1958).
28 Section 34(2) of the British Nationality Act 1948 stipulated that it come into force 'on the first day of January nineteen hundred and forty-nine'.
29 Section 25 of the Company Directors Disqualification Act 1986 stipulates that it come into force on commencement of the Insolvency Act 1986.
30 Section 3(3) of the British Nationality Act 1964 stipulated that it come into force 'at the expiration of two months beginning with the date on which it is passed'.
31 Section 53(3) of the British Nationality Act 1981 stipulates that 'section 49 and this section shall come into force on the passing of this Act' (30 October 1981), and s 53(2) that the rest of the Act 'shall come into force on such day as the Secretary of State may by order made by statutory instrument appoint'. That power was exercised in the British Nationality 1981 (Commencement) Order 1982, SI 1982/933, which appointed 1 January 1983.

than one commencement order, some of which may be years after the enactment which can make it difficult to discover if a particular provision is in force or not[32].

Short Title Provision

7.13   A provision at the end of a United Kingdom Act officially gives it its Short Title (for which, see above) by stating 'This Act may be cited as ... '[33]. No chapter number is given, for this cannot be known until enactment.

Extent Provisions

7.14   Because Acts of the United Kingdom Parliament do not necessarily apply to the whole of the United Kingdom (and, with the arrival of devolution, do so decreasingly) there are commonly 'Extent Provisions, stipulating to which law areas (for instance, England and Wales only, or Great Britain) they do apply. Such provisions can be complicated[34].

Acts may extend beyond the United Kingdom to dependencies. Commonly such Acts are extended to the Channel Islands and Isle of Man (which are not part of the United Kingdom), and to colonies as, for example, does the British Nationality Act 1981, by s 53(5).

An Act may even apply to activities by certain people outwith the territorial extent of the United Kingdom and its dependencies. For instance, the Official Secrets Act 1989 extends to the United Kingdom only, as such, but, by s 15, also applies to specified acts

---

32 The Control of Pollution Act 1974 has had 20 commencement orders and is still not completely in force. The record is thought to be held by the Easter Act 1928 which is still not in force.

33 Thus s 149 of the Constitutional Reform Act 2005 stipulates 'The Act may be cited as the Constitutional Reform Act 2005'.

34 Section 194(6) of the Water Act 1989 specified that Schs 2 and 5, ss 4, 13 and 23 'so far as relating to any scheme under either of those Schedules', s 95 and certain repeals extend to the United Kingdom. Section 194(7) specifies that certain other sections and schedules extend, or extend in part, to Great Britain. Section 194(8) specified that yet other provisions apply only to Scotland, and s 194(9) that yet further provisions extend only to England and Wales. Section 147 of the Constitutional Reform Act 2005 specified that ss 7, 8 and 9 'extend to England and Wales only', '[s]ection 6 and Part 5 extend to Northern Ireland only', but also that '[s]ubject to subsections (1) to (3), this Act extends to Northern Ireland'. It is thus a matter of inference whether ss 1–6, and 9–149 (minus Part 5) apply to Scotland.

done by British Citizens and Crown servants abroad. Acts concerned with the security of the state and terrorism may extend and apply very broadly, usually by international agreement. The Taking of Hostages Act 1982, s 1 (which followed the International Convention Against Taking Hostages of 1979) declares 'A person, whatever his nationality, who, being in the United Kingdom or elsewhere' takes hostages contrary to the terms of the Act, commits an offence in the United Kingdom'. The Criminal Justice (Terrorism and Conspiracy) Act 1998 was co-ordinated with similar legislation in the Republic of Ireland and by s 5 enabled prosecutions in the United Kingdom of conspiracies to commit illegal acts in territories outside the UK.

The most extreme example appears to be the Outer Space Act 1986, which stipulates in s 1 that 'This Act applies to the following activities whether carried out in the United Kingdom or elsewhere ... (c) any activity in outer space'. 'Outer space' is defined in s 14, strangely, to include the moon.

Schedules

7.15   Many United Kingdom Acts have Schedules, which must be specifically incorporated into the Act by a Section. They are appendices, containing detailed matter too complicated for the body of the text, such as lists, tables and incidental rules. The British Nationality Act 1981, for example, has nine schedules[35].

Schedules may have Parts and cross-headings, as the body of an Act does, and are usually drafted in broadly the same manner as sections. The conventional labelling and nomenclature are as follows:

schedule	1	(unemboldened)
paragraph	(1)	(unemboldened)
sub-paragraph	(a)	(unemboldened)
sub-sub-paragraph	(i)	(unemboldened)

Repeal and amendment schedules are often in tabular form[36].

---

35 Respectively: Requirements for Naturalisation; Provisions for Reducing Statelessness; Countries whose Citizens are Commonwealth Citizens; Amendments of the Immigration Act 1971; Form of Oath of Allegiance; British Dependent Territories; Consequential Amendments; Transitional Provisions; and Repeals. The Enterprise Act 2002 achieved 36 Schedules, and the Finance Act 2000 managed 40, but financial legislation is atypical.

36 Typically, a repeal schedule is in the form of a table of three columns, headed respectively 'chapter' (listing the citations of the Acts repealed); 'short title'; and 'extent of repeal' (which may be from a single word to 'The whole Act').

Explanatory Notes

7.16 Since 1999, 'Explanatory Notes' have been produced for almost every Act[37] by the sponsoring Government department. They are an attempt to explain in lay language what each provision of the Act does. They have, however, no official status, although (as discussed in relation to statutory interpretation in Chapter 11) they may be used in statutory interpretation.

THE UNITED KINGDOM PARLIAMENTARY LEGISLATIVE PROCEDURE

7.17 The proposal for legislation presented to the United Kingdom Parliament is called a 'Bill'. Any Bill is itself the result of a lengthy process. Indeed, commonly the changes imposed by the parliamentary process are small compared with what a proposal has already undergone.

Who seeks legislation and why?

7.18 The government's role in the initiation of legislation is central in the United Kingdom constitution. It is expected to legislate, and has something approaching a monopoly of the initiation of parliamentary legislation. Initiation by others is dealt with below under 'Special cases'.

Some government legislation is party political 'manifesto legislation', for example the community charge or poll tax, imposed by the Abolition of Domestic Rates (Scotland) Act 1987, or the introduction of 'human rights' and devolution in the Human Rights Act 1998 and Scotland Act 1998, respectively. Such legislation may be of enormous importance, but represents only a small proportion of all legislation[38]. The current Conservative-Liberal Democrat coalition government has had great difficulty passing some legislation. Both parties have made concessions on their party's pre-election manifestos and in mid-2012 the coalition

---

37 Technically, with every public general Act (for which see above) introduced by the government, and with at least some introduced as private members' Bills.
38 Rose *Do Parties Make a Difference?* (2nd edn, 1984) pp 72–73 concluded that only 8% of the Bills of the Conservative government 1970–72 were 'manifesto Bills', and only 13% of those of the Labour government of 1974–79. For an analysis on somewhat different lines, see Drewry (1989) 10 Stat LR 200. Such proportions are likely still to be broadly true.

clashed over reform of the House of Lords and electoral boundary changes, with the result that a Government Bill to reform the House of Lords had to be dropped. Other legislation emerges as reaction to events. The Dangerous Dogs Act 1991 was a reaction to public pressure over a number of attacks by dogs; the Anti-Terrorism, Crime and Security Act 2001 was a reaction to the events of 11 September that year; the Terrorism Act 2006 was a response to the decision of the Appellate Committee of the House of Lords in *A v Secretary of State for the Home Department* [2004] UKHL 56, [2005] 2 AC 68, which decided that detention under the Anti-Terrorism, Crime and Security Act 2001 was in breach of Article 5 of the European Convention on Human Rights (as effected through the Human Rights Act 1998). Much legislation in relation to asylum-seeking, in a number of Acts over several years (most recently the Borders, Citizenship and Immigration Act 2009) is a reaction to increased asylum-seeking. Such legislation may on occasion be symbolic as much as instrumental, but in any case represents only a small proportion of all legislation[39]. Yet other legislation, not clearly foreshadowed by the manifesto, or as obvious reaction to events may also appear, and be of considerable significance[40].

But the great majority of Bills originate in the normal processes of government. The constitution requires annual legislation to allow the government to raise and spend money. It also now requires the government to produce legislation to put into effect EU policy when EU institutions require it (although this is principally done by Delegated Legislation). Nevertheless, most legislation simply emerges from the departments of government. As they administer their responsibilities, they discover that the law is not having the desired effect, so legislation is promoted to change it. An important category of this is Statute Law Revision and Repeal and Consolidation which are discussed as 'Special cases' below.

It is useful to break up the legislative process into 'pre-Parliamentary' and 'post-Parliamentary'[41].

---

39 See previous note.
40 The Constitutional Reform Act 2005 is of very great significance, but emerged for very unclear reasons.
41 There are some moves towards 'post-legislative scrutiny': see Law Commission 'Post-Legislative Scrutiny' (Law Commission Consultation Paper No 178 (2006) and Anon 'Post-Legislative Scrutiny' (2006) 27 Stat LR iii-vi; see also, Office of the Leader of the House of Commons, Post-legislative scrutiny – The Government's Approach, March 2008, Cm 7320, http://www.official-documents.gov.uk/document/cm73/7320/7320.pdf which outlined the Government's response. Acts are to be looked at by the department responsible for them within three to five years of receiving Royal Assent and a Memorandum produced to be sent to a Select Committee.

Pre-parliamentary stages of United Kingdom parliamentary legislation – 'the Whitehall stage'[42]

7.19 The pre-parliamentary stages of United Kingdom parliamentary legislation are of the utmost importance. It is then that the government decides what legislation it wishes, consults with interested parties, formulates specific proposals, and has them drafted by the Parliamentary draftsman into the Bill which will be presented to Parliament. Because the government has invested considerable resources into producing the Bill, it will be loath to accept amendments to it (though it may introduce amendments itself, reflecting second thoughts, or unfortunate results of the pressure the draftsman was under). Usually the executive enjoys dominance of the legislature and it will almost always get the Bill through Parliament in a form it wants, though often at a cost. The current Conservative-Liberal Democrat coalition has complicated the issue as both parties must agree on the legislation and its content for it to be passed through Parliament without too much challenge. Also, there is a limited amount of parliamentary time available for legislation, and governments would like to introduce much more legislation than there is parliamentary time for. In consequence, there is always a Committee of the Cabinet to rank proposals for the coming parliamentary session.

Consultation is a major part of the pre-parliamentary stages (a topic dealt with in more detail in Chapter 15[43]). Advice is obtained from *ad hoc* or specialised bodies in highly institutionalised ways. Royal Commissions, composed of disinterested members of the great and good, were once a common method of investigating problems and suggesting solutions, but have largely fallen out of favour[44]. Committees of Inquiry, which are less high-powered, and

---

42 For fuller, readable accounts, see Miers and Page *Legislation* (2nd edn, 1990) chs 4 and 5 (now a little dated) and Zander *The Law-Making Process* (6th edn, 2004), ch 1 (from which the phrase 'the Whitehall stage' is taken).

43 And see previous note.

44 A major example was the Wheatley Commission, chaired by the then Lord Justice-Clerk, which reported in 1969 (Cmnd 4150), and resulted in the Local Government (Scotland) Act 1973 which set up a new local government structure in Scotland. Another was the Kilbrandon Commission, chaired by a Scottish House of Lords judge, which reported on devolution in 1973 (Cmnd 5460), but ultimately produced no change. Yet a third was the Wakeham Commission chaired by a former Conservative Cabinet Minister, which reported on the reform of the House of Lords in 2000 (Cm 4534), but also appears to have produced no change.

departmental and inter-departmental committees and working parties of civil servants and others are much more common[45]. There has also been recourse to judges in recent years, at least in relation to possible legislation about courts and procedure[46]. The Law Commissions are of considerable importance in relation to certain types of legislation[47].

In addition, departments of government have continuing relations with a variety of interest and pressure groups, and it is in the dialogue with them that, within the government's priorities and predilections, proposals are formulated.

Consultation may be in part public. United Kingdom governments sometimes issue Green Papers or other consultative documents[48], outlining options and soliciting comment (and sometimes also White Papers, that is, statements of firm policy[49], though some White Papers have 'green edges')[50]. Indeed, now some Bills are published in draft, which allows greater scrutiny.

Drafting is done by barristers and a few advocates employed as civil servants, and known collectively as 'Parliamentary Counsel' in

---

45 The Carnworth Report (*Enforcing Planning Control*) in 1989 led to the Planning and Compensation Act 1991. The North Report (*Road Traffic Law Review*) in 1988 led to the Road Traffic Act 1991.

46 The most obvious examples are *Access to Justice: interim report* (1995) and *Access to Justice: final report* (the 'Woolf Report': 1996) on civil procedure, many of the recommendations of which were effected in new Civil Procedure Rules (although this is Delegated, rather than Parliamentary Legislation) and *Review of the Criminal Courts in England & Wales* (the "Auld Report": 2001) on criminal procedure, some of the recommendations of which were effected in the Criminal Justice Act 2003.

47 Especially statute law revision and repeal, and consolidation. See also Ch 15.

48 The Children and Adoption Act 2006 (applying to England & Wales), was seemingly preceded by a consultation paper *Making Contact Work* (2001), an *Interim Response to the Report of the Children Act Sub-Committee* [*ie* the preceding paper] (2002), another consultation paper *Facilitation and Enforcement Group: final report* (2003), a Green Paper *Parental Separation: children's needs and parents' responsibilities* (Cm 6273) (2004), a White Paper *Parental Separation: children's needs and parents' responsibilities* (Cm 6273) (2005), a Parliamentary Committee Report *Report of a Joint Committee on the Draft Children (Contact) and Adoption Bill* (2005), a Government Reply to that (2005), another Parliamentary Committee Report *House of Commons Committee on Constitutional Affairs: Fourth Report for Session 2004–5 'Family Justice: the operation of family courts* (HC 2004–5 No 116 (2005), and a Government Response to that: see Current Law Annotated Statutes annotations.

49 *Smoking Kills* (Cm 1477) preceded the Tobacco Advertising and Promotion Act 2002.

50 However, it may be that Green Papers legislation have become less fashionable, and White Papers have certainly become more glossy, and therefore less useful.

the Parliamentary Counsel Office within the Cabinet Office[51]. At any time some will be on loan to the Law Commission, however. Draftsmen have been transferred to Edinburgh to draft the Bills of the Scottish Government.

The draftsman's role in legislation is pivotal. A United Kingdom government department, when its proposed Bill has a place in the queue, tells its own lawyers the policy the Bill is to promote, and these lawyers draft instructions for Parliamentary Counsel. Initial drafts of United Kingdom or Great Britain Bills are sent to the Advocate-General for Scotland's office for comment.

A team of two or three Parliamentary Counsel draft the Bill, and the 'Explanatory Notes' which accompany Bills, in liaison with the sponsoring department. This process may continue for months, or be hurried, depending upon the parliamentary legislative timetable. It has been suggested that there are five steps to drafting: understanding; analysis; design; composition; and revision[52]: also, that the Minister has the last word on matters of substance, the draftsman on matters of form.

The draftsman works under considerable constraints. Firstly, the instructions must be put into legislative form so as to satisfy the government. This may require deliberate vagueness or ambiguity on occasion. Secondly, the Bill must be, so far as possible, legally effective and fit within the existing law without producing unintended contradictions. Thirdly, the Bill must be competent for the United Kingdom Parliament (and thus, despite parliamentary supremacy, should not unintentionally offend against 'Convention rights' under the Human Rights Act 1998, and must not be against EU law. Fourthly, the Bill must fit into the parliamentary timetable, and shortage of time may lead to bad drafting and consequent need for extensive amendment in Parliament, requiring more of the draftsman's time. Fifthly, draftsmen see themselves as an elite, employing craft skills, which has been said (perhaps unfairly) to lead to a certain conservatism in form and expression.

---

51   See http://www.cabinetoffice.gov.uk/content/office-parliamentary-counsel/: also Bowman 'Why is there a Parliamentary Counsel Office?' (205) 26 Stat LR 69–81.

52   Thornton *Legislative Drafting* (4th edn, 1996) pp 112–13.

Parliamentary stages of United Kingdom parliamentary legislation – 'the Westminster stage'[53]

7.20   The Enacting Formula of an Act records that the three parts of the UK Parliament have agreed. To pass these three parts, several stages must be gone through.

A Bill may be introduced into either House of Parliament first, by any MP or peer (as appropriate). However, most Bills are government Bills (that is Bills introduced by a member of the government), and most (and certainly controversial Bills and those concerning taxation and expenditure) are introduced into the Commons first.

The stages in each House are called 'First' and 'Second Readings' ('1R' and '2R')[54], Committee Stage ('CS'), Report Stage ('RS') and Third Reading ('3R'). After a Bill has gone through all those stages in each House, there is a process of consideration by the House in which the Bill was introduced of the other House's amendments, to produce an agreed version[55]. The Royal Assent follows automatically.

The whole process suffers from the fact that executive dominance of the legislature normally ensures that the Bill is largely unaltered (although hundreds of amendments may have been moved, unsuccessfully, by Opposition MPs) or only altered as the government wishes (by many amendments moved, successfully, by Government MPs). Parliament therefore largely rubber-stamps the government's proposals and, at least in the House of Commons, the legislative process often becomes a forum for the opposition to harry the government instead. To ensure that the current legislation gets through despite the Opposition's efforts to thwart it there is always also a Cabinet Committee, operating through the Whips (that is members of the government whose job is to maintain party discipline and convey to the government the concerns of backbenchers).

---

53   See again Miers and Page *Legislation* (2nd edn, 1990) ch 6 (now a little dated) and Zander *The Law-Making Process* (6th edn, 2004), ch 2 (from which the phrase 'the Westminster stage' is taken): also standard constitutional law textbooks, the lengthy Cabinet Office *Guide to Legislative Procedures* (Cabinet Office, 2004). See also http://webarchive.nationalarchives.gov.uk/+/http://www.cabinetoffice.gov.uk/secretariats/downloads/guide_legislative_procedure.pdf.

54   Unfortunately the 'co-operation procedure' for the European Community legislative procedure has adopted these titles for very different processes, as noted in Ch 6.

55   Indeed, in contentious cases, there can be 'Parliamentary ping-pong', whereby a Bill is passed back and forth several times. The record, seemingly, is six times: see Zander *The Law-Making Process* (6th edn, 2004) p56, n 14.

The First Reading is purely formal, but permits the Bill, traditionally hitherto confidential (though now Draft Bills are sometimes issued), to be published. Before the Second Reading, s 19 of the Human Rights Act 1998 requires the minister in charge of a Bill to make a written statement that, in his view, the provisions of the Bill are compatible with the 'Convention rights' under that Act (for which, see Chapter 3) or, if he cannot do so, state that the government wishes to proceed with the Bill nevertheless[56]. This is one of several devices designed to seek compatibility of legislation with those rights (see Chapters 3 and 5). The Second Reading, perhaps two weeks later, is designed as a debate on the principle of the Bill. Most Second Readings are unopposed, but a government will almost always win a vote, because it is government by virtue of having a majority in the House of Commons (and the House of Lords will not normally attempt to veto legislation which the majority in the Commons favours). The Committee Stage, which will often extend over several weeks, is usually taken by a 'Standing Committee' reflecting the party balance in the Commons[57], and a 'Committee of the Whole House' in the Lords. This stage is designed to examine the Bill in detail to see if it achieves its purpose, and is the chief stage to put amendments. It may allow such examination on an uncontroversial Bill, but in other cases it may be political theatre, possibly with proceedings 'guillotined', that is terminated at a certain point, whether or not discussion has finished. In this case many clauses of the Bill will not be discussed at all. Also, increasingly, governments propose amendments to their own Bills ('legislating on the hoof'), which suggests that they have been ill-prepared, possibly through lack of time. The Report Stage is for the Committee to report its amendments to the Whole House (even if it has been a Committee of the Whole House, when it will be purely formal), although further amendments may be put. The Third Reading gives approval to the House's final formulation of the Bill. Because the first House to take any Bill has not approved any amendments made by the second House, there is a process of consideration of the other House's amendments.

---

56 As was done in respect to the Anti-Terrorism, Crime & Security Act 2001, as discussed below in relation to the 'Special case' of human rights legislation.
57 It may be taken by a 'Committee of the Whole House', as the European Communities (Amendment) Bill 1992–93 (incorporating changes wrought by the Treaty on European Union) was; or by a 'Select Committee', which can take evidence. However, these committees are rarely used.

The House of Lords will usually concede to the reiterated opinion of the Commons. The Royal Assent has been purely formal for generations, but makes the Bill an Act (although it may come into force only later[58]).

A question raised by parliamentary legislative procedure is whether the unelected House of Lords should have a role[59]. One possible justification is that much legislation is not properly discussed in the Commons, so the Lords provides, in effect, a proper Committee Stage. This view has been prominent in discussions on House of Lords reform, and tends to characterise the Lords as a 'revising chamber' for legislation. Another is that it provides a sheet anchor to limit the wilder excesses of the Commons, which is dominated by the government of the day. This has not figured so largely in these discussions.

Enactment, the 'Sewel Convention' and 'Sewel Motions'

7.21   As noted above, and in Chapter 8, there is still legislation in relation to Scotland being enacted at Westminster, although its subject matter is within the devolved legislative competence of the Scottish Parliament.

This is largely because of the existence of 'Sewel Motions'. In brief, during the passage of the Scotland Act 1998, the government, through Lord Sewel, its spokesman in the House of Lords, indicated the expectation that a convention of the constitution would arise. This would be that, while the United Kingdom Parliament had power to legislate within the devolved competence of the Scottish Parliament, it would do so rarely and only with the consent of the Scottish Parliament.

However, the Scottish Parliament has in fact passed a large number of motions invoking the exception. As a result, in the first couple of years of its existence, the Scottish Parliament passed roughly as

---

58 See 'Commencement provisions' above.
59 See *eg* Lord Hope of Craighead 'What a Second Chamber Can Do for Legislative Scrutiny' (2004) Stat LR 3–18.

many 'Sewel Motions' as it passed Acts. Thus, arguably, as much Scots law was changed by Westminster as by Holyrood[60].

This may make sense if it includes Scotland in reforms introduced to the rest of the United Kingdom, applies international obligations, and so on. Nevertheless, it was completely unexpected. The phenomenon shows the strong centripetal United Kingdom tendencies in tension with notions of solutions tailored to Scottish wishes ('one size fits all' in tension with 'post-code solutions'), the more remarkable for being at least cheerfully acquiesced in by the Scottish Government and Scottish Parliament. These centripetal tendencies may have flowed from a desire for uniformity, caused by electoral expectations, a reliance on UK administrative bodies, the need to avoid inconsistency, and a feeling that diversity should not be sought for its own sake. Moreover, there may be other reasons for not using the Scottish Parliament, such as doubt over the boundaries of devolution, impetus for reform coming from Westminster, a desire to avoid dislocation of the Scottish Parliament's legislative programme, avoidance of challenge, and simple economy of effort. Also, there remain enough Scottish MPs in Westminster to take care of Scottish interests.

An important factor, however, may have been the fact that in the first two sessions of the Scottish Government, the UK Government was a Labour one, while the Labour Party was also the larger group in the coalition Scottish Ministers. While the phenomenon of the 'Sewel motion' has been by no means unknown in the era of the Scottish Nationalist Party Government – for example, there was one in 2012 in relation to parts of the Defamation Bill then passing through the Westminster Parliament – centripetal tendencies have been unsurprisingly less apparent.

Special cases

7.22   There are a number of special cases of legislation which must be examined.

---

60 Clearly, one cannot simply compare number of Acts, as they vary in significance (and length), but the point is well made. For an analysis of 'Sewel motions' in the first few years of the Scottish Parliament, see Page and Batey 'Scotland's Other Parliament; Westminster legislation about devolved matters in Scotland' [2002] PL 501–23 (who noted that in the first three calendar years of the Scottish Parliament, 30 Sewel Motions were passed by the Scottish Parliament, which only passed 36 Acts of the Scottish Parliament in the same period!). The following text relies heavily on that analysis. See also Munro 'Thoughts on the "Sewel Convention"' 2003 SLT 194–196.

Human rights legislation

7.23   By far the most important special case is that of human rights legislation. For present purposes, 'human rights' can be taken to refer to the content of a particular treaty, the European Convention on Human Rights and Fundamental Freedoms (or 'ECHR'), made under the auspices of the Council of Europe, as considered in Chapter 3. As noted there, the United Kingdom, as a member of the Council of Europe, was one of the original signatories of the ECHR in 1950, and ratified it in 1951. (There are also amending Protocols which add further rights, but not all of these have been ratified by the United Kingdom.) Further, there is the possibility of 'individual petition' to the European Court of Human Rights asserting a state has breached its obligations under the ECHR. Thus the United Kingdom adheres to the ECHR and one form of remedy for breach. There are also possibilities of enforcement though Community law.

However, what is of present interest is human rights legislation which, in the United Kingdom, effectively means the Human Rights Act 1998. This is, in some senses, simply another Act of Parliament, and to be mentioned, if at all, in relation to Acts of Parliament in general. However, it has a special status, and has had radical effects, which makes it necessary to give it special mention[61].

As noted in Chapter 3, the Human Rights Act does not, as is sometimes said, actually incorporate the ECHR into United Kingdom law, for its terms do not have the 'direct effect' which EU law does (see Chapter 6). Nevertheless, it can be said to 'embed' human rights, for s 1 of that Act cuts and pastes most of the contents of the ECHR[62], and its First and Sixth Protocols[63], into its Sch 1, under the name of 'Convention rights'. These Convention rights are thus part of United Kingdom law by virtue of being in an Act of Parliament.

Further, in broad terms, United Kingdom law is intended to be 'compatible' with them (though not necessarily required to be). There are various means of seeking this compatibility. Firstly, the Act requires 'public authorities' (including United Kingdom

---

61 See also Feldman 'The Impact of Human Rights on the UK Legislative Process' (2004) 25 Stat LR 91–115.

62 It omits Arts 1, 13 & 15. As noted in Ch 3, the omission of Art 13, requiring 'an effective remedy before a national authority', is controversial. The government considered it added nothing, as the very Act itself provided the effective remedy. Another view is that it wished to avoid judges creating new remedies based on the Act.

63 That is, those protocols creating further rights which the UK has signed up to.

Government and the courts) to act compatibly with Convention rights[64]. However, the United Kingdom Parliament is not a 'public authority' for this purpose (though the Scottish Parliament is, as noted below), so does not have to act compatibly[65] (though courts may issue a 'declaration of incompatibility' in litigation on legislation found to be incompatible). Secondly, the Act imposes requirements in relation to parliamentary scrutiny during the process of legislation of all subsequent Acts, whereby every government Bill is required to have either a statement of compatibility or a declaration of non-compatibility[66]. This was noted above. Thirdly, the Act imposes requirements in relation to statutory interpretation[67], which is discussed in Chapter 11. Fourthly, specific requirements are imposed in relation to devolution[68], which are discussed in Chapters 3 and 8.

In addition to this requirement for 'compatibility', the Act also creates rights for victims of breaches of Convention rights, as was discussed in Chapter 3[69].

Financial legislation

7.24   The United Kingdom constitution requires that there be annual financial legislation. Thus, annual Finance Acts permit taxation and Consolidated Fund and Appropriation Acts permit government expenditure. The legislative procedure for these (which takes up much

---

64 Human Rights Act 1998, s 6.
65 As indeed it did not, as noted above, in relation to the Anti-Terrorism, Crime and Security Act 2001 which contained provisions incompatible with the Convention right to liberty and security of persons (Art. 5 ECHR), by permitting indefinite detention of certain persons. This therefore, required derogation from that part of the European Convention on Human Rights itself, seemingly effected by the Human Rights Act 1998 (Designated Derogation) Order 2001, SI 2001 No 3644. However, in litigation considering this derogation, the Appellate Committee of the House of Lords concluded, in *A and others v Secretary of State for the Home Department* [2004] UKHL 56, [2005] 2 AC 68 that it was incompatible with Convention rights and unlawful in UK law. The relevant provisions therefore ceased to be used, and were repealed by the Prevention of Terrorism Act 2005 which introduced 'control orders', a form of 'house arrest', which might be 'non-derogating' or (with the court's consent) 'derogating'. However, some non-derogating control orders might also breach the same Convention rights: see *Secretary of State for the Home Department v* MB [2006] EWCA Civ 1140, [2007] QB 415; *Secretary of State for the Home Department v JJ & Others* [2006] EWCA Civ 1141 [2007] QB 446.
66 Human Rights Act, s 19.
67 *Ibid*, ss 2 & 3.
68 Scotland Act 1998, 29 & 54.
69 Human Rights Act 1998, ss 7 & 8.

parliamentary legislative time) differs somewhat from the usual. It does not provide effective control over taxation and expenditure by government, however, and in any case control is increasingly shared with the European Community. (For the operation of this in relation to the Scottish Parliament, see Chapter 8).

Legislation under the Parliament Acts 1911 and 1949

7.25   The legislative powers of the House of Lords are constrained by the Parliament Acts 1911 and 1949. Firstly, Bills introduced into the United Kingdom Parliament certified by the Speaker as 'money Bills' (such as taxation and expenditure Bills), which by a convention of the constitution must always be introduced into the House of Commons, can be delayed by the Lords for one month only, after which they are deemed to have agreed to them. Secondly, other Bills (unless they fall into the third category) can be delayed for two sessions of Parliament only, after which they are deemed to be agreed. Thirdly, Bills to extend the life of the Parliament, and any private legislation, are unaffected by the legislation.

The Parliament Acts have rarely been formally invoked[70].

Statute Law Revision and Statute Law Repeal legislation

7.26   Legislation in a common law or mixed jurisdiction is *ad hoc*, and grows by accretion. Legislation on a topic may thus be widely scattered, and may become obsolete. While Acts of the pre-1707 Scots Parliament may fall into desuetude, others are considered immortal unless repealed. Later Acts of the United Kingdom Parliament may repeal all or part of earlier ones, but may do so implicitly.

After occasional initiatives over several centuries, in the early years of the 20th century (but somewhat earlier in England) serious

---

70 However, the Lords did reject the War Crimes Bill in 1990, and again when it was reintroduced in 1991, so the Bill was deemed to have been passed and became law as the War Crimes Act 1991. The European Parliamentary Elections Act 1999 had a similar history, as did the Sexual Offences (Amendment) Act 2000, and the Hunting Act 2004. The Higher Education Act 1998 did not use the procedure, but was passed only after the government agreed to review the matter in dispute. For discussion, see *R (on the application of Jackson) v Attorney-General* [2005] UKHL 56, [2006] 1 AC 262 and Ekins 'Acts of Parliament and the Parliament Acts' (2007) 123 LQR 91–114.

attempts at weeding out were undertaken by the Statute Law Committee and others. They produced a number of Statute Law Revision Acts, for example the Statute Law Revision (Scotland) Act 1906. A simplified parliamentary procedure, using a Joint Committee of both Houses for the Committee Stage, and permitting no subsequent amendments, later stages being 'on the nod', was created for them. These Acts collectively repealed thousands of Acts considered no longer in force or obsolete.

Responsibility for such activities was given to the Law Commissions when they were created in 1965. They have produced at the time of writing some 11 Statute Law Repeal Acts, most recently in 2013 following the 2012 Statute Law (Repeals) Report published in April 2012, repealing hundreds more old Acts by the accelerated parliamentary procedure[71]. These Acts repeal those Acts considered 'no longer of practical utility', a somewhat more inclusive definition than used before.

Consolidation legislation

7.27   In conjunction with the weeding-out process, there have been attempts at 'consolidation', that is, at placing all provisions on a topic in a single coherent Act, and a large number of consolidating Acts were passed in the 19th century. However, the process of rendering provisions from a variety of Acts into a single coherent whole is difficult without at least marginally altering those provisions, in other words, without incidentally altering the law. Thus, although the same simplified legislative process, as for statute law revision, was made available, parliamentary jealousy meant it was little used. The Enactments (Procedure) Act 1949 permitted corrections and minor improvements (as defined in the Act) through the accelerated procedure.

The Law Commissions took principal responsibility for consolidation as well as statute law revision. Their initial hopes of large-scale consolidation were not fulfilled before devolution. It may yet be that the Scottish Parliament will be able to realise them through a simplified procedure. Nevertheless, even before

---

71 Thus, its Schedule contained 11 Parts, each concerned with a different subject matter, eg Part I, Benevolent Institutions; Part II, Civil and Criminal Justice; Part III, Indian Railways, and so on. Part 10(2) concerns Scottish Local Taxation and repeals some 16 Acts dealing with the Two Pennies Scots Act taxes in towns ranging from Kelso to Montrose.

devolution, the Scottish Law Commission had generated more than 20 Consolidation Acts applying solely to Scotland, for example the Prisons (Scotland) Act 1989 (indicating, incidentally, that consolidating Acts are not usually explicitly so called in their Short Titles[72]). It has also joined with the (English and Welsh) Law Commission on many more applying to Great Britain or the United Kingdom, including the massive Income and Corporation Taxes Act 1988. Those consolidation measures recommended by the Law Commissions undergo a version of the accelerated legislative procedure even if their incidental amendments go beyond those permitted by the 1949 Act (although the enormous consolidating Companies Act 1985 used an *ad hoc* procedure laid down in the Companies Act 1981).

In addition, any government department may promote its own consolidating Bill, usually as a result of a report by a committee of inquiry, departmental committee or the like, for example the Highways Act 1959 which followed the *ad hoc* departmental *Report of the Committee on the Consolidation of Highway Law* (Cmnd 630). A more recent example is the Wireless Telegraphy Act 2006, consolidating the Wireless Telegraphy Acts of 1949, 1967 and 1998, the Marine Etc Broadcasting Offences Act 1967, part of the Telecommunications Act 1984 and part of the Communication Act 2003. One particular example of this is the 'Tax Rewrite', that is, the attempt to render tax law into a series of more comprehensible statutes, which the Inland Revenue (now HM Revenue and Customs) was obliged to undertake by the Finance Act 1995, s 160. This enormous task has produced legislation (for instance, the Capital Allowances Act 2001 and Income Tax (Earnings and Pensions) Act 2003), but has been a long drawn out process, doubtfully successful and, like all Consolidation legislation, gradually overtaken by amendments.

There are thus several means of introducing Consolidation Bills, and it has been calculated that about a third of all UK legislation since the Law Commissions were set up has been consolidating.

Consolidation is not a panacea. Firstly, an area of law may be large enough to require several consolidating statutes. The consolidation of customs and excise law in 1979 produced seven Acts. In any case, statutes never stand alone, and must cross-refer. Secondly,

---

72 The consolidating Criminal Procedure (Scotland) Act 1995 (replacing the similarly titled 1975 Act was, confusingly, preceded by a Criminal Law (Consolidation) Act 1995.

a Consolidating Act will soon be amended[73], and may require reconsolidation later. The Criminal Procedure (Scotland) Act 1995, was heavily amended in its first ten years such that it acquired, for example, ss 194A-194I, inserted between ss 194 and 195, 234A-234K between ss 234 and 235, and 245A-245H between ss 245 and 246[74]. Thirdly, consolidation deals only with statute law, not common law.

It may be that pressure to consolidate has slackened in recent years[75].

Codification

7.28 Codification, in the sense of a single statute incorporating all the law on the subject from all the sources, legislative and common law, has been sought in some areas. There are a few late 19th-century United Kingdom examples, such as the Bills of Exchange Act 1882, all passed by ordinary legislative procedure. These Acts, however, suffer from similar problems to those of Consolidating Acts. The law continues to develop and is only comprehensible in the light of judicial interpretation of the Act, so the codification becomes outdated.

Such codifying statutes must not be confused with the 'codes properly so-called' found in civil law countries (for which, see Chapter 5). These, taking Justinian's codification of Roman law as their model, not only seek to reduce the entire law on a subject to a single mega-statute, but set it out in reasoned, encyclopaedic form, from first principles. They are the ultimate authority, changed only rarely and then with difficulty.

It is difficult to imagine such a code in a common law or mixed system. The whole grain of such systems runs against comprehensive, final, authoritative statements which reduce the judge's role to a mere mouthpiece.

---

73 The consolidating Wireless Telegraphy Act 2006 was amended in its year of enactment by the Legislative and Regulatory Reform Act 2006.
74 The consolidating Companies Act 1985 was probably amended more in the following four years than the preceding consolidating Companies Act 1949 was in the nearly 40 years of its life.
75 See Samuels, A 'Consolidation: a plea' (2005) 26 Stat LR 56–63

There have, nevertheless been attempts to 'codify' conducted by the Law Commission and others[76].

The Legislative and Regulatory Reform Act 2006

7.29 This remarkable piece of legislation is discussed in Chapter 9. It should be noted here, however, that it allows the Government to amend existing legislation in order to remove vaguely expressed 'burdens', subject to vaguely expressed safeguards, with limited reference to Parliament.

Private Members' legislation

7.30 Although most Bills in the United Kingdom Parliament are introduced by the government, any MP or peer can, in principle, do so, and such legislation is called 'Private Members' legislation'. However, as governments and oppositions (as 'governments in waiting') have carved up parliamentary time, there is little left for private members.

Private Members may introduce Bills by two special methods. Firstly, the 'ten-minute rule' allows a private member on certain occasions to introduce a Bill and speak in favour of it for ten minutes, after which another can oppose it for ten minutes and a vote is taken. This procedure is usually used simply to air a grievance, rather than seriously to propose legislation.

Secondly, the Private Members' ballot is a device for prioritising between Private Members' Bills. Participants give in their names, and 20 are drawn from a hat. Standing Orders of the House of Commons allow up to a dozen Fridays for Private Members' Bills only and procedural rules make it easy to dispose of a Bill undebated, by filibustering. Only those with high places in the ballot are likely to receive enough time. In any case, the government's voting power

---

76 The Law Commissions Act 1965 enjoined the Law Commissions to 'codify', and the Government's White Paper *Criminal Justice: the way ahead* (2001), paras 3.27 and 3.57–59 enjoined 'codification', but it is not clear in either case what meaning is to be attached to that word. See, however, Law Commission *Codification of the Criminal Law – a report to the Law Commission* (Law Com No 143) (HC Paper 1984–5 No 270) (1985) and Law Commission *Criminal Law: a criminal code* (law Com No 177) (HC Paper 1989–90 No 299) (2 vols) (1989): also Toulson, R 'Forty Years On: what progress in delivering accessible and principled criminal law?' (2006) 27 Stat LR 61–72. For attempts in Scotland, see Ch 8.

ensures that no Bill it dislikes will get through Parliament, and Private Members have little access to Parliamentary Draftsmen.

Thus, Private Members' legislation is not a large proportion of all United Kingdom legislation. It has been as much as a third in the recent past, but this proportion is misleading, for what is ostensibly Private Members' Legislation may be covert government legislation, including Law Commission proposals, which has received drafting and other help. The Age of Legal Capacity (Scotland) Act 1991, introduced by Sir Nicholas Fairbairn MP (Perth and Kinross), is an example. So, more recently, is the Climate Change and Sustainable Energy Act 2006, introduced by Mark Lazarowicz MP (Edinburgh North and Leith). Private members coming high in the ballot are likely to be inundated with requests from interest groups to adopt their Bill. The Solicitors (Scotland) Act 1991, introduced by Alistair Darling MP (Edinburgh Central), was a measure sought by the Law Society of Scotland, for example.

Overall, Private Members' Bills provide a continuing trickle of important legislation, perhaps half-covert government Bills, rarely party politically sensitive, but sometimes on campaigning issues which the government is at worst indifferent to or, as with the Abortion Act 1967, may favour without wishing to be seen to promote.

Law Commission Bills

7.31   The UK Parliament in 2009 set up a procedure for politically uncontroversial Bills proposed by the Law Commissions under which the Bill in question begins its parliamentary journey in the House of Lords, where it is mainly considered by a reasonably expert Special Public Bill Committee. That body may take evidence on the intentions and likely effects of the Bill, and even amend it, before passing it on to the House of Commons for further consideration. A number of Bills, many of them the product of joint projects between the English and the Scottish Law Commissions, have now passed into law by this route, eg the Third Parties (Rights against Insurers) Act 2010 and the Consumer Insurance (Disclosure and Representations) Act 2012. The procedure can also be used for purely Scottish Bills, and the first of these, the Partnerships (Prosecution) (Scotland) Bill, was introduced in the House of Lords on 5 November 2012.

Local, Personal, Private and Hybrid legislation

7.32   The public/private distinction is extremely complicated but, broadly, it is used in two separate ways. Firstly, it is used to refer to the public nature of the contents of an Act. The Interpretation Act 1978, s 3 stipulates that every Act is a 'public Act' unless it otherwise states, and that if it is a public Act, when cited in court it does not have to be proved to be the law, but can be taken as read. Only Personal Acts, discussed below, are private in this sense, and given their rarity and limited effect, in practice this is an unimportant distinction.

Secondly, it is used to refer to the parliamentary procedure a Bill goes through. Public Bill procedure is used for legislation promoted by a member of either House, which will commonly be general in its application, but might apply to a locality only (though if it does, it might be hybrid), or even, rarely, to an individual. Private Bill procedure is used for UK legislation promoted by persons outwith Parliament, such as local authorities, who petition Parliament for legislation. This process involves a quasi-judicial procedure, in which promoters and objectors give evidence. Such a private Act in practice will always be 'Local', or 'Personal', not 'general'[77]. Such legislation was common until the 19th century, when promotion of legislation came to be seen as a function of government. It generally sought only to create exceptions to the law. Thus, for example, local authorities might seek exceptional powers through Local Private Acts, and individuals might seek naturalisation (and, in England, divorce) through Personal Private Acts. It is in this sense that the public/private distinction is usually made.

Personal Private legislation is extremely rare nowadays (though there were a few marriage-enabling examples in the 1980s, such as the George Donald Evans and Deborah Jane Evans (Marriage Enabling) Act 1987), for individuals may now achieve naturalisation and divorce through quasi-judicial administrative procedures[78]. Local Private legislation still occurs every year, however (for example, the River Humber (Upper Pyewipe Outfall) Act 1992, the United Reformed Church Act 2000 and the HBOS Group Reorganisation Act 2006), though most of the need for it has gone as local authorities now have most of their powers given under public general legislation, such as the Local Government (Scotland) Act 1973, s 201 (which gives powers to write by-laws).

In any case, accelerated private legislation procedures have been invented to save parliamentary time. The chief one is 'Provisional Order procedure' under the Private Legislation Procedure (Scotland)

---

77 Though the 'local' means, in practice, anything not 'personal', and personal means concerning an individual or small number of individuals.
78 Non-marital examples include, for example, the Niall Mcpherson Indemnity Act 1954, *c 29.*

Act 1936. This largely delegates the consideration of evidence to Commissioners, and the decision to the Secretary of State. If he makes the Provisional Order requested by the promoters, there must be a 'Confirmation Bill' (for example, the Pittenweem Harbour Order Confirmation Act 1992 and the Scottish Borders Council (Jim Clark Memorial Rally) Order Confirmation Act 1996) but it employs an accelerated procedure. There is also a special parliamentary procedure under the Statutory Orders (Special Procedure) Act 1945, which requires no confirmation Bill, but appears never to have been used.

The Scotland Act 1998 continues the Private Legislation Procedure (Scotland) Act 1936 but, by Sch 8, para 5 it cannot be used where the subject-matter is wholly within the competence of the Scottish Parliament. Thus, there was a Comhaírle nan Eilean Siar (Eriskay Causeway) Order Confirmation Act 2000 and Railtrack (Waverley Station) Order Confirmation Act 2000.

Hybrid legislation is that which is partly public general, partly private (and local or personal). The Maplin Development Act 1973 was hybrid. It gave powers to the Secretary of State to acquire land on the Maplin Sands in the Thames Estuary for an airport, but did so in relation to a specific area, thus directly affecting individual interests. Hybrid Bills go through a modified public Bill procedure. Thus, the Maplin Development Act took its place in the Public General Act series as 1973 c64.

PUBLICATION AND CITATION OF GREAT BRITAIN AND UNITED KINGDON PARLIAMENTARY LEGISLATION

Publication of Acts of the Parliaments of Great Britain and the United Kingdom

7.33 Acts of the Parliaments of Great Britain and the United Kingdom (often bound with those of England) appear in a great variety of editions.

Chronological series

7.34 Public general Acts of the United Kingdom Parliament are printed and sold by The Stationery Office ('TSO') in single copies, and bound up in several volumes annually in a series called *Public*

General Acts and Measures[79], which commenced in 1831. For almost all purposes, these can be taken as authoritative[80].

Most earlier legislation is of historical interest only. Diverse editions of earlier Acts were produced by various publishers, such as various editions of *Statutes at Large* covering various periods (for example, Ruffhead's, covering English legislation 1225–1707 and Great Britain legislation 1707–1800), and *Statutes of the Realm 1235–1713*, published by the Record Commissioners. These also contain English, but not Scots, Acts and some older editions are inaccurate.

Public General Statutes Affecting Scotland ('Blackwood's Acts') were published annually from 1848 to 1947, with a further three volumes published in 1948 covering the period 1707–1847. The third edition of *Statutes Revised*, published in 1950, contains Great Britain and United Kingdom (and English) Acts still in force in 1948.

All chronological series contain the original unamended text. This is useful for some purposes, but has the disadvantage that it is impossible to tell whether the provision has been repealed (and if so by what), or amended (and if so how).

Encyclopaedic series

7.35   The *Statutes in Force* volumes were published as a loose-leaf encyclopaedia, continually updated by the Statute Law Committee through the Statutory Publications Office. It attempted to provide the text of all public general Acts still in force and as amended (with minor exceptions). These were digested into 131 groups and sub-groups. A list of groups and Acts appears in the first volume.

New Acts were inserted, repealed ones removed, and amendments incorporated. An annual cumulative supplement noted amendments and repeals, and the text of heavily amended Acts was replaced from time to time. Unfortunately, the series was not easy to use, and was phased out in the 1990s in anticipation of the availability of an authoritative Statute Law Database (considered below). Despite the fact that the updating service ceased in 1991, and the last Acts were added were those for 1996, *Statutes in Force* can occasionally be useful for revealing changes made to older legislation.

79 The 'Measures' are legislation of the Church of England, which, for some reason, are bound in the same volume.
80 See, however, Rankine 'Errors in Acts' (1987) 8 Stat LR 53.

Commercially produced reprints

7.36 The *Current Law Statutes Annotated* volumes (called *Scottish Current Law Statutes Annotated* until 1990) has been published since 1949 (and from 1948 in the case of England and Wales) by W Green and Sweet & Maxwell. The series reproduces all public general statutes chronologically with annotations. These include citation of parliamentary debates and sometimes lengthy and useful commentaries upon each section. Acts of the current year appear in a loose-leaf service file, and each year's Acts are bound into an annual volume or volumes.

Halsbury's Statutes (Butterworths) contains all United Kingdom Acts save those applying only to Scotland. This is unfortunate, as they are digested into subjects, well annotated, and updated through cumulative supplement, current statutes service, and noter-up volumes. Acts concerned with the constitutional structure and government of Northern Ireland, and Northern Ireland Acts which contain cross-border provisions, are reproduced and updated (though not necessarily annotated). In addition, the application of an Act to Northern Ireland is indicated in the preliminary notes. Acts of purely Scottish application, and those provisions of United Kingdom Acts which apply only to Scotland, are excluded.

There are also reprints of all, or most, statutes on a particular area, such as commercial law and family law. *The Parliament House Book* (W Green) is a six-volume loose-leaf encyclopaedia of information useful to practising Scots lawyers, including reprints of Acts of particular interest, in amended form. Acts included are also sold separately as *Parliament House Statutes Reprints*. There are also a number of specific area encyclopaedias, such as *Simon's Taxes* (Butterworths). Unfortunately, not all of these contain the Scots law on the subject.

Textbooks and monographs may contain Acts of Parliament, or parts of them, relevant to their subject-matter. For example, Macdonald and Webber *Immigration Law and Practice in the United Kingdom* (6th edn, 2005) contains most of the relevant legislation, amended to the date of publication. Annotated Acts from the *Current Law* series are also sometimes published as books, as, for example, Himsworth and Munro *The Scotland Act 1998*.

Indexes etc

7.37 Each volume of *Public General Acts and Measures* contains alphabetical and chronological lists of the Acts included. The final volume for each year also contains a table of origins (formerly referred to as 'derivations') and destinations for consolidation Acts (that is, tables showing the relationship of original and consolidated provisions) although it has no official status; and a table of effects of legislation (that is, of repeals and amendments effected during the year).

The Stationery Office also publishes the *Chronological Table of Statutes* annually[81]. This lists chronologically all Scots, Great Britain and United Kingdom (and English) legislation to date, and indicates repeals and amendments.

(Scottish) Current Law Statutes Annotated volumes are individually indexed, as is the loose-leaf 'Service File'. In recent years, individual Acts have been indexed and for some time, the final volume for each year has had an index to all legislation in that year.

Halsbury's Statutes has a companion volume entitled *Is It In Force?*, also issued with the updating service to *The Laws of Scotland: Stair Memorial Encyclopaedia*. Each annual edition records, in respect of all sections of all statutes passed since 1980, whether they are yet in force, and to what extent.

Local, personal and private Acts

7.38   The Stationery Office publishes single copies of local and personal Acts and there is an Index to Local and Personal Acts 1797–1849 (2 volumes) and Index to Local and Personal Acts 1850–1995 (four volumes), a Chronological Table of Local Legislation 1797–1994 (4 volumes) and Chronological Table of Private and Personal Acts 1539–1997 (1 volume, containing all such legislation passed by Parliaments in Westminster). Public General Acts and Measures also contains an alphabetical list of local and personal Acts, but no text.

Local Acts have often been published in local compilations, for instance, Dundee Water Acts 1845–82, Dundee Municipal Statutes 1872–98, Dundee Gas and Corporation Acts 1868–1901, and Dundee Harbour Acts 1811–1912.

From 1992 local, personal and private Acts are published in *Current Law Statutes Annotated*.

Computerised retrieval of legislation

7.39   All Acts of the UK Parliament (and the devolved Parliaments) can be found online through The National Archives[82]. The National

---

81 Until 1990, it produced an *Index to the Statutes* as well.
82 See http://www.legislation.gov.uk.

Archives is a UK government department and an executive agency of the Ministry of Justice. The National Archives is made up of four formerly independent government bodies; Her Majesty's Stationery Office ('HMSO'), the holder of Crown copyright, the Public Record Office, the Office of Public Sector Information and the Royal Commission on Historical Manuscripts. The National Archives is tasked with, among other things, publishing legislation online to make it easily available for everybody. Bills currently before the UK Parliament can be found in full text at the Parliament website, along with annotations on their parliamentary progress[83].

The Westlaw database includes all public general Acts in force, in their amended form as appropriate. The BAILII database combines the coverage of unamended Acts from 1988, with older legislation derived from the Statute Law Database. The LexisNexis Butterworths database, mirroring *Halsbury's Statutes*, includes all Acts applying to the United Kingdom and to England and Wales only, but not those applying to Scotland only.

Justis [*sic*] United Kingdom Statutes database contains the full text of all Acts of Parliament, including repealed legislation.

Citation of Acts of the Parliaments of Great Britain and the United Kingdom

7.40 Before 1963 public general Acts were cited by the extraordinarily complicated regnal year method which the pre-1707 English Parliament used. In this, as well as (or instead of) the reference to the calendar year of enactment, there was reference to the Parliament that passed it, identified by the year or years of the reign of the contemporary Sovereign, calculated from the date of accession. Thus, the Prevention of Damage by Rabbits Act 1939 was correctly cited as '2 & 3 Geo 6 c44', that is, the 44th Act of the Parliament which started in the second year of George VI's reign, and ended in the third.

There were further complications. Until 1940 statutes were bound in volumes for each Parliament although this did not coincide with any calendar year. For example, the session 22 & 23 Geo 5 straddled 1932 and 1933. Thereafter, until 1963, the statutes were bound in annual volumes, although these did not coincide with any parliamentary year. For example, the volume for 1945 contained 8 & 9 Geo 6 c4 to c44 and 9 & 10 Geo 6 c1 to c21.

---

83 See http://www.parliament.uk/.

Since 1963, however, they have been cited in essentially the same fashion as used for Acts of the (original) Parliament of Scotland, by short title, year and chapter number, for example 'Criminal Procedure (Scotland) Act 1987 c46'.

Local and personal Acts are cited in the same form as public general, save that local Acts use lower case Roman numerals (for example, the Price's Patent Candle Co Ltd Act 1992 cxvii), and personal Acts, italic numerals (for example, the Valerie Mary Hill and Alan Monk (Marriage Enabling) Act 1985 c1).

8 Legislation – Acts of the Scottish Parliament

THE INSTITUTIONAL BACKGROUND

8.1   The institutional background of devolution, and the Scottish Government and Scottish Parliament, were dealt with in Chapter 3, and its relationship with Acts of the United Kingdom Parliament was noted in Chapter 7, with United Kingdom delegated legislation in Chapter 9 and with Scottish delegated legislation in Chapter 10. This Chapter deals with the nature and style of Scottish Parliamentary legislation, the Scottish Parliamentary process, and the publication and citation of Acts of the Scottish Parliament.

THE NATURE AND STYLE OF SCOTTISH PARLIAMENTARY LEGISLATION

Devolution and the nature of Acts of the Scottish Parliament

8.2   As noted in relation to Acts of the United Kingdom Parliament, a few Acts of the original pre-1707 Parliament of Scotland are still in force with, effectively, the same status as those of the United Kingdom Parliament[1]. However, this Chapter concerns Acts of the post-1998 Scottish Parliament.

Devolution is making Acts of the Scottish Parliament the normal method of legislating for Scotland (though existing Acts of the United Kingdom will remain the principal source for some

---

1   Though subject to the 'doctrine of desuetude', that is, that they can cease to have effect without explicit or implicit repeal by a later Act, if they have been ignored for a lengthy period, and there is evidence of contrary practice. The oldest Act of the Parliament of Scotland still in force is the Royal Mines Act 1424 (which provides that 'Item: gif ony myne of golde or siluer be fundyn in ony lordis landis of the realme and it may be prowt that thre halfpennys of siluer may be fynit pwt of the punde oe leide The lordis of parliament consentis that sik myne be the kingis as is vsuale in vthir realmys'.

time, and a surprising amount of law for Scotland continues to be enacted at Westminster, for reasons considered above in relation to Acts of the United Kingdom Parliament[2]). The 'legislative competence' of the Scottish Parliament was considered in Chapter 3, and its breadth noted, for, in respect of Scotland, all legislative powers that are not specifically reserved to the United Kingdom Parliament are devolved to the Scottish Parliament. So the Scottish Parliament has a plenitude of law-making power (much greater than if it had been set up under the abortive Scotland Act 1978, which specified the powers to be devolved)[3]. Under the Scotland Act 2012, the law-making powers are also increasing in number. The range of topics for legislation is thus wide. Indeed, as also noted in Chapter 3, in its first three sessions, the Scottish Parliament passed over 150 Acts, on topics as diverse as the abolition of feudal land-holding and of fox-hunting, reform of the means of appointing judges and of the police and fire services in Scotland, prohibition of anti-social behaviour and of prostitution in public places, and support for the Gaelic language and for breastfeeders. Some Acts have been very controversial, covering topics such as minimum alcohol pricing and damages for asbestos-related conditions. The range may also include legislation on Convention rights and EU law[4].

The very concept of 'legislative competence' indicates, however, that Acts of the Scottish Parliament are 'subordinate' or 'delegated legislation' and this is expressly recognised in some legislation[5]. They are delegated legislation as they are made under powers delegated by the sovereign United Kingdom Parliament, in the Scotland Act 1998 and the Scotland Act 2012.

Pre- and post-enactment checks, described below, police those limits to legislative competence, and the Scottish Parliament is

---

2 As with the United Kingdom as a whole, the sheer quantity of (sub)delegated legislation (see Chapters 9 & 10) far outstrips the quantity of parliamentary legislation. See also references to the Sewel Convention and Sewel Motions below.

3 The position is further complicated in that the Acts of the Scottish Parliament may further delegate powers to the Scottish Government and others, just as Acts of the Westminster Parliament may so delegate. Exercises of such powers by the Scottish Ministers, whether sub-delegated under Holyrood powers or delegated under Westminster powers, are called 'Scottish Statutory Instruments'. They are considered with other delegated legislation in Chapters 9 and 10.

4 Thus, for example, the Convention Rights (Compliance) (Scotland) Act 2001 was passed specifically to make aspects of Scots law conform to the European Convention on Human Rights

5 *Eg*, the Human Rights Act 1998, s 21(1).

subject to the *ultra vires* doctrine (discussed elsewhere in relation to human rights, Community legislation, and other delegated legislation). In any case, power to override the Scottish Parliament still rests at Westminster for, as s 28(7) of the Scotland Act 1998 explicitly declares, 'This section does not affect the power of the Parliament of the United Kingdom to make laws for Scotland'.

However, their style of expression is that used by the United Kingdom Parliament, rather than that used in most delegated legislation. Also, they often make provision for areas such as criminal justice and land law which, until devolution, were dealt with in Acts of the United Kingdom Parliament, rather than in delegated legislation. Moreover, they are made by an elected, deliberative, body rather than by civil servants. Indeed, the powers of the Scottish Parliament are of such inherent significance, and the breadth of delegation so remarkable, as to justify separate treatment from other delegated legislation[6].

The 'Sewel Convention' and 'Sewel Motions'

8.3   It is worth recalling, nevertheless, that (as noted in Chapter 7) there has been much legislation enacted by the United Kingdom Parliament in relation to Scotland, even within the devolved legislative competence of the Scottish Parliament, through the medium of 'Sewel Motions', that is motions passed by the Scottish Parliament, in effect, requesting that Scotland be included in the Westminster legislation. Thus, for example, the provisions of the Civil Partnership Act 2004 and s 3 of the Compensation Act 2006 were extended to Scotland and, at the time of writing, some (but not all) provisions of the Defamation Bill 2012 are similarly to be applied to Scotland.

Acts of the Scottish Parliament, their types and form

8.4   The types and forms of Acts of the Scottish Parliament are modelled upon those of United Kingdom Acts (to which reference

---

6 See further on the status of asps *AXA General Insurance Ltd v Lord Advocate* [2011] UKSC 46; 2012 SC (UKSC) 122.

should be made: see Chapter 7)[7]. Most are 'public'[8], and 'general'[9] in the sense that Acts of the United Kingdom Parliament are, and special types of Act are considered below. The normal legislative product in the first eight years of the existence of the Scottish Parliament was some 15 Acts a year, though they varied considerably in length. The very first Act of the Scottish Parliament had but three sections. The number of Acts fell to an average of 10 a year in the third session but this can be partly explained by the Scottish National Party forming a minority government through the period. Clearly, they do not yet vary much in age (though the continuation in force of Acts of the original pre-1707 Scottish Parliament should not be forgotten).

Short title, 'asp Number' and Contents List

8.5   Acts of the Scottish Parliament commence with a Short Title, normally containing brackets embracing the word '(Scotland)'[10], for example, the 'International Criminal Court (Scotland) Act 2001' (and may contain other bracketed words, as does the 'Mental Health (Public Safety and Appeals) (Scotland) Act 1999'). They also bear an 'asp' ('Act of the Scottish Parliament') Number, that is, a sequential number which, with the year of enactment, identifies the Act, for example, 'asp 10'. Thus '2002 asp 10' was the Fur Farming (Prohibition) (Scotland) Act 2002[11].

All but the shortest Acts have an official 'Contents' list of sections with their numbers and their marginal notes.

---

7 See also McCluskie, J 'New Approaches to UK Legislative Drafting: the view from Scotland' (2004) 25 Stat LR 136–143: also the speculative but interesting Jamieson, NJ 'The Scots Statute' (2006) 27 Stat LR 176–184.

8 *Ie* they go through the normal process of enactment unless they fall into the 'Private Bill' category: Standing Orders of the Scottish Parliament, r 9.17.1

9 *Ie* they are 'judicially noticed' so do not require proving in court: Scotland Act 1998, s 28(6).

10 But not invariably, for example if the title is otherwise unequivocal, eg Scottish Public Services Ombudsman Act 2002. Note also that Acts of the Westminster Parliament exclusively concerning Scotland were usually identified by the parenthetic '(Scotland)' in the past (the last pre-devolution Act of the United Kingdom Parliament which applied exclusively to Scotland was the Mental Health (Amendment) (Scotland) Act 1999) and so no doubt will any in the future.

11 Short titles and asp numbers were required by the Scotland Act 1998 (Transitory and Transitional Provisions) (Publication and Interpretation etc of Acts of the Scottish Parliament) Order 1999, SI 1999/1379, arts 4, 5.

Statement of Enactment

8.6   Unlike Acts of the United Kingdom Parliament, there is no incantatory 'Enacting Formula', but each Act has a Statement indicating its parliamentary passage in the form: 'The Bill for this Act of the Scottish Parliament was passed by Parliament on 6th March 2002 and received Royal Assent on 11th April 2002'.

Long title and preamble

8.7   Acts of the Scottish Parliament also have a Long Title, delimiting the scope of the Bill introduced into the Parliament. Thus, the Fur Farming (Prohibition) (Scotland) Act 2002 has the Long Title 'An Act of the Scottish Parliament to prohibit the keeping of animals solely or primarily for slaughter for the value of their fur; to provide for the making of payments in respect of the related closure of certain businesses; and for connected purposes'.

Sections and Marginal Notes

8.8   The Section is the basic unit of Acts of the Scottish Parliament, and they are numbered sequentially through the Act. They may be broken into Sub-sections, Paragraphs and Sub-paragraphs for, as with Acts of the United Kingdom Parliament, the draftsmen aim at exactitude (rules in 'fixed verbal form') rather than comprehensibility, and use typographical devices to express the logic of the section. This also allows precise and unequivocal identification of provisions, for example 'Debt Arrangement and Attachment (Scotland) Act 2002, s 2(3)(a)(iii)'.

The United Kingdom convention of numbering a new Section or Sub-section inserted by an amending Act is employed. Thus the Criminal Procedure (Amendment) (Scotland) Act 2002, s 1(1) inserts new sub-sections 150(3A) and (3B) between the existing sub-sections 150(3) and (4) of the Criminal Procedure (Scotland) Act 1995[12].

Marginal References to legislation referred to in the text have not been used, the draftsman preferring to reproduce short title, year and chapter number or asp number in the text.

---

12 This is an example of an Act of the Scottish Parliament amending an Act of the United Kingdom Parliament (both, however, identified by the parenthetic '(Scotland)').

Headings

8.9   Groups of sections, as in the United Kingdom convention, may be grouped under 'Cross-headings', and into Parts and even Chapters. For example, the Land Reform (Scotland) Act 2003 has its 100 sections divided into 4 Parts, with 6, 2, 7 and 5 Chapters respectively.

No doubt 'Titles' will also be used if considered necessary.

Interpretation sections

8.10   Where words or phrases are inherently vague, or are used in an unusual sense, or have been invented for the purpose, an Interpretation Section may provide a meaning. Thus, the Abolition of Feudal Tenure (Scotland) Act 2000, s 72 defines, among other things 'land'[13].

Repeal and amendment

8.11   The standard United Kingdom conventions apply to Acts of the Scottish Parliament, that is, that Acts continue in force unless repealed or amended and no special process of repeal is necessary, so 'implicit repeal' is possible[14]. Also, while repeals and amendments may appear anywhere in the Act, commonly, a specific section at the end effects them, often in conjunction with a Schedule. For example, the Adults with Incapacity (Scotland) Act 2000, Sch 6 is headed 'Repeals' and contains a table indicating what provisions are repealed, and to what extent, and the Housing (Scotland) Act 2010, Sch 2, headed 'Modifications of Enactments', contains a long list of repeals and amendments.

However, in the case of Acts of the Scottish Parliament, because of their delegated status, particular considerations concerning repeal and amendment should be noted. Firstly, because of the general possibility that they may be found to be outwith the Parliament's

---

13 The Scotland Act 1998 (Transitory and Transitional Provisions) (Publication and Interpretation, etc of Acts of the Scottish Parliament) Order 1999, SI 1999/1379, Sch 2 contained a list of 'General Definitions' (including one of 'land') to be applied to Acts of the Scottish Parliament.

14 On the effects of repeal, see SI 1999/1379 (see previous note), Sch 1, paras 11–14. In principle, repeals are not retrospective and repeals of repeals do not revive the original provision.

'legislative competence', s 107 of the Scotland Act 1998 gives the United Kingdom government, in such cases, the power to make 'necessary or expedient' provision by ordinary delegated legislation (see Chapter 9). This clearly includes the power to repeal or amend. And, secondly, in any case, as s 28(7) reiterates, the United Kingdom Parliament retains the power to legislate for Scotland which even more clearly includes the power to repeal or amend Acts of the Scottish Parliament. (Indeed, the continued use of the United Kingdom Parliament to legislate for Scotland through 'Sewel Motions', considered above in relation to Acts of the United Kingdom Parliament, means that such legislation is in fact a frequent and regular occurrence.) Thus, repeal or amendment of Acts of the Scottish Parliament may well be by means other than further Acts of the Scottish Parliament.

Transitional, Commencement, Short Title and Extent provisions

8.12   In broad terms these operate, or will operate, in the same fashion as with United Kingdom statutes, save that the difficulty which Extent provisions deal with does not arise, as legislating outwith Scotland is beyond the Scottish Parliament's legislative competence. Thus, the University of St Andrews (Postgraduate Medical Degrees) Act 2002, s 2 states that it may be so cited, but contains no reference to commencement, so came into force on the date of Royal Assent[15], while the Scottish Qualifications Authority Act 2002, s 6, declares that it may be so cited, but that (other than s 6 itself) it comes into force 'on such day as the Scottish Ministers may by order appoint'[16].

Schedules

8.13   Schedules are attached to Acts of the Scottish Parliament in the same fashion, and for the same purposes, as to Acts of the United Kingdom Parliament. Thus, the Water Environment and

15 30 July 2002 is indicated in the 'Statement of enactment' (see above).
16 Its royal assent was obtained on 6 June 2002. The Scottish Ministers, under s 6 of the Act, appointed 19 August 2002 for s 1(7)(a)(iii), (8), (9), by the Scottish Qualifications Authority Act 2002 (Commencement No 1) Order 2002, SSI/335, art 3(2). Thus, at that time, s 1(1)–(6), (7)(a)(i),(ii), (b) and ss 2–5 had not been brought into force.

Water Services (Scotland) Act 2002 has four Schedules, two split into two Parts each[17].

Explanatory Notes

8.14   Almost every Act has accompanying 'Explanatory Notes' (as United Kingdom Acts have since 1999), produced by the sponsoring government department and attempting to explain in lay language what each provision of the Act does. As with United Kingdom legislation, they nevertheless have no official status, although presumably they may be used in statutory interpretation (as discussed in Chapter 11).

THE SCOTTISH PARLIAMENTARY LEGISLATIVE PROCESSES

8.15   Proposed Acts of the Scottish Parliament, by s 28(2) of the Scotland Act 1998, 'shall be known as Bills' and are the product of a lengthy process, as are Acts of the United Kingdom Parliament (for which, see Chapter 7), though with certain specialities.

Who seeks legislation and why?

8.16   The role of legislation in Scotland under devolution is intended to be, and likely to be, very much as is its role in the United Kingdom as a whole. Thus, most legislation comes from the Scottish Government. This may be 'manifesto legislation' promised by the party forming (or forming part of) the Scottish Government, for example the Abolition of Feudal Tenure, etc (Scotland) Act 2000. One sort of legislation that was expected to figure largely in the early years (indeed, the expectation of which was part of the justification for devolution), was uncontentious reform for which the United Kingdom had failed to find time. There have been examples, such as the Adults with Incapacity (Scotland) Act 2000.

---

17 'Matters to be included in river basin management plans' (split into 'Matters to be included in every plan' and 'Additional matters to be included in revised plans'); 'Controlled activities regulations' (split into 'List of purposes' and 'Supplementary provisions'); 'Sustainable urban drainage systems: further amendments'; and 'Modifications of Part III of the 1980 Act', respectively.

However, legislation may be a reaction to events, as was the very first Act of the Scottish Parliament, the Mental Health (Public Safety and Appeals) (Scotland) Act 1999. A person had been convicted of culpable homicide some years earlier, and was detained in the State Mental Hospital at Carstairs. Such detention was, under the relevant legislation, competent only where there was treatment capable of alleviating the subject's condition or preventing further decline. It was agreed that, on the facts, this person's treatment could not have this effect. As a result, a sheriff concluded that the detention was unlawful. The 1999 Act was designed to reverse this result.

The Bail, Judicial Appointments, etc (Scotland) Act 2000 and the Convention Rights (Compliance) (Scotland) Act 2001 could also be seen in this light, but perhaps fall into the most common class of legislation, that is, legislation which simply emerges from the processes of government. In the early years of the Scottish Parliament, some of this was legislation simply setting up new institutions and procedures, such as the Public Finance and Accountability (Scotland) Act 2000, instituting governmental financial controls.

Pre-parliamentary stages of Scottish parliamentary legislation

8.17   As with United Kingdom legislation, the procedures before a Bill even appears are critical, for it is then that the Scottish Government consults and decides what legislation it wishes to bring forward. This is discussed further in Chapter 15, though it may be remarked that the Scottish Parliament was set up with the intention of being more open to the population, and less bound by party political considerations, than is the United Kingdom Parliament[18].

The Scottish Government was, until the 2007 Election, a coalition of two political parties, which put additional strain upon the process of deciding what legislation to propose. There is no Queen's Speech in the Scottish Parliament, and the practice in the first Parliament was for the Scottish Government to outline its intended legislative programme in September. However, in the second, proposals were published from shortly after the election. In the third session of the Scottish Parliament the government formed by the Scottish National

---

18 See *Shaping Scotland's Parliament; report of the Consultative Steering Group on the Scottish Parliament* (Scottish Office 1998), section 3.6 'Access and Information'. One specific example of this is the common use of Draft Bills, published for consultation.

Party felt a different type of strain as a minority government needing to garner support from the other parties to pass legislation. The current Scottish National Party government enjoys an outright majority in Parliament and as a result will suffer far less strain in deciding what legislation to propose. An example of this is the Alcohol (Minimum Pricing) (Scotland) Act 2012. As a minority government the Scottish National Party was unable to pass this legislation due to a lack of support from other parties. As soon as they had a majority in the Scottish Parliament they set about re-introducing this legislation and it was duly passed[19].

Parliamentary stages of Scottish parliamentary legislation and 'pre-enactment checks' on legislative competence

8.18 Any member of the Scottish Parliament may introduce a Bill and, when a Bill is introduced, s 31 of the Scotland Act 1998 requires the person introducing it to state that it is within the Scottish Parliament's 'legislative competence' (discussed in Chapter 3), and the Presiding Officer to decide separately, with reasons, whether or not this is the case. These are the first two 'pre-enactment checks' on legislative competence[20]. Since legislation incompatible with the 'Convention rights' under the Human Rights Act 1998 (for which, see Chapter 3) is not permitted, this is also one of the devices used to seek compatibility between legislation and those rights (see again Chapter 3).

The Bill is also required by the Standing Orders of the Scottish Parliament to have 'accompanying documents', that is, a Financial Memorandum giving best estimates of administrative, compliance and other costs, and (unless it is a 'Member's Bill': see below) 'Explanatory Notes' summarising the provisions and giving other necessary information, and a 'Policy Memorandum' giving the policy objectives of the Bill, describing why the Bill took the approach it did, the consultation which was undertaken, and an assessment of its effects on a somewhat mixed bag of factors, including equal opportunities, human rights, island communities, local government, sustainable development and any other relevant matter.

19 The legislation is however subject to challenge in the courts on competence grounds at the time of writing.
20 A position in marked contrast to that of the UK legislature which may not only validly pass legislation within the Scottish Parliament's legislative competence, but may do so inadvertently, as occurred in relation to the (UK) Housing Act 2004.

The Statement of Enactment records the date the Bill was introduced, and the date it received the Royal Assent, but is silent on what passes on and between those dates. However, s 36 of the Scotland Act 1998 lays down a procedure for enactment similar to that of the United Kingdom Parliament, though by no means identical[21]. One difference is clearly that there is no equivalent of the House of Lords. Another is that the various subject-based Committees of Parliament such as Education, and Justice (for which see Chapter 3) are more involved, and involved earlier.

Thus, s 36 requires (subject to exceptions) that standing orders include provision for:

– a general debate (referred to as 'Stage 1', and equivalent to the United Kingdom Parliament's Second Reading);
– a consideration of, and the opportunity for members to vote on, the details of a Bill (referred to as 'Stage 2' and equivalent to the United Kingdom Parliament's Committee Stage);
– a final stage at which a Bill can be passed or rejected (referred to as 'Stage 3' and equivalent to the United Kingdom Parliament's Third Reading).

The Standing Orders of the Scottish Parliament fill in the detail.

Stage 1 effectively falls into two parts. In the first, the Bill is referred immediately to the relevant Parliamentary Committee (the 'lead committee') which considers and reports on the general principles to the Parliament as a whole, and any Policy Memorandum. (Where the Bill straddles the interests of more than one Committee, there is still a 'lead committee', but the other may also consider them, and in any case, the Subordinate Legislation Committee may also consider matters of delegated legislation: see below.) During this consideration, there can be public taking of evidence.

In the second part, the Parliament debates the general principles in the light of the Committee report, and may refer it back for a further report. If the Parliament disagrees with the general principles, the Bill fails. If it agrees, the Bill is remitted to the lead committee, or another committee, or a Committee of the Whole House, for Stage 2.

Stage 2, which must be at least two weeks later, considers each provision of the Bill, which must be agreed to, amended or rejected (though provisions concerning delegated legislation may be referred to the Subordinate Legislation Committee).

---

21 The procedures of other small countries and devolved legislatures were studied before the final procedure was fixed.

Stage 3, which must be at least two further weeks later if there have been amendments, may permit further amendments, and indeed may involve remitting the Bill back to Stage 2, but is essentially the decision as to whether to pass the Bill, as amended in Stage 2. If the decision is pushed to a vote, there is a quorum of one quarter of all MSPs.

Royal Assent is required by s 32, but s 33 gives to certain officials, in the four weeks following Stage 3, the right to refer a Bill to the Supreme Court of the United Kingdom (the final authority on disputes on the Scotland Act: see Chapter 3) for a decision as to whether the Bill is within the Parliament's legislative competence. These officials are the Advocate-General for Scotland (the Scottish law officer of the Westminster government: see Chapter 3) or the Attorney-General (of England and Wales: see Chapter 3), either of whom might be concerned about an encroachment on Westminster's reserved powers, and even the Lord Advocate (the Scottish Government's principal law officer: see Chapter 3), who, though a member of the Scottish Government, might be unhappy with the form the Bill finally took. The Bill may not be presented for royal assent during this period. This is the third 'pre-enactment' check on legislative competence and, like the others, operates as another of the devices seeking to ensure compatibility between legislation and 'Convention rights' under the Human Rights Act 1998.

There is a fourth 'pre-enactment check' in that the Secretary of State (in other words, the United Kingdom government) may issue an order under s 35, forbidding the Presiding Officer from submitting a Bill for Royal Assent. This is different in kind from the other 'pre-enactment checks', for it is not in the hands of an official exercising a quasi-judicial function, but in those of a clearly party political person. However, the Secretary of State may take this grave step only if he believes on reasonable grounds that the Bill will transgress some international obligation (which would include a breach of the European Convention on Human Rights, or of EU law) or with the interests of defence or national security, or that, in modifying the law on reserved matters, it will have an adverse effect on them.

In addition to the 'pre-enactment checks', there are the 'post-enactment checks' considered in Chapter 3, whereby in any litigation concerning legislation which is in force, a 'devolution issue' may arise.

Special cases

Human rights legislation

8.19   There is no Scottish Parliament equivalent of the Human Rights Act 1998, for that Act applies to the whole United Kingdom in any case. One important result of this is, of course, that the legislative competence of the Scottish Parliament is limited by that Act (as noted above).

Financial legislation

8.20 The Scottish Parliament receives a block grant which is paid into the Scottish Consolidated Fund along with any other payments. Out of it the Scottish Government pays all authorised expenditure.

As noted in relation to legislation of the United Kingdom Parliament, financial legislation has a particular constitutional status, and taxation is in any case a reserved matter. However, Part 4A of the Scotland Act 1998 (as amended by the Scotland Act 2012) gives the Scottish Parliament the power to set a Scottish rate of income tax for Scottish taxpayers. This power must be exercised by a Scottish Rate Resolution. This replaced the former tax varying powers in the now omitted Part IV of the Scotland Act 1998. The Scottish Government now also has powers to tax on land transactions and on disposals to landfill.

Tax-spending powers can be exercised only through legislation, following United Kingdom convention of the constitution. Thus, any such legislation requires a 'Financial Resolution' before Stage 2 can be taken. Respecting the constitutional convention requiring annual Acts authorising expenditure, there has been an annual 'Budget (Scotland) Act'.

The Scotland Act 2012 also introduced new borrowing powers for the Scottish Government. They are mainly concerned with meeting unforeseen shortfalls in the budget of the Scottish Government. The Scottish Ministers may borrow from the Secretary of State.

Consolidation, statute law repeal and statute law revision legislation

8.21 'Consolidation' etc Bills are discussed above as special examples of United Kingdom legislation. Although there is insufficient legislation from the Scottish Parliament for these procedures to be needed in respect of it, the Scottish Parliament is, of course, entitled to seek to simplify the statute book by consolidating United Kingdom Parliament legislation within its legislative competence, and there are simplified procedures in the Standing Orders of the Scottish Parliament[22].

Members' legislation

8.22 Most legislation is introduced by government but, as noted in relation to the UK Parliament, any MSP may do so. The Scotland Act 1998 does not specifically refer to such Private Members' legislation, but the Standing Orders of the Scottish Parliament anticipate it, under the description 'Member's Bills'. Indeed, there have been some such Member's Bills, a few of which have been enacted [23]. A significant failure, however, was Margo Macdonald's End of Life Assistance (Scotland) Bill, which was rejected by the Scottish Parliament in 2010.

Committee legislation

8.23 In addition, in an interesting innovation, committees themselves may introduce Bills on matters which they have enquired into, provided the Parliament agrees (and in which case the first part of Stage 1 is dispensed with). There have been few examples of this, however, as Committees have found the pressure of other business too great[24].

Local, personal, private and hybrid legislation

8.24 Existing forms of Private Bill procedure are retained for those matters not within the competence of the Scottish Parliament. Thus,

22 These powers have been exercised. In 2003, following the Scottish Law Commission Report 'Report on the Consolidation of Certain Enactments concerning Salmon and Freshwater Fisheries' (Scot Law Com 188), the Salmon and Freshwater Fisheries (Consolidation) (Scotland) Act consolidated one Act of the Scottish Parliament (the Theft Act 1607), 23 Acts of the United Kingdom Parliament (the oldest dating from 1804) and four pieces of delegated legislation.
23 *Eg* the Council of the Law Society Act 2003 (introduced by David McLetchie MSP) and the Dog Fouling (Scotland) Act 2003 (introduced by Keith Harding MSP).
24 The Commissioner for Children and Young People (Scotland) Act 2003 was a Committee Bill, following the Education, Culture and Sport Committee's Report 'An Inquiry into the Need for a Children's Commissioner in Scotland' (2nd Report of 2002, SP Paper 508, 14 February 2002) and 'Report on the proposed Commissioner for Children and Young Persons Bill' (11th Report of 2002, SP Paper 617, 3 July 2002): the proposal was accepted by the Parliament on 25 September 2002 and introduced on 4 December 2002, and was successfully enacted 26 March 2003, receiving its royal assent on 1 May 2003.

for reserved matters (which include oil and gas and most transport matters), the Private Legislation Procedure (Scotland) Act 1936 (discussed above in relation to United Kingdom Private, Personal etc legislation), continues unchanged, still requiring the decision of the Secretary of State and a UK Parliament Confirmation Act. The alternative procedure under the Statutory Orders (Special Procedure) Act 1945, which is partly devolved, also remains (though it appears never to have been used in Scotland, even before devolution).

However, for fully devolved matters, the public/private distinction applies to legislation of the Scottish Parliament as it does to the United Kingdom Parliament. There is provision in the Standing Orders of the Scottish Parliament for 'Private' legislation in this sense, that is, for Bills introduced by a promoter who is an individual person, a corporate body (such as a local authority or a trading company) or an unincorporated association (such as a club, society or trust which is not incorporated) for the purpose of obtaining particular powers or benefits in excess of, or in conflict with, the general law. This includes Bills relating to 'estate, property, status or style or otherwise relating to the personal affairs of the promoter'. In such case, the lead committee requires the promoter to deposit documents, give notice, deposit copies of the Bill for public inspection, give notice to interested parties and invite objections[25].

Emergency legislation

8.25   There is special provision for 'emergency Bills' in the Standing Orders of the Scottish Parliament providing rapid enactment. No definition of 'emergency' is attempted[26].

---

25 Thus there were the Robin Rigg Offshore Wind Farm (Navigation and Fishing) (Scotland) Act 2003, promoted by Offshore Energy Resources Ltd and Solway Offshore Ltd, and designed to allow them to interfere with public rights of navigation and fishing in order to construct and maintain the wind farm, and the Stirling-Alloa-Kincardine Railway and Linked Improvements Act 2004 promoted by Clackmannanshire Council and designed to construct a rail connection to Longannet Power Station and related works, including closing level crossings and roads, and purchasing land compulsorily.

26 However, the Criminal Procedure (Legal Assistance, Detention and Appeals (Scotland) Act 2010, designed to implement changes to Scottish criminal procedure following the decision by the Supreme Court in *Cadder v HMA* [2010] UKSC 43, 2011 SC (UKSC) 13, was passed by this means. The court decision was on 26 October 2010, and the Bill was drafted by, and passed all its stages, on 27 October. The Bill received Royal Assent on 29 October.

PUBLICATION AND CITATION OF ACTS OF THE SCOTTISH PARLIAMENT

Publication of Acts of the (pre-1707) Parliament of Scotland

Chronological series

8.26   Acts of the original Parliament of Scotland, a few of which are still in force, are printed in a number of modern series. The *Acts of the Parliaments of Scotland 1124–1707* (alias the 'Record Edition') was published in the 19th century by the Commissioners of Public Records[27]. It has been largely superseded by the digital *Records of the Parliaments of Scotland*, accessible at http://www.rps.ac.uk/. Acts and related documents, such as Charters, from 1135 are published in the several volumes of *Regesta Regum Scottorum* (Edinburgh University Press) which commenced in 1960. Each deals with the output during the reign of a monarch.

Those Acts still in force in 1964 appear in an HMSO reprint also called *Acts of the Parliaments of Scotland 1424–1707*.

Computerised retrieval of Acts of the (pre-1707) Scottish Parliament

8.27   The National Archives (see Chapter 7) makes available the text of those Acts still in force, as amended. Note also the *Records of the Parliaments of Scotland*, accessible at http://www.rps.ac.uk/.

Citation of Acts of the (pre-1707) Scottish Parliament

8.28   Acts of the Parliament of Scotland are usually cited by Short Title and year, for example the 'Union with England Act 1706'. Different editions do not always agree on the chapter number[28] but, as so few are still in force, it is possible to omit it. In historical contexts they are sometimes cited by reference to the volume and page of the Record Edition, for example 'APS [ie 'Acts of the Parliaments of Scotland'] VIII, 80'. The *Records of the Parliaments of Scotland*, accessible at http://www.rps.ac.uk/, are abbreviated 'RPS'

---

27 Earlier editions include the *Laws and Acts of Parliament 1424–1681*, published by Sir Thomas Murray of Glendook ('*Glendook's Edition*'), itself based on those published a century earlier by Skene.

28 The Royal Mines Act 1424, the oldest Scots Act still in force, is described in the Record Edition as c13, but in *Glendook's Edition* as c12. See RPS 1424/15.

and provide their own system of calendar year and statute number, eg APS II 3, chapter 1, is RPS 1424/2.

Publication of Acts of the Scottish Parliament

Chronological series

8.29 Acts of the Scottish Parliament are printed and sold in individual copies by The Stationery Office ('TSO') and are bound into annual volumes so entitled, and these can be taken as authoritative.

Commercially produced reprints

8.30 The *Current Law Statutes Annotated* series reproduces all Acts of the Scottish Parliament, including private legislation.

The *Parliament House Book* and *Parliament House Statutes Reprints* include relevant Acts of the Scottish Parliament, and some text-books and monographs will do likewise. In addition, the *Passage of Bills* series published by Astron most usefully contain all relevant accompanying documents, including Scottish parliamentary debates, and indeed the Bill as amended at different stages, with the Act itself in final form

Indexes etc

8.31 Annual volumes of *Acts of the Scottish Parliament* are indexed, but no indexes as such have yet been published.

Computerised retrieval of Acts of the Scottish Parliament

8.32 Acts of the Scottish Parliament are available online from The National Archives at http://www.legislation.gov.uk. Bills currently before the Scottish Parliament can be found in full text, and with links to 'accompanying documents' and 'policy memoranda' and references to the relevant Committees, at the Scottish Parliament website[29].

---

29 See www.scottish.parliament.uk/.

The Westlaw, LexisNexis Butterworths and Justis [*sic*] databases include all Acts of the Scottish Parliament in force, in their amended form as appropriate, with sophisticated search facilities. The BAILII database also contains all such Acts.

Citation of Acts of the Scottish Parliament

8.33   Acts of the Scottish Parliament are cited by Short Title, year and 'asp' ('Act of the Scottish Parliament') number, for example 'Regulation of Care (Scotland) Act 2001 asp 8. Bills are cited as 'SP Bill', with the title, number, session and (in brackets) year, for example 'SP Bill 12 National Parks (Scotland) Bill [as introduced] Session 1 (2000)[30].

---

30 Style and Example taken from 'A Guide to recommended Citations for Scottish Parliament Publications' (May 2001).

9 Legislation – United Kingdom delegated legislation

9.1 In the United Kingdom context, delegated legislation is legislation made by a body other than Parliament using powers delegated to it by that Parliament. It is not a novel phenomenon. Its modern use dates from the early 19th-century but it has become increasingly important as a source of law over the last 50 years.

The institutional background of delegated legislation was touched on in Chapters 3 (concerning the distinction between Parliament and Government) and 5 (concerning sources of law). As discussed in Chapter 8, the laws made by the devolved legislatures, such as Acts of the Scottish Parliament, are technically delegated legislation but these are not discussed in this chapter.

Not all grants of powers in Acts of Parliament are delegations of legislative powers, that is, of powers to write laws. There are often grants of executive or administrative powers, that is, powers to take decisions[1]. But this chapter will focus on the delegation of power to make legislation and will discuss the nature of delegated legislation, its types and their form, judicial control of it, and its publication and citation.

---

1 For example, powers are granted by the Immigration and Asylum Act 1999, s 83(1), (2) to the Secretary of State to appoint (after consultation with the Lord Chancellor and the Scottish Ministers) an Immigration Services Commissioner with a duty to operate a register of persons qualified to provide immigration advice and services, and by s 85(3) and Sch 6 powers are granted to the Commissioner himself to determine whether a person is competent to provide such advice and services and, if so, to register that person as so qualified.

THE NATURE OF DELEGATED LEGISLATION

The origins and purpose of delegated legislation

9.2   The power to make law lies with Parliament. But Parliament alone could not hope to deal with the enormous burden of making all the legislation required to regulate a modern state. Much regulation is also detailed and technical; with political controversy, if any, being about the governing principles rather than detail. Other legislation must cover circumstances applicable only to a particular location, where those with local knowledge, such as local authorities, are best placed to set exact rules[2]. And many aspects of legislation inevitably require frequent minor changes to allow for changes in technical standards or, where financial figures are involved, the rate of inflation or other similar economic factors.

Delegating the power to make some legislation allows authorities with the time and correct expertise to make the detailed rules; whilst Parliament, at least in theory, retains control of the governing principles. Delegated legislation is also subject to abbreviated approval processes, meaning legislation can be brought into force quickly and without the limits imposed by the capacity of Parliament.

Delegated legislation is sometimes referred to as *subordinate legislation* or *secondary legislation*. This implies that it is less powerful than other forms. This is misleading: legislation made under delegated powers is as authoritative and powerful as an Act of Parliament[3].

Uses of delegated legislation

9.3   In principle, the primary use of delegated legislation is to create detailed schemes of regulation over technically complex areas. For example, the rules requiring headlamps of a certain size and

2   For example, whether drinking alcoholic beverages in public in the centre of cities should be controlled or not is probably best left to local decision: see for example, the City of Dundee District Bylaws for Prohibiting the Consumption of Alcohol in Designated Places 1995 and equivalents elsewhere.
3   As discussed later in this Chapter, one exception is that delegated legislation is not immune to being struck down by the courts as it is not protected by the doctrine of Parliamentary Sovereignty.

power on cars[4], establishing speed limits[5], fixing fees for various services or other matters which may require frequent amendment.

Delegated legislation is also used to bring Acts of Parliament into force[6], enabling Ministers to stagger the introduction of new legislation. This can smooth the transition to a new statutory regime or allow for delays in establishing the necessary supporting structures. Controversially, this means a subsequently elected government can decline to bring into force provisions of an Act of Parliament passed before they came to power[7].

Some delegated legislation is very significant and affects matters of major importance. The European Communities Act 1972 empowers Ministers to make Statutory Instruments ('Sis') to give legal effect to Directives of the European Union. Several thousand SIs have been made under these powers. These include many very significant measures originating from the EU. Examples include the Commercial Agents (Council Directive) Regulations 1993 which imposed a very European approach to agency law over some parts of an area previously governed, in the UK, by common law rules; and the Transfer of Undertaking (Protection of Employment) Regulations 2006 which confer extremely important rights to employees[8].

4 For example, Road Vehicles (Construction and Use) Regulations 1986, SI 1986/1078 (as amended); Road Vehicles (Authorisation of Special Types) General Order 2003, SI 2003/1998) (as amended); Motor Vehicles (Tests) Regulations 1981, SI 1981/1694 (as amended) etc; and even the Pedal Cycles (Construction and Use) Regulations 1983, SI 1983/1176, made under various powers, now chiefly the Road Traffic Act 1988.

5 Chiefly the Motor Vehicle (Variation of Speed Limits) Regulations 1947, SR&O 1947/2192; Motorway Traffic (Speed Limit) Regulations 1974, SI 1974/502; 70mph, 60mph and 50mph (Temporary Speed Limit) Order 1977 and Temporary Speed Limit (Continuation) Order 1978, SI 1978/1548; and Motor Vehicle (Variation of Speed Limits) Regulations 1986, SI 1986/1175, made under various powers, chiefly now the Road Traffic Regulation Act 1984. Note that most of the Statutory Instruments imposing speed limits apply to very specific areas, eg the A34 Trunk Road (Chievely Interchange) (40 Miles Per Hour Speed Limit) Order 2007, SI 2007/233.

6 In other words, although the Act is law, having passed through Parliament, it has no effect until a further piece of legislation, the power to make which was delegated by the Act (typically to the government), is exercised: see 'Commencement provisions' in Chs. 7 & 8 and, for example, the Scotland Act 1998 (Commencement) Order 1998, SI 1998/3178.

7 For instance, s 1 of the Equality Act 2010, contains a duty on public authorities to consider the impact of their decisions on narrowing socio-economic inequality. Following the 2010 General Election, the new Government announced they would not be commencing this provision.

8 See 'EU legislation without direct effect and United Kingdom law' in Chapter 6.

Delegated legislation gives the ability to separate the principles of legislation from its detailed application. Governments are sometimes accused of drawing this boundary at too high a level, seeking for themselves very wide powers of delegation. Arguably this gives too much power to the executive and inhibits the proper scrutiny of legislation by Parliament. For instance, the now repealed Education (Student Loans) Act 1990[9] had only four sections and three brief schedules. But it empowered the Secretary of State to 'make arrangements' to enable eligible students to receive loans towards their maintenance. The Secretary of State was also authorised to impose 'such other conditions as may be prescribed by regulations made by him' on eligible students and make regulations to prescribe the maximum annual loan, the timing and manner of repayment, deferment or cancellation of liability with few restrictions. In this way, all the significant details of the scheme were placed in the hands of Ministers, subject only to the limited scrutiny given to delegated legislation.

Acts of Parliament sometimes give power to Ministers to make amendments to primary legislation by delegated legislation. Such provisions are sometimes called *Henry VIII clauses*. This alludes to the Proclamation by the Crown Act 1539, by which Parliament empowered Henry VIII to legislate by decree. The practice is open today to the criticism that it may flout the principle of the separation of powers and allow the normal Parliamentary scrutiny of primary legislation to be circumvented. However, such powers are commonly granted to permit Ministers to make the myriad of consequential amendments to existing legislation that may be required by a new Act of Parliament. This avoids each and every amendment needing to be contained in the new Act itself, something that would vastly increase the size and complexity of new legislation. These powers have also been granted as a legislative short-cut where amendment of primary legislation is required to comply with EU law[10]. A similar power exists to allow Ministers to rectify issues where the courts have made a declaration of incompatibility under the Human Rights Act 1998[11]. More controversially, Henry VIII clauses are also used to allow Ministers to amend legislation at their discretion. There have been several examples of very widely expressed powers of amendment in recent years. For instance, the Scotland Act 1998 includes several very powerful Henry VIII clauses which allow the Act itself to be amended by Ministers. The boundary between reserved and

---

9 Now replaced by the Teaching and Higher Education Act 1998.
10 This is the effect of s 2(2) and 2(4) of the European Communities Act 1972.
11 Under s 10 of the Human Rights Act 1998.

delegated matters is set by Schedules 4 and 5 to the 1998 Act and is clearly an extremely significant feature of the devolution settlement. But s 30(2) of the Scotland Act grants Ministers the power to amend these schedules by secondary legislation. Other provisions allow amendment of the Act and other primary legislation where it is deemed 'necessary and expedient' in particular circumstances[12].

Even more powerful is the Legislative and Regulatory Reform Act 2006. This Act gives Ministers power to make orders repealing or restating any enactment, including primary legislation, to remove or reduce any regulatory burden. The concept of regulatory burden includes financial cost, administrative inconvenience or 'any obstacle to efficiency, productivity or profitability'. It also allows Ministers to remove sanctions, whether criminal or civil that affect the carrying on of any lawful purpose. There are some limitations imposed by the Act but these are arguably vaguely stated[13].

Types of United Kingdom delegated legislation

9.4   Many thousand pieces of delegated legislation are produced every year although many replace or amend already published legislation so the actual quantity in force is not rising so steeply. Some apply only in Scotland, some only in Wales, some only in England, some only in Great Britain, and others in the whole United

---

12 For instance, s 104 allows any provision to be made which is 'necessary or expedient' in consequence of the Scotland Act or delegated legislation under it; s 105 allows modifications to legislation made before the Scotland Act 1998 which are 'necessary or expedient' in consequence of the Scotland Act; s 106 allows modification of the functions exercisable by the government which is 'appropriate' to enable it to be transferred to the Scottish Executive. Moreover, s 114 allows amendment by delegated legislation of some of those very provisions which give the power to amend by delegated legislation. No doubt this can be justified in so far as the draftsmen could plead that it was impossible for them, or the Members of Parliament, to foresee all the necessary provisions. Certainly, some of these powers have been used extensively.

13 In s 3 there are, admittedly, pre-conditions to an Order, that is, that the 'policy objective intended to be secured ... could not be satisfactorily secured by non-legislative means', 'the effect of the provision is proportionate to the policy objective', and the provision 'strikes a fair balance between the public interest and the interests of any person adversely affected by it', 'does not remove any necessary protection', 'does not prevent any person from continuing to exercise any right or freedom which that person might reasonably expect to continue to exercise' and 'is not of constitutional significance'. Nevertheless, it remains that for vaguely stated purposes, and subject to vaguely stated safeguards, the Government can largely by-pass Parliament in amending existing legislation.

Kingdom[14]. They also vary enormously in length, from one page orders to detailed social security rules stretching over hundreds of pages.

Delegated legislation may be described as *Orders, Orders-in-Council, Regulations* or *Rules*. There is no clear policy on which title to use, but Rules are usually procedural, Regulations of general application and Orders brief. Other titles are occasionally used, such as *Scheme, Directions* and *Instrument*. Confusion is possible: the title Order-in-Council is used for delegated legislation of constitutional significance but the same title is also given to legislation made by the Privy Council under prerogative powers, which is not delegated legislation; whilst *Regulations* are also the name of the most powerful form of European Union legislation[15].

The most familiar type of delegated legislation is the *Statutory Instrument*. There is a complicated definition of Statutory Instrument in the Statutory Instruments Act 1946[16] but, essentially, a piece of delegated legislation is a Statutory Instrument if the enabling Act says it must be. Legislative powers delegated to the government are usually required to be in Statutory Instrument form. However, in principle, the United Kingdom Parliament can delegate to anybody. In practice, delegation is largely to four types of delegate: the government; local government; the courts; and to other statutory bodies.

- **Delegation to government**. Most delegation is to the Secretary of State[17] or other minister; in other words, to the

14 Scottish Statutory Instruments are discussed separately in Chapter 10.
15 The potential for confusion is worsened by the fact that EU Regulations are of direct effect and do not need to be enacted at a national level. EU directives do need to be enacted and, often, a SI taking the form of a Regulation will be used. For instance, the Transfer of Undertakings Directive (2001/23/EC) is implemented in the UK by the previously mentioned Transfer of Undertakings (Protection of Employment) Regulations 2006.
16 Section 1 of the Act states: 'Where by this Act or any Act passed after the commencement of this Act power to make, confirm or approve orders, rules, regulations or other subordinate legislation is conferred on His Majesty in Council or on any Minister of the Crown then, if the power is expressed (a) in the case of a power conferred on His Majesty, to be exercisable by Order in Council; (b) in the case of a power conferred on a Minister of the Crown, to be exercisable by statutory instrument, any document by which that power is exercised shall be known as a "statutory instrument" and the provisions of this Act shall apply thereto accordingly.'
17 The title *Secretary of State* is attached to most Cabinet ministers in charge of departments, as noted in Chapter 3. There may therefore be nearly a dozen Secretaries of State. In principle, any Secretary of State could exercise the delegated powers.

government. The civil servants in the relevant department draft the actual legislation with the assistance of government lawyers.

- **Delegation to local authorities.** Delegation to local authorities is common, giving powers to write laws for the good government and suppression of nuisance in their areas. This may include creating schemes for licensing of abattoirs, public houses or taxi operators; or to regulate public spaces. Such legislation is usually in the form of *byelaws*. Power for local authorities to make byelaws are contained in a range of Acts including those relating to public health and transport and, for Scottish local authorities, the Local Government (Scotland) Act 1973[18]. Breach of a byelaw is commonly a criminal offence. Local authorities may also make *management rules* for the control of their premises[19].

- **Delegation to courts**. Courts have delegated powers to make rules for their own organisation and procedure. The Lord President and other judges of the Court of Session are delegated such powers in respect of the Court of Session by the Court of Session Act 1988, s 5, and the legislation they produce is called *Acts of Sederunt*[20].

- **Delegation to public corporations and utilities**. Some public corporations and statutory bodies may be granted the power to make law. With the transfer of many utilities and other service from public to private hands, this now often extends to private companies. For instance, the Railways Act 2005, s 46 gives railway operating companies the power to make byelaws to regulate the use and working of railways and Sch 9, para 2 of the same Act allows the operating companies to make breach of byelaws a criminal offence.

- **Delegation to other bodies**. There are many examples of delegated legislation which do not fit easily into the above categories. A good example is the statutory scheme for regulating the legal profession. The Solicitors (Scotland) Act 1980, s 34 grants powers to the Council of the Law Society of Scotland the Council to 'make rules for regulating in respect of any matter

---

18 Specifically, ss 201–203.
19 Under the Civic Government (Scotland) Act 1982, s 112. Breach of them is not of itself criminal, but may lead to ejection and (after a hearing) an exclusion order, breach of which may be criminal.
20 They are granted similar powers under the Sheriff Courts (Scotland) Act 1971 in relation to the sheriff court. The same judges in criminal guise are given parallel powers in respect of the High Court of Justiciary by the Criminal Procedure (Scotland) Act 1995. Since devolution, these are now issued as Scottish Statutory Instruments, discussed in the next Chapter.

the professional practice, conduct and discipline of solicitors'. These standards may appear to be internal professional rules rather than laws, and breach of them is not criminal. However, they are created under powers granted by Parliament, and breach can lead to professional disciplinary proceedings under statutory procedures[21].

The form of United Kingdom delegated legislation

9.5 In their form, Statutory Instruments and other forms of delegated legislation mimic parliamentary legislation, though the details vary according to the type in question. Some or all of the following features will be found in most types of delegated legislation:

- **Citation**. Statutory Instruments commence with their citation in the form of a year and sequential number, for example '2002 No 3204' (commonly abbreviated to 'SI 2002/3204'). This may be followed by brackets enclosing a further reference number preceded by 'S', 'W' (or 'Cy'), 'NI', 'C', or 'L'. These indicate respectively that the instrument applies only in Scotland, Wales (or Cymru) or Northern Ireland (as do some each year even with devolved government[22]); is a Commencement Order (see Chapters 7 and 8); or is a procedural instrument applying solely in England and Wales. Thus, 'S.3' would indicate the instrument is the third of that year applying solely to Scotland.
- **Subject Matter and Name**. In official editions of Statutory Instruments, after the citation, appear one or two headings, for example, 'FOOD' followed by 'MILK AND DAIRIES'. These are not part of the name but a guide to the subject-matter. The name, equivalent to an Act's Short Title, is given thereafter, for example 'The Milk (Special Designations) (Scotland) Order 1988' or 'The Advice and Assistance (Scotland) (Prospective Cost) (No 3) Regulations 1988'[23]. Brackets are much favoured,

---

21 The regulation of solicitors is discussed in detail in Chapter 14.
22 For instance, the Scottish Parliament (Constituencies and Regions) Order 2010 was made by UK ministers as the relevant electoral arrangements are a reserved matter but the SI naturally only has effect in Scotland.
23 There is a good deal of innocent amusement to be had in discovering the most unusual Statutory Instrument name. See for example, the Housing (Grants for Fire Escapes in Houses of Multiple Occupation) (Prescribed Percentage) (Scotland) Order 1990, SI 1990/2242, and the Water Bylaws (Milngavie Waterworks, Loch Katrine, Loch Arklet, Glen Finglas) Extension Order 1990, SI 1990/2250. See also Reid (correspondence) (2003) 24 Stat LR 93.

enclosing 'Scotland', 'Amendment', 'Variation' and other things[24], including numerical sequences, as where an Act has several commencement orders[25].

- **Dates**. After the name, Statutory Instruments list three dates, those of making, laying before Parliament, and of coming into force (unless the instrument is not required to be laid before Parliament).

- **Arrangement of Regulations, Articles or Rules**. A Statutory Instrument of more than a few provisions is likely to have contents list or *Arrangement of Regulations* (or similar) at the beginning. The titles used there reappear as headings to the actual provisions.

- **Recital of delegated powers**. Most delegated legislation will identify the powers under which it was made and may also describe any consultation carried out. For example, 'The Secretary of State, in exercise of the powers conferred on him by sections 37(1)(b), 38(1) and 143(1) of the Roads (Scotland) Act 1984 and of all other powers enabling him in that behalf, and after consultation with representative organisations in accordance with sections 37(6) and 38(2) of that Act, hereby makes the following Regulations …'. This bears on the question of *ultra vires*, but its significance is reduced by the common use of 'and all other powers in that behalf'.

- **The substantive provisions**. The terms used to describe substantive provisions of a Statutory Instrument depend on the type of instrument but often includes *Regulation* (in a Regulation), *Article* (in an Order) or *Rule* (in Rules). Structure is in the same form as an Act, but sub-divisions of the basic unit are always called Paragraphs, Sub-paragraphs (and even Sub-sub-paragraphs). Parts and Part headings are used in much the same way as in primary legislation. Operating instructions such as interpretation, amending and repealing (known in Statutory Instruments as *revoking*) provisions may appear and, while most

---

24 For example, the Town and Country Planning (Determination of Appeals by Appointed Persons) (Prescribed Classes) (Scotland) Amendment Regulations 1989, SI 1989/577. It is surprising that 'Amendment' is not bracketed.

25 For example, by mid-2007, the commencement orders for the Immigration and Asylum Act 1999 ran from the Immigration and Asylum Act 1999 (Commencement No 1) Order 1999, SI 1999/3190 to the Immigration and Asylum Act 1999 (Commencement No 16) Order 2004, SI 2004/297, without the whole Act yet being in force. Indeed, the twelfth Commencement Order (in 2003) actually followed the Nationality, Immigration and Asylum Act 2002 (Commencement (No 1) Order 2002, SI 2003/1, starting to bring into force the next major piece of immigration legislation.

are placed at the end, as with Acts, interpretation paragraphs are usually placed at the beginning.

- **Schedules**. Schedules are very common and are often used to present complex or tabulated information which forms part of the Statutory Instrument.
- **The Explanatory Note**. Invariably, official editions of Statutory Instruments have an Explanatory Note appended. This does not form part of the legislative text.

CONTROL OF DELEGATED LEGISLATION

Parliamentary and Executive Control

9.6 To ensure parliamentary control of delegated legislation, the delegation by Parliament of any power to legislate must itself be contained in primary legislation, known as the enabling Act[26]. This sets out the purposes, limits and terms of the delegation and the identity of the delegate. When the enabling Act is considered, Parliament will examine any proposed delegations and, in passing or amending a bill, will accept the terms and extent of the delegation. To help strengthen this scrutiny, a specialist House of Lords Committee on Delegated Powers and Regulatory Reform examines proposed delegations of power in Bills and reports to the House.

The most familiar classification of delegated legislation, that is, Statutory Instruments must meet the requirements of the Statutory Instruments Act 1946[27]. This includes stipulations on their dating, numbering and publication[28] but also makes them subject to certain parliamentary procedures designed to allow Parliament to be informed of their existence, and apply a veto if it wishes. (It cannot, however, amend other than in certain exceptional cases.) These procedures can include the following:

- Statutory Instruments may be required to be laid before the Parliament (that is, made available to any MP) a set period before coming into effect, showing the dates when it was made, when it was laid, and when it is intended to come into force. In some cases they must be laid in draft, in some cases in final form.

---

26 In practice, the use of delegated legislation is so widespread that almost all Acts are enabling Acts to some degree, even if the only power delegated is the power to bring the Act into force by a commencement order.

27 A separate, although similar, regime now operates for Scottish Statutory Instruments. This is discussed in the next chapter.

28 The basic requirements are contained in ss 2–4.

- Statutory Instruments may be examined by the Joint Committee on Statutory Instruments, which conducts technical scrutiny of Statutory Instruments to ensure they are properly made and do not purport to do something constitutionally inappropriate.
- Statutory instruments may be subject to a parliamentary vote by either the *negative* or *affirmative resolution procedure.* Negative resolution procedure, which is the most common and is generally applied to routine or uncontroversial legislation, means the Statutory Instrument will be deemed approved by Parliament if no motion to annul it against it is raised and passed within a specified time, usually 40 days. Affirmative resolution procedure means the Statutory Instrument does not come into force unless affirmed by a parliamentary motion.
- Other Acts of Parliament may impose their own specific approval regimes although most are variations of the negative or affirmative resolution procedures. Controls over powers of delegation under the Scotland Act 1998 are particularly complex with eleven different procedures to be applied in different circumstances: from 'Type A' (draft instrument has been laid before, and approved by resolution of, each House of the UK Parliament and laid before and approved by resolution of the Scottish Parliament) to 'Type K' (instrument subject to annulment by a resolution of the House of Commons).

An enabling Act may also stipulate specific conditions on the exercise of delegated power. For instance, delegates may be required to consult before legislating. For instance, the Legislative and Regulatory Reform Act 2006 requires a Minister, before making a Statutory Instrument, to consult with 'such organisations as appear to him to be representative of interests substantially affected by the proposals', the Law Commissions (for which, see Chapter 15) and 'such other persons as he considers appropriate'.

Parliamentary controls are, of course, subject to the fact of executive dominance of the legislature. Governments are therefore free to draft Bills delegating powers and making delegated powers subject to such procedures, and can anticipate that, except in exceptional circumstances, their majority removes the likelihood of their proposed legislation being overturned.

Other types of delegated legislation are subject to similar types of control. Local authority and other byelaws are generally subject to approval by a *confirming authority*, the powers of which may be very wide, including powers to modify or reject on various grounds. The confirming authority is commonly stated in pre-devolution legislation to be the Secretary of State, that is, the United Kingdom government, but this is now commonly devolved to the Scottish Ministers in relation to Scotland by the general transfer of functions under the Scotland Act 1998, s 53.

Judicial control and ultra vires

9.7   Under the British constitutional doctrine of parliamentary sovereignty, the courts are not able to strike down primary legislation. But delegated legislation is not made by Parliament, it is made by others under the authority of Parliament and, as discussed above, Parliament always limits delegation. Enabling primary legislation may delegate specific powers to specific persons, for specific purposes, to be exercised through specific procedures, possibly subject to specific publicity requirements and a veto.

If those limits are exceeded, the purported laws are beyond the powers of the delegate (or *ultra vires*) and a court may rule them invalid.

For example, *Malloch v Aberdeen Corporation* 1974 SLT 253 turned on the Education (Scotland) Act 1962 which delegated to the Secretary of State certain powers to make regulations for certain purposes[29]. Under these powers he made a regulation, the Teachers (Education, Training and Certification) (Scotland) Regulations 1967, SI 1967/1162, among other things purportedly requiring teachers retrospectively to register with the General Teaching Council for Scotland. Malloch, a teacher employed by Aberdeen Corporation, was dismissed for failure to register. He sued the Corporation, and the Inner House upheld his claim that the 1962 Act did not delegate the power to make such regulations, so that they were *ultra vires*[30].

---

29 There was considerable related litigation, in part of which Mr Malloch most remarkably appeared as a litigant in person, in other words without benefit of legal representation, in the House of Lords: see 1973 SLT (Notes) 5.

30 See also *Marshall v Clark* 1957 JC 68 and *Magistrates of Ayr v Lord Advocate* 1950 SLT 102. An interesting English case is *Bugg v Director of Public Prosecutions* [1993] QB 473. RAF Alconbury By-laws 1985 and HMS Forest Moor and Menwith Hill Station Byelaws 1986, made by the Secretary of State under Pt II of the Military Lands Act 1892, purported to exclude the public from certain military sites. Bugg was convicted of the offence of entering a place protected by the byelaws without permission, and convicted. On appeal, the Divisional Court of Queen's Bench held that there were two types of invalidity, substantive (where the byelaw was invalid on its face because *ultra vires* or unreasonable) and procedural (where a procedural requirement, such as consultation, had not been followed). In the instant case, neither byelaw set out with sufficient clarity the area it covered, and the Alconbury byelaws covered the area within a perimeter fence, but the fence had been moved in an attempt unilaterally to extend the area.

In practice such striking down is rare, as delegation is generally widely worded. The courts have also regarded some procedural requirements as merely directory rather than mandatory, that is they are required, but failure to follow them does not annul the regulations[31].

PUBLICATION OF UNITED KINGDOM DELEGATED LEGISLATION

9.8   In general, Statutory Instruments ('SIs') must be published and sold by the Controller of Her Majesty's Stationery Office ('HMSO') in her capacity as the Queen's Printer of Acts of Parliament. SIs are also bound up and published in several annual volumes entitled *Statutory Instruments*.

All SIs issued since 1 January 1987 are available in full text on the legislation.gov.uk website which also contains a partial data-set of SIs published between 1948 and 1987. Any SIs pre-dating 1948, and still in force at the time of publication are available in *Statutory Instruments Revised*, published in 1950.

It is still possible to obtain hard-copy, commercially published, compendiums of SIs. *Halsbury's Statutory Instruments* contains all SIs of general application to England and Wales and stretches to 22 volumes. More frequently, specialist practitioner reference books and textbooks will contain a compilation of any SIs relevant to that specialist area. The number of SIs and the frequency with which they are issued or amended means that these books often come with special subscription services providing regular updates.

Comprehensive databases of SIs are also available through subscription-based online legal databases, such as *Westlaw*, *LexisNexis* or *Justis*. These services will often include value-added features such as search functions, regular implementation of amendments and updates, and cross-referring links to relevant case reports or associated legislation. However, each publisher may make different decisions about which SIs will be included or excluded, so any given service may not be entirely comprehensive.

There are no general requirements for publication of delegated legislation which is not in Statutory Instrument form, but the requirements of publicity of by-laws and local management rules mean that they are likely to be reasonably available in the area to which they apply.

---

31 In English cases, requirements for publication were held directory in *Sheer Metalcraft Ltd* [1954] 1 QB 114, but requirements for consultation were mandatory in *Agricultural Training Board v Aylesbury Mushrooms Ltd* [1972] 1 WLR 190.

10   Legislation – Scottish Delegated Legislation

THE SOURCES OF SCOTTISH DELEGATED LEGISLATION

10.1   Delegated legislation in Scotland may come from a wide range of sources. Delegated legislation made by UK ministers (discussed in Chapter 9) may apply to Scotland simply because it applies to the whole of the United Kingdom, or to Great Britain. This may be because it relates to reserved matters or simply because it was made prior to devolution and has not yet been replaced or superseded.

Upon devolution, Scottish Ministers were given many powers to make delegated legislation. These powers may be conferred by Acts of the Scottish Parliament but, frequently, the powers originate from UK Acts of Parliament. These may be pre-devolution Acts of Parliament: under the general delegation of executive powers for devolved matters, Scottish Ministers now exercise many powers previously held by UK Ministers. Alternatively, the UK Parliament retains the power to legislate on devolved matters. Where it does so, any powers to make delegated legislation will be conferred on Scottish Ministers.

Other Scottish bodies, including the courts and local authorities, may have powers to make delegated legislation. Again, these powers may come from either UK or Scottish primary legislation.

The institutional background of delegated legislation was touched on in Chapter 3 (concerning devolution) and Chapter 5 (concerning sources of law). This Chapter deals with the nature of such legislation within the context of devolution, legislative control over it, its types and form, *ultra vires* and judicial control over it, and its citation and publication.

THE NATURE OF SCOTTISH DELEGATED LEGISLATION

Delegation, the Scotland Act 1998 and Acts of the Scottish Parliament

10.2 Devolution itself involves a massive delegation, as the Scotland Act 1998 delegated to the Scottish Parliament and Scottish Executive all powers, legislative and executive, except for those concerning a defined list of *reserved matters*[1]. As the delegation of legislative power to the Scottish Parliament is defined, with limits, by statute, Acts of the Scottish Parliament are technically delegated legislation[2]. However, the devolution settlement and Acts of the Scottish Parliament are discussed in Chapter 8, and so are not dealt with in this Chapter.

Delegated legislation in Scotland and devolution

10.3 The principles which apply to United Kingdom delegated legislation, discussed in Chapter 9. also apply to delegated legislation in relation to Scotland. But, the devolution settlement produces some additional complications, as delegated legislation for Scotland can be authorised by either UK Acts of Parliament or Acts of the Scottish Parliament; and can be enacted by UK Ministers, Scottish Ministers and other Scottish public bodies.

UK delegated legislation on reserved matters

10.4 Where UK Acts of Parliament delegate powers to the UK government (typically to 'the Secretary of State') and other bodies in relation to reserved matters, the delegated legislation produced is normally in the form of Statutory Instrument ('SI'), although other forms such as byelaws, are common. Mostly, this will be delegated legislation applying to the whole of the UK. Occasionally, it may

---

1 For discussion of the difference between reserved matters and devolved matters, see Chapter 3.
2 They are explicitly described as so in the Human Rights Act 1998, s 21(1), but the courts have clarified that they have a special status and cannot be considered as 'just' delegated legislation (see, for instance, *Axa Insurance, Petitioners* [2011] UKSC 46, 2012 SC (UKSC) 122).

apply solely to Scotland, typically because it concerns the devolution settlement[3].

Although such UK delegated legislation is not itself affected by devolution, the way that it is used may be. As noted in Chapter 3, some reserved functions can in fact be devolved by the UK government to the Scottish Ministers by the process known as *executive devolution*, under powers in the Scotland Act 1998[4]. Others, while not transferred, can be used by Scottish Ministers under an *agency agreement* with the United Kingdom government, also under powers in the Scotland Act 1998[5]. Thus Scottish Ministers may well exercise some powers relating to reserved matters, operating under the authority of a UK SI, which itself relies on a UK Act of Parliament.

Delegated legislation and devolved matters

Existing delegated legislation on devolved matters

10.5   Acts of the United Kingdom Parliament, of course, also delegated powers before devolution concerning what have become *devolved matters*, to the Secretary of State, Scottish local authorities, Scottish courts and other persons and bodies within Scotland[6]. Devolution did not remove this delegated legislation at a stroke; much of it is still in force and will remain in force unless and until replaced.

But devolution has substantially changed the way this delegated legislation is used. As noted in Chapter 3, s 53 of the Scotland Act 1998 performs a general transfer of functions from the United Kingdom government to the Scottish Ministers in relation to Scotland. Thus, Scottish Ministers now hold the governmental functions previously granted to the Secretary of State and other members of the United

---

3   For instance, the Scottish Parliament (Disqualification) Order 2002, SI 2003/409 (S4) which specifies persons disqualified from being MSPs.

4   The general delegation of executive powers on devolved matters is in s 53 of the Scotland Act 1998. There are also a whole series of SIs made under s 63 of the 1998 Act transferring additional functions to Scottish Ministers which may be exercised with or without the agreement of UK Ministers, or sharing functions between UK and Scottish Ministers.

5   A series of Agency Arrangement Orders, made by SI under s 93 of the 1998 Act allows Scottish Ministers to make arrangements on behalf of the UK government.

6   Obvious examples are the delegation of powers to the Scottish courts to write their own procedures in the form of Acts of Sederunt and Acts of Adjournal.

Kingdom government, in so far as they apply to Scotland[7]. Thus, where UK delegated legislation gives powers and responsibilities to the Secretary of State, it must now be read as giving them to the Scottish Ministers[8]. So, where previously, the Secretary of State might be given the power to take a decision, or the responsibility for carrying out a duty, it is now normally the Scottish Ministers who may, or must, do so[9].

New delegated legislation on devolved matters

10.6   The devolution settlement envisages that, over time, existing UK SIs will be replaced by Scottish Statutory Instruments ('SSIs') in relation to devolved matters. The replacement occurs in three separate ways.

Firstly, it occurs by means of the Scottish Ministers exercising powers under existing United Kingdom legislation. The basic provisions of the Scotland Act 1998 just referred to, conferring upon the Scottish Ministers the functions previously granted to the Secretary of State, include not just powers to take decisions but also powers to make delegated legislation. Thus, where the United Kingdom government used to exercise these powers under United Kingdom Acts of Parliament, now the Scottish Ministers do, and they do so by means of SSIs rather than SIs[10]. Some of these powers are very extensive: for instance the power under the

---

7 Or rather, within the 'devolved competence' of the Scottish Ministers.

8 To the extent that powers to make delegated legislation on subjects which are now devolved matters were delegated to a person or body other than the UK government (for instance, a local authority), such delegation would be unaffected.

9 Thus, for example, the Police (Scotland) Act 1967, s 4 requires that a police authority obtain the approval of the Secretary of State before appointing a new Chief Constable. This now means they must obtain the approval of the Scottish Ministers.

10 Thus, for example, the pre-devolution Land Registration (Scotland) Act 1979 (Commencement No 12) Order 1998, made under powers in the Land Registration (Scotland) Act 1979, s 30(2), was issued by the Secretary of State for Scotland and was an SI (SI 1998/2980), while the post-devolution Land Registration (Scotland) Act 1979 (Commencement No 13) Order 1999 made under precisely the same powers was issued by the Scottish Ministers and is an SSI (SSI 1999/111).

European Communities Act 1972 to make delegated legislation in conformance to give effect to EU directives[11].

Secondly, new UK Acts of Parliament may, even after devolution, affect devolved issues. In practice, this legislation is always enacted after agreement between the UK and Scottish Governments (as discussed in Chapters 7 and 8). In these Acts, powers may be explicitly granted to the Scottish Ministers to make delegated legislation. When they do so, it will be by SSI[12]. Finally, replacement of SI by SSI occurs when Scottish Ministers exercise powers under Acts of the Scottish Parliament. Over time, these acts will gradually replace the remaining United Kingdom legislation which previously delegated equivalent powers. Of course, where the delegate is a local authority, and in some other cases, the delegated legislation was not in SI form before devolution, so will not be replaced by SSIs[13].

Use of delegated legislative powers in Scotland

10.7   There are hundreds of SSIs issued every year so, as at a UK level, they generate a much greater volume of law than primary legislation[14]. Although a significant number relate to narrow, technical areas, such as local traffic orders or amendments to fee levels in legal aid cases, they touch on nearly every aspect of the Scottish Government's competence, including the major subjects of health, education and the courts. And as discussed above, many SSIs will deal with aspects outwith the Scottish Parliament's normal competence, with Scottish Ministers acting under powers transferred to them by UK Ministers. Beyond SSIs, much delegated legislation made by the United Kingdom government continues to apply in Scotland, and indeed there may be more SIs than SSIs each year applying to Scotland[15].

---

11 Under the European Communities Act 1972, s 2(2): *eg* the very first SSI, *ie* the Environmental Impact Assessment (Scotland) Regulations 1999, SSI 1999/1 (implementing an EC Directive).

12 Often this will be achieved by primary legislation giving powers to 'the appropriate Minister' which will then be defined within the act to mean 'the Scottish Ministers' in relation to Scotland.

13 Thus, byelaws made by Scottish local authorities under the Local Government (Scotland) Act 1973, ss 201–203 remain byelaws.

14 Well over 400 SSIs are normally produced per year. There are usually between 10 and 20 Acts of the Scottish Parliament in any year.

15 Figures produced by Reid 'Who Makes Scotland's Law?' (2002) 6 EdinLR 8 380–384, suggest as many as a quarter of all SIs apply to Scotland; this equates to between 500 to 750 SIs per year. It is not likely that this proportion has changed much.

The form of delegated legislation in Scotland

10.8 Delegated legislation made by Scottish Ministers is in essentially the same form although cited using the prefix SSI, for example 'SSI 2003/143', and use the 'C' abbreviation and sub-sequence of numbers for Commencement Orders.[16] No distinction is made between SSIs made under Acts of the United Kingdom and those made under Acts of the Scottish Parliament, although the relevant legislation is often referred to in the preamble of the SSI.

The form and publication procedure for SSIs is laid down in the Scottish Statutory Instrument Regulations,[17] themselves a piece of delegated legislation made under the Interpretation and Legislative Reform (Scotland) Act 2010. This requires that they must be published to the website of the Queen's Printer[18] and printed and delivered to the National Library of Scotland. Lists of SSIs must also be published, as must an annual edition, containing all of each year's SSIs.

CONTROL OF DELEGATED LEGISLATION IN SCOTLAND

Control by the Scottish Parliament

10.9 Control by the Scottish Parliament of Scottish delegated legislation is similar to that applied by the UK Parliament to SIs. Firstly, provisions in bills proposing the grant of new powers to make delegated legislation are scrutinised by the Scottish Parliament's Subordinate Legislation Committee. Secondly, the same committee must scrutinise any draft delegated legislation laid before the Scottish Parliament.

---

16 There is, again, innocent amusement to be had in discovering the most unusual statutory instrument name. See *eg* the Food Protection (Emergency Provisions) (Amnesic Shellfish Poisoning) (West Coast) (No 12) (Scotland) Order 2005, SSI 2006/6. (Note, incidentally, an example of an SSI title referring to one year, and the citation referring to the next).

17 Scottish Statutory Instruments Regulations (SSI 2011/195).

18 This now means the www.legislation.gov.uk website administered by The National Archives on behalf of the UK and devolved governments. Commercial providers of legal information (discussed in Chapter 13) also publish SSIs as part of their offering of legislative material. These offerings often include added-value services, such as updating and amendment of published SSIs, not usually provided as part of official services.

The draft measures themselves are subject to similar *negative* and *affirmative resolution procedures* to those applied by the UK Parliament to UK Sis[19]. The exact approval process for each piece of delegated legislation will be specified in the enabling legislation.

Controls over byelaws remain as they were before devolution, except where the Secretary of State was the confirming authority, it will now be the Scottish Ministers, by operation of the 'general transfer of functions'.

Where the power to issue delegated legislation is in an existing UK Act of Parliament, then the requirement for laying before Parliament, and for negative or affirmative resolution procedure, is applied to the Scottish Parliament instead of the United Kingdom Parliament (or either House of it)[20].

Judicial control and ultra vires

10.10 Scottish Ministers and the Scottish Parliament act under clearly defined limits; specifically, delegated legislation must be within their competence (either because it relates to a devolved matter or they have explicitly been granted to power to make legislation on reserved matters) and must not breach Convention rights or EU law. The same criteria of legislative competence applying to Acts of the Scottish Parliament apply also to the making of SSIs.

Clearly, these limits of the powers of the Scottish Government provide a number of routes by which delegated legislation may be challenged by way of judicial review. Similar limits, and opportunities for challenge, apply to delegated legislation created by other Scottish authorities[21].

---

19 The detailed rules for parliamentary procedure are contained in the Standing Orders of the Scottish Parliament, available online at www.scottish.parliament. uk.

20 Scotland Act, s 118.

21 For instance, in *KP and MRK v Secretary of State for the Home Department* [2012] CSIH 38, the court held that a rule made by Act of Sederunt was *ultra vires* as it went beyond making a procedural rule for the court.

11 Legislation – application, construction and interpretation: statutory interpretation

THE APPLICATION, CONSTRUCTION AND INTERPRETATION OF LEGISLATION

11.1 Previous chapters considered the various types of legislation which may apply in the United Kingdom generally, or Scotland in particular. This chapter turns to the difficulties of applying legislation to real-life situations: a process often termed *statutory interpretation*.

Most statutory interpretation is not conducted in a court setting or even by qualified lawyers. On a day-to-day basis it is done by officials such as civil servants, local government officers and the police, as well as by ordinary people in the course of their business and personal lives. However, legal attention is usually directed exclusively at the way judges apply the law. There is good reason for this: judges' decisions are uniquely authoritative. They are signals to officials, including civil servants, local government officers, the police, tax inspectors, company secretaries, personnel managers, and the public at large, as to the correct view on the application of the legislation in question. They have the final word[1].

This Chapter will discuss why statutory interpretation is needed and the processes of construction and interpretation which underly it. It will then discuss the approaches to statutory interpretation historically taken by courts in UK jurisdictions and how these have evolved. However, the increasing prominence of European Union law, much of which is drafted in a form originating in the

---

1 The courts can occasionally cause practical problems when they overturn what those working in the sector have always taken to be the correct practice. For instance, in *Royal Bank of Scotland v Wilson* [2010] UKSC 50, 2011 SC (UKSC) 66, the Supreme Court decided that 40 years of practice in conveyancing had been based upon a misinterpretation of the law, with immediate implications for many cases which were then being pursued under the now incorrect procedures.

European civil law tradition, has required the UK courts to adopt new approaches to statutory interpretation of European law. These influences will be described and discussed. Finally, the Human Rights Act 1998 and Scotland Act 1998 embed new approaches to statutory interpretation which are arguably altering the way in which the courts see their role in the application of legislation.

THE APPLICATION OF LEGISLATION

11.2   Much effort goes into the preparation and production of legislation, so it might be thought that it is easy to apply. Often this is the case, but by no means invariably, and there are remarkably few attempts to analyse what problems the application of legislation involves[2]. The reasons for the problems probably lie in the interplay of several factors. Some are inherent: rules concerning complicated matters will be complicated; no language is an instrument of complete precision; no drafter can foresee all eventualities, and sometimes drafters make mistakes. Others are not: the United Kingdom tradition in drafting is to seek to cover all possibilities, at the expense of comprehensibility, while the civil law tradition (more obvious in EU law) involves looser drafting, giving more discretion to those applying it. Equally, the legislation may be an unhappy compromise or have been formulated more for political expediency[3].

These difficulties produce various problems. On the one hand, complexity may make legislation very resistant to comprehension. The legislative text may be unclear on its face, typically through numerous conditions and exceptions, exacerbated by frequent cross-reference, but also through ambiguity. On the other, it may be clear on its face, but produce a result which seems absurd, for example by apparently failing to cover certain situations (often described as a *lacuna*[4] or loophole). Arguably statutory interpretation involves two processes. Firstly, the text must be scrutinised to establish what the

---

2   See, however, Kirby 'Towards a Grand Theory of Interpretation: the case of statutes and contracts' (2003) 24 Stat LR 95-111; Hunt 'Plain Language in Legislative Drafting: an achievable objective or a laudable ideal?' (2003) 24 Stat LR 112-124; and Barnes 'The Continuing Debate About "Plain Language" Legislation: a law reform conundrum' (2006) 27 Stat LR 83-132.

3   It has even been suggested that the obscurity of legislation is sometimes deliberate. For instance, The Equal Pay (Amendment) Regulations 1983, SI 1983/1794, was regarded by some as an unwilling response to the demands of EU law, drafted in obscure fashion, and involving a tortuous procedure in order to deter those seeking a remedy under them.

4   *Lacuna* is the Latin word for a missing part or blank.

rule actually is; this is known as *construction*. Secondly, the rule must be *interpreted* to establish what it actually means in that particular case. This terminology is not fixed and the terms construction (or, in verb form: to *construe*) and interpretation are often used interchangeably.

Construing legislation

11.3 Legislation must be written, so there is always a text from which the rules created by the legislation must be extracted using the rules of logic, grammar and syntax. The UK drafting tradition seeks exactitude, and expresses the logic through typographical devices such as indentations; division into sections and sub-sections; as well as the words themselves.

A useful approach is to remember that rules can be seen as 'if ... then' statements. The terms *protasis* (the 'if' part of the rule) and the *apodosis* (the 'then' part of the rule) are sometimes used in this context[5]. Construing the text means identifying the various different 'if' and 'then' parts (of which there may be many) and determining their relationship, to establish a set of logical rules applicable to the facts of the case.

One commentator, an experienced drafter of legislation, has taken this process further, suggesting that legislative provisions can be analysed into five aspects: case, condition, subject, declaration and exception[6]. In slightly modified form, his example, taken from the legislative provision on the production of driving licences, is as follows:

- **Case**. Who is under consideration?
  'Where a person is in charge of a motor vehicle...'.

- **Condition**. What must be true before the obligation or right applies?
  '...if so required by a constable...'.

- **Subject**. On whom does the obligation or right fall?
  '...that person...'.

- **Declaration**. What is the obligation or right created?
  '...shall produce his licence...'.

- **Exception**. What is the obligation or right created?
  '...unless he is exempt from holding a licence.'.

5   See Appendix 1.
6   *Bennion on Statute Law* (3rd edn, 1990): see also his *Statutory Interpretation: a code* (4th ed 2007) and *Understanding Common Law Legislation* (2nd ed. 2009).

In straightforward cases, such analysis is done intuitively, but many cases are not straightforward. They are complicated by amendment; by cross-reference within the legislation (such as to Interpretation Sections); by cross-reference between pieces of legislation (particularly, in the United Kingdom context, between Acts of Parliament and delegated legislation); and where amendment is done by inserting references rather than amending the text of the legislation itself[7].Where rules are buried in complex provisions, there is often no shortcut: patient and diligent analysis is the only route to a clear understanding[8].

Interpreting legislation

11.4 Construing legislation is often only the start. Even where the rule established by a legislative provision is clear, it may be far from clear whether it applies to the facts of the case. Even where important terms are clearly defined, words are inherently ambiguous, leaving room for doubt as to whether certain situations were are covered or not. And, more often than might be hoped, legislation may use vague terms or not define important terms. Sometimes this is deliberate: a recognition that the courts are better equipped than Parliament to deal with the variety of scenarios that may emerge[9]. Other times it is simply an omission: the courts must

---

7   An example of the awkward readings occasionally required is the (now repealed) Criminal Procedure (Scotland) Act 1975, itself inserted by the Criminal Justice Act 1982, which read: 'Where the penalty or maximum penalty for an offence to which s 457A(1)(b) of this Act applies has not been altered by any enactment passed or made after 29th July 1977 [the date of the passing of the Criminal Law Act 1977], this section applies as if the amount referred to in subsection (5)(a) below were the greatest amount to which a person would have been liable on any conviction before that date'.

8   See also Twining and Miers *How To Do Things with Rules* (5th edn, 2010), especially Appendix 2, which offers analysis in terms of algorithms.

9   For instance, legislators did not attempt to prescribe the extent of a phrase like 'in charge of a motor vehicle' in s 4 of the Road Traffic Act 1988. It would be impossible to formulate a definition that could capture the totality of possible situations. Instead, the courts have been left to develop principles from the real life cases that appear before them.

then try to reverse-engineer rules of general application from the specific case in front of them[10].

Ultimately, there is no single approach to interpretation. Instead, a number of rules, presumptions, principles and guidelines have been developed over the years. These have historically been applied inconsistently, have been given different weight by different judges and at different times, and are often incompatible. In many ways, they reflect the continually developing relationship between the legislature (which makes the legislation) and the courts (who interpret it) under the unwritten and evolutionary British constitutional arrangements. And, as discussed in the introduction, developments in this constitutional relationships, brought about by membership of the European Union (EU), the Human Rights Act 1998 and the devolution settlement have also influenced the way legislation is interpreted.

So far as the United Kingdom is concerned, there appears to be no significant difference between the approaches adopted in Scotland and England. Certainly, writers on the subject in Scotland cite English cases without remark. This similarity of approach reflects not just a similar legal system but 300 years of a shared legislature and, for civil and human rights matters, a shared final appellate court in the shape of the Supreme Court, previously the House of Lords[11].

10 For example, the Race Relations Act 1976 made it unlawful in certain situations to discriminate against people on 'racial grounds', defined in s 3(1) as the ground of their 'colour, race, nationality or ethnic or national origins'. In *Mandla v Lee* [1983] AC 548 the question was whether discrimination against a Sikh was on this ground. The House of Lords finally decided that it was. Sikhs constitute an ethnic group, so discrimination against them is on the grounds of their '... ethnic ... origins'. In *Nyazi v Ryman Conran* [1988] Race Discrimination Law Reports 85, the same question arose in relation to Muslims, and it was decided that it was not unlawful discrimination. Muslims are a religious group, so discrimination against them is not on the grounds of their 'colour, race ... [etc]'. Thus, legislation requires to be interpreted in respect of any set of facts, which may show the precise meaning is unclear, so has to be resolved by the courts.

11 In the field of criminal law, the Supreme Court has no jurisdiction in Scotland, unless considering an EU law or Convention rights question, so occasionally Scottish and English courts give different interpretations to statutes which apply in both jurisdictions. An example is *Kelly v MacKinnon* 1982 JC 94 where the Scottish courts held that a weapon that could easily be adapted to fire bullets was not a firearm in terms of the definition in the Firearms Act 1968 s57(1). The English courts had previously decided differently on this point.

INTERPRETATION OF LEGISLATION BY UNITED KINGDOM COURTS: THE TRADITIONAL APPROACH

11.5   Historically, the UK courts have seen their role in interpreting legislation as discovering the intention of Parliament. In doing this, they have at times developed a number of rules and presumptions. Some of these are expressions of logic and common sense; others reflect particular approaches taken by different judges in different eras. The extent to which judges have been willing to refer to material outside the legislation itself has also varied over legal history.

Principles employed by United Kingdom courts in construing and interpreting legislation

The Intention of Parliament

11.6   Traditionally, statutory interpretation has been driven by the UK constitutional principle of parliamentary sovereignty. Under this analysis, Parliament can legislate as it wishes and the role of the courts is subservient to this, merely applying this law. In keeping with this tradition, courts commonly saw statutory interpretation as a process of applying the *intention of Parliament* and that it was not open for the courts to read too much into the words of a statute. This view is expressed in a well-known exchange between senior judges. Lord Denning (famous for his lack of respect for orthodoxy), commenting on a case as a Court of Appeal judge said he had 'no patience with an ultra legalistic interpretation which would deprive [the plaintiffs] of their rights altogether'. On appeal to the House of Lords, this brought a sharp rebuke from Lord Simonds: '[t]he duty of the court is to interpret the words that the legislature has used; those words may be ambiguous but, even if they are, the power and duty of the court to travel outside them on a voyage of discovery are strictly limited', and referred to Lord Denning's approach as a 'naked usurpation of the legislative function under the thin disguise of interpretation'[12].

Whilst courts still say that they seek to apply the intention of Parliament, there is no doubt that Lord Denning's approach is probably more representative of the way in which statutory interpretation developed in the second half of the twentieth century.

---

12 *Magor and St Mellons RDC v Newport Corporation* [1950] 2 All ER 1226 (CA) at 1236 (Lord Denning) and [1952] AC 189 (HL) at 191 (Lord Simonds).

Certainly, the attitude adopted by the courts to discussions of parliamentary sovereignty show that at least some judges see that the need for deference to the will of Parliament has important limits[13]. In particular, the courts now have little hesitation taking a broad approach to interpretation where they are convinced that the drafting of the provision is in error[14].

Rules of Statutory Interpretation

11.7 Against the background of the task of discovering the intention of Parliament, three rules of statutory interpretation have been said to exist: the *Mischief Rule*, the *Literal Rule* and the *Golden Rule*.

The *Mischief Rule* was expressed as far back as the sixteenth century, in the English *Heydon's Case* (1584) 3 Co Rep 7a. It is usually said to mean that, if a provision is unclear, the judge should look to the mischief the Act was designed to overcome, and interpret it in order to 'suppress the mischief and advance the remedy'. Although it is often seen as a warrant for judges to rewrite legislation in a fashion they find more palatable, it has been suggested that it is quite the contrary, having been developed as a means of compelling judges to focus on what Parliament intended rather than what they wish it had intended[15]. The rule has been explicitly applied in Scotland. For example, the High Court considered that its power, granted in an 1859 statute, to forfeit any 'boat, cart, basket or package' used for salmon poaching applied where a motorcycle combination had been employed, 'so as to cope with the mischief'[16].

The *Literal Rule* emerged later, encouraged by the increased precision and formality legislation as the UK's parliamentary

---

13 As expressed in the concept that the courts might consider that judicial review or the role of the courts was a 'constitutional fundamental' such that the courts would decline to apply legislation abolishing it *(per* Lord Steyn in *R(Jackson) v Attorney-General* [2005] UKHL 56, [2006] 1 AC 262, at [102]).

14 House of Lords authority (*Inco Europe Ltd and Others v First Choice Distribution and Others* [2000] 1 WLR 586) was followed in *Scottish Water v Clydecare Ltd* 2003 SC 330, with the judge being willing to read words into the statute on the ground that they considered it was clear that the draftsman had omitted them in error. It was noted, at [30], that the court would require to be persuaded that 'a fundamental error or draftsmanship has occurred in the legislation under consideration'.

15 Miers and Page *Legislation* (2nd edn, 1990) p 171.

16 *Leadbetter v Hutcheson* 1934 JC 70. The statutory provision in question was s 10 of the Tweed Fishing Act 1859.

democracy matured. It is simply an expression of the idea that the courts may only look to the legislative text itself. At points, judges have felt constrained to apply the literal meaning of the legislation even if the result is absurd, or at least something common sense suggests Parliament did not intend. For example, the Finance Act 1933 taxed certain 'profits'. In *Ayrshire Employers Mutual Insurance v IRC* 1946 SC(HL) 1, the House of Lords considered whether this included 'surpluses' generated by mutual insurance companies. Even though reasonably sure that the Government, the drafters and Parliament all intended the legislation to tax them, it held that such surpluses were not regarded as profits elsewhere in the law, and it consequently applied a literal interpretation, thereby excluding them. In another example, the Misuse of Drugs Act 1971, s 5 made it an offence to possess cannabis resin. In *Keane v Gallagher* 1980 SLT 144, the High Court decided to apply 'the plain unqualified words' to uphold conviction of possessing a minute quantity, totalling 11 milligrams, which was too small to be usable.

The *Golden Rule* is arguably not a separate rule, merely a compromise based on the rules above. It says that the literal meaning should be applied unless it produces, in Lord Blackburn's classical exposition of the rule 'an inconsistency, or an absurdity, or inconvenience so great as to convince the court' that the intention of Parliament must have been different. Such an outcome will justify the court in applying another meaning which the words will bear[17]. In *K v Craig* 1997 SLT 748, a case involving the discharge of a mental patient into community care, the literal wording of the Act required that a person who did not need to be detained must be released. In the circumstances, the court held this would be an absurd result and declined to apply it.

The problem with the Mischief, Literal and Golden Rules is that they are clearly not rules at all. They are alternative guidelines and there is no clue as to which should be preferred and when, giving the impression that they may be fig-leaves to cover the embarrassment of conclusions arrived at by other means. In any case, commonly judges do not refer explicitly to any rule and, when they do, sometimes it is to explain that fortunately all three point in the same direction. Academic commentators tend to explain them with examples promiscuously chosen from different judges, in different periods, in different courts, in different jurisdictions.

17 *River Wear Commissioners v Adamson* (1877) 2 App Cas 743, .

Some commentators have suggested that the Rules should be seen as examples of two alternative approaches. One, the *literal approach*, regards the language of the text as primary, and tries to apply the actual words of the legislation, come what may. The other, the *purposive* approach, assumes that the legislator had a purpose which has to be applied, and that the words of the legislation are one piece of evidence of that purpose.

A synthesised view which has been suggested in both England and Scotland is that there is a single basic rule with five parts[18]. This is expressed as:

* the judge must give effect to the grammatical and ordinary or, where appropriate, technical meaning of words, given their context;
* if the result is absurd, or contrary to the purpose of the statute, he may apply a secondary meaning;
* if necessary, the judge can read in missing words implied by words which are present and, to a limited extent, add to, ignore or alter words to prevent unintelligibility, absurdity, complete unreasonability, unworkability, or irreconcilability with the rest of the statute;
* in applying the above rules, the judge may have resort to the various materials and presumptions available (discussed below);
* the judge must interpret a statute so as to give effect to directly applicable EU law (also discussed later).

Linguistic presumptions in statutory interpretation

11.8 A number of important presumptions are sometimes drawn from the language and construction of legislative provisions.

The first is that the courts accept that the legislation may, on occasion, misuse the conjunctions 'and', 'or' and 'and/or' when listing conditions. If the result of the literal interpretation appears to defeat the intention of the legislation, the courts will not necessarily hold to the literal use of the conjunction. For instance, the Food and Environmental Protection Act 1985 permits the Scottish Ministers to prohibit 'fishing for **and** taking fish' (emphasis added) under certain circumstances. The courts held they could legitimately make

---

18 See Cross *Statutory Interpretation* (3rd edn, 1995) p 49 and Wilson 'Trials and Try-Ons: Modes of Interpretation' 1992 Stat LR 1.

a regulation to prohibit 'fishing for **or** taking scallops' (emphasis added)[19].

Lists and examples are also governed by a number of linguistic principles, usually expressed by their Latin names. Firstly, there is a presumption that the meaning of a term is restricted by the common features it shares with other terms in a list. This is known as *noscitur a sociis* (literally, it is known from its associates). In *Imperial Tobacco, Petitioner*, the Inner House had to consider whether an Act of the Scottish Parliament regulated the 'sale and supply of goods' for consumer protection[20]. By reference to the other nine items listed as elements of consumer protection, the court held that this section of legislation was concerned only with economic or contractual protection of consumers, not product safety[21].

A special case of this, *eiusdem generis* ('of the same kind'), applies to a commonly used statutory formulation, 'any A, B, C, or other X'. This strongly implies that A, B, and C share common features that define X. For example, a court required to decide whether a structure built from stone and brick and housing a gas meter fell within the definition of 'building' for the purposes of the Representation of the People (Scotland) Act 1832. As the full definition referred to 'any house, warehouse, counting house, shop, or other building', the court held that, in this context, 'building' included 'residential, commercial and agricultural premises' so did not stretch to the gas meter house[22]. Sometimes legislation will include the phrase 'without prejudice to the forgoing' to attempt to disapply these presumptions.

A final example of a presumption sometimes applied to lists is *expressio unius, exclusio alterius* (simply, 'if you don't say it, you don't mean it'). This reflects a more literal or stricter approach which will apply where a list is apparently definitive rather than illustrative[23].

---

19 *Colley v Poland* 2005 SLT 436. A literal use of 'or' means the Order would prohibit both fishing for scallops (even if none were caught) and the taking of fish (even inadvertently when not fishing for them) while, arguably, the Act only permitted prohibition of catching fish when fishing for them.

20 [2012] CSIH 9, 2012 SC 297. The decision was subsequently upheld by the Supreme Court at [2012] UKSC 61, 2013 SLT 2.

21 *per* Lord President Hamilton at [8], discussing the list at Section C7(a) of Schedule 5 to the Scotland Act 1998.

22 *Duncan v Jackson* (1905) 8 F. 323.

23 In *R(Jackson) v Attorney-General* [2005] UKHL 56, [2006] 1 AC 262, at [138], Lord Rodger quotes the rule when disposing of an argument that Parliament intended to exclude any bill amending the Parliament Act 1911 from the category of Public Bills to which the 1911 Act applied, when s2(1) of the 1911 Act applied the provisions of the act to 'any Public Bill (other than a Money Bill or a Bill containing any provision to extend the maximum duration of Parliament beyond five years)'.

The words *shall* and *may* deserve attention. 'It **shall** be an offence ... ' really means 'It **is** an offence ... ', emphasising obligation rather than futurity. Also, used in relation to a procedure, 'shall' generally makes it mandatory (that is, obligatory), so failure to follow the procedure invalidates the outcome (rather than directory, that is, merely recommended)[24]. However, the presumption can be rebutted, as, for example, in *HM Advocate v Graham* 1985 SLT 498 (which concerned the lodging of copy indictments under the Criminal Procedure (Scotland) Act 1975). Where legislation says someone 'shall' do something, it also implies he is given the power to do so. 'May' in legislative discourse generally denotes power or permission, without any obligation to use it, as held, for example, in *Patmor Ltd v City of Edinburgh District Licensing Board* 1988 SLT 850 (concerning gaming licences under the Gaming Act 1968). On occasion, however, permissive words have been interpreted as obligatory, as, for example, in *Gray v St Andrews and Cupar District Committees of Fife County Council* 1911 SC 266 (concerning the Highways (Scotland) Act 1771).

Legal presumptions in statutory interpretation

11.9   A number of presumptions are often said to operate unless explicitly or implicitly excluded. In general they apply when there is doubt as to the meaning of the legislation, though some are so strong as to displace an apparently clear meaning. There is no exhaustive or official list of any of them, they may contradict each other and different authorities give different examples[25].

Examples of these presumptions are: against unclear alteration of settled law; against absurd results; against criminalising behaviour; against retrospectivity and against injustice. A famous example of the application of these presumptions is *Sweet v Parsley* [1970] AC 132, an English case concerning the Dangerous Drugs Act 1965. This Act created the offence of 'being the occupier' or 'concerned in the management' of premises used for the offence of 'smoking of

---

24 As held by the House of Lords in *London and Clydeside Estates v Aberdeen District Council* 1980 SC(HL) 1, concerning planning appeal procedures.
25 Competing lists are proposed in *Stair Memorial Encyclopaedia* Vol 12 paras 1126–1133; DM Walker *The Scottish Legal System* (8th edn, 2001) pp 428–430 (which only offers the 'principal' presumptions; Paterson, Bates and Poustie *The Legal System of Scotland: cases and materials* (4th edn, 2001) pp 384–386 (where legal presumptions are desecribed as the 'judicial principles'); and Cross *Statutory Interpretation* (3rd edn, 1995) Ch 7.

cannabis resin'. It was silent on whether such a person committed the offence if unaware of the smoking by others on the premises. Sweet, a non-resident landlord, wholly ignorant of the actual smoking by others on the premises, was convicted of the offence. The House of Lords quashed the conviction on appeal, deciding that only the clearest words could create a new criminal offence that did not require a criminal intent. Lord Reid, a notable Scottish judge, observed that 'there has for centuries been a presumption that Parliament did not intend to make criminals of persons who were in no way blameworthy...'.

A further legal presumption is the *doctrine of implied repeal*. This applies where two statutes apparently conflict but there is no explicit repeal of the earlier statutory provision in the later Act. The consequence of the fact that no Parliament can bind its successors (a feature of the sovereignty of Parliament) is that the later rule takes precedence over the earlier which is, by implication, repealed. This doctrine was limited in *Thoburn v Sunderland City Council* [2003] QB 151 (the so-called *metric martyrs* case). In their judgments, the court said that where statutes were clearly of fundamental legal importance (described in *Thoburn* as a *constitutional statute*) they could not be impliedly repealed but would require clear and express repeal by a subsequent statute[26].

Materials considered by United Kingdom courts in construing and interpreting legislation

11.10 The concept of the intention of Parliament is a theoretical one. The UK Parliament comprises over 600 MPs plus many more unelected peers. Many of these may have voted against the legislation in question; those who voted for it may have done so for various reasons, often on an incomplete or inaccurate understanding of the provisions and certainly without being able to anticipate each and every situation to which the law may be applied. In the face of this, the courts have historically adopted the principle that the text of the legislation approved by Parliament, and that text alone, is the source from which a judge may infer the intention of Parliament. This approach also reflects the UK legislative tradition of drafting

26 It was argued that a 1985 Act of Parliament, which permitted the use of imperial measurements, had impliedly repealed or restricted s 2(2) of the earlier European Communities Act 1972 to the extent which it could no longer be relied upon by Ministers to empower them to subsequently amend the 1985 Act (by secondary legislation) to remove the permission to use imperial measures.

legislation with the aim of achieving verbal exactitude. The alternative approach taken with European Union legislation which, following the civilian tradition, is drafted much more loosely, is discussed later in this chapter.

This section will first discuss the traditional interpretive approach to the legislative text itself. It will then discuss the other material that is sometimes employed by the courts in an exception to the general rule of considering only the words of the statute.

The legislative text

11.11 A piece of legislation is generally considered as underpinned by a unifying purpose or intention. So, where the meaning of a particular provision is unclear, the courts will consider it in its context with the overall piece of legislation. An obvious consequence is that, generally, any given word or phrase will be taken as having the same meaning throughout a piece of legislation; although, as with all principles of statutory interpretation, this is not a fixed rule and the courts have sometimes felt it necessary to depart from this[27]. Legislation often contains *interpretation provisions*. Thus, vague or unusual terms may be explained, for example 'race' and 'racial groups' in the Equality Act 2010, s 9, or 'gender reassignment' in s 7 of the same Act. There may be also lists and examples.

However, interpretation provisions can only assist where the drafter has foreseen the difficulty, and are sometimes hedged by the use of words such as 'unless the context otherwise requires'.

In keeping with the traditional approach of giving supremacy to the legislative text itself, the courts have traditionally been much more reluctant to take into account text that is not actually part of the wording of the provisions themselves. Even the long titles of Acts, which explicitly contain a statement of the aim of legislation, are only used to remove doubts[28]. Less weight is given to the marginal notes and headings found in legislation. These are referred to as the *unenacted parts* of an Act as they are not discussed in Parliament but it has been held that these should not be disregarded, as they were there for guidance (in particular, in relation to the mischief the

---

27 The English Court of Appeal found that the word 'discrimination' bore different meanings in ss 1 and 4 of the Sex Discrimination Act 1975.

28 *R (on the application of Quintavalle) v Secretary of State for Health* [2003] UKHL 13 [2003] 2 AC 687, *per* Lord Millett at [41]. In reality the long titles of Acts are generally written in vague terms so are not helpful for drawing fine distinctions in interpreting provisions of the Act.

legislation was intended to cure) so were part of the context of the Act which assisted in interpretation[29]. Short titles have been held, in contrast, to be mere 'statutory nicknames' and given no weight in interpretation[30]. *Preambles* can be used[31], but are very rare (except in private legislation).

Records of Parliamentary proceedings

11.12 The proceedings of the UK Parliament and its committees are recorded and published in Hansard. For the Scottish Parliament, the Official Record of the Scottish Parliament performs the same function. So it might be thought that the obvious material to shed light on the intention of Parliament is the record of what was said in Parliament at the time the legislation in question was being discussed. In fact, there was until the 1980s a complete rejection of this idea. This rule was founded on both principle and pragmatism. In principle, it was said to be both irrelevant and unreliable to read too much into discussions in Parliament: it was unlikely that the precise question before the court was discussed and could not reliably be said that the content of any given speech or statement, even from the minister promoting the legislation, was fully accepted by Parliament corporately unless it was enshrined in the final words of the statute[32]. From a pragmatic point, the courts hesitated at the thought that all litigation would be complicated by both sides delving into the huge mass of Parliamentary material seeking out statements supporting alternative interpretations of legislation or throwing doubt on otherwise clear provisions.

---

29 In *Hill v Orkney Islands Council* 1983 SLT (Lands Tr) 2, the Lands Tribunal resolved an ambiguity by reference to a cross-heading following the House of Lords authority of *DPP v Schildkamp* [1971] AC 1 (especially the remarks of Lord Reid, a Scottish judge; although the case was English, the statute concerned was equally applicable in Scotland). See also Simamba, B 'Should Marginal Notes be Used in the Interpretation of Legislation?' (2005) Stat LR 125-130.
30 *Vacher & Sons v London Society of Compositors* [1913] AC 107; *R v Boaler* [1915] 1 KB 21.
31 *Anderson v Jenkins Express Removals Ltd*, reported in *James Kemp (Leslie) Ltd v Robertson* 1967 SC 229 at 233–234 *per* Lord Mackintosh; and *A-G v Prince Ernest Augustus of Hanover* [1957] AC 436, especially *per* Lord Normand (a Scottish judge) although the role of Scots law was overlooked in that case.
32 Lord Diplock in *Hadmor Productions v Hamilton* [1983] 1 AC 191 at 232 criticised Lord Denning in the Court of Appeal for seeking to justify the construction he placed on s 17(8) by referring to 'the report in Hansard of a speech made by a peer...when moving an opposition amendment (which was defeated) to delete the subsection from the Bill'.

A significant softening of this strict rule was however accepted in *Pepper v Hart* [1993] AC 593[33]. In this case the House of Lords, by a majority, accepted that, as the courts' job is to apply the intention of Parliament and that Parliament cannot have intended an ambiguity, it was legitimate to vary the exclusionary rule. Conscious of the difficulties, the House of Lords were careful to limit the variation to the rule, stating it would only apply where a statute is ambiguous, obscure or leads to an absurdity. Any Parliamentary material employed, preferably statements by a minister or other promoter of the Bill, must be clear.

The *Pepper v Hart* approach was quickly adopted in Scotland in *Short's Trustee v Keeper of the Registers of Scotland* 1994 SLT 65. In this conveyancing case the reports which preceded legislation on the registration of titles, as well as aspects of the parliamentary process, were referred to in both the Outer and Inner Houses[34].

Explanatory Notes

11.13 *Explanatory notes*, written by the sponsoring Government Department, have long been attached to Statutory Instruments and, since 1999, to Acts of Parliament. They are designed to give a straightforward explanation of the meaning of the various provisions but might be expected to be excluded on the same grounds as the record of Parliamentary proceedings. If this was the rule, then a more relaxed approach has been taken in recent years. In *R (on the application of Westminster City Council) v National Asylum Support Service* [2002] UKHL 38, [2002] 1 WLR 2956, Lord Steyn at [4]-[6] explicitly invoked *Pepper v Hart*, stating that explanatory notes should always be admissible in relation to establishing the 'contextual scene of the statute and the mischief at which it is aimed'.

---

33 Here the tax authorities argued that teachers in a private school should pay tax on the discounts they received on their children's school fees as a benefit-in-kind, based on the value assessed by the (large) fees charged to other parents, rather than the (marginal) cost to the employer of accommodating a small number of additional children. Although this question had specifically been addressed in Parliament, the wording of the final provision was ambiguous.

34 Although the Inner House found them to be of limited assistance. In other cases, such as *AIB Finance v Bank of Scotland* 1995 SLT 2 and *Customs and Excise Comrs v Robert Gordon's College* 1995 SLT 1139, the court declined to apply *Pepper v Hart* since it was held there was no ambiguity or obscurity in the relevant statutes.

Other documents and reports

11.14   Arguments for excluding documents such as Government White Papers, Royal Commission reports and other documents related to legislation are similar to those in relation to Parliamentary materials, but are stronger as these documents may shed light on the intention of the drafter but not necessarily the intent of parliament.

This position was taken in an English case on United Kingdom legislation before the Appellate Committee of the House of Lords, *Assam Railways and Trading Co Ltd v IRC* [1935] AC 445 (see Lord Wright at 457–458) and in a Scottish case, *Inglis v British Airports Authority* 1978 SLT (Lands Tr) 30. However, in a complicated judgment in another English case the House of Lords preserved the rule in *Black-Clawson International Ltd v Papierwerke Waldhof Aschaffenburg AG* [1975] AC 591. Some of its members were prepared to accept that in certain circumstances a draft Bill attached to a report, and possibly other documents, might be considered.

The reports of the Law Commissions which precede some legislation are arguably a special case. These customarily rehearse the law before the legislation, identify its defects and offer a remedy in the form of a draft Bill with supporting arguments. If Parliament has in all material respects enacted the Bill drafted by the Commission, its Report would seem a useful means of discovering the meaning of the Act. In *McWilliams v Lord Advocate* 1992 SLT 1045, Lord Morton made full use of two Commission reports on the question whether a child had a right of action for injuries sustained before birth. However, the more common attitude of the judges, as exemplified in *Barratt Scotland Ltd v Keith* 1994 SLT 1343, has been to restrict reference to Law Commission publications to cases of ambiguity or other doubts. But, as has been pointed out[35], statutory language is neither clear nor unclear in the abstract. It depends on the context, and part of that context is the mischief for which the Commission recommended a remedy. In *MacDonald v HM Advocate* 1999 SLT 533, it sufficed that it would be 'helpful' to refer to a Commission report.

Other legislation

11.15   The courts have traditionally been even more conservative about allowing themselves to look outside the statute in question.

---

35 Maher 'Statutory Interpretation and Scottish Law Commission Reports' 1992 SLT (News) 277.

However, there have always been exceptions to this rule in certain cases and it has been moderated significantly in more modern times.

Firstly, the courts will often consider other legislation on the same subject (such legislation sometimes being described using the Latin phrase *in pari materia*) as it is assumed Parliament means the same thing if it uses the same words. In some cases, an Act specifically stipulates that it is to be construed with another. This is implied where Acts are given collective Short Titles[36]. Consolidation Acts are a special case of legislation *in pari materia* with the Acts consolidated. They re-enact, though may do so with minor amendment.

The *in pari materia* concept is a flexible one. For example, the Sex Discrimination Act 1975 and Race Relations Act 1976 concerned different subjects but were drafted in large measure identically. Cross-reference to one was therefore sometimes made by the courts in order to interpret the other[37]. (The issue is less likely to arise since the Acts have been replaced by the Equality Act 2010). On the other hand, Acts on the same subject may have differing interpretation provisions, so cannot be used to interpret each other.

There is also difficulty with delegated legislation, since it is not written for, nor normally expressly approved by, Parliament, so the words can be said to be the intention of Parliament only with extreme difficulty. In *Hanlon v Law Society* [1981] AC 124, an English case before the House of Lords on the English legal aid legislation, Lord Lowry (at 193–194) suggested half a dozen principles to apply. These indicate that delegated legislation can be used to interpret its parent Act or related Acts, provided those Acts are ambiguous, or provided it can amend them. In the former case, they cannot control the meaning of the Act but, if consistent, can confirm an interpretation, and are particularly reliable if they flesh out a skeleton Act. In the latter case (and if they are to have effect as if enacted in the Act), they are a clear guide.

Finally, the Interpretation Act 1978 is explicitly designed to govern the interpretation of certain standard definitions and establish standard rules. This includes confirming that gendered words apply equally to both genders or that references to time mean Greenwich Mean Time or British Summer Time, as appropriate. The Interpretation and Legislative Reform (Scotland) Act 2010 performs the same function

---

36 For instance, the Companies Acts of 1976, 1985, 1989 and 2006. Where subsequent legislation has not corrected decisions of courts as to interpretation of earlier Acts on the same subject, the courts may consider that Parliament has impliedly approved the interpretative approach applied in the earlier case and adopted that in the later legislation.

37 As the English Court of Appeal did in *Singh v West Midlands Passenger Transport Executive* [1988] IRLR 186.

for Scottish Parliament legislation. Whilst these general rules are important, their application is limited[38] and subject to the legislation under consideration expressing a contrary intention[39].

Precedent

11.16 It is the legislation which determines the meaning, not other judges' views. However, earlier cases interpreting the same legislation may be used to extract its meaning and only a bold judge would depart from a series of similar decisions interpreting an Act, or even from a single decision of a higher court. Previous interpretations are difficult to avoid as a means of seeking meaning, and are one of the most commonly used. They operate as precedents in essentially the same way as in the common law, as the Inner House decided, albeit with some difficulty, in *Dalgleish v Glasgow Corporation* 1976 SC 32. However, as the Inner House also decided, in *AIB Finance Ltd v Bank of Scotland* 1995 SLT 2, subsequent amending legislation cannot be so used, as it cannot shed light on the intention of Parliament at the time of enactment of the legislation which is to be interpreted.

In general, however, this principle means that cases concerning the legislation '*in pari materia*' can be used as precedents. Reinforcing this is a presumption, based on the Appellate Committee of the House of Lords' decision in *Barras v Aberdeen Steam Trawling and Fishing Co Ltd* 1933 SC(HL) 21, of 'statutory endorsement'. If a word or phrase has received a particular interpretation by the courts, and it is incorporated in subsequent statutes, then it may be assumed that Parliament was endorsing that interpretation. However, some doubt was cast upon this by the High Court in *Kelly v MacKinnon* 1982 SCCR 205.

International Treaties

11.17 Some legislation is designed to give effect in national law to rules enshrined in international treaties agreed between governments[40]. This is becoming more important with an increasing

---

38 See Duperron 'Interpretation Acts – impediments to legal certainty and access to the law' (2005) 26 Stat LR 64-68.
39 For an example of which, see Lord Chancellor Loreburn and Lord Robertson in *Nairn v St Andrews and Edinburgh University Courts* 1909 SC(HL) 10, at 13 and 15–16 respectively.
40 This is required by the UK's dualist legal system, as only national law could be enforced by the courts. This does not apply to much EU legislation which has direct effect (although, arguably, this relies on the European Communities Act 1972, a UK statute).

number of multilateral treaties directly affecting individuals[41]. Often, the text of the treaty is directly imported to the text of the legislation[42]. In these cases, there is, in principle no modification required to the normal rules: the court need not look outside the words of the statute. In practice, the broader wording often used in treaties may require more interpretation than the more precise wording traditionally used in UK legislation.

English courts have in some cases considered that they might look at other, unincorporated versions of the treaty; commentaries on it (which might involve translation); and even the background documents, report and material that preceded the treaty (often known by their French term *travaux préparatoires*)[43]. Such practice may be justified by the need for consistent interpretation in different countries (as is required of EU law).

Scottish authority on the issue exists in *Gatoil International v Arkwright-Boston Manufacturers Mutual Insurance* 1985 SC(HL) 1. This concerned the Administration of Justice Act 1956 and the Brussels Convention Relating to the Arrest of Seagoing Ships. It was held that even where the treaty is not expressly incorporated, so is external to the Act, it can be examined, and so possibly could some of its *travaux préparatoires*.

Dictionaries and textbooks

11.18   Dictionaries have always been admitted to find the ordinary meaning of words. However, they are not often helpful[44]. Textbooks

---

41 See eg Berman 'International Treaties and British Statutes' (2005) 26 Stat LR 1-12 and Eaton 'Enacting Treaties' (2005) 26 Stat LR 13-21.

42 For instance, the Child Abduction and Custody Act 1985, s 1 says 'Subject to the provisions of this Part of this Act, the provisions of that Convention set out in Schedule 1 to this Act shall have the force of law in the United Kingdom'. Schedule 1 merely reproduces the Convention.

43 Literally, 'preparatory works'. The term refers to the published documentation of the negotiations leading to the treaty. The advantage of them is that they may show the reasoning which produced an agreed form of words. The disadvantage is that they are not what was actually agreed.

44 In *Mandla v Lee* [1983] QB 1 at 9–10, Lord Denning in the English Court of Appeal relied upon three dictionaries to assign a meaning to 'ethnic' in the Race Relations Act 1976. His interpretation, relying heavily upon etymology, was roundly rejected as absurd by Lord Fraser of Tullybelton on appeal to the House of Lords [1983] AC 548. In *Reed International v IRC* [1976] AC 336 at 359, Lord Wilberforce, having found Dr Johnson's *Dictionary* (1755) unhelpful, referred to *Palgrave's Dictionary of Political Economy* (1896).

on law are sometimes referred to, but they are evidence of what commentators thought[45], rather than guides to Parliament's intention.

Construction and interpretation of European Union law

11.19   The accession of the United Kingdom to what is now the European Union (EU), brought with it the obligation to apply EU law (referred to as Community law prior to 2009) at a national level. This has meant the courts have had to adopt new approaches to construing and interpreting legislation which is often written in a style very different from that normally found in UK legislation. EU legislation must also be applied uniformly in all member states and the Court of Justice of the European Union (CJEU)[46] is the ultimate arbiter of interpretation. The courts of the Member States, including Scottish courts, are therefore required to adopt the interpretive approach of the CJEU when dealing with EU law, with any questions of doubt referred to the CJEU for a binding ruling.

This section will discuss the approach to construction and interpretation adopted by the CJEU and then discuss how that approach has affected the UK courts.

The Interpretive Approach of the CJEU

11.20   The CJEU adopts an unashamedly *purposive* (sometimes called *teleological*) approach to construction and interpretation. In part, this reflects the nature of the legislation it deals with. The fundamental treaties of the EU are instruments of international law and tend to be written in terms of general principle rather than exhaustive detail[47]. Even more detailed EU legislation tends to be modelled on the civil law codes and statutes common in much of Europe which is usually much less precise than UK statutes. This

---

45 Until relatively recently, there was a convention that legal textbooks could not be considered as an authority until the author was dead. 'The law books give no assistance, because the work of living authors, however deservedly eminent, cannot be used as authority' *per* Lord Buckmaster in *Donoghue v Stevenson* 1932 SC(HL) 31 at 35.

46 The CJEU, previous known as the European Court of Justice (ECJ), includes the Court of Justice (CJ), the General Court (GC) and various specialist tribunals.

47 For example, Article 45(1) of the Treaty on the Functioning of the European Union (TFEU) declares that 'Free movement of workers shall be secured … ' but does not define 'worker', the key term of the Article. The definition had to be worked out by the European courts through a series of decisions.

apparent vagueness may be unavoidable with many equally authentic texts in different languages[48], which are often the result of political bargaining[49]. But the CJEU's purposive approach is not just driven by the nature of EU legislation: it also reflects the CJEU's view of its own role. Whilst the UK courts talk in terms of deference to the legislature, the CJEU sees itself as *communautaire*[50], pushing forward when Member States have dragged their feet. This is evident in the court's inventiveness in generating the 'general principles of law common to all Member States', and in a number of decisions which have been frankly legislative, such as Case 41/74 *Van Duyn v Home Office* [1974] ECR 1337, in which the court decided Directives might be directly effective, despite the apparently contrary wording of Article 189 and the intention of the (then) Treaty itself. Indeed, in Case 9/70 *Grad* [1970] ECR 825 at 839, for example, the court said 'It is true that a literal interpretation of ... Article 4 ... might lead to the view that this provision refers to [a certain date]. However, such an interpretation would not correspond to the aim of the directives in question ... '.

The court tends also to look at any piece of legislation as part of a general scheme containing a reservoir of principles expressed in various legislative texts, rather than as a single free-standing text in fixed verbal form. An example of this approach, sometimes termed a *schematic* approach, is Case 283/31 *CILFIT Srl v Ministry of Health* [1982] ECR 3415. The court said 'every provision of Community law must be placed in its context and interpreted in the light of the provisions of Community law as a whole, regard being had to the objectives thereof and to its state of evolution at the date on which the provision in question is to be applied'. The last words imply that interpretation can change over time.

The court also looks at other materials as well. The EU is a body of limited competence so, to be valid, any EU legislation must relate to an area of competence. This leads to the lengthy recitals at the beginning of legislation required by Article 253 TFEU. These contain a list of the Treaty provisions under which the legislation is made, the legislative history of proposals and opinions ('having

---

48 Clear differences of meaning can occur between translations and may indeed be used to throw light upon meaning, as for instance in Case 29/69 *Stauder v City of Ulm* [1969] ECR 419, where there was a difference between Dutch and German texts on the one hand, and French and Italian on the other.

49 In Case 136/79 *National Panasonic (UK) Ltd v Commission* [1980] ECR 2033, at 2066, the Advocate General observed that 'what members of the Council [of the Union] do when they adopt regulation is to agree upon a text. They do not necessarily all have the same views as to its meaning'.

50 *Communautaire* is a term that translates, roughly, as 'Community-minded'.

regard to ...'), and a statement of the reasons for the provision itself ('whereas ...'). This expressly directs the court's attention to other specific documents and *travaux préparatoires*.

Not all *travaux préparatoires* are examined, however. Those related to the Treaties themselves, and the proceedings of the Commission and Council, are not published. Debates of the European Parliament, though published, are rarely referred to by the court. The opinions of individual members of the Commission, Council or Parliament or of their staff are not admissible, even if they negotiated or prepared the text in question[51].

The court has also drawn on the constitutions of Member States, and national courts' interpretations of them, and on international treaties, in particular the ECHR, to produce 'general principles of law common to all Member States' such as certainty, proportionality and the concept of the fundamental status of citizenship of the EU, which it has gone on to apply in many cases. The Treaty of the European Union (TEU), which started life as a draft constitution for the EU, and the Charter of Fundamental Rights have now formalised many of the general principles of law established by the CJEU and may become a source of more. The accession of the EU to the ECHR also formalises the role of ECHR principles and jurisprudence in the interpretative approach of the CJEU.

Interpretation of EU law by the UK courts

11.21 EU law may bear on any legal issue in one of two ways. Firstly, EU law may have direct effect, in which case it should be applied directly by the UK courts. Second, EU law not of direct effect will generally be implemented by United Kingdom legislation[52]. In either case, the court is required by the European Communities Act 1972, to interpret the law in the same fashion as the CJEU would. The effect of this requirement became clear in a Scottish House of Lords case, *Lister v Forth Dry Dock and Engineering Co Ltd* 1989 SC(HL) 96. This concerned the rights of employees during the takeover of a company. The UK legislation applied protection only to those employed immediately before the takeover. When certain employees were sacked only one hour before the transfer of ownership of the company, the House of Lords referred to the EU Directive implemented by the UK legislation. Lord Oliver, giving the leading

---

51 *Per* the opinion of the Advocate General in Case 136/79 *National Panasonic (UK) Ltd v Commission* [1980] ECR 2033 at 2066.
52 These concepts are discussed in Chapter 6.

judgment, referred to the recital of the Directive and, briefly, to the French version of it, and said, at 105:

'If the legislation can reasonably be construed as to conform with [EU obligations] – obligations which are to be ascertained not only from the wording of the relevant Directive, but also from the interpretation placed on it by the European Court of Justice … – such a purposive construction will be applied even though, perhaps, it may involve some departure from the strict and literal application of the words the legislature has elected to use.'

This still leaves open to doubt the position where the United Kingdom legislation cannot 'reasonably be construed to conform with' them, although in *Litster* the House of Lords was prepared to read in words which were not in the text. Lord Templeman went even further, saying that United Kingdom courts are under 'an obligation to follow the practice of the European Court of Justice by giving a purposive construction to Directives and Regulations issued for the purpose of complying with Directives'[53].

Special rules of construction and interpretation: the Human Rights Act 1998 and the Scotland Act 1998

The Human Rights Act 1998

11.22   Prior to 1998, the European Convention on Human Rights (ECHR) had not been enshrined in UK national law so could not confer any rights or obligations on individuals, or on state institutions, enforceable in the national courts[54]. Initially, the Scottish courts took the traditional view that, as the ECHR was not part of the law of Scotland, but merely an international treaty, they were not entitled to have regard to it, even as an aid in interpreting United Kingdom legislation[55]. However, even before the Human Rights Act, judges had begun to accept that it could be used to help resolve ambiguity,

---

53 Nevertheless, in *Stirling District Council v Allan* 1995 SLT 1255, at 1259 D–E, the Inner House observed, *obiter* that, 'The [terms of the very same Directive] cannot affect the construction of the [the very same statutory instrument] except to the extent that there may be an ambiguity which may be resolved by reference to the Directive'.

54 Although, unlike most international treaties, the ECHR does provide a separate adjudication and enforcement mechanism, the European Court of Human Rights (ECtHR), which can be used by individuals.

55 See *Kaur v Lord Advocate* 1980 SC 319, per Lord Ross, approved in *Moore v Secretary of State for Scotland* 1985 SLT 38.

arguing that it should be assumed that Parliament intended to legislate in conformity with their international obligations[56].

All this was changed by the Human Rights Act 1998. This enshrined most of the key provisions of the ECHR into national law as *Convention rights* and required any court or tribunal to take into account 'any judgment, decision, declaration or advisory opinion' of European Court of Human Rights (ECtHR) when deciding any question of Convention rights[57]. But, although significant, it is how Convention rights interact with other legislation that has created a whole new approach to the interpretation of legislation. The first key provision is s 3(1) which states that all legislation from whatever source 'must so far as is possible be read and given effect to in a way that is compatible with Convention rights'. The second key provision is s 4, which states that when it is not possible to read legislation as being compatible with Convention rights the courts may strike it down as *ultra vires* (for all but UK Acts of Parliament) or make a *declaration of incompatibility* (for UK Acts of Parliament[58]).

Even at its most modest, s 3 allows the courts to depart from the constraints of their traditional approach, which required at least some ambiguity or uncertainty before reference could be made to external sources and where the purported objective is to discover the intention of Parliament. Instead, they are required instead to interpret legislation to create compliance with the ECHR where it might never have, and never have been intended to exist[59]. The main question is how far courts would go in interpreting the concept of what was 'possible' to read into existing legislation. And where they would draw the line beyond which they would instead use their declaratory power to state that legislation could not be read as compatible, highlighting the problem but – for UK primary legislation – leaving it to Parliament to resolve the issue.

---

56 In *T, Petitioner* 1997 SLT 724 at 733, Lord President Hope stated that where there was an ambiguity in United Kingdom legislation it would be appropriate to look at the ECHR so as to produce an interpretation in conformity with it, noting that under EU law, to which the Scots courts were bound to give effect, the EU 'general principles of law' included fundamental human rights.

57 Also the opinions of the European Commission on Human Rights and the Committee of Ministers of the Council of Europe under the earlier ECHR procedure (for which, see Chapter 3).

58 For the purposes of the Human Rights Act 1998, Acts of the Scottish Parliament are delegated legislation, so may be struck down by the courts if incompatible with Convention rights.

59 It could be said that this merely represents an assumption that Parliament intends always to legislate compatibly with Convention rights, maintaining a link to the will of Parliament. But this concept cannot apply to pre-Human Rights Act legislation, and s 3 applies to all legislation of any kind.

So far, the high water mark of the courts' interpretive efforts is probably represented by the case of *R v A* [2001] UKHL 25, [2002] 1 AC 45. This concerned statutory prohibitions in an Act of Parliament removing the ability of judges to exercise their discretion to allow the questioning of rape victims about previous sexual history. The courts applied section 3 and decided it was 'possible' to read judicial discretion back into this legislation, blowing apart the statutory scheme which had been designed to exclude it. By holding s 3 (and specifically 'so far as possible') to include the ability to depart from (or add to) the words of the statute, the court was arguably creating or amending legislation, not interpreting it.

A more limited approach is exemplified by *Ghaidan v Godin-Mendoza* [2004] UKHL 30, [2004] 2 AC 557. Here, the House of Lords had previously decided on the basis of conventional principles of statutory interpretation that the description of a person living 'as his husband or wife' did not extend to same-sex cohabitants. In *Ghaidan*, this fell to be considered after the coming into force of the Human Rights Act 1998. The House of Lords overturned its previous decision, holding that it was 'possible' to interpret the definition as extending to same-sex cohabitants, despite the fact it was demonstrably not the will of Parliament at the time of enactment[60].

The Scotland Act 1998

11.23 The Scotland Act 1998, s 101 also imposes a special requirement upon courts interpreting legislation, arguably conveying similar powers to s 3 of the Human Rights Act 1998. This provision applies to any provision of an Act of the Scottish Parliament which could be read in such a way as to be outside the Parliament's legislative competence (or any provision of delegated legislation made by Scottish Ministers). These provisions must be 'read as narrowly as is required for it to be within competence, if such reading is possible'. If such reading is not possible, clearly the legislation is *ultra vires*, so void[61], however, the aim is equally clearly

---

60 *R v A* and *Ghaidan* are both English cases. A more limited approach has been taken by the Scottish courts in *Smith v Scott* [2007] CSIH 9, 2007 SC 345, where the Inner House declined to adopt alternative interpretations of the Representation of the People Act 2000 to give Convention rights compatibility, as they were too strained to be 'possible'. Instead the court granted a Declaration of Incompatibility, the alternative remedy in such cases.

61 Indeed, if it is a provision of an Act of the Scottish Parliament, it is specifically stated in s 29 to be 'not law'.

to preserve the provision from this fate if at all possible, through a reading down mechanism.

The drafting is different from that of s 3 of the similar Human Rights Act 1998. First, it specifically requires an ambiguity before the rule is invoked, which might suggest that this rule is not intended to operate on clear provisions, unlike the provision under the Human Rights Act. Secondly, it specifically enjoins a narrow interpretation which might have the effect of preserving provisions more readily than the provision under the Human Rights Act. Thirdly, s 29(3) of the Act requires that, on a question of whether a provision concerns a reserved matter, this is to be determined by reference to its purpose.

Where legislation has been challenged, the relevant provisions have generally been found within competence[62] although, in two cases[63], statutes have been found to be incompatible with human rights and therefore outwith competence with no limited, compatible reading possible.

---

62 See in particular *Martin v HM Advocate* [2010] UKSC 10, 2010 SC (UKSC) 40, also showing, however, the difficulties in this area arising from Sch 4 para 2. See especially the dissenting judgments of Lord Rodger of Earlsferry and Lord Kerr of Tonaghmore.

63 *Cameron v Cottam* [2012] HCJAC 19, 2012 SLT 173, and *Salvesen v Riddell* [2012] CSIH 26, 2012 SLT 633. The latter is subject to appeal to the Supreme Court at the time of writing.

12 Precedent – *Ratio Decidendi*, *Obiter Dicta* and *Stare Decisis*

12.1 This Chapter considers the nature of precedent[1] as a source of law and the key concepts of *ratio decidendi*, *obiter dicta* and *stare decisis*. It then examines how they are applied in practice in the courts (including the Court of Justice of the European Union and the European Court of Human Rights). Published law reports, an essential feature of any system of precedent, are dealt with in the next Chapter.

PRECEDENT AS A SOURCE OF LAW

The Nature of Precedent

12.2 Precedent is a formal source of law[2] within the Scottish and English legal system. It emerges from the justifications that judges provide for their decisions. As such it has an existence entirely independent of legislation and is a distinctive feature of legal systems with a common law heritage.

Rules of law established by precedent are not explicitly created; nor are they written down in a single authentic text. Instead, they are established by the principles applied by judges in deciding cases and have to be extracted from their written *opinions*[3]. Judges may be explicit in explaining the rule they are applying; at other times

---

1 'Precedent' is spelt thus, and has the meaning described below. 'Precedence' and 'president' are perfectly respectable words, but mean something different. The surprisingly common tendency to confuse them is to be resisted.
2 See Ch 4.
3 In the Scottish tradition, the reasons given by judges in deciding a case are called opinions. In other jurisdictions, including England and Wales, the term judgment is generally used.

they are not. In either case, they are not laying down a rule in fixed verbal form[4], and their words are often not designed to encapsulate the rule precisely but to describe its operation given the facts of the case being decided. Usually they are only extending an existing rule but it is not always clear what the historical source of the rule is. It may come from custom, the judge's sense of morality, or elsewhere.

Thus, reasonable people may disagree on what rule has actually been laid down, and how it might apply to another case. The rule may have to be inferred from the decision. Indeed, it may only be possible to make this inference with confidence when a series of decisions on the same topic has been given; in other words, only from a series of precedents.

Nonetheless, as a formal source of law, precedent carries its own authority. Lawyers and other users of the law will respect it as genuine law. Courts in the same judicial hierarchy will hear arguments based on similar cases already decided, and are obliged, or at least encouraged, to follow the rule that seems to emerge from an earlier case with similar facts.

The Origin of Precedent

12.3 A system of precedent emerges from the instinctive demand of justice that like cases are treated alike, even where no clear written law covers the situation and from the nature of the court system as a system of *adjudication*[5]. This decision of the court is determinative and is not a compromise (so there are winners and losers), and is justified by reference to a rule of general application rather than personal preference[6] or some random method. The decision must therefore fit into the matrix of previous similar cases and also becomes a precedent for later cases of similar type. The decisions therefore form a more or less coherent system.

These considerations are strengthened where the courts are arranged in a clear hierarchy. Respect will be felt for the more senior

---

4   See Appendix 1 for discussion of the concept of rules in fixed verbal form.
5   Adjudication means dispute resolution where a third party imposes a solution upon the disputants, whether they agree with the decision or not. This can be contrasted with other dispute resolution mechanisms such as mediation or conciliation.
6   'Why does the judge not make his reason explicit by granting Mrs McTavish her divorce just because she has a ravishingly pert retroussé nose? Because such are not accepted as good reasons within the system for ... granting divorces', MacCormick *Legal Reasoning and Legal Theory* (1978) p 15. Lord Atkin is believed to have consulted his young children before deciding *Donoghue v Stevenson* 1932 SC(HL) 31, however.

judges. If, as appellate judges, they have the power to overrule the decision of a lower court, judges in the lower court will only reject the rule on some strong ground, such as that new social conditions have rendered an ancient rule unworkable or out of date.

Not all systems of law accept precedent as a formal source but many fundamental areas of law were largely created by precedent (albeit sometimes building upon the work of the Institutional Writers), and may still be developed by this means. Contract, delict and criminal law, for example, are primarily of this nature: their basic rules are not to be found in Acts of Parliament but have to be extracted from precedents. Thus, the basic rules on what contract is, how a contract is made, what the effect on it is of error by one party as to any of the terms, and so on, are found in, or inferred from, precedents. Acts of Parliament, such as those relating to the sale of goods and consumer credit, may be regarded as making modifications to this basic structure[7].

A problem about precedent is that the law can only develop if there are new precedents, and that depends upon litigants bringing cases to court in the areas needing development[8]. As Scotland has a population about one-tenth of that of England and Wales, the potential for elaborating the law by means of judicial decisions is that much less. By the same token, the development of the law through cases requires that there be people with the resources and the determination to have their disputes settled by courts.

Nobile officium and declaratory power

12.4   Two exceptional exercises of legislative power by the courts require special mention, that is, the *nobile officium* and the declaratory power. The *nobile officium* is an exceptional 'equitable' power exercised by the Court of Session and High Court of Justiciary to provide a remedy where none exists, but the court feels it should. In the Court of Session, the power goes back to at least the time of Stair, at the end of the 17th century. He mentions in his *Institutions*, at IV, 3, 2, seven miscellaneous exercises of it. That varied character has continued to the present day. A modern, much cited, description of that is by Lord

---

7   'The common law is a canvas on which a picture is being painted. The cloth may be obscured by layers of pigment, but it is ever apt to show through and without it the whole image crumbles', McBryde *The Law of Contract in Scotland* (3rd edn, 2007) para 1–15.
8   On the social limitations on Scottish case law, see Willock 'Making Law and Keeping to the Law' 1982 JR 237 at 250.

President Emslie: 'It may be exercised in highly special or unforeseen circumstances to prevent injustice or oppression. It cannot however be invoked in such a way as to defeat a statutory intention, express or implied, or to extend the scope of an Act of Parliament'. Petitions are heard by three judges of the Inner House.

On the criminal side the *nobile officium* (not always so described) is referred to by Alison in his *Practice* of 1833 as used 'in circumstances unforeseen for which the law makes no provision'. The Crown may seek its exercise as well as an accused. Modern criminal instances of this power do tend to emphasise the avoidance of injustice or oppression as a justification for its use. Examples of the absence of a remedy as such injustice or oppression include *Wylie v HM Advocate*, 1966 SLT 149, where the then lack of provisions on sentencing for contempt of court was held to justify invoking the *nobile officium*.

The declaratory power is an exceptional power held by the High Court of Justiciary to declare behaviour which it considers morally wrong to be a criminal offence, even though it was not, or not unequivocally, regarded as criminal before. This could be a wide and unpredictable power, and was so used in the formative years of Scots criminal law. It is now very rarely invoked, if indeed it still exists. It is only invoked in cases closely analogous to existing crimes, and is difficult to distinguish from the application of existing vague offences to new circumstances, as for example in *Khaliq v HM Advocate* 1984 JC 23 which rendered criminal the selling of glue-sniffing kits as the wilful supply of potentially noxious substances.

Precedent and the common law

12.5   Precedent and common law are intertwined. Originally, at least in England, 'common law' meant custom which was common to the whole country, rather than purely local. Now, however, custom having crystallised into law through the decisions of judges, the basic meaning has come to be law which has been made by precedent, and this English law-based meaning has largely displaced any others. In a slightly extended form, the phrase refers to the minor sources as well, in other words, to all law that is not legislation. In both these meanings common law is contrasted with statute law.

Systems of law which accept precedent as a formal source are known as 'common law systems'. They are widespread because English law, the original common law system, was exported to most British colonies (not least those which later formed the United States of America). Thus, there is said to be a family of common law systems. It is contrasted with the family of civil law systems, that is, those which claim Roman law as their intellectual progenitor and which, generally speaking, do not recognise precedent as a formal source of law. This family includes most European states, and countries formerly their colonies (such as the whole of South America).

Scots law is said to be one of a few 'mixed' or 'hybrid' systems, because it claims some Roman ancestry (like the civil law systems), but now uses precedent (like the common law systems). Other such systems are the state of Louisiana, the province of Quebec, South Africa and Sri Lanka.

European Union law, because it has been created largely in a milieu of civil law countries, operates essentially as a civil law system, with limited reliance upon precedent. 'Human rights law', as expressed in decisions of the European Court of Human Rights, also bears evidence of civil law reasoning.

There are other uses of the term 'common law'. For example, in English law, it has a technical meaning more restricted than the basic meaning. For centuries in England there were two parallel sets of courts. The basic common law courts generated common law in this most restricted sense. The supplementary 'courts of Chancery' generated 'equity'. The two court systems were amalgamated in the 1870s, and English courts are now both common law and equity courts, but common law and equity are still said to be separate sets of rules or principles. Also, histories and theories of the common law (in any of its senses) are usually histories and theories of English law, and thus 'the common law' is sometimes taken to mean simply 'English law'.

Precedent and Scots law

12.6　Before the 19th century, Scottish courts were applying customary law (native and feudal), fortified by concepts of Canon law and Roman law, reinforced and modified by statute, and consolidated by legal writers (Scottish, French, German and others), including, as time went on, those later regarded as institutional.

Decisions were not reported but began to be recorded in *practicks*, written records of decisions that which judges created for their own use. These were later published by them and others in collections. Previous decisions were cited in court and Stair referred to many in his *Institutions*. However, they were not the formal source of the law, but merely evidence of what it was. Indeed, the way the *practicks* and early series of law reports were edited meant that nothing like the modern system of precedent could operate. For example, cases were commonly recorded without giving the judges' reasoning. It can be very unclear, therefore, what rule or principle the judges considered they were applying.

In the 19th century reliance on institutional works did not wane, but reliance on previous decisions increased, and precedent became recognised as a formal source of law. This reflected a number of factors, including change in the perception of the nature of law[9], and the reorganisation of the Court of Session[10] and, following the Act of Union in 1707, the influence of English law through the availability of appeal to the House of Lords[11]. The growth of law reporting in the modern form can only have encouraged recourse to precedent[12], although only in the second half of the 20th century did explicit reliance upon precedent become a major feature[13].

JUDICIAL REASONING: *RATIO DECIDENDI* AND *OBITER DICTA*

12.7 Because every case adjudicated is decided according to a rule or principle, the decision must reflect that rule or principle, which must therefore be discoverable from the opinion or judgment itself. This rule or principle is referred to as the *ratio decidendi*[14] or, often, just *ratio*. Ratios[15], being law, bind later judges under certain

---

9 Legislation in its modern guise emerged at this time, and the creation of a distinct class of Institutional Writers, with Stair pre-eminent, emerged: see *The Laws of Scotland: Stair Memorial Encyclopaedia* vol 22, para 256 and Blackie 'Stair's Later Reputation as a Jurist' in *Stair Tercentenary Studies* (ed Walker) (Stair Society, vol 33, 1981). Law was seen less as immemorial custom, and more as the expression of sovereign will. A parallel change in the status of precedent was also occurring in England: see *The Laws of Scotland: Stair Memorial Encyclopaedia* vol 22, para 252.

10 The Court of Session sat as a single court of fifteen judges (the 'Haill Fifteen') until the reforms of early 19th century. These reforms made possible inconsistent opinions by different judges, Divisions or Houses created a hierarchy and thus posed questions of relative authority.

11 Although it has been suggested that this factor is less important than sometimes said. See *The Laws of Scotland: Stair Memorial Encyclopaedia* vol 22, para 255.

12 Lord Cockburn in his *Memorials of His Times* (1856, reprinted 1971) attributed the rise in accurate reporting to the fact that 'the public, or at least the independent proportion of the legal profession, had begun to require something more [than the reporting of merely the results of cases]'.

13 Doubt as to its operation within Scotland has remained: see *eg* Maher 'Sir Thomas Smith, *stare decisis* and sheriffs' 2004 SLT (News) 85–89.

14 The first word is pronounced 'ray-she-oh' or 'rah-tea-oh', the second 'dess-ee-dend-aye' or 'dess-ee-dend-ee'.

15 The plural in Latin would be *rationes decidendi* but this is rarely used.

circumstances. In other circumstances, ratios are simply more or less persuasive and may or may not be applied at the discretion of the later judges. The principle that ratios may bind is called *stare decisis*[16].

The *Ratio Decidendi*

12.8   *Ratio decidendi* means the reason for deciding. A more nuanced definition is that it is the rule or principle of law for which a competent observer considers the case to be authority. This acknowledgement that identifying a ratio requires an external, subjective viewpoint reflects two important concepts. Firstly, no ratio stands alone. It can only make sense within the matrix of other relevant precedents. Secondly, ratios are not rules in fixed verbal form. Although an authentic version of the judges' words is available, there is no single authentic version of the actual rule or principle. Judges may not even be explicit as to what rule or principle they believe they are employing. Often, it may be possible to view the *ratio* as having a wide application across related areas of law; alternatively, it may be possible to see the *ratio* as applying narrowly to cases with similar facts. Finally, a *ratio* is often decided not by that case itself but by how subsequent judges have interpreted, applied, limited and extended the principles in any given case.

Identifying the ratio

12.9   The place of precedent in the legal system means that the skill of identifying ratios for previous decisions is a vital one for legal practitioners. This does not mean that it will often be straightforward to identify a single ratio for any case or series of cases; in fact, much legal argument is centred on either challenging ratios or arguing for a more favourable version of the ratio. The problem is best approached by considering four things: what the relevant facts are; what their appropriate level of generality is; how multiple ratios are to be dealt with; and wide and narrow ratios and the development of principles.

The Relevant Facts

12.10   A legal rule can be seen as a statement that a certain legal consequence will apply if a condition, or series of conditions, are

---

16 Usually pronounced 'star-ray dee-sigh-sis'.

fulfilled by the relevant facts[17]. Consequently, a ratio can be sought by identifying the facts and the conditions that the judges stated or implied to be relevant and excluding those which he stated or implied were not relevant. This approach has been elaborated largely in relation to English law and United States law[18] but can be applied to Scots law[19].

For example, a contract is constituted by an offer and its acceptance. In a case turning on whether a valid offer or valid acceptance was made, it is useful to consider what actual communications were considered relevant or material by the judges in the relevant precedents, and what they considered not. Perhaps they considered an advertisement in a newspaper, or the placing of priced goods in a shop window? Perhaps they discussed acceptance by actions without words, or leaving a voicemail message on a mobile phone. What common features of purported offers or acceptances were, or appear to have been, relied upon by those judges in deciding as they did? Can these common features be synthesised into a rule or principle? If so, this can be considered the (or at least one) ratio.

The Level of Generality

12.11 Identifying the right facts often leaves the problem of determining the right level of generality of the facts. Narrowly expressed, the decision in *Donoghue v Stevenson* was that a soft drinks manufacturer was liable for harm done to the ultimate consumer when their negligence allowed a noxious substance to be concealed in a drinks bottle. But does the ratio extend to drinks manufacturers only; or to manufacturers of any consumable substance; or to anybody distributing anything which might contain hidden faults?[20] The judge who laid down the precedent may have limited the range of

---

17 See Appendix 1.
18 See, for example, Goodhart's 'The *Ratio Decidendi* of a Case' in *Essays in Jurisprudence and Common Law* (1931), and Llewellyn's very readable *The Bramble Bush* (1951), as well as Twining and Miers *How To Do Things With Rules* (5th edn, 2010).
19 *The Laws of Scotland: Stair Memorial Encyclopaedia* vol 22, para 344 expresses doubt but, subject to caveats, MacCormick in *Legal Reasoning and Legal Theory* (1978) appears to approve Goodhart's approach. Perhaps in modern conditions the assertion that Scots law relies on principle rather than precedent, while English law does the reverse, means that Scots lawyers are prepared to generalise further.
20 See further para **12.14**.

possibilities, but only later judges will determine how far the principle is taken. The rule of thumb is to simply ask what, in the light of the judges' actual words, and all other precedents, is plausible. Where, as will often be the case, uncertainty remains, it will only be removed when a subsequent case re-examines the boundaries of the ratio.

Multiple Ratios

12.12 Often discussion of *ratio decidendi* assumes that there is one judge in the court. Especially in appellate courts, there is often more than one. The common law tradition, followed in Scotland, permits every judge to publish their own separate opinion. They may dissent from the ultimate decision[21]; alternatively, they may agree with the decision but have come to the same conclusion through an alternative line of reasoning[22]. Where this occurs, it inevitably confuses the search for a clear ratio[23]. A few principles can assist. Firstly, the views of a dissenting minority can bind no-one but may throw light on those of the majority and can be resurrected if the majority reasoning is overturned by a superior court. Where

21 The dissenting opinion is an important feature of common law systems: see Kirby 'Judicial Dissent – common law and civil law traditions' (2007) 123 LQR 379–440.

22 Multiple ratios may also arise where a single judge gives alternative lines of reasoning but does not state which is preferred. Increasingly, in Scottish appellate courts, both civil and criminal, a single opinion is issued where there is no dissenting judge.

23 A good example of the problem is *Macfarlane v Tayside Health Board* 2000 SC(HL) 1. A couple with four children, a number they considered sufficient, relied on a negligently inaccurate report on the success of a vasectomy, and produced a fifth. The mother sued for damages for pain and suffering from pregnancy and birth, consequential expenditure, and loss of earnings. The House of Lords held that the claim for pain and suffering was relevant (unanimously); the claim for expenditure consequential upon the pregnancy and birth was relevant (Lords Clyde and Millett dissenting) but that for expenditure consequential upon bringing up the child was not (unanimously); and the claim for loss of earnings consequential upon the pregnancy and birth were relevant (Lords Clyde and Millett again dissenting). In respect of the consequential expenditure claim unanimously held irrelevant, in brief, Lords Slynn and Hope so concluded because they saw it as 'pure economic loss'; Lord Steyn relied on 'principles of distributive justice'; Lord Clyde on 'disproportionality'; and Lord Millett on the benefits of having a child invariably outweighing any detriments. Even on the merely majority issues, there was much variation as between the reasoning of the majority. Two other, more recent, complicated examples are the separate, but linked *A & Ors v Secretary of State* [2005] UKHL 71, [2006] 2 AC 221 and *A & Anr v Secretary of State* [2004] UKHL 56, [2005] 2 AC 68.

judges agree on an outcome, but deliver separate opinions, their reasoning may differ or it may be difficult to tell whether they agree completely or not[24]. Sometimes, this will have been addressed by later judges who will have refined the ratio in subsequent cases[25]. Otherwise, if there is a leading opinion, that is, one more fully argued than the rest, and to which the other opinions merely add variations or emphases, it is more likely to be drawn on for the ratio of the case, especially if that judge is more senior or more respected. The variations to it may be treated as persuasive rather than binding, or simply ignored. If there is no leading opinion, and all opinions are broadly consistent, then the ratio of the case is likely, according to some Scottish commentators[26], to be taken to be the highest common factor among the judges sitting and other parts of the opinions are ignored[27]. According to a commentator on English law[28], in such circumstances, the ratio of the case might be taken to be the sum of all ratios of the judges sitting[29]. A third possible view is that the ratio is that which fits most neatly into the existing law[30]. In any case, clearly a wide discretion is left to judges in later cases. If no synthesis of the competing ratios is possible then a case is sometimes said to be 'authority only for its own facts' and is little help as a precedent[31].

24 In *Manuel v A-G* [1982] 3 All ER 786, an English case before the Chancery Division, Sir Robert Megarry VC (the President of the court), at 798, observed 'During the argument it was not surprisingly suggested to me on this point: (a) there was a majority for Lord Denning's view and that Kerr LJ was in a minority and (b) that there was a majority for the view of Kerr LJ and Lord Denning was in the minority. A third contention was that May LJ was agreeing with Lord Denning in his general view, but with Kerr LJ in his particular application. A variant is that May LJ ... '.

25 Paterson, Bates and Poustie *The Legal System of Scotland: Cases and Materials* (4th edn, 1999) at p 441 remark ' ... juggling with multiple ratios is one more technique which the wise judge acquires'.

26 *Ibid* p 440, and *The Laws of Scotland: Stair Memorial Encyclopaedia* vol 22, para 342. No authority is cited.

27 So, if Judge 1 finds facts A, B & C material, Judge 2 finds facts A, B & D material, and Judge 3 finds facts A, B & E material, the *ratio* is A+B.

28 Goodhart in 'Determining the *Ratio Decidendi* of a Case' in *Essays in Jurisprudence and the Common Law* (1931). Examples are given, but no authority cited.

29 That is, if Judge 1 finds facts A, B & C material, Judge 2 finds facts A, B & D material, and Judge 3 finds facts A, B & E material, the *ratio* is A+B+C+D+E.

30 *The Laws of Scotland: Stair Memorial Encyclopaedia* vol 22, para 342 describes this procedure as 'dubious'.

31 Commonly quoted are the words of Lord Dunedin in the English case of *Great Western Railways Co Ltd v Owners of the SS Mostyn* [1928] AC 57 at 73 '... if [the ratio of a case] is not clear, then I do not think it is part of the tribunal's duty to spell out with great difficulty a ratio decidendi in order to be bound by it'.

The development of ratios

12.13 Later judges must interpret the apparent ratio of a case when deciding subsequent cases. Often, this interpretation will develop and evolve over time. It is an important truth that a precedent is what later judges say it is, and they decide upon the width of the ratio. All the judge actually laying down the precedent can do is seek to restrict the range of possibilities.

This evolutionary process can best be understood by recalling the nature of adjudication. A judge must decide the case before him according to some rule or principle. The judge may find the existing rules and principles, discoverable from the ratios of precedents clear enough to be determinative. In such a case, the judge's ratio in the new case adds nothing but another illustration to the existing law. In other cases, the rules and principles may not so clearly apply, in which case the judge has the opportunity and duty to extend or restrict existing rules and principles, or lay down some new ones to decide the case. Here, the ratio of the new case will develop the law. But, unless a court is in the position to overturn precedent, it is constrained by the need to fit into the matrix of the existing common law.

Donoghue v Stevenson: A case study on the development of a ratio

12.14 *Donoghue v Stevenson*[32] has for decades been cited as authority for certain propositions, and has been the basis of most of the modern law of negligence in Scotland and England. The decision does not, of course, stand alone. Like any other precedent, it has to be seen against the background of the earlier law. Before the decision, for example, it was not clear whether a manufacturer was liable to someone with whom he had no contract, and much of the judgment in *Donoghue* is spent reviewing the earlier precedents (different judges coming to different conclusions as to their significance). *Donoghue* settled the question, within limits, in the affirmative. The current view of *Donoghue*, and how far the principle attributed to it goes, equally can only be understood in the light of the numerous later decisions which have developed it.

As is the way with ratios, not all those of the judges in *Donoghue* are clear. Lord Atkin, for example, gives two different versions of his. One, his neighbour principle, is broad. It includes few facts,

32 1932 SC(HL) 31

and those at a high level of generality, and can be expressed as: 'If you act in such a way as to make it reasonably foreseeable that you will injure someone, if that person ought reasonably to be in your contemplation, and if such a person is in fact injured, then you are liable to compensate that other person for the injury suffered'[33]. The other is narrower. It includes more facts, and at a lower level of generality, and could be rendered as the following: 'If you are a manufacturer of food and drink for consumption by the public, and if you produce such food or drink in sealed containers, then you are liable ...'[34].

However, later judges, have generally asserted the broader version to be the ratio. This is the more surprising because, firstly, the decision was by a bare majority of 3 to 2; secondly, it is not clear on the face of it that Lord Atkin's is the leading judgment; and thirdly, the other two judges of the majority produced principles close to Lord Atkin's narrow version[35]. This broad ratio has been used to give compensation losses caused by negligent misstatements by banks, which were losses of profit rather than physical losses[36] and losses caused by the escape through negligence of young offenders[37]. It is far from clear that even Lord Atkin would have accepted all such subsequent developments of his principle, while Lord Thankerton and Lord Macmillan's more limited views have effectively been discarded.

Not all such developments have proved lasting, however. *Donoghue* was used by the House of Lords to justify the liability not only for wrongful acts, but also for the failure to act, in an English case concerning local authority building inspectors, *Anns v Merton Borough Council*[38], only for it to decide in *Murphy v Brentwood District Council*[39] that it had decided *Anns* wrongly.

Thus, the views expressed in *Donoghue v Stevenson* have been a fruitful source of law. This has developed in some directions, but been restricted in others, but in all cases at the instance of later judges, and despite the fact that most of these developments could hardly have been foreseen by the original judges.

---

33 Most succinctly expressed at 44.
34 Most succinctly expressed at 57.
35 Lords Thankerton, especially at 59–60, and Macmillan, at 71.
36 *Hedley Byrne v Heller & Partners* [1964] AC 465).
37 *Dorset Yacht Co v Home Office* [1970] AC 1004.
38 [1978] AC 728.
39 [1991] 1 AC 398.

Obiter Dicta

12.15 *Obiter dicta*[40], usually translated as 'things said by the way', is a phrase describing any reasoning of a judge which is not part of the ratio. These often include observations upon the law or hypothetical examples. As they do not relate directly to the facts being adjudicated, they are not considered part of any precedent established by the decision.

Although never binding, they may be considered by subsequent courts as persuasive (a concept discussed later in this chapter). Also, given the difficulty of determining the ratio of a case, there is often disagreement as to whether a particular piece of reasoning is *ratio* or *obiter*.

STARE DECISIS

12.16 If precedent is a source of law, the ratios of precedents will determine how a case is to be decided by later courts. This doctrine is known as *stare decisis*, that is, 'to stand by what has been decided'[41].

The Language of Precedents

12.17 Not all precedents are binding. This principally depends upon two factors: firstly, whether or not the ratio in question is *in point*, and secondly, upon the relative position in the court hierarchy of the court examining the precedent, to the court which laid down the precedent.

Precedents which are not binding may be *persuasive*, that is, they do not bind, but may persuade a judge to decide in conformity with them. Persuasiveness is a matter of degree, unlike bindingness, which is categorical. A precedent is said to be *in point* or *on all fours* when the issues in that case are the same, at an appropriate level of generality as the issues in the case to be decided (often referred to by judges as the *instant case*). Where a precedent is binding, the question of whether it is in point will be determinative of the case. Much legal argument therefore focuses on whether a case is in point

---

40 *Obiter dicta*, pronounced as spelt, is plural; the singular is *obiter dictum*. The term *dicta* or *dictum* is also used generally to describe a noteworthy remark or remarks by a judge; this does not mean that it is an *obiter dictum*.

41 More fully rendered '*stare decisis et quieta non movere*', the additional words meaning 'and not disturb settled matters'.

with previous decisions and thus whether the judge is required to *follow* or *apply* the precedent. A superior court which might have discretion to overturn an existing precedent may, when following it, describe itself as *approving* the precedent.

A judge who decides a precedent is not in point is said to *distinguish* it[42]. There is more than one way of distinguishing. There may be a factor in the rule or principle of the precedent which is absent in the case under consideration[43]; or there may be a significant factor in the current case which was absent in the precedent[44]. The latter form is sometimes called *restrictive distinguishing*, because its effect may be to restrict the width of the *ratio* of the precedent, whether by creating an exception, or more generally.

A superior court may also *doubt* a precedent established by a previous decision and may *disapprove* or *overrule* precedents they believe to be wrong or no longer valid in light of changed circumstances. A court may also *explain* a precedent where it thinks the ratio of the precedent insufficiently clear.

Where a court determines that a precedent is not binding, it may still consider it *persuasive*. It may then be taken into account in the court's reasoning (often termed *considering* a precedent) but it will not be determinative. Various factors may influence the persuasiveness of any precedent including: how convincingly the judges in the precedent have expressed themselves; how well respected those judges are; how high in the hierarchy the decision was taken; whether it was unanimous or not; and the subsequent judicial history of the precedent.

Stare Decisis and the hierarchy of courts

12.18   As discussed, relative position in the hierarchy of courts will determine the treatment by one court of precedents created by another. There is a vertical dimension to these hierarchies, created by the possibility of appeals and the greater seniority of appeal court judges and their specialist role in deciding complex or difficult areas of law. This dimension is important because not only may higher courts be able to overrule lower ones, but also, even when not overruling, higher courts send out stronger signals to lower courts and other users of the law as to what the law is on a given issue. The horizontal dimension is created by the need for multiple local

---

42 That is, he finds it distinctly different, not that he makes it admirable.
43 The precedent has material factors A, B & C: the instant case has only A & B.
44 The precedent has material factors A, B & C: the instant case has A, B, C & D.

points of entry to the system but not to have competing final courts of appeal.

There are also possible relationships between the civil and criminal court hierarchies[45]. Scottish courts often quote and give significant weight to precedents established by the English courts whilst both Scottish and English courts occasionally refer to precedents established by courts within other legal systems. And, as part of the UK's participation in the European Union and European Convention of Human Rights, UK courts are bound to consider the determinations of those institution's courts authoritative.

The hierarchy is not entirely simple. The Court of Session is above any Sheriff Court, although their jurisdiction is remarkably similar. Within the Court of Session, the Inner House is in some sense above the Outer House, for it hears appeals from it, but the court is a collegiate court and Courts of Five Judges (or other odd number) may be convened. It is difficult to say succinctly in hierarchical terms what the relationship between the Outer House and Sheriffs is.

Also, while civil and criminal courts are separate, there may be cross-reference of precedents. For example, whether a certain action is the crime of theft may depend upon who owned the item, which is a question of the civil law of property.

It is difficult to fit either the Court of Justice of the European Union or the European Court of Human Rights into the hierarchy. The CJEU must effectively be seen as above any Scottish court in matters of EU law, for preliminary references to it under Article 267 (ex Article 234) TFEU are binding, and where one is not made, that court's interpretations must be followed[46]. By the Human Rights Act 1998, courts determining cases involving 'Convention rights' (see Chapter 3) must 'take into account' all decisions of the ECtHR (and of the former European Commission on Human Rights)[47]. While this makes clear that the domestic court is not absolutely bound by the ECtHR, it would not be sensible to ignore or oppose its decisions, especially if made by a full chamber of the Court[48].

---

45 There may be cross-reference of precedents. For example, whether a certain action is theft may depend upon who owned the item, which is a question of the law of property.

46 This is a rule imposed by statute: s3(1) of the European Communities Act 1972.

47 Human Rights Act 1998 s2(1).

48 See *Cadder v HM Advocate* [2010] UKSC 43, 2011 SC (UKSC) 13. Note also the famous dictum of Lord Rodger of Earlsferry in *Secretary of State for the Home Department v F (No 3)* [2009] UKHL 28, [2010] 2 AC 269 para 98: 'Even though we are dealing with rights under a United Kingdom statute, in reality, we have no choice: *Argentoratum locutum, iudicium finitum* – Strasbourg has spoken, the case is closed.'

Precedents from another jurisdiction

12.19 Precedents from English courts are frequently cited in Scottish courts, for instance in cases on delict, where the law is largely common law in both jurisdictions. Those from some other common law jurisdictions such as Australia, Canada, New Zealand and the United States are cited occasionally. Thus, in *Morgan Guaranty Trust Co v Lothian Regional Council* 1995 SC 151 decisions from superior courts in Australia, Canada, and South Africa were mentioned by Lord President Hope as 'instructive'. Despite the apparent parallel of Scots law with other mixed systems, such as South Africa, precedents from such jurisdictions are not frequent.

All are in the same position in that, coming from a different jurisdiction, they cannot bind Scottish courts, though they may be persuasive. In any case, in judicial decisions and legal textbooks, not only are English cases often cited, but they are often cited without specific warning that they do not determine Scots law. In relation to EU law, special considerations arise, as such law with direct effect must have the same meaning throughout the EU. Thus, decisions of the Court of Justice of the European Union bind United Kingdom courts, and decisions of courts in other Member States may be cited.

In relation to human rights cases, other special considerations apply, as decisions of the European Court of Human Rights must be 'taken into account', and decisions from courts of other countries applying the European Convention on Human Rights and like documents are inevitably and frequently cited.

Exceptional cases where a precedent is not binding

12.20 There are exceptional cases where an otherwise binding precedent may be disregarded by a court. These can be summarised as:

- **Subsequent Legislation**. Where the precedent has been overtaken by legislation, it is no longer to be applied.
- ***Per Incuriam***. Secondly, where the precedent was laid down by a court which had not considered all the relevant law, and had therefore come to an erroneous conclusion, it is described as *per incuriam* and is not binding[49]. Especially in these days of comprehensive case reporting, this rule is rarely applicable.

---

49 In *Mitchell v Mackersy* (1905) 8 F 198, the Inner House overruled its own decision in *Gray's Trustees v Royal Bank of Scotland* (1895) 23 R 199, on the ground that it had been decided without reference to the House of Lords' decision in *Globe Insurance Co v Mackenzie* (1850) 7 Bell App 296.

- **Age and Defective Reporting**. Thirdly, age and defective reporting may render a precedent not binding. Age of itself is insufficient, for instance, in *Morgan Guaranty Trust Co v Lothian Regional Council* 1995 SC 151, cases of 1959 and 1975 were overruled, but the 1733 case of *Stirling v Earl of Lauderdale* Mor 2930 was approved. A determined court may go a long way to examine alternative reports and other records of an ancient case, as the House of Lords did in *Wills' Trustees v Cairngorm Canoeing and Sailing School Ltd* 1976 SC(HL) 30, where *Grant v Duke of Gordon* (1781) Mor 12820 was considered.
- **Societal Changes**. Fourthly, a precedent may be robbed of authority where a court decides that the maxim *cessante ratione legis, cessat ipsa lex* applies. The phrase means, roughly, 'where the reason for a law ceases to exist, so does the law itself'. This enables the courts to respond to changed societal or economic realities[50].

THE SYSTEM IN PRACTICE – THE CIVIL COURTS

12.21 Each Sheriffdom forms its own small hierarchy. Thus, a Sheriff (including a Sheriff Principal) is bound to follow precedents from: the Sheriff Principal of his Sheriffdom (if he is not Sheriff Principal himself)[51]; the Outer House, possibly[52]; the Inner House, or any Court of Five or more Judges; the Supreme Court (previously the House of Lords or, for devolution issues the Judicial Committee of the Privy Council). A Lord Ordinary in the Court of Session is bound by precedents from: the Inner House; a Court of Five or more Judges; and the Supreme Court. A Division of the Inner House is

---

50 A clear example of its use is *Commerzbank AG v Large* 1977 SC 375, in which the Inner House rejected the House of Lords' decision in *Hyslops v Gordon* (1824) 2 Shaw's Appeals 451 that judgments for money must be expressed in sterling. In the opinion of the court, at 328, 'the case of *Hyslops*, decided as it was in the context of conditions which no longer apply, does not now bind this court. We are accordingly free to consider, in the context of the age of floating currencies and rapidly fluctuating exchange rates, the true objectives of our law ...'.

51 See, incidentally Maher 'Sir Thomas Smith, *stare decisis* and sheriffs' 2004 SLT (News) 85–89.

52 In *Jessop v Stevenson* 1987 SCCR 655 the High Court of Justiciary decided that a decision of a single High Court judge in a trial bound a sheriff. In *Cromarty Leasing v Turnbull* 1988 SLT (Sh Ct) 62 Sheriff Wilkinson held, by parity of reasoning, that in civil matters an Outer House judge bound a sheriff, and Sheriff Principal Ireland has said 'I have to accept [*Jessop*] as binding upon me': see 1990 SCLR 388. However, Sheriff Stoddart in *Farrell v Farrell* 1990 SCLR 717 took a different view. The matter remains unresolved.

bound to apply precedents from: either Division of the Inner House, probably[53]; a Court of Five or more Judges; and the Supreme Court. A Court of Five or more Judges is bound by precedents from: another Court of the same or greater number of judges, probably[54]; and by the Supreme Court.

The Supreme Court of the United Kingdom is the apex of the hierarchy of Scottish civil courts, and those of England and Wales, and of Northern Ireland. This raises two problems in relation to *stare decisis*, namely: whether a precedent laid down in a case appealed to the Supreme Court from one hierarchy binds courts in another; and, secondly, whether the Supreme Court binds itself. Generally, decisions of the Supreme Court (or its predecessors) in English cases are considered binding on Scottish courts where it is accepted that English and Scottish law are identical[55]. Whether this is the case may well be a matter of argument in areas governed by common law but negligence is commonly quoted as an example where the law is, for all practical purposes, identical. The House of Lords historically considered itself bound by its own precedents, subject to the concept of *per incuriam*.

Particularly because of the enormous social changes, this position became irksome and was changed in 1966 through a Practice Direction[56] issued by the Lord Chancellor. But, reflecting the desire for certainty and finality, there have been few cases, and only one in a Scottish appeal, where the House of Lords availed itself of this power[57]. The Supreme Court has not adopted any statement to parallel the 1966 Practice Direction but equally has so far been silent on the extent to which it regards itself as bound by its own or previous House of Lords decisions.

---

53 Although the Inner House has never specifically pronounced on the matter, neither Division has departed from such a precedent for more than 50 years)

54 See *The Laws of Scotland: Stair Memorial Encyclopaedia* vol 22, para 289.

55 The matter was discussed by Lord Normand in the House of Lords in *Glasgow Corporation v Central Land Board* 1956 SC(HL) 1, and by Lord Justice-Clerk Wheatley in the Inner House in *Dalgleish v Glasgow Corporation* 1976 SC 32.

56 [1966] 1 WLR 1234. A Practice Direction is an administrative rule on the running of the courts. Not the least interesting aspect of this change was that it was effected by a mere Practice Direction.

57 The Scottish appeal was *Dick v Burgh of Falkirk* 1976 SC(HL) 1, where it overruled *Darling v Gray* (1892) 19 R(HL) 31. Paterson, Bates and Poustie *Legal System of Scotland: Cases and Materials* (4th edn, 1999) p 431 estimated that, between 1966 and their date of publication, it had been asked to reverse one of its precedents once or twice a year and, between 1996 and 1983, actually did so in nine cases (on average about once every three years). Since 1966, the House of Lords has heard well over 2,000 cases (though few of them Scottish appeals).

Several courts of special jurisdiction and tribunals exist, such as the Land Court and the Employment Tribunal. These courts and tribunals have their own hierarchies which may involve appeals to superior tribunals or the Inner House of the Court of Session and thence the Supreme Court. These courts and tribunals are not bound by their own precedents, but are bound by precedents established by the courts or superior tribunals above them in their own hierarchy. Most law applied by tribunals is common to the whole of Great Britain or the United Kingdom, and many more decisions are taken by them in England and Wales, so decisions of the English Court of Appeal are very persuasive[58].

THE SYSTEM IN PRACTICE – THE CRIMINAL COURTS

12.22   JP Courts are bound by precedents from: a Sheriff possibly[59]; the High Court of Justiciary as a trial court probably[60]; the High Court of Justiciary as an appeal court; and the Supreme Court on a devolution issue.

Sheriffs are bound by precedents from the High Court of Justiciary as a trial court and as an appeal court[61]; and the Supreme Court on a devolution issue.

The High Court of Justiciary, like the Court of Session, is a collegiate court, so hierarchy does not work within it in a straightforward way. The High Court of Justiciary, sitting as a trial court, is bound by precedents from the High Court of Justiciary sitting as an appeal court. The High Court of Justiciary sitting as an appeal court is bound by precedents from itself sitting as an appeal court with a bench of the same size, or larger. For this reason, a larger court may be formed to overrule a precedent which has been

---

58 In *Brown v Rentokil Ltd* 1992 IRLR 302, Lord Mayfield, sitting in the Employment Appeal Tribunal, said 'this court, being part of a United Kingdom body in the field of employment law, would only depart from an opinion of the Court of Appeal on a matter which was purely related to an aspect of Scots law. Accordingly, we find [a certain decision of that court] binding upon us'.

59 This is asserted by DM Walker *Scottish Legal System* (8th edn, 2001) p 447, but no authority is offered. *The Laws of Scotland: Stair Memorial Encyclopaedia* vol 22 is silent. There is a certain parity of reasoning with the position of the sheriff and the High Court as a trial court.

60 By a parity of reasoning with the position of the sheriff court.

61 It used to be orthodox to say that a Sheriff was not bound by the High Court sitting as a trial court (with which it has a considerably overlapping jurisdiction). However, in *Jessop v Stevenson* 1987 SCCR 655 , the High Court, sitting as an appeal court from a Sheriff's decision, held that Sheriffs were bound by it sitting as a trial court.

found unacceptable or otherwise clarify the law. For instance, a court of five judges revisited diminished responsibility in *Galbraith v HM Advocate (No 2)* 2002 JC 1 to consider whether a lengthy period of physical abuse could justify that plea. A court of nine judges was used in *McCutcheon v HM Advocate* 2002 SLT 27 to overrule a decision of seven judges concerning cross-examination in *Morrison v HM Advocate* 1990 JC 299. An extreme example is *Elliott v HM Advocate* 1995 JC 95 where, on 24 March 1995, five judges met and overruled the decision on 10 February 1995 of three judges in *Church v HM Advocate* 1995 SLT 604.

PRECEDENT AND THE COURT OF JUSTICE OF THE EUROPEAN UNION

12.23 The Court of Justice of the European Union (CJEU) (consisting of the Court of Justice, the General Court and specialist tribunals) does not readily fit into the hierarchy of courts. There is no appeal to them from any UK court, nor appeal from them. The CJEU is the guardian of EU law, and its pronouncements on the interpretation of that law are authoritative and must be followed by national courts regardless of any national rules of interpretation or precedent. If in any doubt as to the CJEU's view of an aspect of EU law, the national courts must make a *preliminary reference* so that the CJEU can decide the issue. As a court bound by written law, the CJEU does not operate a system of precedent; however, it will frequently refer to previous decisions as illuminating the principles to be drawn from specific provisions of EU law. But, as discussed in Chapter 11, the CJEU has, from its decisions, developed certain 'general principles of law common to all Member States' which it requires to be applied to any decision on EU law. It has thus generated something approaching a EU law doctrine of precedent[62].

On the other hand (as also discussed in Chapter 6), the CJEU has decided that it is not actually bound by its own decisions[63] and it does not cite other cases in its judgments, even when relying on them or when consciously rejecting them. The problem is aggravated by the fact that only a single judgment is given, which may reflect a

62 As is evident from cases such as Cases 28–30/62 *Da Costa en Schaake NV and Others v Nederlandse Belastingadministratie* [1963] ECR 31 and Case 283/81 *Srl CILFIT and Another v Ministry of Health* [1982] ECR 3415 (as discussed in Chapter 6).
63 For example, in Case 4/69 *Alfons Lüttike GmbH v EC Commission* [1971] ECR 325.

compromise between several lines of reasoning, making it difficult to determine what principles are being applied. The Advocate General's opinion is printed with the judgment, and is able to avoid many of these difficulties. Thus, it is often cited as a form of precedent, though it lacks the full authority of a court.

PRECEDENT AND THE EUROPEAN COURT OF HUMAN RIGHTS

12.24 The European Court of Human Rights (ECtHR) fits even less well into the hierarchy of courts. It is the authoritative interpreter of the European Convention on Human Rights (ECHR), most of which is enacted as *Convention rights* by the Human Rights Act 1998. Section 2 of that Act requires its decisions to be taken into account by UK courts when deciding cases on Convention rights. Thus, its decisions are highly persuasive for the UK courts. However, unlike for EU law, the doctrine of the *margin of appreciation* means that it is accepted that a democratically elected government has some room for manoeuvre in balancing opposing interests and taking account of national conditions in complying with the ECHR[64]. While the ECtHR strives for consistency, it is not bound by itself. The Articles of the ECHR are generally brief[65], and even the most specific is drafted in the form of a principle rather than a rule[66]. In any case, it is expressly asserted that the ECHR is 'a living instrument ... which must be interpreted in the light of present-day conditions'[67].

---

64 For instance, the court acknowledges that there is not necessarily 'a uniform European conception of morals' (*Handyside v United Kingdom* (1979–80) A/24, 1 EHRR 737, para 48).

65 Art 3 is simply 'No one shall be subjected to torture or inhuman or degrading treatment'.

66 See *eg* Arts 5 and 6.

67 *Tyrer v United Kingdom* (1979–80) A/26, 2 EHRR, para 31.

13 Precedent – Law Reports

13.1 The previous Chapter considered precedent as a source of law. This Chapter considers the publication of judicial decisions and law reporting, essential features of any system of precedent. It will discuss the publication of judicial decisions, law reporting, the principal series of law reports, the citation of cases, the form and content of law reports and electronic reporting and computerised retrieval of law reports.

Although the need to report court decisions might be thought a characteristic mainly of common law or precedent-based systems, it also exists in civil law countries, even although precedent is not, generally speaking, accepted as a formal source of law, and where at most a very weak doctrine of stare decisis operates. Its role in these countries is rather to illustrate how a code or other enacted law is being understood and applied. The form of law reports reflects this, being often more laconic, and reasoned in a formal stereotyped way in terms of the enacted law with usually no reference to precedents.

The form of law reports of European Union courts, or from the European Court of Human Rights are, however, far from laconic, although otherwise more akin to the civil law countries in their approach. This may reflect the difficulty of obtaining a single opinion from a disparate body in the one case, and allowing broad discussion of principle from a disparate body in the other.

THE PUBLICATION OF JUDICIAL DECISIONS

13.2 Any system of precedent relies upon the availability of previous judicial decisions. Unless the decisions in at least the most important cases, and the reasoning which produced them, are readily available, no doctrine of *stare decisis* can operate.

Despite this, the reporting of the outcome of cases has not been seen as an obligation of the state or even the courts themselves[1]. Until the arrival of the Internet in the 1990s, no formal, public systems for publishing the results of cases or the text of decisions[2] was established. Instead, decisions of the court, and the reasons for them, were given to the parties at the end of the individual case without any attempt to publicise them more widely[3].

In Scotland, some judges in the Court of Session began, in the mid-16th century, to record their own decisions in notebooks, known as *practicks*. Some of these were then circulated among legal practitioners and subsequently published. These published decisions were then available to inform subsequent judicial decision making and provided a valuable resource for those institutional writers and later compilers of the first law reports[4]. In some ways they are more like the early reports in civil law countries than those also found at the same period in England[5].

With the development of precedent as a formal source of law, individuals and commercial publishers began to collect and publish important judicial decisions to meet the demand from the legal profession for regular reporting of the way in which the law was being applied and developed.

Only recently, with the ease of publishing information online, have the courts moved to establish comprehensive systems for the publication of decisions. The Scottish Court Service introduced electronic publication in 1999, making decisions available on its website[6]. The opinions of judges in the Court of Session and High Court from September 1998 are contained on that site. Opinions

---

1 With a very limited number of exceptions. For example, *Reports of Patent, Design and Trade Mark Cases* and *Immigration Appeal Reports*, both published by The Stationery Office.

2 In Scotland, the written decisions are referred to as the *opinion* of the court. Other jurisdictions, including England, tend to refer to the written decision as the *judgment*.

3 The courts historically considered that delivering decisions in open court was sufficient recognition of their public nature. This has been done since the 17th century, originally orally but, as legal procedures become more formalised, oral reasons were supplemented by the issue of written opinion to the parties concerned.

4 The earliest reports took the form of dictionaries of decided cases arranged by topic.

5 See Dolezalek, 'The Court of Session as a ius commune court – witnessed by Sinclair's Practicks', Miscellany IV (Stair Society vol 49), pp 51–84.

6 www.scotcourts.gov.uk.

in important civil cases in the Sheriff Courts from September 1998 (and Court of Session commercial cases from January 1998) and Fatal Accident Inquiries from March 1999 are also included.

Courts of other jurisdictions have established similar systems, as have the Court of Justice of the European Union and the European Court of Human Rights[7]. The UK Supreme Court has, from its beginning, published not just the decisions themselves, but also a distillation intended to summarise the key issues of the judgment for the press and public[8].

The routine electronic publication of decisions has also allowed the development of free-to-access websites bringing together important decisions into a single database as a resource for the public, students, academics and the profession. The best example of this is BAILII[9] which forms part of a world-wide network of similar sites providing unprecedented access to the decisions of many courts across the world.

In UK courts, it is common for a court constituted of more than one judge to deliver multiple opinions, even where all judges agree (although the opinion may consist of only a single line indicating agreement). Dissenting opinions are relatively common, always published and play their own role in the development of precedent, as discussed in the previous chapter. More recently, it has become more usual for a single opinion of the court to be given if all judges are in agreement on both the outcome and the reasoning for reaching it. In the Court of Justice of the European Union, there is only ever a single judgment of the court and never any dissenting judgments. The European Court of Human Rights usually attempts to reach a single judgment of the court but additional and dissenting judgments are sometimes published.

LAW REPORTING

13.3 As discussed above, the whole system of precedent was historically reliant on law reports produced by publishers for legal practitioners on a commercial or semi-commercial basis. Decisions and judgments believed to be important in terms of the development and application of the law would be collated by law reporters, edited,

---

7 www.curia.europa.eu (CJEU) and www.echr.coe.int (ECtHR).
8 www.supremecourt.gov.uk. Uniquely among UK courts, hearings and decisions of the Supreme Court are also routinely webcast.
9 www.bailii.org.

and published in volumes along with supplementary information to assist legal practitioners.

Despite the increased availability of judicial decisions in raw form, law reports continue to be an important resource. The added value provided by the reports, through selecting, editing and compiling the decisions and adding useful supplementary information, means that practitioners will still pay for this service even if the underlying information is, in principle, available for free.

In Scotland, the most authoritative reports are produced by the Scottish Council of Law Reporting, a non-profit-making semi-official body[10]. An equivalent body, the Incorporated Council of Law Reporting, performs the same function in England. But the majority of reporting is still undertaken by commercial legal publishing companies who, between them, produce around 70 different series of law reports covering UK courts and tribunals. Each of these series will adopt a different approach to the cases reported and the nature of the report. Some aim for comprehensive and authoritative coverage of the most important decisions in either Scots law or English law; some aim for speed of reporting; others at significant cases in a particular or niche area of law, irrespective of the court or tribunal concerned.

Many of these series of reports are concerned primarily or exclusively with cases decided in England and Wales. However, because so much law is now in legislation, and so much legislation extends over Great Britain or the United Kingdom, such reports are often of value in Scotland. Equally, series of reports on English law will carry reports of decisions of the UK Supreme Court on matters of Scots law where that law is seen as sufficiently similar to English law or for the sake of a comprehensive coverage of the decisions of that court.

Scottish Law Reports

13.4   The major law reports dealing generally with Scottish cases are described below. This list is far from exhaustive and there are a number of specialist series of reports dealing with cases on particular issues not discussed here.

---

10 The Scottish Council of Law Reporting website (www.scottishlawreports.org. uk) contains more information and links to a series of short, informative video films discussing precedent and law reporting.

Session Cases

13.5   The principal law reports in Scotland are *Session Cases*. These reports are produced by the Scottish Council of Law Reporting and published by W Green. It aims for authoritative coverage of all important Scots law cases, including decisions of the Supreme Court (previously the Privy Council and House of Lords), the High Court of Justiciary and the Court of Session. The reports from each of the courts each form a separate series within the overall *Session Cases* reports (and the reports on criminal matters, whilst still part of the *Session Cases* reports, are referred to as *Justiciary Cases*). These series have for many years been generally bound together in a single annual volume, misleadingly marked *Session Cases* on the spine, the different series being separately paginated within it[11]. The separate series are cited by the designations SC or JC (for first instance cases in the Court of Session and High Court of Justiciary respectively[12]). Bracketed suffixes are added to indicate the series of reports from the Supreme Court (UKSC) or, formerly, from the House of Lords (SC(HL)) and Privy Council (SC(PC)) cases[13].

The particular authority of *Session Cases* is derived from the semi-official nature of the Scottish Council of Law Reporting and the fact that the judges delivering the opinions reported on have the opportunity to comment on a pre-publication draft of the *Session Cases* report. *Session Cases* therefore take priority over all series of reports for use in court[14].

The *Session Cases* series in its present form commenced in 1907 (covering 1906–7). It was, however, the continuation of privately produced reports in broadly the same form, in five sequential series sometimes collectively referred to as the *nominate reports*, but individually known by the name of the five editors: Shaw, Dunlop,

---

11 Prior to devolution, there were no Privy Council cases affecting Scotland, so these were not reported in Session Cases. In 2000, there were only House of Lords, but no Privy Council cases reported; in 2001, there were Privy Council cases, but no House of Lords cases reported, so 2002 is the first year in which all four series appeared.

12 From 1906 to 1916, Justiciary cases were cited 'SC(J)'.

13 Thus, there are three separate sections each beginning at p 1 in most volumes of *Session Cases*: e.g. 1942 SC(HL) 1 (*Crofter Hand Woven Tweed Co Ltd v Veitch*), 1942 JC 1 (*Duguid v Fraser*) and 1942 SC 1 (*Swaire v Demetriades*) respectively.

14 Court of Session Practice Note No. 5 of 2004 states: 'For the avoidance of doubt, the Court of Session requires that where a case has been reported in Session Cases it must be cited from that source. Other series of reports may only be used when a case is not reported in Session Cases.' A similar direction in respect of cases cited before the High Court of Justiciary and Court of Criminal Appeal is given in High Court of Justiciary Practice Note No. 2 of 2004.

Macpherson, Rettie and Fraser[15]. Nominate volumes are identifed in citations by the editor's name or, more commonly, the initial letter of their name. As with the later series, House of Lords cases and Justiciary cases, where present, are usually paginated as a separate series in the same volume[16], although there are also some separate series of reports, such as Macqueen's reports of House of Lords cases running from 1851 to 1865 (cited Macq), and Adam's reports of Justiciary cases from 1893 to 1916.

Scottish Criminal Case Reports and Scottish Civil Law Reports

13.6   The *Scottish Criminal Case Reports* (SCCR) and *Scottish Civil Law Reports* (SCLR) are two separate series published by the Law Society of Scotland, on a commercial basis, since 1981 and 1987 respectively. They cover cases considered worth reporting from any court in Scotland, and some have a commentary on them added by the editor or other commentator.

The SCLR series also contains brief notes of cases of interest not deserving of a full report and a separate series of *quantum* notes on cases for which the chief interest is the amount of damages awarded, or the means of its calculation.

These series commenced in part because of the then chronic delays in the production of *Session Cases*. They are produced in loose parts six times a year, and bound into an annual volume at the end of each year.

Scots Law Times

13.7   The *Scots Law Times* is, like *Session Cases*, published by W Green, but as a purely commercial enterprise. It contains professional information and articles, but also law reports on important recent cases from all courts and other tribunals within the Scottish jurisdiction[17].

---

15 The volumes of the nominate series are: Shaw 1821–38; Dunlop 1838–62; Macpherson 1862–73; Rettie 1873–98; and Fraser 1898–1906.

16 House of Lords cases begin to be included from 1850 (that is, from volume 13 of Dunlop's reports). The bracketed suffix convention is generally adopted, so such reports are cited D(HL). Justiciary reports are included from 1874 (that is, from the first volume of Rettie's reports). They are cited R(J) instead of R.

17 Including devolution cases and appeals going to the Supreme Court (or formerly the Privy Council or House of Lords) and cases from the Court of Session, High Court of Justiciary, Sheriff Courts, Scottish Land Court and Lands Tribunal and the Lyon Court.

One series (cited simply as SLT) is used for cases in the Supreme Court (previously the House of Lords and the Privy Council), Court of Session and High Court of Justiciary. Separately paginated series exist for the lower courts and tribunals (using suffixed abbreviations such as SLT(Sh Ct) or SLT(Land Ct) for Sheriff Court and Land Court reports, respectively). The *Scots Law Times* also contains a series of articles and professional information, also separately cited as 'SLT (News)'.

The *Scots Law Times* is published in weekly editions through the year, except when the Court of Session is on vacation. It thus provides relatively rapid publication of reports. Usually, two annual volumes are produced[18]: one containing the compiled reports from the Court of Session, High Court of Justiciary and the Supreme Court; the other containing all other reports and the news section.

Greens Weekly Digest

13.8 *Greens Weekly Digest* (GWD) has also been produced by W Green since 1986. It contains brief notes, though not a report, upon recently decided cases, under topic headings. It appears in weekly loose-leaf parts thus providing rapid, but limited, information. Some libraries bind these into annual volumes.

Earlier reports and compilations

13.9 Many reports other than the nominate ones were produced in the 19th century and later[19]. These include the *Scottish Jurist* (SJ) from 1829 to 1873 and the *Scottish Law Reporter* (SLR) from 1865 to 1924. They sometimes cover cases not found in other reports, or provide alternative reports. Before the 19th century several major series existed to which reference is made, such as that of Lord Stair, that of Forbes and the *Faculty Collection* (cited as FC or Fac Col).

---

18 From the 1920s to 1990, only one annual volume was produced although some editions marked the news section and reports from different courts by different coloured edges to the page. Citation of earlier volumes is confusing. The earliest volumes were cited by sequential number of the annual volume number, often preceded by the year in round brackets, for example 15 SLT or (1907) 15 SLT. For some years until 1921, two annual volumes were produced, cited by year, but including the volume number, for example (1915) 1 SLT.
19 Full lists of Scottish law reports which have existed, the dates they cover, and the abbreviated form of the name used for citation purposes, are to be found in Walker *The Scottish Legal System*.

Reference may be made instead to the reports in *Morison's Dictionary* which, with synopses and supplements, covers cases from the 16th to the early 19th centuries in some 40 volumes ordered alphabetically by subject[20]. Most of these reports are very short and without reasoned judgments. Some modern editions of practicks, such as *Balfour's Practicks*, are available. Selected cases from *Morison's Dictionary*, the *Faculty Collection*, the earlier *Session Cases* and some other pre-1873 reports were reprinted as *Scots Revised Reports*.

Other sources of law reports

13.10 Much informed comment and analysis of recent cases can be found online in legal blogs. Although these tend to be personal opinions and will be of varying quality and depth of analysis, some are authored by leading practitioners in the field, and frequently provide a rapid response and analysis of recently published cases.

Important decisions may also be reported, although usually with limited analysis, in online news or digest services such as *Scottish Legal News*[21] or *Casecheck*[22].

Court of Justice of the European Union

European Court Reports

13.11 Unlike in the UK, the courts of the European Union have always published their decisions as one of the official publications of the European Union. These are now generally accessed online[23] although the *European Court Reports* are still produced as a three-volume annual set. Every case also has a unique identifying number allocated by the court to assist with citation[24].

---

20 Citations of reports in *Morison's Dictionary* are given to the page numbers, which run continuously throughout all volumes, after the abbreviation 'Mor Dic', 'Mor', 'Mo' or (likely to cause confusion with Macpherson's reports) 'M', the whole often preceded by the year in brackets), for example '(1714) M 14757'.

21 *Scottish Legal News* is a daily, free email bulletin containing the latest from the Scottish legal world: www.scottishlegal.com.

22 *Casecheck* provides short digests of recently decided cases across a very wide range of topic areas. It is free to register: www.casecheck.co.uk.

23 http://europa.eu/eu-law/case-law/index_en.htm.

24 This is often necessary as so many cases involve the same parties. The identifying number is the sequential number of the case and the year. Since the introduction of the Court of First Instance (now the General Court), the sequential number is preceded by 'C' for the European Court; 'T' for the General Court or Court of First Instance; and 'F' for the civil service tribunal.

European Court Reports are the most authoritative reports, but have been slow to appear (although unbound copies of judgments rendered in English may be much faster), and are produced without the editorial assistance of headnotes in the United Kingdom fashion.

The form and content of EU decisions differ somewhat from the common form in the United Kingdom. They include a summary with key words and a précis of the principle applied. The opinion of the Advocate General (which has no analogy in United Kingdom practice) is normally included (and may be published separately before final determination of the case). The judgment of the court is given in more formal terms than in United Kingdom practice, specifying the nature of the proceedings and parties, then dealing with each aspect of the case considered. It ends with a formal conclusion preceded by words such as 'On these grounds ...'.

Common Market Law Reports

13.12 The *Common Market Law Reports* series is published by Sweet & Maxwell, on a commercial basis. It has similar but fuller coverage than the *European Court Reports*, including cases heard before national courts as well as those before the Court of Justice of the European Union. They are published in numerous loose parts during the year, bound into a number of volumes at the end of the year, and reports have headnotes in the United Kingdom fashion.

The form and content are closer to United Kingdom practice than the *European Court Reports*, as in place of the summary there is usually a fuller précis of the issues, and the facts are more clearly spelled out. However, its basic form is determined by the form of the Advocate-General's opinion and the court's judgment. The actual translation of those items into English is not identical to that in *European Court Reports*.

All England Law Reports European Cases

13.13 This is an addition to the standard English set of *All England Law Reports* commercially produced by LexisNexis, and contains decisions of the Court of Justice of the European Union.

European Court of Human Rights

13.14 As with the Court of Justice of the European Union, electronic publication has become the primary means by which the official reports of the court are published and cases are referred to by sequential number and year as well as the names of the parties. However, the official reports are still also available as a published series of *Reports of Judgments and Decisions*, of which there are multiple volumes for each year, and the relevant volume and year may be quoted along with the case reference. Prior to 1996, the publications were in two series: Series A for judgment and decisions; and Series B for pleadings, oral argument and other documents.

European Human Rights Reports

13.15 The main commercial English language series of law reports on the application of the European Convention on Human Rights is the *European Human Rights Reports* (EHRR) published by Sweet & Maxwell. It contains full reports of judgments of the Court (and, historically, admissibility decisions of the now defunct European Commission on Human Rights). It is published in numbered annual volumes.

LAW REPORTS: ENGLAND AND WALES

The Law Reports

13.16 The most authoritative English law reports are those produced by the Incorporated Council of Law Reporting. They are commonly referred to in England and Wales simply as the *Law Reports*. These comprise five series of reports:

- **Appeal Cases (AC)**. Appeals heard by the UK Supreme Court (or, formerly, the Judicial Committee of the Privy Council and the Appellate Committee of the House of Lords). This includes appeals from Scottish courts.
- **Queen's Bench (QB), Chancery (Ch) and Family (Fam) series**[25]. Reports of cases heard by the three divisions of the High Court in England and Wales, including appeals to the Court of Appeal.
- **Weekly Law Reports (WLR)**. These are published weekly in loose leaf format but then made up into three annual volumes: volumes 2 and 3 contain initial reports of those cases to be more

---

25 What is now the Family Division was before 1971, the Probate, Divorce and Admiralty Division (the citation abbreviation was P).

fully reported later in the other four series; volume 1 contains reports of other cases.

For a period in the 19th century, a similar but more complicated system operated[26]. Before that, there were nominate private reports known by the name of the editor, rather as in Scotland. The more important were collected in various compilations, including the *English Reports* (ER) and the *All England Reports Reprint* (All ER Rep).

All England Law Reports

13.17 The *All England Law Reports* are produced by LexisNexis, a commercial legal publisher. It reports all cases considered worth reporting from any court in England and attempts more rapid production than the *Law Reports*. It is produced in weekly loose parts, bound into several volumes per year.

USING LAW REPORTS

Citation of Cases

13.18 In the UK, there was historically no official case reference assigned by the court system, so citations are not related to the case itself, but to the report of it. These citations are governed by convention rather than any strict rules, so there are sometimes variations in usage, even within jurisdictions[27].

The citation of a report generally consists of three parts.

- **A year and/or a volume number**. Sometimes volumes are just known by the year; others are given sequential numbers for each year, in which case the practice is to also give the year when citing. Scottish reports generally just state the year. English practice is usually to include the year in [closed brackets] if it is essential to the citation; and to include the year in (open) brackets if there is also a sequential volume number. Where there is more than one volume for any given year, the identifying number of the volume is given after the year.

---

26 For details, see Sweet & Maxwell *Guide to Law Reports and statutes*.
27 For a discussion of some of the principles of citation, see White 'Bracketing the Target: the citation of multi-volume Session Cases' 2006 SLT (News) 37–40.

- **The designation of the series of reports**. This is an abbreviation indicating the series of reports to which the citation refers. A fuller list is given in the table below.
- **A page number.** The citation concludes with the page number on which the report starts. If the reference is to a specific part of the opinion, then this page number is also given (for instance 1949 SLT 230 at 235)[28].

Any case may, if reported in more than one series of law reports, have several citations, presenting a forbiddingly prolific combination of names, numbers and letters. For example, the case of *Wilsons and Clyde Coal Co v Scottish Insurance Corporation* could be cited as 1949 SC(HL) 90, 1949 SLT 230, [1949] AC 462, [1949] LJR 1190, 65 TLR 354, 93 SJ 423, [1949] 1 All ER 1068.

As courts began to publish decisions systematically online they introduced their own systems which allocate a unique reference to each case. These *neutral citations* are increasingly used as the primary means of referring to cases, certainly outwith courts. The broad form of neutral citations is similar to that of traditional citation, but indicates the year, the court and the case, rather than year, report and page. Thus '[2005] CSOH 1' indicates the first case of 2005 from the Court of Session, Outer House[29]. Similarly, '[2003] EWCA (Civ) 1' indicates the first case of 2003 from the (England and Wales) Court of Appeal, Civil Division[30]. Further, every opinion has numbered paragraphs (the numbers running through the whole opinion, even if there are several judges). Thus, reference is made to

28 The abbreviation 'p' is not used for page numbers in citations.
29 The full list of abbreviations used in Scotland is UKSC for the Supreme Court (formerly UKPC D the Privy Council, the D indicating Devolution cases or UKHL for the House of Lords); CSIH for the Inner House of the Court of Session; CSOH for the Outer House of the Court of Session; HCJ or HCJAC for the High Court of Justiciary at first instance or when acting as an appeal court (see Court of Session Practice Note No 5 of 2004 and High Court of Justiciary Practice Note No 2 of 2004). The neutral citation has brought square brackets into Scottish citations for the first time.
30 Practice Direction on the Form of Judgments, Paragraph Marking and Neutral Citation of 11 January 2001 ([2001] 1 WLR 194, [2001] 1 All ER 193) and Practice direction – Neutral Citations of 14 January 2002 ([2002] 1 WLR 346, [2002] 1 All ER 351). The full list of abbreviations used is: UKSC, UKHL or UKPC (for the Supreme Court and its predecessors); EWCA (Civ) or EWCA(Crim) for the two divisions of the Court of Appeal; EWHC (Ch) for the Chancery Division; EWHC (Pat) for the Patents Court; EWHC (QB) for the Queen's Bench Division; EWHC (Admin) for the Administrative Court; EWHC (Comm) for the Commercial Court; EWHC (Admlty) for the Admiralty Court; EWHC (TCC) for the Technology and Construction Court; and EWHC (Fam) for the Family Division.

a paragraph rather than a page, in the form '2005 CSOH 1 at [7]', or '2001 EWCA Civ 10 at [59]'. The paragraph number is bracketed to avoid confusion with page numbers, which are not used as the text in electronic format is generally not paginated.

Names of the Parties

13.19 Cases are usually known by the names of the parties, for example, *Junior Books Ltd v The Veitchi Company Ltd*[31]. These names are often abbreviated (for example, simply to *Junior Books v Veitchi*, or just *Junior Books*). In a case at first instance the pursuer's name comes first, but if the defender appeals, his name may come first. If the parties are acting in a particular capacity this may be recorded in the citation, such as in *Aitken's Trustees v Aitken*[32], *Drummond's Judicial Factor v HM Advocate*[33] or *Taylor's Executor v Thom*[34]. Cases from the Court of Justice of the European Union (CJEU) present special problems as names may often be ambiguous, as in *Commission of the European Communities v United Kingdom of Great Britain and Northern Ireland*, for there are several cases of that name. Most CJEU case names are not in English (and if translated, are not always consistently translated), so are often referred to by abbreviated names, as in *Van Gend en Loos*[35], or unofficial ones, such as '*the Isoglucose case*' (or just *Isoglucose)*[36], even though that word may not be part of the name of either party. In any case the CJEU case reference number is the most important part of the citation.

Importance is sometimes attached to the word used in place of the 'v' between parties' names. In Scottish cases, the convention is that it is spoken as 'against'; in English cases 'and' is preferred; whilst cases from the United States are 'versus'. The first named party is not necessarily the pursuer, because if the defender loses at first

---

31 1982 SC (HL) 244.
32 1927 SC 374. *Trustee* and *trustees* are usually abbreviated to *Tr* and *Trs*.
33 1944 SC 298. *Judicial Factor* is usually abbreviated to JF.
34 1914 SC 79. *Executor, Executrix* (the feminine form) and *Executors*, are usually abbreviated to *Ex, Exx, Exrs* or similar.
35 This case appears in the official European Court Reports at [1963] ECR 1 as Case 26/62 *NV Algemene Transport en Expeditie Onderneming van Gend en Loos v Nederlandse Administratie der Belastingen* (which means roughly, *Ghent and Loos General Transport and Export Co Ltd v Dutch Tax Commission*). In Common Market Law Reports ([1963] CMLR 105) the respondent appears reported in the table of cases as *Nederlandse Belastingadministratie*, and in the body of the volume as *Nederlandse Tariefcommisie*.
36 *Royal Scholter-Honig v Intervention Board* [1977] 2 CMLR 449.

instance and appeals, the names are often reversed. Occasionally there is more than one reported decision between two parties in the course of a litigation, in which case it will be referred to with *'No 2'* after the names, for example, *Weir v Jessop*[37] (concerning search of premises) and *Weir v Jessop (No 2)*[38] (concerning entrapment)[39]. But an appeal decision does not fall to be treated as 'No 2' (or even 'No 3') in relation to the decision at first instance. The practice is needed only when a fresh point arises for decision during a litigation which has already produced decisions on other points at an earlier stage.

There are variations. Where there are reporting restrictions, as with some cases involving children, or others whose identity is not to be publicised, initials may be used, as with *E v T*[40]. This can be confusing, as with the famous and very important *A v Secretary of State for the Home Department*[41], (concerning the legality of detention under the Anti-Terrorism, Crime and Security Act 2001) which is not to be mistaken for the equally famous and important *A v Secretary of State for the Home Department*[42] (concerning the inadmissibility of evidence obtained by torture)[43].

Where procedure is by petition, as with the *nobile officium*, the case may be referred to in the form *McLachlan, Petitioner*[44]. Also, because it has been common in Scottish reports to record a married woman's maiden name as well, both may appear in the citation, at least in English-based sets of reports. Indeed, for this reason, in the English series called *Appeal Cases, Donoghue v Stevenson* 1932 SC(HL) 31 is cited as *M'Alister*[45] *(or Donoghue) v Stevenson* [1932] AC 562, Mrs Donoghue's maiden name having been McAlister. Likewise *Darling v Gray & Sons* (1892) 19 R(HL) 31 is also *Wood v Gray & Sons* [1892] AC 576. Historically, the married name is preceded by 'Mrs'.

In criminal cases, the names used are those of the nominal prosecutor and the accused. For summary cases, the prosecutor is

---

37 1991 SCCR 242.

38 1991 SCCR 636.

39 The *Factortame* litigation probably takes the prize, as it runs to some ten cases: *R. v Secretary of State for Transport, Local Government and the Regions ex parte Factortame Ltd (No. 8)* [2002] EWCA Civ 932, [2003] QB 381, plus *Factortame Ltd v Secretary of State for the Environment, Transport and the Regions (Costs) (No.2)* [2002] EWCA Civ 932, [2003] QB 381.

40 1949 SLT 411.

41 [2004] UKHL 56, [2005] 2 AC 68.

42 [2005] UKHL 71, [2006] 2 AC 221.

43 Indeed, at the beginning of 2013, LexisLibrary revealed 285 cases of 'A' (or some variant thereof, such as 'AB')and 'Secretary of State' names.

44 1987 SCCR 195. *Petitioner* is usually abbreviated to *Petr*. There are further variations, such as *Minuter*.

45 M', is an old-fashioned version of Mc.

the senior Procurator for that Sheriff Court district. In the past, the actual name of the Procurator Fiscal was used but, more recently, they have been referred to instead by their role (for example: *McKenzie v Procurator Fiscal Edinburgh*). For solemn cases the prosecutor is always *Her Majesty's Advocate*, usually abbreviated to *HM Advocate* or simply *HMA*[46]. If the accused is convicted and appeals, the names are again usually reversed, for example, *Khaliq v HM Advocate*[47].

Similar conventions apply to English cases, but three variations are worth noting. Criminal cases are cited as '*R*' (short for *Regina* or *Rex*) but the English equivalent is used when speaking the name of the case, for example, *R v Dudley and Stephens*[48] is spoken as 'The Queen against Dudley and Stephens'). Judicial review cases (where the court reviews a decision of government or a tribunal) are in England technically brought by the Crown against the relevant person, on behalf of (*ex parte*) the complainer, so are cited as, for example, *R v Secretary of State for the Home Department, ex parte Zamir*[49], often shortened to *R (Zamir) v Secretary of State for the Home Department*. In proceedings where there is not a straightforward action by one person against another, the name of the principal party or other information is preceded by '*Re*' or '*In re*' (both meaning 'concerning' in Latin), for example, *In re an Arbitration between Polemis and Another and Furness Withy & Co Ltd*[50] (often abbreviated to simply *Re Polemis*, after the name of the ship centrally involved in the case).

Form and Content of Law Reports

13.20 Law reports have traditionally included a variety of information supplementing the text of any opinion, with the aim of assisting practitioners to assess the content, subject matter and relevance of any case report without having to read each in full. The nature and amount of supplementary information will depend on the series of law reports. Some aim for speed of publication over depth of analysis; whilst others attempt to provide a wide range of information to assist with highlighting key issues or cross-referencing with other cases or relevant legislation. However, the information contained in the following sections is often included in law reports.

46 In civil cases, HM Advocate is referred to as the Lord Advocate, even when female.
47 1984 JC 23, 1984 SLT 137, 1983 SCCR 483.
48 (1884) 14 QBD 273, 15 Cox CC 624.
49 [1980] AC 930.
50 [1921] 3 KB 560.

- **Names of the parties, their roles, and counsel.** Reports commence with the names of the parties and their role in the proceedings: such as petitioner, pursuer, defender, appellant or reclaimer. Often their representatives, counsel and sometimes solicitors, are explicitly noted. The abbreviations QC and AD mean *Queen's Counsel* and *Advocate Depute*, respectively. Some reports list representation at the end of the report.
- **Case number and date.** The court's own reference number for the case and the date heard may be noted, for example, 'No 1' and 'Oct 1 1985'.
- **Names of judges and court.** Usually the names of the judges and the court hearing the case will be specified.
- **Catch words.** Many case reports include a series of key words or phrases (known as *catch words*) to highlight the subject matter of the opinion. These are usually italicised or emboldened, and separated by dashes, and if the case concerns several disparate issues, there may be more than one series of references.
- **Headnote.** The headnote is inserted by the editor to summarise the key points of the case. It is sometimes called the *rubric*. The first section of the headnote is a summary of the facts and general argument in the case. The reporter or editor will then summarise the decision of the court and what appears to be the *ratio decidendi* of the case. By convention this is done in a series of statements introduced by the word *Held*. A headnote may contain other italicised words, such as *aff.* or *affirmed*, followed by the name of the court from which the appeal came, and *opinion per* a named judge, which indicates a view expressed by that judge alone. It will also record if any judge dissented, usually by giving his name after the italicised abbreviation *diss.*, and possibly with some indication of his reasoning. A headnote may also indicate that a precedent cited has been followed, distinguished, approved or otherwise, and end with the decision, such as 'appeal dismissed'. Although the headnote provides a very valuable summary of the case report, it has no authority and should always be used as a guide to, not a substitute for, reading the opinion of the court.
- **Recital of facts and procedure and argument of counsel.** Fuller reports contain a recital of relevant facts, of the procedure which brought the case to that court, and an abbreviated account of the arguments deployed by counsel[51]. This may be several

---

51 It is important to note that argument of counsel is not the opinion of the judge. As noted in Chapter 12, it is an embarrassing error to quote the former under the impression that it is the latter.

pages long, and possibly longer than the actual opinion. It may explain why the dispute took the form it did. For example, one party may have conceded certain issues, which therefore do not have to be argued. Thus, it may throw light upon the breadth of the *ratio decidendi* or its persuasiveness.

- **Cases and legislation cited**. Some reports list the cases and legislation referred to by the judges in their opinions, and sometimes others cited by counsel in argument.
- **Opinions**. The body of the report is formed by the opinion of the court, or separate opinions, where the judges have delivered them. These are in the judges' own words, and are not written by the editor of the reports, as the rest of the report is. Thus, they are that part from which all legal reasoning, including extraction of *ratio decidendi* and assessment of persuasiveness, chiefly flows. In recent years, judges have generally adopted a common structure to opinions, helpful in extracting ratios. Thus, they often comprise informal sections, identified by headings, such as 'Introduction', 'Relevant legislation', 'Submissions of parties', 'Discussion' and 'Conclusion', 'Result' or 'Disposition'. Not all of an opinion may be reported, however, if the report of the case is concerned with only part of the dispute. A judge's recital of the facts may be omitted if an adequate summary exists, or they are recounted by another judge. Dissenting opinions will be reported, so care must sometimes be exercised to ensure that passages are not mistakenly quoted from a minority opinion.
- **Disposal**. Every piece of litigation must end in a decision. This appears in the opinion of the judge or judges, but may be separately recorded at the end by the editor.
- **Commentary**. Some specialised reports try to put the case in context and explain its implications.
- **Reporter's identity**. Reports often identify the reporter who produced the report.

Electronic Law Reporting

13.21 Over recent years, modern information technology has allowed legal publishers to move towards publishing case reports in electronic format; first using CDs and then through online databases.

These services are generally provided on a subscription basis by legal publishers and contain the case reports from the series of reports produced by that publisher. Often, the databases will also contain reports licensed from other sources, comprehensive databases of legislation, articles from legal journals, citation searches, PDF versions of the hardcopy reports, the text of leading practitioners' textbooks and other information. Whilst the major database services aspire to be as comprehensive as possible, the exact content of each database depends on the publisher, the licensing arrangements and the level of service for which the user elects to pay[52].

The most well-known databases are *Westlaw*, *LexisNexis* and *Justis*. As discussed previously, BAILII provides a similar database but drawing on the officially published versions of opinions and judgments, so the additional information, analysis and cross-referencing provided by commercial publishers is absent.

These databases have revolutionised legal research for practitioners, academics and students. Powerful search functions, hyperlinking of cited cases and legislation and the sheer mass of information available means relevant material can quickly be identified, analysed and assessed in its context. Tasks which previously would have taken many hours and access to a comprehensive law library can be achieved in a fraction of the time from a single computer.

---

52 For instance, at the time of writing, *Westlaw* did not carry the SCCR series of criminal case reports. *All England Law Reports* are only available on *LexisNexis*. *Fleet Street Reports*, published by Sweet & Maxwell, are only available on *Westlaw*. However, the principal series (*Session Cases* in Scotland and the *Law Reports* for England and Wales) feature on all the main databases.

14   Legal services

THE NEED FOR LEGAL SERVICES

14.1   Although much modern law offers some kind of advantage to people, they may miss the benefits if they do not take them up in the right way. And the kind of law that holds out threats over people who do not obey them can easily be abused by the officials wielding the threats – in criminal law, the police, the prosecutors, the judges and the penal authorities who actually apply the sentences. In other words, laws may be abused or miss their intended objectives.

To avoid this it is important that the subjects of the law should know what the law is – or at least be able to discover it, to find out how it applies to their particular situation, and then to utilise it, if that seems to be in their interests, and comply with it if it has a penalty attached. They need knowledge, advice and sometimes representation.

In a simple society where the law is largely custom they could probably do all this for themselves. But as law becomes more comprehensive, it becomes less accessible. The sheer bulk of it is intimidating. How to find one's way about it is a problem. Even when one has found what seems to be the right bit of law, the words used may be technical and obscure. The draftsmen of statutes often seem to defeat their own ends; in trying to cover every possible situation, they end up with laws that are beyond the understanding of those who are expected to use them – even the lawyers and officials.

The laws in the statute books may not be enough, for they may have been interpreted in a certain way by senior judges if there has been a similar dispute in the past which has reached the stage of a court hearing. For instance, if a house purchaser claims he was misled by a favourable report by a surveyor instructed by a building society and is entitled to compensation, questions of what actually happened and the terms of contracts, of statute and of case law and the value of his loss will all have to be considered. Then if the claim seems a sound one, it may be pursued by negotiation, arbitration or litigation (in a court). Given that the defenders will be advised by legal experts, the house purchaser would not get very far without the help of a lawyer.

When an individual is on the receiving end of laws, then the need for knowledge, advice and representation is still greater, for there is an inequality between him and the professionals who are doing the job daily. This is especially so in criminal cases where prosecution is a daily activity for prosecutors, but is usually a rare or unprecedented occasion for the accused and moreover one which may lead to the loss of his liberty.

To meet these needs a class of experts in the law has arisen in all mature systems of law, ones which have reached such a stage of complexity that people cannot make their way through them unaided. They may be called by various titles. In Scotland lawyers come in two classes: advocates and solicitors. No-one can belong to both classes at the same time, though transfers from solicitor to advocate are quite common and solicitors can seek certain powers of advocates. In carrying out their functions they all act under law and have various privileges and duties. However, they do not necessarily meet the entire need for legal services and we shall examine later other more informal responses to that need.

HISTORY OF THE LEGAL PROFESSION

Advocates

14.2　How do we come to have two mutually exclusive categories of lawyer, both enabling people to make the best use of the law? In medieval Scotland, two specific needs for legal services emerged. These were speaking in a court on behalf of a person called before it, and authenticating the documents which described occurrences under feudal law, upon which the all-important titles to land depended.

It seems very likely that court pleaders, from whom the later profession of advocate emerged, appeared first in the ecclesiastical courts. By the 13th century they had elaborate procedural rules and a largely written procedure which obviously called for literacy. It was not peculiar to Scotland. It derived from the universal canon law of the Catholic Church. Canon law provided until the Reformation the Scots law on marriage and its annulment, legitimacy, succession to items other than land, and contracts supported by an oath. On other matters too its courts were often resorted to, as being impartial and usually free from the influence of local magnates.

Many of the occasional references to lawyers before the 15th century seem to have some connection with church courts. Thus, a

Glasgow cleric, Adam Urri, was criticised in 1288 for practising civil law (ie Roman law) for personal profit, but repented before he died[1]. The records of the Great Cause[2] around 1290 over the succession to the throne of Scotland and later those of a long litigation on titles to land in the Court of the Bishop of Aberdeen (as a secular lord) in 1382[3] show that men with a wealth of knowledge of civil in the sense of Roman law and of Canon law were available in Scotland. One such, Baldred Bissett, was a graduate of Bologna and an official or ecclesiastical judge in the Diocese of St Andrews in 1282. Later, in 1301, with two others he was in Rome presenting legal arguments in the Scottish case against Edward I to the Papal Curia[4].

In 1425, after James I returned from captivity in England and set about remodelling the Scottish legal system, there must have been sufficient lawyers around in the royal courts for judges to ensure that, as Parliament enacted, poor persons should have 'a leill and wyse advocate to folow sik pure creaturis causes'[5]. Advocates and 'forspeakers' were also to swear that their cause was a 'gude and leill'(or true) one[6]. By 1455 advocates must have been recognised as professional participants in courts of some formality, for by an Act of that year forspeakers 'for meide' (or reward) were to wear 'habits of grene of the fashion of a tunicle and the sleeves to be open as a tabard'[7]. In 1479 there is the first mention of the King's Advocate, the ancestor of the Executive's chief law officer in Scotland today, the Lord Advocate[8].

When the Court of Session was established about 1532, eight men of 'best name, knawlege and experience' were selected to be 'general procurators', their number not to go above ten[9]. Others were admitted as individuals to practise before the court on satisfying the

---

1 *Chronicle of Lanercost for 1288.*

2 DM Walker *A Legal History of Scotland* vol II (1990) p 267; see para **2.8**.

3 Stein 'The Influence of Roman Law on the Law of Scotland' 1963 JR 205.

4 DER Watt *A Biographical Dictionary of Scottish Graduates Before 1410* (1977). See generally HL MacQueen *Common Law and Feudal Law* (1993) ch 3. A court is painted on the tower of Dunkeld Cathedral.

5 *Records of the Parliaments of Scotland to 1707* (RPS; www.rps.ac.uk), 1425/3/25.

6 RPS 1430/20.

7 RPS 1455/8/13.

8 RPS 1479/10/6. In 1579 the King's Advocate acquired his role as prosecutor of grave criminal offences on behalf of the Crown. See further J Finlay *Men of Law in Pre-Reformation Scotland* (2000), ch 7.

9 See RK Hannay *The College of Justice* (1933) p 137. In 1567 the Lords of the Articles narrated the great number of advocates in Edinburgh and sought to restrict the number authorised to appear before the Session to ten, thus releasing others to appear in the other courts of Edinburgh (RPS 1567/12/162).

judges of their competence[10]. The first sign of an organisation of these advocates is a mention in 1582 of Master John Sharp, 'dene of the advocattis of sessioun'[11]. Gradually they seem to have acquired a corporate identity and a monopoly of representation in the Court of Session. Their earliest extant minutes are of 1661[12], but the Faculty of Advocates had some form of existence as part of the College of Justice long before then – certainly by 1582, if not earlier[13].

Solicitors

14.3 The development of the advocates' profession is fairly simple to chart, as with the judges they have formed part of the College of Justice since its creation in 1532 and have thus been based (until recently) in Edinburgh. Solicitors on the other hand were and are to be found throughout Scotland and their corporate existence began as local societies of lawyers. Many of these still exist, but all practising solicitors must now be members of the Law Society of Scotland, which is the creation of statute.

The formation of societies of solicitors in the provincial towns is not well documented, except in Glasgow and Aberdeen. The term 'solicitor' is a relatively modern one. Lawyers in Glasgow specifically rejected it, preferring to be known as procurators, originally those who were licensed to appear before the Commissary Courts of the pre-Reformation Archdiocese of Glasgow. Reborn under a Charter of Queen Mary in 1563, the Commissary Court of Glasgow continued to dominate the legal life of the city. Lawyers in Glasgow, whether or not they regularly practised before the court, called themselves procurators and belonged to the Royal Faculty of Procurators in Glasgow, which still exists[14].

In Aberdeen the men of law called themselves advocates and belonged to the Society of Advocates in Aberdeen, which also still exists. It traces its origin to 1633 when the Sheriff of Aberdeen recognised 16 practitioners as being alone qualified to appear before

---

10 See generally Finlay, *Men of Law*.
11 RK Hannay *The College of Justice* p 144.
12 See The *Minute Book of the Faculty of Advocates* (Stair Society, vols 29, 32, 46, 53).
13 Generally on the development of the Faculty of Advocates see JW Cairns, 'History of the Faculty of Advocates to 1900', Stair Memorial Encyclopaedia vol 13 paras 1239-1285; J Finlay, *The Community of the College of Justice: Edinburgh and the Court of Session 1687–1808* (2012) ch 5.
14 See JS Muirhead *The Old Minute Book of the Faculty of Procurators in Glasgow*.

him, but a list of advocates going back to 1549 survives[15]. A society was formed in 1685 and it received Royal Charters in 1774, 1799 and 1862[16]. The Dundee Faculty of Procurators and Solicitors was incorporated by Royal Charter in 1819. The members of none of these bodies, despite their titles, concentrated exclusively on court practice, but it was the right to appear in court that gave them their standing.

At the level of the Supreme Courts in Edinburgh non-advocates were also becoming involved in procedures. Advocates drafted the written pleadings or allegations and arguments on which they were to base their oral representations, but these documents had to be sealed with the Royal Signet. The Clerks of the Signet received fees for this transaction, which continued until 1933. They formed the Society of Writers to the Signet, which is now an organisation of solicitors, mainly in Edinburgh, where it has a fine hall and library. The Society of Solicitors in the Supreme Courts had a less auspicious beginning in the throng of 'agents' as they called themselves who throughout the 17th century crowded the courts offering to help litigants with their cases. The advocates resented their intrusion and obtained several Acts against the agents. Eventually they were tolerated and by the mid-18th century individual agents were formally admitted to assist litigants before the Supreme Courts[17]. As the Society of Solicitors in the Supreme Courts of Scotland they now operate under private Acts of Parliament. They have no special privileges but speak for the interests of many of those solicitors in Edinburgh who regularly instruct advocates to appear on behalf of their clients and those of firms outside Edinburgh.

Another common ancestor of the modern Scottish solicitor is the medieval notary. Notaries were licensed by the Pope or the Holy Roman Emperor (and usually by both) to record transactions of legal significance. Their record was enough to prove that the transaction had taken place as stated. The office of notary was recognised in courts throughout Europe. A supplication to the Pope in 1425 complained that there were few notaries in Scotland, to the detriment of the people, especially when documents had to be authenticated by a notary in order to be sent to the courts in Rome. Six new notaries were then created who might be priests[18]. In 1469 King James III decided to remedy this shortage by taking powers as,

---

15 See article in (1969) 14 JLSS 325.
16 Collected in *Records of the Society of Advocates in Aberdeen* (New Spalding Club); Henderson Begg *Law Agents* p 12.
17 Henderson Begg *Law Agents* p 8.
18 Henderson Begg *Law Agents* p 10.

in effect, Emperor of Scotland to create notaries to operate within Scotland[19].

Notaries kept copies of all the deeds they drew up in what were called Protocol Books. These were preserved after the notary's death and formed a kind of public register and a safeguard against loss of or alterations to the originals. The many surviving ones give a vivid account of the variety of a notary's work[20]. The conveyancing and drafting side of the solicitor's work has its origin in the work of the notary. Their deeds still have international recognition. Until 1896 the office of notary was an additional qualification which many solicitors sought. Since then only enrolled solicitors have been eligible to become notaries. Most solicitors now do so[21].

There are thus two historic strands in the background of the present-day solicitor: admission by judges to provide services in their courts and the power to create authentic documents. Both of these privileges were sought by individuals. But there was no means of checking on the qualifications of those who applied and no means of training them. A first step towards remedying this deficiency was taken in 1825 when the Court of Session decreed that anyone seeking admission as a procurator before any court must first have served an apprenticeship for three years with a procurator, writer to the signet or solicitor.

There was still a lack of a prescribed curriculum and a means of testing proficiency in it. This was remedied in the Procurators (Scotland) Act 1865, which provided an easy means by which lawyers in every county could form an incorporated society. Having done so they were to hold examinations in general knowledge and law, with the approval of the local sheriff. But as the users of the law began to include companies and other organisations which operated nationally or in many localities, it was plainly unsatisfactory that the qualifications of new lawyers should be left to the initiative and variable competence of local societies. So, following a Royal Commission Report, their training and admission were closely regulated in the Law Agents (Scotland) Act 1873. Applicants for admission to a local society had to have served a five-year apprenticeship under a registered indenture or three years if they held a degree in arts or law. The

---

19 RPS 1469/20.

20 See, eg, *Selkirk Protocol Books 1511–1547* (Stair Society, vol 40).

21 The admission and regulation of notaries public is now controlled by the Solicitors (Scotland) Act 1980, Pt V, as amended by the Law Reform (Miscellaneous Provisions) (Scotland) Act 1990, s 37. On the history of notaries in Scotland, see J Finlay, 'The history of the notary in Scotland', in Schmoeckel and Schuber (eds), *Handbuch zur Geschichte des Notariats der europäischen Traditionem* (2009).

Court of Session would nominate examiners to hold examinations in general knowledge and law. A registrar was appointed to keep a roll of enrolled law agents. The universities which had played little part in the education of lawyers were now given a role, in that applicants, whether or not graduates, must have attended the classes of Scots law and conveyancing in a Scottish university.

The law agents as a whole had no voice. Having no collective say on who should be admitted to their number they were lacking in one of the essential indicators of a profession, which in the early 20th century they aspired to be. In 1933 by the Solicitors (Scotland) Act (giving official recognition to their now usual name) a General Council of Solicitors in Scotland was created, to be elected by all their local societies. It had power to hold examinations and to regulate the admission and enrolment of solicitors. It also made nominations to the Solicitors' Discipline (Scotland) Committee. In 1949, when a system of civil legal aid to help finance court actions was about to be introduced, it was decided that the legal profession should operate the scheme on behalf of the government. Yet the existing structure which did not represent all solicitors was felt to be inadequate. So a Law Society of Scotland was created by the Legal Aid and Solicitors (Scotland) Act 1949 to replace the General Council and exercise its powers and more. All solicitors wishing to practise as such must now hold a current practising certificate from it. The law concerning solicitors is to be found in the Solicitors (Scotland) Act 1980, which has been amended and supplemented by much recent legislation.

Thus, their separate histories explain the existence of two branches of the legal profession in Scotland. But they do not necessarily justify it. The advent of solicitor-advocates in the 1990s is one example of the drawing together of the two branches (as discussed later in this Chapter).

LAW AS A PROFESSION

14.4   From the standpoint of the state the main purveyors of legal services in Scotland are regarded as a single profession. The title of the Conservative Government's Consultation Paper of 1989 on the supply of legal services was *The Legal Profession in Scotland*, which it states 'comprises both solicitors and advocates'. In their responses to this document, which challenged many of their assumptions, the Faculty of Advocates and the Council of the Law Society of Scotland (speaking for solicitors) agreed that their members form two branches of the one profession.

But what is a profession? What justifies the use of this traditional title? Sociologists who range over the whole world in their scrutiny of societies find the term problematical, to the point of admitting defeat in trying to encapsulate the term in one meaning. But we can single out certain features of a profession as the term is habitually used in Scotland (and England too).

For our purposes a profession is taken to comprise those who possess a specialised body of knowledge and skills related to it. It sustains an organisation which enables it to define with greater precision that knowledge and those skills; to admit to its membership those who possess them to a sufficient degree; to impose on its members certain standards of behaviour; and to discipline those who fail to maintain them. The maintenance of these standards is regarded as a matter of such public benefit that the organisation is by law conceded certain privileges to be enjoyed by its members.

We shall examine each of these characteristics in turn, in relation to advocates and solicitors, and then look at the internal stresses and strains and the external pressures to which the legal profession is subject.

ORGANISATION OF THE LEGAL PROFESSION

Advocates

14.5   The Faculty of Advocates consists of those who have been admitted by the judges of the Court of Session to practise before it. They thereby have access to the other superior courts of Scotland, most importantly the High Court of Justiciary, the UK Supreme Court, the European Court of Human Rights and the Court of Justice of the European Union. They can also appear before all the lower courts of Scotland, but they share that right of access with solicitors. Certain solicitors may also appear in the superior courts[22].

The Faculty is in law a corporation, that is, it has a legal existence separate from that of its individual members. But it enjoys that status by custom. No statute created it. Nor does it have a written constitution. The conduct of its members was, until 1988, a matter of unwritten custom but is now governed by *Guide to the Professional Conduct of Advocates*, which, being available to the public, enables breaches of that conduct to be complained of[23].

---

22 See p 412 below.
23 A copy of the Guide is available on the Faculty of Advocates website: www. advocates.org.uk

There are around 460 practising members of the Faculty[24]. Each advocate practises on his or her own as a self-employed sole trader. Partnerships are not permitted[25]. Practising advocates are either seniors or juniors. They enter as juniors and after about 12 to 15 years of successful practice they may apply through the Lord President to be appointed by the Queen to the Roll of Queen's Counsel in Scotland, which, following English custom, was formed in 1897. As a QC or senior an advocate is entitled to require that he be accompanied by a junior to assist him in the conduct of a case, but need not be.

Advocates are to be found in and around the Advocates' Library in Parliament House, Edinburgh, where consulting rooms are available and at the High Court in Glasgow. Almost all advocates share in administrative support, clerking services and other communal provision through Faculty Services Limited, a company funded through a deduction to fees paid. Within this arrangement, advocates do form groups, called *stables*, each run by a separate clerking team who maintain the diaries of the members, receive instructions from solicitors and negotiate and collect fees[26]. More recently, these stables have been given greater freedom to develop their own identity and promote their members but the Faculty remains a single collegiate body rather than the *chambers* arrangements adopted by barristers in England where accommodation and overheads are shared by groups of barristers[27]. Negotiations on fees in Scotland are conducted by the stable clerks. Fees are unregulated, except by statutory instrument in civil and criminal legal aid cases, where it is the state that pays. But they should be 'reasonable'.

The Faculty is headed by its Dean, who is its elected leader and also makes rulings on professional conduct and has disciplinary powers and duties. He is assisted by an advisory Dean's Council. The other elected officers are the Vice-Dean, Clerk of Faculty, Keeper of the Library and Treasurer. They are elected at an annual meeting of

---

24 The Faculty of Advocates also includes many non-practising members. These may be retired advocates or those who have moved into other areas of legal practice or employment (including judges, sheriffs or academic lawyers). They take little or no part in the running of the Faculty.

25 Although this is no longer enforced by statute, the Faculty have so far been successful in persuading the Scottish Government to allow them to retain this restriction.

26 A small number of advocates have elected not to be part of this arrangement. They remain members of the Faculty.

27 Some of the stables describe themselves as chambers as this term is more familiar to those accustomed to the English system.

advocates held in January although, by convention, once elected they serve indefinite terms.

Solicitors

14.6 By law, all practising solicitors qualified in Scotland must be members of the Law Society of Scotland and hold a practising certificate. Around 10,000 solicitors hold a practising certificate.

The society is governed by its Council. This body, currently of 46 members, made up pre-dominantly of members elected from various geographical constituencies; there are also a small number of co-opted members to represent particular groups within the profession. Finally, nine lay members are appointed by Scottish Ministers to reflect the society's public regulatory role. Each year, the Council elects a President, who is the main spokesman of the Society, and a Vice-President, who usually becomes the next President.

The statutory objects of the Law Society include the promotion of '(a) the interests of the solicitors' profession in Scotland and (b) the interests of the public in relation to that profession'[28]. The Council conducts the business of the Society and, with the concurrence of the Lord President, the senior Scottish judge, can make regulations affecting its members, which have the force of law.

The Council puts much of its business through a plethora of committees and working parties which report to it. They are composed of Council members and others, the President and Vice-President being members of them all. Many of the committees have specific functions within the regulatory scheme of the profession and, by law, must contain a stipulated number of non-solicitor members to represent the public interest in the proper regulation of solicitors.

There are also other societies of solicitors, local and national, many of which pre-date the Law Society of Scotland and which carried out regulatory functions before the consolidation of the profession into a single national body. Membership is voluntary and members do not now have any public statutory privileges. They include the Scottish Law Agents Society, the Society of Writers to the Signet, the Society

---

28 Solicitors (Scotland) Act 1980, s 1(2). There is a body of opinion, both within and outwith the profession, that the dual functions of the Society, both regulating the profession but also representing the interests of the public, is a fundamental conflict of interest. In England and Wales, this function is split with the Law Society representing solicitors and the Solicitors Regulatory Authority performing the regulatory function.

of Solicitors in the Supreme Courts and local societies such as the Glasgow Bar Association and the Society of Advocates in Aberdeen.

Certain solicitors also have the additional qualification of being entitled to practise in the supreme courts and as such are known as solicitor-advocates[29].

Whilst advocates must practise alone, solicitors conduct their business in a variety of ways. As with other professional services firms, such as accountants, most firms of solicitors are partnerships (or, since their introduction, Limited Liability Partnerships (LLPs)). But solicitors may also practice as sole traders or, since 2001, as limited companies.

Prior to the entry into force of the Legal Services (Scotland) Act 2010, solicitors were not permitted to share income from fees with non-qualified individuals. This effectively prevented solicitors forming partnerships that included non-solicitors as partners, or working in companies not wholly owned by solicitors. The 2010 Act introduced a new class of licensed legal services provider. These providers are not subject to the same restrictions and may include non-solicitor partners or part-ownership by non-solicitors. These Alternative Business Structures (ABS) are intended to allow solicitors to form multi-disciplinary practices with other professionals, such as surveyors or accountants, or to take advantage of external capital investment as available to most other businesses. When initially proposed, this initiative was referred to as 'Tesco Law', reflecting the possibility that organisations such as supermarkets might seek to directly provide a legal services market as they have done in the banking sector. However, the eventual legislation was not as radical as some desired[30], and still limits non-solicitor involvement in licensed providers to a 49% interest, maintaining majority control by qualified solicitors of any legal services provider. Other regulatory safeguards, including a 'fit and proper person' test for non-solicitors involved in ownership of a licensed provider have also been put in place[31].

---

29 See para **14.10**.
30 The changes were driven in part by consumer organisations which felt that restrictions on business structures stifled innovation and reduced competitive pressures. The proposals were divisive within the profession but the eventual compromise position requiring majority ownership by solicitors was the position eventually adopted by the Law Society of Scotland.
31 At the time of writing, arrangements for regulating licensed legal service providers were only just being finalised, so no ABS had yet commenced trading. Opinion differs on whether these changes go too far, or do not go far enough; or whether the impact on the profession will be relatively limited, or lead to very significant changes in the way legal services are provided.

LEGAL EXPERTISE

14.7   The body of specialised knowledge which advocates and solicitors profess to have is the law of Scotland. This includes all law effective in Scotland, including European Union law. That includes both the substantive law and the procedural law. They should not advise on the law of any foreign jurisdiction – including that of England and Wales – unless they are qualified in it.

Advocates

14.8   Advocates tend to be ready to accept instructions on any branch of the law of Scotland. But, increasingly, many advocates specialise in particular areas as they increase in seniority and experience. Only a few work in both civil and criminal spheres. With some exceptions[32] they may receive instructions only from a solicitor, never directly from an individual client. They thus have no contractual relationship with the client, as the solicitor does. They have a professional loyalty to the client, but subject to the rules of professional practice, which include obligations to the court[33]. This has several consequences. They are not supposed to pick and choose among clients but should accept instructions when given, if free to do so and offered a reasonable fee, giving priority to the party who applies first. This is called the *cab-rank* rule and is intended to ensure that the expertise of the bar is equally available to all litigants, regardless of identity or ability to pay enhanced fees. Sometimes, of course, they are double-booked, for instance when a trial takes longer than expected. Then they will have to drop out of one commitment, often at very short notice, and the instructing solicitor will have to find a replacement.

Advocates have the right to appear in any court and tribunal within Scotland and long enjoyed a monopoly in representing clients in the Court of Session, High Court of Justiciary, and equivalent courts. They now have to share representation in the Scottish superior courts with Solicitor-Advocates. Members of Bars of European Union Member States may also appear in these courts, in conjunction with advocates and now qualified solicitors[34].

---

32 From public authorities, their heads and members, from legal professionals outside Scotland, from certain charities, voluntary bodies, trade unions and from specified professionals, including surveyors. More information is available from the Faculty website: www.advocates.org.uk
33 *Anderson v HM Advocate* 1996 JC 29 at 35.
34 European Communities (Services by Lawyers) Order 1978, SI 1978/1910.

As well as their public appearances in courts of all levels, advocates are frequently consulted on questions of doubt which have arisen in the course of legal practice; for example, on the legality of a proposed course of action or the meaning of a will or, most commonly, on the prospects of success in raising or defending an action. This is known as taking the opinion of counsel. The consultation is initiated by a written document, drafted by a solicitor, called a memorial, in which the facts are stated and copies of any documents are produced, possible legal authorities cited and then a number of questions posed. The advocate will answer these one by one, supporting his response by legal authority and argument. Advocates may also be consulted on the drafting and revision of documents intended to have legal effect, such as important contracts. Advocates frequently also take part in arbitrations, which are hearings of disputes by an arbiter in private, according to procedure agreed by the parties and at a time and place to suit them. They may also be instructed to represent interested parties at public inquiries including planning applications.

Solicitors

14.9 Solicitors are sometimes described as the general practitioners of the law. This is true to the extent that they are often the first point of contact for a member of the public with a legal question. But most solicitors are not generalists and they are warned in their Code of Conduct not to undertake work for which they lack the necessary knowledge and experience[35]. Whilst many of the biggest firms will offer a full service across all areas of law and client groups, the vast bulk of their business will be for their commercial and corporate clients, rather than individuals, whilst each individual area of law will be dealt with by specialists in that area. Smaller firms often specialise in particular aspects of law such as family or employment law or the buying and selling of houses. This specialism is most apparent in the divide between civil and criminal law, with most criminal defence work conducted by smaller firms which deal with this work exclusively or nearly exclusively. Away from the big towns and cities, the volume of work will be lower, so firms are often smaller but tend to be more generalist.

Much of a solicitor's work is non-contentious. They provide advice and assistance on legal matters to ensure transactions are conducted in accordance with the law and in a manner that avoids

---

35 As discussed below under *Standards of Conduct*.

legal doubt or dispute. In some areas, the law is relatively clear and work can be routinised in a standard set of steps. In these areas, *paralegals*, who are not qualified solicitors, may carry out much of the work, under the supervision of a qualified solicitor. Very many solicitors' firms engage in the buying and selling of property, both residential and commercial, and in drawing up the documents of offer and acceptance, called missives, the deed of transfer called the disposition, and the security, if any, over the property which enables the transaction to be financed. These and certain less frequent property transactions are called *conveyancing*. Nearly all also deal with *executry*, the distribution of the estates of deceased people, which sometimes leads to the setting up and administration of a trust, under which assets are held for the benefit of someone or some public purpose. Many will form companies for clients. This often leads to advising on all aspects of the law as it affects companies. Many are now also licensed under the relevant financial services schemes to advise on financial investments, with their tax implications. Commercial law firms advise business parties on their transactions and the management of such assets as intellectual property, as well as preparing any necessary documentation (which may be voluminous and call for careful legal analysis in high value deals). Some firms avoid court work, some do it when their established clients require it, and a minority engage in it in a substantial way. Solicitors who have acquired expertise by specialising in a particular branch of law may apply to have this recognised by the Law Society by being known as Accredited Specialists. They include agricultural law, child law, employment law, intellectual property, medical negligence law and pensions law. Holders of these qualifications are available to advise their fellow solicitors in their area of expertise.

Many solicitors also qualify as notaries public, for which no extra training or qualification is necessary. The notary public was originally a separate branch of the legal profession; more recently, only qualified solicitors can gain this status. Notaries public perform such functions as receiving under oath written statements called affidavits which form the basis of the evidence in undefended divorces; receiving sworn statements from executors as to the items of property left by deceased persons; and drawing up and signing wills and other documents for blind people. Because of the international credibility of notaries they may also be asked by foreigners in Scotland to deal with documents under foreign legal systems[36].

---

36 See Brand 'The Modern Notary in Scotland' 1997 JLSS 50.

The traditional way in which legal disputes are settled is by the judgment of a court[37]. Recently, much attention has been given to Alternative Dispute Resolution (ADR) which can include arbitration, mediation and conciliation, among others. Especially given the high costs, risks and publicity of the legal process, solicitors have increasingly been offering these alternative routes to resolving disputes; many of these require additional training and certification.

Solicitor-advocates

14.10 Solicitors may appear in any sheriff or district court and tribunal in Scotland. Before 1993, solicitors could not appear in the High Court of Justiciary, the Court of Session and other superior courts, though they were usually much involved in the preparation of cases in these courts and would sit in court, while their client was represented by an advocate.

But solicitors with five years' continuous experience of court work may now apply to practise in the superior civil or criminal courts or both. They must undergo an induction course, observe cases in the appropriate court(s), attend (subject to certain exemptions) a training course in the work of the courts, and pass examinations on subjects related to practice in the superior courts[38]. When appearing in court, solicitor-advocates enjoy the same professional responsibilities and privileges as advocates although they remain regulated by the Law Society of Scotland.

TRAINING FOR AND ADMISSION TO THE LEGAL PROFESSION

The Route to Qualification as a Solicitor

14.11 Admission as a solicitor is controlled by the Law Society of Scotland as the profession's regulator[39]. The normal route requires a three stage process of education and training known as *Professional Education and Training* (PEAT).

---

37 See Ch 4.
38 For more information, see the website of the Society of Solicitor Advocates: www.solicitoradvocates.org.
39 The regulations are contained in the Admission as a Solicitor (Scotland) Regulations 2011. Reference should be made to the Law Society of Scotland website for further information: www.lawscot.org.uk.

The foundation programme for PEAT is usually achieved by studying for a degree in law (LLB) at an accredited Scottish University. The degree programme must include certain core subjects of Scots Law[40]. The degree is usually taken as an Honours degree although, for students who have an honours degree in another subject, a 2 year long ordinary LLB is available.

The first stage after the foundation phase is known as PEAT1 and is to complete the postgraduate Diploma in Professional Legal Practice (DPLP). This one year course is designed to act as a bridge to the profession and involves students learning to apply legal principles in a practical context. The DPLP also involves introductory teaching on many of the more procedural elements of legal practice and the basics of professional ethics and conduct. Students are also introduced to the more general professional skills, such as client interviewing and negotiation, which they will be expected to develop as solicitors.

The final stage, PEAT2, consists of on-the-job training whilst working in an approved legal office under a two-year training contract. In larger firms this will often consist of three or four *seats*, placements in different areas of the firm to provide exposure to various areas of law. As well as training and mentoring provided by the employing firm, trainees must complete a set amount of *Trainee Continuous Professional Development* (TCPD). The competence of trainees is assessed on a six-monthly basis and reported on through a log book maintained by the trainees and their supervisors.

In addition to the professional training requirements, an aspiring solicitor must demonstrate that they are a 'fit and proper person' to be admitted as a solicitor. Criminal convictions must be declared and a Disclosure Scotland form must be completed. Satisfactory completion of these checks will result in issue of an *Entrance Certificate*; this must be held before commencement of the PEAT2 traineeship. Admission as a solicitor normally occurs at the half-way point of the traineeship where, subject to satisfactory progress, a *Restricted Practising Certificate* will be granted. On successful completion of the traineeship, a full *Practising Certificate* marks qualification as a solicitor.

In general, studying for the LLB is covered by the same student support and funding arrangements that apply to study of any first

---

40 Including: the Scottish legal system; obligations (contract, unjustified enrichment and delict); family law; EU Law; public and constitutional law; company and commercial law; criminal law; the law of evidence; succession law; trust law; property law. Each University will divide these subject areas differently.

degree[41]. This will not be the case for graduates studying for the two-year ordinary LLB; fees for this degree must be met by the students themselves. Currently, Scottish domiciled students are entitled to a small loan towards part of the fees of the DPLP; but no student loans for support are available. A small number of the larger commercial firms recruit trainees prior to commencement of the DPLP and a minority of these will offer their prospective trainees some assistance with DPLP fees. Otherwise, commercial loans or family funding will be required to pay for the costs of this year of study.

The traineeship is not employment but training[42]. Trainees must, however, be paid[43]; the Law Society of Scotland specifies a recommended salary for each year of the traineeship. This is just a recommendation although some larger commercial firms and public bodies pay more. Once discharged as a trainee, newly qualified solicitors must then seek employment (or, in principle, form their own firm) and a training contract does not guarantee employment with the firm providing the training.

The Route to Qualification as an Advocate

14.12 In general terms, those aspiring to become advocates must generally first qualify as a solicitor[44]. In recent years, the great majority of those seeking to become advocates will first have worked as solicitors for at least a short period[45]. The Faculty of Advocates requires some additional subjects to have been studied at degree level[46] but otherwise the academic requirement is the same. Successful completion of the DPLP and the traineeship is also

---

41 Hence, arrangements differ for Scottish students, those from the rest of the UK, those from EU countries, and those from non-EU countries.

42 The Law Society of Scotland states that it is therefore not possible to make a trainee redundant.

43 This is a relatively recent innovation although, historically, most traineeships were paid. The Law Society of Scotland will refuse to register any traineeship that does not pay at least the national minimum wage.

44 The full regulations are contained in *Regulations as to Intrants*, available on the Faculty of Advocates website: www.advocates.org.uk.

45 The situation is very different in England, where a student will generally decide after graduating whether to train as a barrister or as a solicitor; although transfer between the branches of the profession is possible.

46 Specifically, International Private Law and Roman Law (sometimes taught as Civil Law). With appropriate choice of subjects, these can normally be studied within the LLB syllabus or taken at a later date, including during the DPLP and traineeship. The Faculty of Advocates also sets its own exams in these subjects but no tuition is provided.

required[47]. The intending advocate then has to spend a further nine months approximately as a *devil*[48], learning from and assisting an established advocate. Prior to this period he or she has to pass the Faculty's examination in evidence, practice and procedure. During devilling, he or she will also undertake the Faculty's intensive skills programme.

Devils receive no payment although there is no charge for the nine months of professional training or the Faculty skills course.

Alternative Routes to Qualification

14.13 A number of alternative routes to qualification exist. For both solicitors and advocates, there are complex rules for transferring between branches of the profession, between jurisdictions in the UK and between jurisdictions in the EU and elsewhere.

In addition, the Law Society of Scotland sets its own examinations, completion of which will satisfy the academic requirements normally met by the LLB, where a candidate has also completed a special 3 year pre-diploma training contract. The PEAT1, DPLP and PEAT2 traineeship must still be completed.

Flexible study options are available for the LLB, including several part-time options and a distance-learning option. The DPLP can be taken part-time over 2 years, rather than the normal one year course.

REGULATION OF THE LEGAL PROFESSION

14.14 As with many professions, the legal profession remains largely self-regulating; that is, the standards of professional conduct and performance are enforced by the membership of the profession, acting through the professional body. As with other systems of self-regulation, these standards and procedures have become increasingly formalised and transparent. This section will discuss the standards of conduct for legal professionals, the formal methods of complaint

---

47 Technically, the Faculty of Advocates requires only a 21 month traineeship, a period which may be reduced to as little as 12 months for those with the highest academic results. It used to be common for aspiring advocates to take advantage of this route. However, in recent years, only one firm of solicitors has been willing to offer this specialist, shorter traineeship.

48 The word *devil* probably originates from the archaic use of the word to refer to an apprentice in some trades. The English term pupillage is sometimes used in preference, including in the Faculty's own *Regulations as to Intrants*.

and redress, disciplinary procedures and the possibility of pursuing redress through legal action.

Professional Standards

14.15 Solicitors are regulated under the Law Society of Scotland Practice Rules 2011. These form part of a comprehensive set of documentation called *Rules and Guidance*, which covers both fundamental rules of standards of conduct and client care, detailed rules on work of a particular nature and best practice advice on general and particular topics[49]. In particular, Rule B1 covers the key elements of a solicitor's professional conduct including: trust and integrity; independence; acting in the interests of the client; avoiding conflicts of interest; confidentiality; and relationship to the courts.

The concept of providing adequate professional services is extensively defined. It includes the requirement not to undertake work unless the entrant can perform it adequately. That means they must have the requisite legal knowledge and skill, be able to complete the work within a reasonable period of time, and communicate effectively with the client and others. Having once undertaken work, they must not withdraw from it without good cause and, if the matter is before a court, normally with the agreement of the court.

A *Code of Conduct for Criminal Work* forms part of Section F of the Practice Rules. It is supplemented by a Scottish Legal Aid Board Code of Practice affecting those solicitors who are registered to provide legal services remunerated by Criminal Legal Aid[50]. This stipulates in detail the manner in which these services are to be provided and the records which are to be kept.

Solicitors frequently hold significant amounts of money on behalf of clients. Detailed financial and accounting rules are also laid out in the Practice Rules, reflecting the need for strict procedures to safeguard these funds from misuse, especially in insolvency situations. The Law Society of Scotland administers a financial compliance regime which includes regular returns, audits and inspections of a solicitor's handling of client money. In extreme cases, the Society can apply to the courts for the imposition of a Judicial Factor to

---

49 An online version of the Rules and Guidance is available on the Law Society of Scotland website: www.lawscot.org.uk. A comprehensive hard-copy compilation of related legislation, and the Rules and Guidance, is published by W Green as Section F of the *Parliament House Book* and, separately, as the *Solicitors Professional Handbook*.

50 See para **14.19**.

administer the financial affairs of a solicitor or firm, in order to safeguard clients' funds.

For advocates, standards of professional conduct are laid down in the Faculty of Advocate's *Guide to the Professional Conduct of Advocates*[51]. This publication sets out the status, rights and obligations of an advocate; the general principles of professional conduct; and the advocate's duties towards fellow advocates, the instructing solicitor, the client and the court. Detailed guidance is also provided on issues such as feeing, confidentiality, advertising, dress and continuous professional development[52].

Complaints, Redress and Discipline

14.16 Where a client, or another person, believes a lawyer has failed to deliver an adequate service or has fallen below the standards of conduct required by the profession, a formal system of investigation and redress exists.

The basic principle is that complaints should be dealt with directly between the practitioners in question and the dissatisfied client. Under the Law Society Practice Rules, all practitioners and firms must have established complaints procedures and a named Client Relations Partner. If a complaint is not resolved to a client's satisfaction, the Scottish Legal Complaints Commission (SLCC) has been established by statute as a body independent of both government and the profession, to investigate and determine complaints and provide redress[53]. Where a complaint is solely related to the level of fees charged, a separate procedure, administered through the Law Society of Scotland, will allow the fees to be challenged and assessed, either an adjudicator appointed by the Society (known as *determination*) or directly, or on appeal from determination, by the Auditor of Court, an official of the Court of Session whose remit is

---

51 Available from the Faculty's website: www.advocates.org.uk.
52 Prior to 1988, standards of conduct were set informally and by convention. This approach is still reflected in the introductory line of the *Guide to the Professional Conduct of Advocates*, which states 'the work of an Advocate is essentially the work of an individual practitioner whose conscience, guided by the advice of his seniors, is more likely to tell him how to behave than any book of rules'.
53 The SLCC was introduced by the Legal Profession and Legal Aid (Scotland) Act 2007, replacing the Scottish Legal Services Ombudsman. Although independent of the profession, the SLCC is entirely funded by an annual levy paid by each practising lawyer (or on their behalf by their firm). More information is available on the SLCC website: www.scottishlegalcomplaints.org.uk.

to resolve disputes over legal costs. Assessment of fees by the Auditor of Court is known as *taxation*.

Where the SLCC receives an eligible[54] complaint, it will first determine whether the complaint is related to the standard of service required or to the personal or professional conduct of the lawyer concerned. The former, known as *service complaints*, will be considered by the SLCC itself. The latter, *conduct complaints*, are not dealt with by the SLCC but are referred to the Disciplinary Committee of the Law Society of Scotland, or the Dean of the Faculty of Advocates, as appropriate.

For service complaints, the SLCC may offer mediation in an attempt to resolve a complaint. Otherwise, an SLCC investigator will examine the complaint, calling for evidence, if necessary. The investigator will then report their findings and propose a settlement. This may be agreed between the parties without further procedure or, if agreement on the report cannot be reached, will be placed before a Determination Committee, made up of members of the Commission[55]. The Committee's determination is final, subject to appeal to the Court of Session. Where a complaint is upheld, the sanctions may be: an order reducing the client's bill, including a reduction to nil; an order requiring specific action or to rectify errors or omissions at the practitioner's own expense; a requirement to pay compensation of up to £20,000 for loss, inconvenience or distress. If issues of competence or conduct are raised, then the SLCC may also refer the matter to the professional body as a conduct complaint.

For solicitors, conduct complaints referred to the Law Society of Scotland will be investigated by the Society's Complaints Investigation Team. A report will then be submitted to a Professional Conduct Sub-Committee[56]. Where a complaint is upheld, it may be categorised as *unsatisfactory professional conduct* and dealt with by the Sub-Committee, who have power to censure solicitors, require

---

54 Complaints may be ineligible if, among other factors, they are: premature (made before the practitioner has had a fair opportunity to respond directly to the client); not made within certain time limits (although waivers may be granted); the subject of the complaint is outside the SLCC jurisdiction; or the complaint is 'vexatious, frivolous or totally without merit'.

55 The commissioners are between seven and fifteen strong and are appointed by the Scottish Ministers. The commissioners will always include both legally qualified and lay members, but lay members will always be in the majority and the Chair will always be a lay member.

56 In principle, this is a sub-committee of the Council of the Law Society of Scotland but these sub-committees always contain an equal balance between legally qualified members and lay members, who are co-opted to represent the public interest.

them to undertake specified education or training, pay a fine of up to £2,000, or pay compensation of up to £5,000. In more serious cases of *professional misconduct*, the Law Society of Scotland report a solicitor to the Scottish Solicitors' Disciplinary Tribunal (SSDT). This tribunal has powers to strike-off solicitors, suspend or impose restrictions on practising certificates and impose fines of up to £10,000[57]. The SSDT will also hear appeals against decisions of the Professional Conduct Sub-Committees and consider the cases of solicitors convicted of crimes involving dishonesty.

The Faculty of Advocates administers a similar system for conduct complaints against advocates. A Complaints Committee, with two members each from the Faculty and a panel of lay members appointed by the Scottish Ministers, performs an equivalent role to the Professional Conduct Sub-Committee and can impose various sanctions including censures, fines, compensation orders and suspension for up to one year. A Disciplinary Tribunal, chaired by a retired Judge or Sheriff appointed by the Lord President and consisting of two members of the Faculty of Advocates and three lay members nominated by Scottish Ministers, considers more serious cases and can impose sanctions including permanent expulsion from the Faculty[58].

Where a complainer is unsatisfied with the actions taken by either professional body following a conduct complaint, they are able to raise a separate handling complaint to the SLCC for the action taken by the professional body to be investigated.

Civil Liability of Legal Services Providers

14.17 Solicitors, in common with other professional people, are bound to exercise the standard of skill and care which can reasonably be expected of a competent practitioner in their profession. If they do not, they may be sued for consequential loss, certainly by a client, and possibly by affected third parties as well[59]. Delay in performing legal transactions is the commonest form of such negligence: for example, failing to raise an action for damages for personal injuries within three years, failing to make an application for unfair dismissal compensation within three months, failing to register security

---

57 More information, and copies of the findings of tribunals, is available on the SSDT website: www.ssdt.org.uk
58 The Faculty of Advocate's *Disciplinary Rules* are available on the Faculty website: www.advocates.org.uk.
59 See *The Laws of Scotland: Stair Memorial Encyclopaedia* vol 13, para 1189.

documents. As well as such negligence, deliberate fault, such as fraud, will give rise to a claim for compensation.

Although a claim against a solicitor may eventually have to be decided in court, the great majority are settled by negotiation, under the threat of court action. Since November 1978 the Law Society has required all its members to be covered by a Master Policy of professional indemnity insurance, thus ensuring that legitimate claims will be met. Proof that the premium has been paid must be exhibited each October when applications for renewal of the practising certificate are made. The number and size of claims has soared and so inevitably there have been regular increases in the premiums. Premiums are calculated on a complex formula related to number of partners and staff. To encourage care, there is a low claims discount financed out of loadings on the premiums of those who have had above average claims. There is also an excess per partner, a sum which must be paid by the insured before the liability takes effect. The insurers are advised by a panel of solicitors on the more difficult claims, for it is by the standards of the average competent solicitor that liability is established.

The Law Society of Scotland is also legally obliged to maintain the *Guarantee Fund*, out of which grants of compensation may be made to people who have suffered loss because of the dishonesty of solicitors where there is no other way of recovering the money[60]. The dishonesty may, but need not, have led to a criminal conviction. The scheme is a last resort, so any other remedies have to be pursued first. This Guarantee Fund is maintained by annual contributions from solicitors, plus levies to meet exceptionally large claims and borrowing.

By comparison with those against solicitors, the remedies of clients against advocates are less. This is because, when appearing in court, the advocate owes his duty to the court and must be independent of his client[61].

However, it now seems clear that advocates can be liable in negligence for actions out of court. Recent cases have seemed to indicate that the immunities previously enjoyed by advocates in court

---

60 Solicitors (Scotland) Act 1980, s 43.
61 The classic expression of this rule is in the case of *Batchelor v Pattison & Mackersy* (1876) 3 R 914, where Lord President Inglis stated of advocates: 'His legal right is to conduct the cause without any regard to the wishes of his client, so long as his mandate is unrecalled, and what he does *bona fide* according to his own judgment will bind his client, and will not expose him to any action for what he has done, even if the client's interests are thereby prejudiced.'

may be further restricted[62]. Certainly, advocates are now obliged by the Faculty of Advocates to obtain insurance against claims for negligence.

LEGAL AID

14.18 Pursuing or defending legal action can be an extremely expensive business. Yet, the rule of law requires that all who need to, have access to justice and the courts to bring or defend cases.

To provide access to the legal system for those who could otherwise not afford it, legal aid provides state funding for various legal activities for those determined to be eligible. Assistance with the costs of litigation can be traced back to the Poor's Roll, which came into being in 1424 and under which legal professionals gave their services free-of-charge. State funding of legal services replaced this system in 1950 (1964 for criminal cases).

The Forms of Legal Assistance

14.19 Legal Aid may be provided in various forms, collectively described as *legal assistance*, but all are administered by the Scottish Legal Aid Board (SLAB), a body operating in accordance with the rules and regulations formulated by the Scottish Government[63]. The various forms of legal assistance are:

- **Advice and Assistance**. *Advice and Assistance* helps pay for advice from a solicitor on any aspect of Scots law or assistance with a legal matter that does not require an appearance in court. This can include initial discussions and investigations to establish whether a client has a valid case which can be pursued and negotiations to resolve or settle a case out of court. Advice and Assistance also applies in criminal cases, so may include advising a client as to whether to accept a fixed penalty or advising a client not in custody

---

62 In *Arthur JS Hall & Co v Simons* [2002] 1 AC 615, Lord Hope, a former Lord President, speaking *obiter* in a House of Lords case, opined that the 'core forensic immunity' (as to conduct in court) should remain in criminal cases in which the advocate might be harassed by a client who might well be 'devious, vindictive and unscrupulous'. However, in civil cases he regarded the core immunity as 'disproportionate' though it might be difficult to prove negligence.
63 The regulations on Legal Aid are complex and detailed. Further information can be obtained from the SLAB website: www.slab.org.uk.

- **Civil Legal Aid**. *Civil Legal Aid* pays towards the cost of preparing and pursuing a civil case in the courts. A system of *Children's Legal Aid* provides free advice and representation to children and adults involved in Children's Hearings where the Children's Panel considers that the case is sufficiently serious or where legal representation is required to permit that child or adult to participate fully in the hearing.
- **Police Station Duty Scheme**. Where a suspect is detained by the police, they must receive legal advice before interview[64]. This may be provided by a duty solicitor or, provided that tight time limits can be met, a named solicitor. Attendance (or telephone advice) is funded by SLAB.
- **The Duty Solicitor Scheme**. When an accused person is held in custody, or released from custody by the police on an *undertaking*, before their first appearance in court, they are entitled to make free use of a duty solicitor assigned to that court[65]. This entitlement extends to sentencing following a plea of guilty, or the setting of dates for future diets following a plea of not guilty.
- **Assistance by Way of Representation (ABWOR)**. Where an accused has an existing professional relationship with a lawyer, they may elect to be represented by that lawyer rather than the duty solicitor. Legal Aid will fund this assistance through the ABWOR scheme.
- **Criminal Legal Aid**. This covers the cost of preparing an accused person's defence and providing representation in court.

Most legal assistance is provided by solicitors in private practice who then claim payment from SLAB. But SLAB also funds the Public Defence Solicitors Office (PDSO) and the Civil Legal Assistance Office (CLAO) which employ solicitors to deliver elements of legal assistance in some geographical areas alongside solicitors in private practice. Although funded differently, clients receive the same level of service and, where appropriate, are required to make the same contributions, when dealing with PDSO and CLAO as they would when dealing with solicitors in private practice.

---

64 This was introduced into Scottish criminal procedure following the landmark Supreme Court case of *Cadder v HMA* [2010] UKSC 43, 2011 SC (UKSC) 13, and the subsequent legislation.
65 There are some minor differences between the legal aid rules in summary and solemn procedure.

Eligibility and Contributions

14.20 With the exception of representation through the duty solicitor scheme and advice to persons in custody, all legal aid is provided only to those who meet certain eligibility criteria. The main tests are:

- **Financial Eligibility.** With the exceptions above, all legal aid is subject to means testing. Above certain income levels, legal aid will not be available. At lower levels of income, clients will be expected to contribute to the cost of the legal services they are using. As with any means-testing, the rules are complex and the thresholds are subject to regular adjustment and different for each type of legal assistance. In civil cases, legal aid will not be provided if equivalent help is available from other sources, such as a trade union, professional body or insurance company.
- **Interests of Justice**. In criminal cases, the seriousness of the offence charged or the complexity of the case must justify the provision of legally qualified assistance and representation. For solemn cases, or where an accused person is in custody, this is assumed; for summary cases, a detailed statutory test applies which involves consideration of the consequences of conviction, the complexity and nature of the case and the ability of the accused to appear unrepresented[66]. For civil cases, the equivalent test is that the client has both *probable cause* (that is, a sufficient prospect of success to justify bringing the case) and that, in the circumstances, it would be reasonable to bring the action[67].

In addition to possibly paying contributions towards the cost of legal aid, successful legally aided clients in civil actions may be subject to *clawback*, where SLAB will seek to recover the net costs paid out in legal aid, after any expenses covered by the losing side, from the amount won in the case.

The grant of legal aid also has implications for the opponent of a legally aided person. In the event the legally aided person loses

---

66 The test is set out in the Legal Aid (Scotland) Act 1986 s 23(3). Factors that will be taken into account include: the possibility of loss of liberty or livelihood; whether questions of law and evidence are involved; whether the accused is prohibited by law from questioning witnesses; and any inability of the accused to understand the proceedings due to incapacity, language difficulties or mental health issues.
67 For instance, civil legal aid will not be granted to pursue an action for payment against someone who has no prospect of paying or if the case would cost more to pursue than it is worth.

their case, legal aid will not pay towards the expenses of a successful opponent unless it would cause 'severe financial hardship' not to do so; however a losing, legally assisted person will be unable to meet any award of expenses against them[68].

Problems with Legal Aid

14.21 The provision and level of legal aid has been a frequent source of conflict between the legal profession and the government. Many solicitors, especially in larger firms, have ceased to deliver any services under legal aid arrangements as the rates paid by SLAB are far lower than can be charged in normal private practice[69]. Many solicitors also find the administrative and record-keeping requirements imposed by SLAB overly onerous and costly, given the relatively low value of claims involved. And where, in some cases, block fees that do not require complex record keeping are available, the fees arguably do not reflect the actual time taken to complete the work properly.

The financial thresholds at which legal aid is withdrawn, or subject to contributions, also leaves a potential gap between those who are insufficiently poor to obtain legal aid, but insufficiently wealthy to contemplate the expense of bringing legal action[70].

ALTERNATIVE DELIVERY OF LEGAL SERVICES

14.22 The legal profession is the most conspicuous provider of legal services. However, solicitors and law firms are not charities but businesses and therefore must concentrate on activities that generate profits, without which lawyers would not remain in business. Many

---

68 This means that, even where successful, litigants such as insurers in personal injury cases will generally be unable to recover any expenses, even if they successfully defend this case. This arguably leads to an incentive to settle cases out of court even in unmeritorious cases, to save on legal expenses.

69 Dependent on one's point of view, this may simply be that legal aid work is insufficiently lucrative; or that the fees are set at such a low level that they do not even cover the legitimate costs of delivering the services.

70 At the time of writing, Government proposals to introduce contributions towards criminal legal aid for all except those on the lowest incomes, and to require solicitors to collect those contributions (bearing the risk of non-payment) have resulted in unprecedented industrial action by criminal defence solicitors. Nevertheless the scheme has been enacted under the Scottish Civil Justice Council and Criminal Legal Assistance Act 2013.

firms inevitably concentrate on those services such as conveyancing, financial services, commercial transactions, and the distribution of the assets of the deceased.

But need for legal services is not limited to these issues. And there may be many other factors that mean potential clients are unwilling or unable to obtain legal advice or assistance direct from a solicitor. This may be as simple as the lack of a solicitor local to a remote rural area or a public perception that lawyers are expensive or unwilling to deal with small cases. The relatively low income thresholds for the withdrawal of legal aid also potentially creates a whole category of the public who are unable to afford to pursue legal remedies to which they may otherwise be entitled.

Whilst many solicitor firms have attempted to address some of these access to justice issues through, for example, the provision of basic legal information on their websites or through offering free or reduced-price initial consultations, other means of delivering legal services are extremely important in helping to meet these gaps in provision. These include:

- **Advice Centres**. Arguably, advice centres, such as Citizens' Advice Bureaux (CAB), are the single largest provider of basic legal services. They are generally funded by local authorities or specific government funding to deliver basic advice and assistance to the public, especially to disadvantaged communities. They are often managed by full-time employees but typically rely on trained volunteers to deliver most advice. The majority of enquiries at advice centres have some level of legal involvement: debt issues, problems with benefits, housing, employment and family breakdown. Most will be answered on the basis of a basic knowledge of the relevant law, in which advisers are trained. More complex legal issues, or those requiring the involvement of a qualified solicitor, may be referred to a local firm of solicitors although, frequently, solicitors will run clinics within the advice centre itself, usually drawing on the Advice and Assistance scheme and sometimes working on a *pro bono* basis[71]. Some advice centre volunteers also receive special training to provide representation at certain tribunals, such as Employment Tribunals or summary cause

---

71 *Pro bono* is the Latin term used to describe lawyers providing qualified advice or assistance without charge. Many solicitors' firms and the Faculty of Advocates encourage lawyers to provide some *pro bono* work and some provide schemes through which this can be done as part of their Corporate Social Responsibility commitments.

hearings in the Sheriff Court, where this is permitted.

- **Law Centres**. Law centres are non-profit-making charitable bodies, staffed by legally qualified staff and support staff. They exist to make up the lack of traditional legal services in deprived areas and concentrate on the branches of the law that could most benefit the residents of such areas, such as social security, housing, consumer protection and immigration. They generally depend on local and central government access to justice or social inclusion funding to cover the majority of their costs. As well as advising individuals and groups, they give training to other users of the law, such as tenants' associations and disabled groups, and they raise awareness of the law and legal issues among residents generally. Some strive to change the law to the benefit of disadvantaged people by taking up test cases or campaigning for reforms in statutory law and law enforcement. Other law centres focus on a particular client groups (including the Ethnic Minorities Law Centre or the Scottish Child Law Centre) or specific areas of law (such as the Legal Services Agency which operates a specialist unit covering mental health law).

- **Trade Unions and Professional Bodies**. Many trade unions and professional bodies provide legal services for their members, either through their own staff or by standing arrangements with certain firms of solicitors to provide a free interview for members with any legal problem, whether or not related to employment. Often, the union or professional body will also assist with financing action related to employment.

- **Insurance Policies**. Certain insurance policies include the provision of legal advice by telephone or, in certain circumstances, the costs of taking legal action. Similar cover may be available as a benefit of certain membership organisations or other products such as premium bank accounts.

- **University Law Clinics**. Many of the Scottish Universities provide law clinics which operate on a similar basis to advice centres but use volunteer law students, working under the supervision of qualified lawyers (usually working on a *pro bono* basis) to provide an initial consultation and basic legal advice or assistance. This provides a valuable learning opportunity for students whilst delivering public benefit. At some universities participation in a clinic is a requirement of the course.

- **Specialist Executry and Conveyancing Practitioners**. Historically, solicitors held a monopoly on the provision of executry and conveyancing services. In an attempt to increase competition, it became possible to train and register to deliver executry or conveyancing services without being otherwise legally qualified. It was intended that this would introduce competition to the market for these services and drive down costs to the consumer. However, there have never been more than a handful of these specialist practitioners operating in Scotland.

Note should also be taken in this context of the *speculative action*. It is unlawful for an advocate (or solicitor) to enter an agreement with a client to be paid a proportion of, and out of, the proceeds of an action. This is however widely used in the United States, where the arrangement is known as a *contingency fee*. In Scotland, it is permissible for an advocate or solicitor to agree to provide services on the basis of payment if the action is successful. There must be a reasonable prospect of success. This is called a 'speculative action'. It is permissible by this means for the lawyer's agreed fee to be raised by up to 100 per cent.

15   Law reform

WHY LAW REFORM?

15.1   To be effective a law must be capable of being discovered and understood, so that people can know what is required of them. But there is no point in a law having these attributes if it is incapable of meeting changing human needs and wants or is plainly out of date. So an efficient law system must make provision for its own development. There has to be a mechanism for making brand-new laws, repealing outdated laws, and amending laws that are no longer able to achieve their goals.

Most changes in the law are of a minor character, adding to what is there already. A section in an Act turns out to be ambiguous and courts are interpreting it in different ways. Or it has left a loop-hole of which people, perhaps tax-payers or motorists, are taking advantage. The Misuse of Drugs Act 1971 has a provision enabling new drugs to be added to the list of controlled drugs by a resolution of both Houses of the UK Parliament. The highest court may resolve the problem by upholding one of the conflicting interpretations applied in lower courts. Or a department of government may secure an amendment of an unsatisfactory section by Parliament.

Apart from such deliberate changes, whenever existing law is applied by a court to new circumstances and a reasoned judgment is delivered and published, the law has been developed, even if only to a trivial extent. We can call this normal legal development. The law never stands still. It is always on the move, as it keeps being applied to new situations.

However, a law system should be capable of striking off in new directions or making a fresh start to some outmoded form of regulation. This is law reform and it is usually confined to the enacted law that Parliament produces, though occasionally judges can engage in law reform in what turns out to have been a dramatic way. Thus, in *Stallard (or S) v HM Advocate* 1989 SLT 469, 1989 SCCR 248 the judges decided that a wife could no longer be said to surrender herself to her husband's sexual demands. They were equal partners and he could be charged with raping her, as with any other person. Law reform is usually prompted by some assumptions as to what is right or good or necessary and thus to reflect a presumed social need. But sometimes, as in laws against racial and sexual discrimination, the law has an educative role and sets new standards that are in advance of social behaviour.

PRESSURES FOR LAW REFORM

Technological change

15.2   What are the cues that signal a need for law reform? Perhaps the most tangible is when some new technology or technique becomes available that has a potential for harm as well as good. The most obvious example is the advent and expansion of motor traffic, which revolutionised the transport of goods and people, but at the cost of killing and maiming many road users. A vast array of laws and regulations has been devised to try to contain these unwanted consequences. The introduction of a 30mph speed limit in built-up areas in 1934 was followed by a dramatic drop in road deaths. The advent of the breathalyser in the Road Safety Act 1967, now followed, under the Road Traffic Act 1988, ss 6 to 8, by a test of the alcoholic content of breath, blood or urine, avoided the difficulties of proving unfitness to drive through drink or drugs.

Sometimes the law's reaction is of a less coercive and punitive kind than road traffic law. Medical science has advanced rapidly in two ethically problematical areas: the transplanting of human organs and the use of embryos in assisting pregnancy and medical experiments. The general public has shown some concern at these developments and the medical profession itself looked for a clear statement of what is ethically permissible. The Human Tissue Act 2004 attempts to answer these questions.

Yet sometimes the new development appears out of the blue without human volition. The HIV virus, which is believed to cause the life-threatening condition of AIDS, raised questions as to whether there is a role for law in charting its advance and impeding its transmission and whether tests for HIV should be performed, and if so, with or without consent. Under the AIDS (Control) Act 1987, health authorities had to make reports on HIV and AIDS to the Secretary of State to facilitate the collection of statistics on their spread, and allows the detention of apparent sufferers. The Act has however now been repealed and replaced by much more general public health legislation on notifiable diseases (see in Scotland the Public Health etc (Scotland) Act 2008).

Political pressure

15.3   Often the demand for law reform is put forward as part of the programme of a political party. Parties in a multi-party society such as ours exist to promote their vision of a better society (or, as some of them would say, to advance the interests of a class within it). So whatever they propose in and out of government is likely to meet with resistance from the other parties. Together they help through public debate to clarify the options for change. The reform, when it comes, will nearly always take the form of new law. Thus, throughout the 1980s industrial relations and the powers of trade unions were a highly contentious political topic. The prior law was transformed by six employment and trade union Acts between 1980 and 1990. Most were consolidated in the Employment Rights Act 1996 which was amended, in accordance with the policies of the Labour Government, in the Employment Act 2002. (But some of these amendments were themselves then repealed by the Employment Act 2008, because they had been found unworkable in practice even before the change of government in 2010.)

A further form of pressure for law reform is created when a law system is expanded and the bounds of the territory in which it operates are redrawn. This has been one major consequence among many of the United Kingdom's membership of the European Union. As a Member State the United Kingdom obliged itself to give effect to directives by the Commission. The implementation of the Single European Act by the end of 1992 with the object of equalising trading conditions throughout the EU impinged on innumerable areas of domestic law by setting uniform standards, such as on water quality and pollution.

Political and moral values

15.4   Behind many of these demands for change there lie tacit or explicit changes in values or conflict among rival value systems. Thus, the policies of the Labour Party, for example, in education and health, tend to exhibit a preference for equality and community action which translated into the public provision of services, show a tendency which became less distinct in the 'New Labour' era. Those of the Conservative Party show a preference for individual choice and thus encourage a variety of services privately supplied. Sometimes, as on the suppression of dealings in dangerous drugs by the criminal law, the parties share a common stance. But some calls for law reform show straight clashes of values held by citizens, unmediated by political institutions. Thus, attempts to change the law on abortion, to make it either easier or more restrictive, reflect differing beliefs on the value of human life and the point from which it merits protection. The lowering to 16 of the age at which consensual male homosexual acts are permitted has cut across party political boundaries, as also the issue of whether or not to legalise 'same-sex' marriage.

THE INSTRUMENTS OF LAW REFORM

15.5 How is this requirement that the law be kept up to date achieved? As shown above, the normal means is through legislation. But before examining how enacted law is used to revise the law, we should first examine what scope other sources of law play in this task.

Custom

15.6 Custom is so diffuse and uncoordinated that one would not expect it to be of use in the purposive enterprise which law reform requires. But on rare occasions concerted and sustained action may have the effect of changing the law. Thus, before the passing of the Abortion Act 1967, abortion was an offence at common law only. But most gynaecologists in Scotland did perform abortions in hospitals to save the life or avert serious risk to the health of pregnant women; and in so far as they did not incur prosecution, it could be said that a custom had emerged among leading gynaecologists and the Crown Office, tacitly amending the criminal law on abortion so as to exclude those performed by medical practitioners for therapeutic reasons. Under the guidance of a Scottish Office circular the medical profession until the Age of Legal Capacity (Scotland) Act 1991 had a firm practice of requiring the written consent of parents and guardians to treatment of children only up to the age of 16, which ignored the common law of minority in Scots law[1].

Institutional writers

15.7 Institutional writers purported to declare and expound the law, including customary law, whether unwritten or evidenced in the

---

1 See Scottish Law Commission, Report no 110, para 27.

decisions of courts. They did not therefore claim to be making law, though in gathering it, organising it and drawing inferences from it, they certainly developed it. But it would be misleading to describe this activity as an exercise in law reform.

Judges

15.8 Judges do from time to time have opportunities to reform the law in a deliberate way. Whether they seize the opportunity depends in part on their temperament and in part on the scope that existing law affords them. It is mainly judges in the appellate courts who have the chance to reform the law. If the parties are able to pay for the full pleadings and exhaustive debate that civil appeals are given, it is likely that more is at stake than the outcome of the one case. An insurance company may want a ruling to settle some point concerning the assessment of damages. A local authority may want the legality of a financial practice followed by several others determined. (See eg *Morgan Guaranty Trust Co v Lothian Regional Council* 1995 SC 151, 1995 SLT 299.) Judges will give a ruling arising out of the closest scrutiny of the facts of a genuine dispute. They are not considering the question, as Parliament does, in abstract terms. But if the matter is one in which the government of the day takes an interest, there is a risk that it will introduce a Bill to undo the change in the law, or even exceptionally to nullify the court's decision[2].

The response of the judiciary to the opportunity to reform the law can be expressed in some generalisations. Broadly speaking, Scottish judges in civil appeals are less willing to declare that they are changing the law than some English judges. This may be because they know there is the possibility of a further appeal to the UK Supreme Court. Certainly some Scottish judges when sitting in the House of Lords have been at least as innovative as their English colleagues. Lord Kilbrandon, Lord Fraser and Lord Reid (though he was never a judge in Scotland) are examples. On the other hand, the criminal law of Scotland, which has not been subject to appeal to the Supreme Court or its predecessor, the House of Lords, and most of which is the creation of judges, not statute, is regularly developed by judges, though often without their declaring that they are doing so. Thus, in a few unpretentious cases the law of theft was expanded to embrace situations where there was only a temporary removal of

---

2 This occurred when the decision of the House of Lords in favour of the company in *Burmah Oil Co Ltd v Lord Advocate* 1964 SC(HL) 117 was overturned in the War Damage Act 1965. See Stott *Lord Advocate's Diary* p 145.

another's property with no intention to appropriate it[3], or merely unlawful retention of it[4]. The conduct in question was denounced as 'nefarious' and that was enough to make it criminal by extension of the law of theft. But the judges are sometimes bolder, as when rewriting the old common law offence of 'shameless indecency' as 'public indecency' (*Webster v Dominick* 2005 1 JC 65), or in overturning the view that an accused could not plead 'diminished responsibility' except where his or her state of mind at the time of the act in question bordered on insanity (*Galbraith v HM Advocate* 2002 JC 1). There are limits, however: in *Petto v HM Advocate* 2012 JC 105, for example, Lord Justice Clerk Gill remarked (para 22):

> [A] comprehensive re-examination of the mental element in homicide is long overdue. That is not the sort of exercise that should be done by ad hoc decisions of this court in fact-specific appeals. It is pre-eminently an exercise to be carried out by the normal processes of law reform.

It is no coincidence that Lord Gill spoke here as a former chairman of the law reform body, the Scottish Law Commission (for which see further below), and that he was therefore aware that the reform of the law of homicide was (and is) on the Commission's future agenda.

Signals to Parliament

15.9 The responses of judges to an invitation explicitly to develop the law may be arranged on a scale from timidity to boldness. Firstly, a judge may note a gap in the law or an unjust consequence of the law, but declare that it is for Parliament to remedy it. Thus, the Adoption Act 1930 required that a minor child consent to his or her own adoption. In *B and B* 1965 SC 44 the child was mentally incapable and unable to give consent. Although the adoption would be to the child's benefit, Lord Clyde declined to approve it as to do so would in effect be to amend an Act of Parliament. But the case did draw attention to the need for reform and following the Law Reform (Miscellaneous Provisions) (Scotland) Act 1966, s 4 the child's consent could be dispensed with (now Age of Legal Capacity (Scotland) Act 1991, s 2(3)). Since the creation of the Scottish Law Commission judges have been able to point to it as able to give more

---

3   *Milne v Tudhope* 1981 JC 53.
4   *Kidston v Annan* 1984 SLT 279, 1984 SCCR 20. And see *Black v Carmichael* 1992 SLT 897, 1992 SCCR 709, where the wheel-clamping of a vehicle without removing it was held to be theft.

thorough consideration to the need for law reform than can judges adjudicating in a single dispute[5].

Overruling

15.10 Secondly, judges may overrule an unsatisfactory past decision. Thus, in *Dick v Burgh of Falkirk* 1976 SC(HL) 1 the question was whether a widow, as well as taking over as executor her late husband's action of reparation for injuries sustained at work, could also seek an award for herself for solatium and loss of support. The Court of Session judges felt constrained to follow a decision of the House of Lords in *Darling v Gray & Sons* (1892) 19 R(HL) 31 'despite the injustices which may follow from it' (per Lord Wheatley). But in the House of Lords the judges readily overruled the decision of their predecessors in *Darling* as 'wrongly decided', Lord Kilbrandon pointing out that 'your Lordships are here to do justice between the appellant and the respondents and should not leave it to Parliament to act on the recommendations of the Scottish Law Commission in Report 31 on the subject'. It was perhaps also significant that it was the Law Lords who created the injustice and it was therefore appropriate that they should remedy it at the first opportunity.

Reformulating case law

15.11 Thirdly, judges of the highest courts may reformulate case law in a new and broader manner and thus open up the way to a new line of cases. The best known and most dramatic example of this practice is the celebrated snail-in-the-gingerbeer-bottle case of *Donoghue v Stevenson* 1932 SC(HL) 31. In the case of *Mullen v Barr* 1929 SC 461 the Inner House of the Court of Session had held that the law did not require bottlers to maintain an infallible system to exclude mice from ginger beer bottles. But in *Donoghue* Lord Atkin in the House of Lords not only held that the manufacturer of a product not open to intermediate inspection owed a duty of care to the consumer of it; he also stated a general principle of negligence, to the effect that 'you must take reasonable care to avoid acts or omissions which you can reasonably foresee would be likely to injure your neighbour' (at 44). Though the majority in the Lords was only 3 to 2, *Donoghue v*

---

5 See Lord Reid in *McKendrick v Sinclair* 1972 SC(HL) 25; Lord Kissen in *Dick v Burgh of Falkirk* 1976 SC(HL) 1 at 7.

Stevenson has been as significant a reform of consumer protection law in the United Kingdom and many Commonwealth countries as any statute, and has also been the springboard for the development of liability for several other forms of negligence.

In another House of Lords 'reformulating' case, *RHM Bakeries v Strathclyde Regional Council* 1985 SC(HL) 17, Lord Fraser showed himself to be anxious to dispel any suggestion that a person who creates a structure on land, such as a dam, is strictly liable for any consequential damage. Single-handed (the other Lords concurring), he re-interpreted an earlier case, *Kerr v Earl of Orkney* (1857) 20 D 298, described the suggestion that the English strict liability case of *Rylands v Fletcher* (1868) LR 3 HL 330 was part of Scots law as 'a heresy which ought to be extirpated', distinguished the House of Lords decision of *Caledonian Railway Co v Greenock Corporation* 1917 SC(HL) 56 as involving not a dam but a diverted stream, and thus reversed the decision of the Inner House.

Prospective change

15.12   Fourthly, judges can go beyond the factual bounds of the case before them and address those who they foresee may face similar but not identical questions in the future. To them they give an indication of the court's thinking on such prospective questions. This can be justified as making a lengthy and expensive recourse to the courts unnecessary. But it has the drawback that the judges deprive themselves of hearing the arguments of counsel on the issue. Lord Denning was an enthusiastic exponent of this practice. In *Jefford v Gee* [1970] 2 QB 130 the Court of Appeal had to interpret a new Act on the award of damages in personal injuries. But Lord Denning as Master of the Rolls said

> 'Parliament has quite understandably left it to the courts to decide the principles on which they should act. Up and down the country people want to know the answer. Trade unions, insurers, accountants, solicitors, barristers, all want to know .... Such is the confusion that we feel it our duty to set out the guide-lines.'

Such a practice comes close to judicial legislation and was almost unknown in Scotland. But in *Smith v M* 1982 SLT 421 Lord Wheatley, who in his time as Lord Justice-Clerk considered nearly all Scottish bail appeals, set out guidelines for all lower judges in saying that where 'the accused was in a position of trust to behave as a good citizen and not to break the law he should be refused bail unless there were cogent reasons for deciding otherwise'. But that the police were making further inquiries was not a sufficient reason for refusing bail. This guidance was not, however, well received by defence lawyers and social workers. In a case which carries the authority of a bench of seven judges, *Morrison v HM Advocate* 1991 SLT 57, 1990 SCCR 235, where the admissibility of a statement by an accused which was both incriminating and exculpating was in issue, Lord Justice-Clerk Ross, giving the opinion of the court, said 'The following is a statement of the law which applies to all such statements', that is, statements made by an accused after the offence and prior to trial, if accurately recorded and fairly obtained. However this clarification of the law in advance in the broadest of terms was not wholly successful. In *McCutcheon v HM Advocate* 2002 SLT 7 a court of nine judges was formed which disapproved of *Morrison* in part as being capable of creating injustice. And in the civil case of *West v Secretary of State for Scotland* 1992 SC 385 at 392 Lord President Hope, noting that guidance should be given as to the scope of judicial review, said he would 'set out what we consider to be the principles which may be used to define the limits of the supervisory jurisdiction of this court'.

Procedural legislation

15.13   In the last of these practices judges come close to legislating. Through their power to control the procedure of the courts, they can widen remedies and thus give new access to the law. Through Acts of Sederunt in civil matters and Acts of Adjournal in criminal matters judges do engage in a specialised form of legislation and from their creation until 1756 the Court of Session and High Court produced a mass of law, much of it changing the substantive law[6]. Nowadays such Acts usually merely spell out the consequences for Scottish court procedure of some innovation in the law elsewhere. For example, the power of a court of a Member State of the European Union to seek a ruling on a point of EU law from the Court of Justice led to the Court of Session amending its Rules of Court by Act of Sederunt. But occasionally the court will be bolder. Thus, the lack of effective remedies against unlawful administrative action had been the subject of criticism in Scotland for many years without response. Lord Fraser (obiter in the House of Lords) in the case of *Brown v Hamilton District Council* 1983 SC(HL) 1, a case on the Housing (Homeless Persons) Act 1977, observed 'It is for

---

6   According to the House of Lords, in later condemning this tendency. See *An Introduction to Scottish Legal History* (Stair Society, vol 20, 1958) pp 27, 53.

consideration whether there might not be advantages in developing special procedures in Scotland for dealing with questions in the public law area'. Lord President Emslie leapt into action and set up a working party under Lord Dunpark which quickly produced a simple scheme for judicial review of administrative decisions, that came into effect as Rule of Court 260B in 1985. A similar rapid reform was the provision of simplified commercial procedure in 1994 by amendment of the Rules of Court, following the recommendations of a Committee under Lord Coulsfield.

The UK and Scottish Parliaments

The UK Parliament

15.14 On the surface the most suitable vehicles for changing the law are the legislatures. The individual members that constitute the UK Parliament and the government which controls much of its activity are in touch with most aspects of public life and receptive to complaints of things that are wrong and which the law might remedy. Through select committees MPs who are not in the government can inform themselves on the current state of affairs in most government departments. The law that emerges from Parliament is general in its terms and seeks to determine some form of human conduct for the future. The manner in which it is expressed can be thoroughly considered through the legislative process. Its links with adjacent law can be checked. Finally, the ideology which holds that Parliament expresses the will of the majority of the people who have elected it, gives to measures of law reform approved by it a legitimacy lacking in changes made to law by other means, such as the judgments of judges.

However, most of these points are subject to some qualification. Governments are in fact usually elected by a minority of the electorate and obtain power through their ability to command a majority in the House of Commons. The exigencies of the parliamentary timetable and in particular the crude device of the guillotine by which parts of a Bill may receive no scrutiny at all mean that statutes can turn out to be unworkable in some respect. Sometimes too much activity at the committee or report stages can mean that late amendments are inserted without the draftsmen having a chance to consider fully their impact on other parts of the Bill. The conventions of legislative drafting make the resultant law often incomprehensible to the people who are supposed to comply with it. Nevertheless, the parliamentary process does provide a semblance of popular participation through representatives and an opportunity for careful forethought. It is thus better than any alternative method of law reform. And as we shall see shortly, in some areas of the law Parliament is assisted by the careful preparatory work of the Law Commissions.

Most UK parliamentary time is controlled by the government and in so far as it is used for drafting legislation is taken up with the enactment of the government's own programme as announced in the annual Queen's Speech. Much of that will take the form of new areas of legal coverage. But some kinds of government activity are constantly being monitored by the department concerned and new legislative proposals are frequently brought forward in the hope of improving the existing law and keeping it in line with the government's objectives. Thus, between 1980 and 1989 ten social security Acts were passed (including ones on contributions), an average of one a year. In the same period there were seven Acts on aspects of road traffic.

The Scottish Parliament has no equivalent to the Queen's Speech, and the Government has simply issued a statement of its legislative intentions, usually each September.

Law reform Acts

15.15 One kind of statute promoted by the government declares itself to be a law reform measure. This is the law reform act. The low priority given to Scottish legislation led to many matters of Scots law being changed by this device. The last example of this genre, which aroused much criticism from the legal profession and other quarters, is the Law Reform (Miscellaneous Provisions) (Scotland) Act 1990, which has 75 sections and 9 Schedules. It includes what amounted to whole statutes on charities, on arbitration, and on legal services, including the restructuring of the legal profession, substantial amendments to the law on liquor licensing, provisions on the giving of blood samples in civil proceedings, on the giving of evidence by children and many other lesser matters. Given the heterogeneous character of such Bills, it is difficult to ensure that the standing committee which will scrutinise it in detail is staffed with members who will have an interest in or knowledge of its coverage or to avoid excluding members who are strongly concerned about one of its ingredients. Its miscellaneous character also makes it vulnerable to unexpected amendments and additions from MPs during its parliamentary progress. Such unpredictability is anathema to those who manage parliamentary business for the government of the day.

The Scottish Parliament

15.16 The limited opportunities for the examination of legislation affecting Scotland in the Westminster Parliament and the problems Scots people and organisations had in lobbying MPs and attending proceedings there were among the reasons why a devolved form of government for Scotland was created in the Scotland Act 1998. The Consultative Steering Group on the Scottish Parliament in its Report entitled *Shaping Scotland's Parliament* laid down as a key principle that 'the Scottish Parliament should be accessible, open, responsive and develop procedures which make possible a participative approach to the development, consideration and scrutiny of policy and legislation'. To promote these objectives it recommended that a structure of specialist Committees of MSPs should be set up. They should be able to influence the formulation of policy emanating from the Executive even before a Bill is drafted. In this role they should be accessible to interested organisations and individuals. If authorised to do so under s 23(8) of the Scotland Act 1998 a Committee might require 'any person' to attend its proceedings to give evidence and to produce relevant documents. The Steering Group recommends that these specialised committees should also have the power to initiate legislation. Under the Scotland Act, 1998, Sch 3, para 6, the Parliament has created 16 committees.

The Scotland Act 1998 envisages modification of existing Scots private law or Scots criminal law which bears upon reserved matters as described in s 29(4). A simplified procedure can be created by standing orders under s 36(3) for Bills which merely restate the law and ones which repeal spent laws and for private bills.

The procedures of the Scottish Parliament have on the whole fulfilled these objectives. It is possible for any individual or organisation to petition the Procedures Committee with some grievance which may result in a new or amended law. All Bills promoted by the Scottish Government are examined in detail by one or more relevant committees which under the Scotland Act 1998, s 23 have been given the power to summon witnesses including, with certain qualifications, ministers and civil servants and to call for documents to be produced.

Commissions and committees

15.17 Governments were formerly often prompted to introduce legislation by the reports of Royal Commissions and departmental committees, composed of people from various walks of life, which they set up to inquire into some particular problem. Major inquiries included the Crowther Committee on Consumer Credit, which led to the massive Consumer Credit Act of 1974, and the Clayson Committee on Scottish Licensing Law on whose report the Licensing (Scotland) Act of 1976 was based. Under the administrations of Margaret Thatcher this method of law reform fell out of favour as being too slow and liable to produce proposals unacceptable to the government. The major reform of social security in the Social Security Act 1986 was based on the work of small review teams chaired by ministers. Where, exceptionally, external bodies are created to recommend changes in public policy they are now given a clear indication of the direction of the reform expected of them and set a time limit within which to report[7]. The Scottish Government made relatively little use of ad hoc committees in its early years, but important examples since 2007 are the Review of Scottish Civil Courts chaired by Lord Gill (2009) and the Carloway Review of criminal law and practice (2011). The typical mode of paving the way for law reform practised by the Scottish Government otherwise has been the issue of consultation papers and draft Bills, to which any interested party can respond, as for example with the Marriage and Civil Partnership (Scotland) Bill consultation on the introduction of same sex marriage and the religious registration of civil partnerships (12 December 2012: www.scotland.gov.uk/publications/2012/12/9433).

Private members' Bills

15.18   At Westminster individual MPs who have limited access to the legislative process through the annual ballot for the chance to introduce a Bill can bring about law reform. Usually it takes the form of a limited amendment to existing law, which has been shown to be defective[8]. Large-scale innovations requiring new administrative structures and increasing public expenditure are unlikely to be supported by the government. But the Housing (Homeless Persons)

---

7   Eg the Sheehy Inquiry into Police Responsibilities and Rewards (1993) (Cm 2280); the Maclean Committee on Serious Violent and Sexual Offenders (1999). A slightly different example is the Report of the Leveson Inquiry into the Culture, Practices and Ethics of the Press, published in November 2012. The Government may have had legislation on press regulation in mind when commissioning the Inquiry but seemed to have had second thoughts by the time the report was published.
8   Eg the Badgers Act 1991.

Act 1977 is an example of an important social reform introduced by a Liberal MP, Stephen Ross, although in its early years it suffered from a lack of government funding and local government support[9]. Sometimes major matters on which the government does not wish to take up a position are left to the initiative of individual MPs. Thus, the Abortion Act 1967 was steered through the Commons by David Steel MP (now Lord Steel).

The Scottish Parliament also makes provision for members' legislation; of which the Dog Fouling (Scotland) Act 2003 is an example of general application. In the 2007–2011 session Margo MacDonald MSP brought forward a controversial proposal to make it lawful for someone to seek assistance to die. The End of Life Assistance (Scotland) Bill was, however, eventually rejected by the Parliament in 2010 after prolonged debate.

THE LAW COMMISSIONS

15.19 In preparing comprehensive schemes of law reform on subjects which are neither of concern to political parties, nor likely to attract the interest of individual MPs, the United Kingdom and Scottish Parliaments have the benefit of the Scottish Law Commission. There is also a Law Commission for England and Wales. A wide area of law exists, covering, for example, contract, delict, succession and property, which is the everyday concern of members of the legal professions, but impinges only rarely on the lives of ordinary people. As such it is often called 'lawyers' law', misleadingly so, for of course it would not exist without the problems of the general public and its rules can dramatically affect their lives. If for instance a person is rendered paraplegic in the course of an operation, legal definitions of what constitutes medical negligence and how it can be proved will have a vital impact on his future standard of living. But such questions are not the everyday concern of the general public. The Law Commissions provide a process by which what the law ought to be on these matters can be exhaustively considered.

The genesis of the Law Commissions is to be found in a book entitled *Law Reform Now*, written by a barrister, Gerald Gardiner, and an academic lawyer, Andrew Martin, in 1964. In it they argued that the Lord Chancellor's Office (for England and Wales) should have attached to it a unit composed of five highly qualified lawyers,

---

9   See now Homelessness etc. (Scotland) Act 2003, as amended by Homelessness (Abolition of Priority Need Test) (Scotland) Order 2012 (SSI 2012/33).

independent of government and civil service, to be called Law Commissioners. Their main task would be 'to review, bring up to date and keep up to date what may be called the "general law"'. In the same year Gerald Gardiner gained the opportunity to turn his vision into reality, for he was appointed Lord Chancellor in the Labour government which took office in October 1964. The Law Commissions Act 1965 was one of its first pieces of legislation.

Because of the wide differences between English and Scots law in the areas to be the concern of the Commissioners it was decided that there should be a separate Law Commission for Scotland. But the two Commissions should act in consultation. Scotland had had since 1954 a Law Reform Committee, but it was a part-time body with no permanent secretariat. It had no power to take an overview of the law but could act only on references from the Lord Advocate. Like its English counterpart its output was small. Its main achievement was the important Occupiers' Liability (Scotland) Act 1960, which followed its first report.

In 1965 the Scottish Law Commission was created, with, as its first Chairman, a judge, Lord Kilbrandon, best remembered for leading the committee whose report on children and young persons led to the setting up of children's panels (but who also chaired the Royal Commission on the Constitution, which reported in 1973 and foreshadowed the beginnings of the process of devolution). The numbers of the two Commissions are the same, at five. But the Scottish Commission has usually included two part-time members. Academic lawyers, seconded from the universities or combining work for the Commission with their university duties, have been prominent in the work of the Commission. There has also usually been one advocate and one solicitor.

Powers of the Commissions

15.20 The powers of the two Commissions are laid down in s 3 of the Law Commissions Act 1965. They have a general duty:

> 'to take and keep under review all the law with which they are respectively concerned with a view to its systematic development and reform, including in particular, the codification of such law, the elimination of anomalies, the repeal of obsolete and unnecessary enactments, the reduction of the number of separate enactments and generally the simplification and modernisation of the law'.

In fulfilment of that duty, they have the positive function of submitting programmes of law reform to the Scottish Government.

Otherwise their functions are of a reactive nature. When requested by these ministers, they are to examine specified branches of the law and make proposals for reform by draft Bills or otherwise, and to prepare schemes for the consolidation and revision of statute law. They are also to respond to requests for advice and information from government departments on law reform. They are to receive proposals for law reform from anyone. To facilitate their work they may seek information on the law systems of other countries.

The Scottish Law Commission

15.21 The Scottish Law Commission consists in 2013 of five commissioners appointed by the Scottish Ministers. The part-time Chairman is Lady Clark of Calton, a judge seconded from the Court of Session. There are three full-time Commissioners, Patrick Layden QC, Professor Hector MacQueen and Dr Andrew Steven, and one part-time Commissioner, Ms Laura Dunlop QC. Thus within its small number the Commission has representation from the judiciary, the legal profession, and academic lawyers. There are no members who do not have some professional involvement with law. Section 2(2) of the Law Commissions Act 1965 so limits the appointments. However, the Commission has been scrupulous in seeking responses to its proposals from all interested bodies and persons and on some subjects commissioning social research. The Commission has a core staff of six lawyers, drawn from the Scottish Government Legal Directorate, four legal assistants appointed for a year at a time, and a Parliamentary draftsman.

Its method of working

15.22 Each law reform project is assigned by the Commission to a Commissioner (occasionally more than one), who leads a team drawn from the Commission's staff. Their first task is to ascertain exhaustively the existing state of the law and uncover its deficiencies. Some, but not necessarily all, of these may have led to the reference to the Commission. Occasionally this research on the relevant law is entrusted to outside experts. Thus, Sheriff (later Lord) ID Macphail, later a member of the Commission, produced an extensive research paper on the law of evidence, which was revised and published as a book on the subject. Social surveys are sometimes commissioned on the way the existing law is used and perceived by users. The most extensive use of this technique was in preparation for consultative memoranda on debt recovery and diligence. Eight studies were conducted by or for the Central Research Unit of the then Scottish Office. Since then there have been surveys on public attitudes to succession law, on the financial arrangements made on divorce, as shown in a sample of 1,104 divorce actions, on the legal powers of young people and on attitudes to corporal punishment. Commissioners meet fortnightly to debate and approve the work in progress and individual teams meet more frequently to advance their projects.

Once the Commissioners have formed provisional views on the options for change, they issue a discussion paper (formerly called a memorandum) to all organisations and persons likely to be knowledgeable and interested in the subject. These are all published on the Commission's website. Summaries are issued to legal periodicals and the press. More popular pamphlets aimed at the general public have occasionally been issued. Examples are the law regarding young people and that on inheritance and incapable adults. Any member of the public is entitled to a copy of a discussion paper on application to the Commission. Responses, often in the form of answers to specific questions, are invited by a certain date. Sometimes, on very specialised topics, for example the recognition of foreign nullity decrees, consultation is by means of consultation papers issued to a few selected experts.

When the Commissioners have considered the replies and come to a final view on the nature of the reforms, the team produce a draft report for consideration by the Commission, often mentioning the views of respondents. A Commissioner who disagrees with the final recommendations is entitled to dissent and add a note of dissent to the report. Where legislation is recommended, the report will be accompanied by a draft Bill. Thus, the Commission has addressed itself not only to what reforms are desirable, but also to how they can be achieved. Finally, the government, as the recipient of the report, may choose to issue its own consultative document on how it should respond to the report.

This is the most visible part of the Commission's work and arguably the most important. But it also engages in some painstaking and less dramatic tasks. In its interpretation of its remit in the Law Commissions Act 1965, s 3 (see above) it examines old Acts to see which are ripe for repeal in a Statute Law Repeals Act. There have been 18 of these emanating from the two Commissions and enacted by the UK Parliament, repealing over 2,500 spent statutes altogether. The consolidation of laws covering a certain subject but still needed is another form of 'tidying up' in which the Commission engages. The process allows for obsolete words to be replaced by contemporary ones to make the enactment more comprehensible. For example, the law on criminal procedure in Scotland was consolidated in the Criminal Procedure (Scotland) Act 1995. But one cannot be certain that all the law relating to the topic in the title of the Act is there. That Act by 2006 had been amended nearly thirty times, as well as being interpreted in 35 reported cases. The Court of Session Act 1988 consolidates only certain enactments relating to the Court of Session and repeals only some. A statute law revision report was published in April 2012 with the Bill enacted in early 2013 while a consolidation of the law of bankruptcy is also (see para **7.26**) under active consideration, with a consultation published in August 2011, and a report anticipated in 2013.

Its achievements

15.23   In its early days the Commission issued ambitious Programmes of Reform for the approval of the Lord Advocate, as it might be required to do under the 1965 Act, s 3(1)(b), undertaking to reform areas of law as extensive as obligations and succession. Some foresaw in this power the possibilities of codification on the scale of European systems of law, such as the French and German. But difficulties of achieving agreement on such complex areas, where continental and English models were at odds, doubts about the desirability of such a comprehensive reform, with its implications of permanence, and the number of small-scale referrals to the Commission combined to make progress on Programmes very slow. A major report on the law of succession, testate and intestate, was issued in 1990, as part fulfilment of the Second Programme of 1968 was never implemented in legislation, and a further report was published in 2009. But it too now awaits implementation. A series of innovative Acts did bring closer to possibility a comprehensive restatement of family law in a single consolidating Act, but this has not happened. Diligence (debt enforcement) was in part codified in the Debtors (Scotland) Act 1987, which was however heavily amended in the Debt Arrangement and Attachment (Scotland) Act 2002.

Since 1997 the Commission's mode of operation has been for each of its Programmes to be 'rolling' in nature, that is, each one gathering up whatever has not been completed from previous ones. The projects are arranged under most of the main branches of law. Timetables are set for each. A short-term project should take just one year; a medium one, two or more years; a long-term one is not time-limited. The Annual Report highlights what progress has been made with each project in these three categories.

Another factor which can determine the allocation of the resources of the Commission is the collaboration in which it is bound to engage with the other Law Commission. Certain topics are referred by Whitehall departments jointly to the two Commissions and result in joint reports; for example, on commercial law topics, such as partnership, insurance and the sale of goods, on consumer law such as unfair contract terms, and on questions of private international law. Legislative change may go forward in a single Bill or parallel Bills. Then there are draft English measures which may impinge upon the law of Scotland and which have to be considered within the English Commission's timetable. Requests for informal advice from government departments, often at short notice, add to the Commission's workload and can alter its timetable.

The recommendations and draft Bills of the Law Commissions remain no more than aspirations until they are turned into law by Parliament. Except for consolidation (under the Consolidation of Enactments (Procedure) Act 1949), Bills have to go through the normal legislative process with the possibility of amendment. They have to compete for space in the government's legislative programme, but usually lack any political glamour. But sometimes a sympathetic MP, often a lawyer, who has been fortunate in the private members' ballot, or a member of the House of Lords, will take up a ready-made Commission Bill. For example, the Age of Legal Capacity (Scotland) Bill was introduced in the Commons by Sir Nicholas Fairbairn MP and piloted through the Lords by Lord Macauley QC in 1991. As mentioned in chapter 7, a procedure for the implementation of politically uncontroversial Law Commission Bills has been successfully introduced at Westminster, and this can be used for Scottish Law Commission proposals. The first example was the Partnerships (Prosecution) (Scotland) Bill, introduced in the House of Lords in November 2012. The Scottish Parliament should be a forum with greater understanding of the objectives of the Scottish Law Commission's proposals and the means of accomplishing them. But no special procedure is laid down in the Scotland Act for enacting its Bills, except, under s 36(3), those that restate the law or repeal obsolete laws. The abolition of the feudal system of land tenure[10], as proposed by the Commission in its Report No 168, is one recommendation of the Commission which received a strong ground-swell of support from most interested bodies and most political parties. It was given effect in the Abolition of Feudal Tenure etc (Scotland) Act 2000, s 1 and consequential legislation.

10 See Reid, *Abolition of Feudal Tenure in Scotland* (2003).

But government and parliamentary interest tends to be greater in relation to criminal rather than civil law, and the former is the area where the Commission's reports have tended to be most readily implemented in recent years, for example in the Criminal Justice and Licensing (Scotland) Act 2010 and the Double Jeopardy (Scotland) Act 2011. In its Annual Reports the Commission lists the Reports that have been implemented, sometimes with their assistance.

Once a report has been enacted it may be referred to in court to help to clear up an ambiguity in the statute or to discover what mischief it was designed to remedy. For example in *MacDonald v H.M.Advocate* 1999 SLT 533 the court, in considering whether a prior statement should be admitted in evidence when a witness refused or was unable to give testimony in court, quoted extensively from a Commission report which had led to this being permitted in the Criminal Procedure (Scotland) Act 1995, s 259.

The Scottish Law Commission has firmly established itself as the paramount means of keeping Scots law in line with changing social needs. The coming of a Parliament wholly dedicated to Scottish affairs has not however improved the rate and speed of implementation of its reports as much as might have been expected.

Appendix 1

A NOTE ON THE NATURE OF RULES[1]

Two models of rules

Law is generally thought of as comprising rules. Rules can, however, be usefully divided into more than one type.

Rules in fixed verbal form and rules not in fixed verbal form

Some rules are written, usually in formal, even stilted, language. They are usually written to encapsulate, as exactly as may be, the intentions of those drafting them, and they attempt to cover all likely eventualities. Often they are broken down into sections, subsections, and the like, and these may be indicated by arabic or roman numerals, or letters, and indented. These are draftsman's devices to express the rule logically and unequivocally. Rules of golf clubs and other societies are generally of this nature, as are the rules within a university on who may be awarded an LLB degree. They are what we usually expect rules to look like. They have been referred to as 'rules in fixed verbal form'.

Some rules are not of this nature, however, and we are familiar with the idea of unwritten rules. One of the commonest ways of making a rule is by saying 'don't do that!' (or 'do it this way!', or 'watch me!'). Rules within families and workplaces are commonly of this kind. Here there is no written form of the rule, indeed quite possibly no attempt to articulate at all closely what the rule is. Nevertheless, a rule may be inferred, by observing the prohibition (or requirement) made and the behaviour which precipitated it, against a general knowledge of the relationship between the parties involved. It may be that no clear inference is possible from a single instance, and impartial observers might differ as to what inference

---

1 See W Twining and D Miers *How To Do Things with Rules* (5th edn, 2010). The debt owed to them in what follows will be obvious to those who read that book.

is correct. Clarification might be sought by asking for a 'fixed verbal form' of it; in other words, for this unwritten rule to be written down. However, this may not be possible or reasonable in practice. In this case, only further examples are likely to specify more closely what the rule is. These have been called 'rules not in fixed verbal form'.

The significance of the two types of rule

Both types of rule exist within the legal system. Legislation is generally speaking in fixed verbal form. It is laid down in advance, with reasonably precise instructions to cover foreseeable cases. Common law is not in fixed verbal form. It is inferred from a series of decisions by judges on more or less similar facts, and a clear view may emerge only after quite a number of decisions. These two types of rule require different handling.

With those in fixed verbal form, there is a text which has a single authoritative version. A person applying it cannot alter this text, but only apply what it requires. This may be straightforward, but where it is not, the interpretation applied must be one the text can reasonably bear. It follows that it is all-important to have an accurate version of the text, and that any text departing from the original is not authentic, and cannot be relied upon.

With those not in fixed verbal form, there is no authoritative text in the same sense, although there are decisions, expressed in words. It is important to have an accurate report of what the judge said, but the rule lies not in his precise words. It must be inferred from those words, for he is not constructing a rule in fixed verbal form. The inference can only be made in the light of the dispute which gave rise to the judgment, against the background of the already known rules of the system. Indeed, a clear view of the rule may often emerge only when a series of decisions has been made[2]. In any case, such rules are never in final form, for they can always develop through further precedents, and there can be reasonable argument as to the precise applicaton of the inferred rule to a new set of facts. Each case can indeed be seen as a 'rule-fragment'.

Dealing with rules in fixed verbal form is akin to dealing with a fixed standard like Greenwich Mean Time. There is a correct version

---

2   Jeremy Bentham, a great legal philosopher of two centuries ago, observed (in relation to English law), that common law, working through precedent, operates in the same way as you train a dog. You do not draft precise rules for it in advance. You wait till it does something you regard as wrong, and then punish it. Bentham's mummified body can be viewed in University College, London.

which is to be applied, and all other calculations of time of day are accurate only in so far as they accurately reflect it. Dealing with rules not in fixed verbal form is more like building a dry-stone dyke. Rules of thumb, born of long experience, must be applied to the materials to hand, which are less than ideal, in order to produce a structure which will stand up to the weather and keep the sheep in.

The structure of rules

Rules, whether in fixed verbal form or not, can be said to have a certain structure. They are one class of 'if ... then' statements. In other words, they appear, or can always be redrafted to appear, as statements which say 'if a certain thing or things happen, then there will be a certain result'. In the case of legal rules the result is a legal result, for example a permission or a penalty[3].

Protasis and apodosis

The 'if' part of the statement is sometimes called the protasis, and is descriptive. That is, it describes those facts or conditions which have to be fulfilled if the result is to occur. The 'then' part can be called the apodosis and, in a legal rule, it is prescriptive. That is, it prescribes the legal result of the fulfilment of the facts or conditions in the protasis.

This structure may be obvious, for rules in fixed verbal form, particularly offences, are sometimes actually drafted in something close to this mould. For instance, s 3(1) of the Prevention of Terrorism (Temporary Provisions) Act 1989 read:

'Any person who in a public place –
  (a) wears any item of dress; or
  (b) wears, carries or displays any article,
in such a way or in such circumstances as to arouse reasonable apprehension that he is a member or supporter of a proscribed organisation is guilty of an offence and liable on summary conviction to imprisonment for a term not exceeding six months or a fine not exceeding level 5 on the standard scale or both.'

---

3 Not all 'if ... then' statements are rules, let alone legal rules. 'If you hit a person without legal excuse, then you commit an offence' is a simplified legal rule. 'If you hit him, then you will be sorry' is a prediction.

Commonly, however, the structure is less than obvious[4], particularly so with rules not in fixed verbal form. Thus the rule laid down in *Donoghue v Stevenson* 1932 SC(HL) 32 could be rendered as something like: If you act in such a way as to make it reasonably foreseeable that you will injure someone, if that person ought reasonably to be in your contemplation, and if such a person is in fact injured as a result of your act, then you are liable to compensate that person for the injury suffered[5].

It is often useful to analyse rules in terms of this structure in order to understand them. Firstly, it may be useful in specifying what the facts in the *protasis* actually are[6]. Secondly, it may be useful in specifying the relationship between the various facts[7]. The relationship between the facts in a *protasis* is either cumulative (all must be true) or alternative (either must be true). Thirdly, it draws attention to, and requires specification of, the *apodosis*[8].

This form of analysis can usefully be done by constructing algorithms, although these are rarely found in legislation[9].

---

4 'No entry', 'Keep out' and 'Trespassers will be prosecuted' can all be redrafted into something like 'If a person enters, then he will be punished'.

5 But see Ch 12.

6 The prevention of terrorism offence includes 'wears ... any article' as well as 'wears any item of dress', so badges are included as well as uniforms.

7 Thus 'wears' or 'carries' or 'displays' are alternatives, so any one of them suffices. On the other hand, the requirement that it be 'in such a way or in such circumstances as to arouse reasonable apprehension ...' of certain things is cumulative, and must be fulfilled in all cases, or no offence is committed. The important words (expressed or implicit) are 'and' and 'or'.

8 The penalty is imprisonment, or a fine, or both, subject to certain maxima.

9 One example found in quasi-legislation is Chart I in Annex 2 (NHS Charges to Overseas Visitors: Manual for Hospital Staff) to Scottish Home and Health Department Circular 1982 (GEN) 29 (NHS Treatment of Overseas Visitors: Summary) (reference NFE/4/2) dated 15 December 1982 to health board secretaries. These attempted to explain the effect of the National Health Service (Charges to Overseas Visitors) (No 2) (Scotland) Regulations 1982, SI 1982/898.

Appendix 2

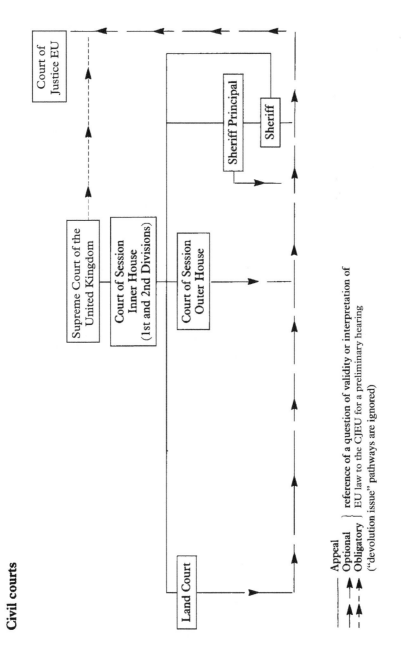

SCOTTISH COURTS (SIMPLIFIED)

Civil courts

- Court of Justice EU
- Supreme Court of the United Kingdom
- Court of Session Inner House (1st and 2nd Divisions)
- Court of Session Outer House
- Sheriff Principal
- Sheriff
- Land Court

Appeal

Optional ⎫ reference of a question of validity or interpretation of
Obligatory ⎭ EU law to the CJEU for a preliminary hearing
("devolution issue" pathways are ignored)

Criminal courts

Solemn procedure (with jury)

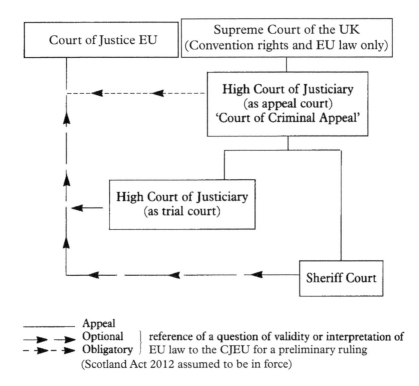

_____ Appeal

➤ ➤ Optional ⎫ reference of a question of validity or interpretation of
- ➤- ➤ Obligatory ⎭ EU law to the CJEU for a preliminary ruling

(Scotland Act 2012 assumed to be in force)

Summary procedure (without jury)

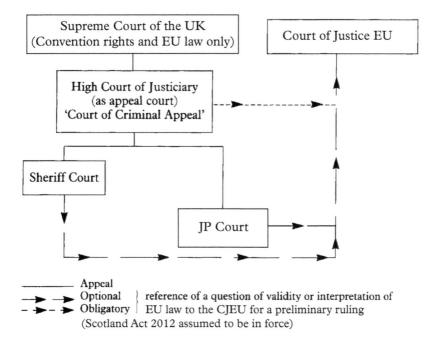

——————— Appeal
Optional   ⎫ reference of a question of validity or interpretation of
Obligatory ⎭ EU law to the CJEU for a preliminary ruling
(Scotland Act 2012 assumed to be in force)

ENGLISH AND WELSH COURTS (SIMPLIFIED)

Civil courts

Appeal
Optional } reference of a question of validity or interpretation
Obligatory } of EU law to the CJEU for a preliminary ruling

Criminal courts

Indictable procedure (with jury)

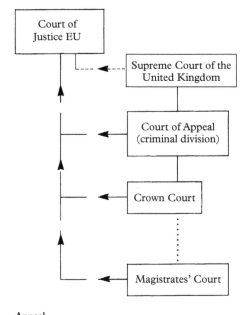

_____ Appeal
◄— ◄— Optional ⎫ reference of a question of validity or interpretation of
◄ –◄ – Obligatory ⎭ EU law to the CJEU for a preliminary ruling
. . . . Committal for trial i e preliminary sieving process

Summary procedure (without jury)

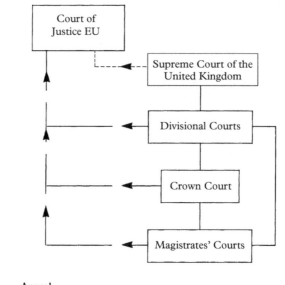

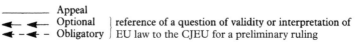

_____ Appeal

◄─ ◄─ Optional } reference of a question of validity or interpretation of

◄- -◄- - Obligatory } EU law to the CJEU for a preliminary ruling

NORTHERN IRELAND COURTS (SIMPLIFIED)

Civil Courts

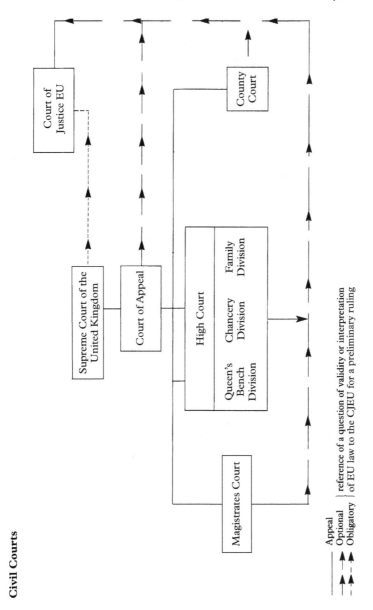

Appeal
Optional ⎫ reference of a question of validity or interpretation
Obligatory ⎭ of EU law to the CJEU for a preliminary ruling

Criminal courts

Indictable procedure (with jury)

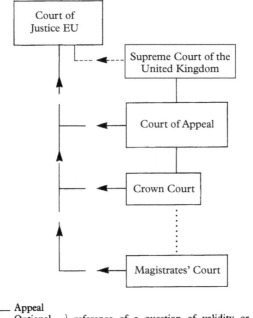

_____ Appeal
◄— ◄— Optional ⎤ reference of a question of validity or interpretation of
◄ –◄– – Obligatory ⎦ EU law to the CJEU for a preliminary ruling
.... Committal for trial i e preliminary sieving process

Summary procedure (without jury)

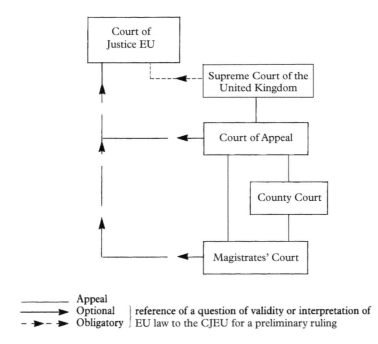

_____ Appeal

————▶ Optional ⎫ reference of a question of validity or interpretation of
– ▶– ▶ Obligatory ⎭ EU law to the CJEU for a preliminary ruling

Appendix 3

'EUROPE'

COUNCIL OF EUROPE	EUROPEAN UNION (since 1 December 2009 merging the former 'three pillars' of European Community, Common Foreign and Security Policy, and Police and Judicial Co-operation on Criminal Matters)
47 Members (2013) (founded 1948, UK founder member)	**27 Member States (2013)** (founded 1950s, UK joined 1 January 1973)
Strasbourg	**Brussels** European Commission Council of the European Union COREPER European Parliament (committees) **Strasbourg** European Parliament (plenary sessions) **Luxembourg** European Parliament (secretariat) Court of Justice of the European Union
	European Commission
Committee of Ministers	**Council of the European Union** **European Council**
Parliamentary Assembly	**European Parliament**
European Court of Human Rights	**Court of Justice of the European Union**
Congress of Local and Regional Authorities	
Commissioner for Human Rights	**European Court of Auditors**
Conference of International Non-Governmental Organisations (INGOs)	**European Central Bank**

Over 200 treaties between various members including principally: – **European Convention on Human Rights and Fundamental Freedoms** ('ECHR') – but also a variety of matters from social security to cybercrime, via patents, extradition, travel by young persons on collective passports, exchange of blood grouping reagents, liability of hotelkeepers for property of guests, protection of archaeological heritage, protection of pet animals, cinematographic co-production, etc.	**Various treaties,** including: – **Treaty on the Functioning of the European Union** ('TFEU') – **Treaty on European Union** ('TEU', alias 'Maastricht Treaty') – **Treaty of Amsterdam** ('ToA') – **Treaty of Nice** ('ToN') – **Treaty of Lisbon** ('ToL') Also 'secondary legislation' under TFEU (main means of legislating): – **Regulations** (thousands every year) – **Directives** (hundreds every year) – **Decisions** (hundreds every year) **TFEU, TEU, + secondary legislation = 'European Union (EU) law'**
No 'direct effect' of human rights or other law (i.e. no direct incorporation into UK law), but: – **most of rights under ECHR transferred into UK law by Human Rights Act 1998** and contents of various other treaties similarly taken into account in UK legislation – **right of individual petition** to European Court of Human Rights, which may produce a favourable decision (including compensation), which the state is obliged by the ECHR to effect, but which is unenforceable in domestic law.	**'Direct effect'** (i.e. direct incorporation into UK law of some EU law, i.e. – **parts of Treaties** – **all Regulations** – **Directives under some circumstances** – **Decisions** EU law **without 'direct effect'** transferred into UK law by: – **statutory instruments under European Community Act 1972, s 2** or – **Act of Parliament**

Index

[all references are to paragraph number]